P9-EEA-117

THE CRAFT OF
SOFTWARE
ENGINEERING

INTERNATIONAL COMPUTER SCIENCE SERIES

Consulting editors   **A D McGettrick**   University of Strathclyde
                        J van Leeuwen   University of Utrecht

OTHER TITLES IN THE SERIES

Programming in Ada (2nd Edn.)   *J G P Barnes*
Computer Science Applied to Business Systems   *M J R Shave and K N Bhaskar*
Software Engineering (2nd Edn.)   *I Sommerville*
A Structured Approach to FORTRAN 77 Programming   *T M R Ellis*
An Introduction to Numerical Methods with Pascal   *L V Atkinson and P J Harley*
The UNIX System   *S R Bourne*
Handbook of Algorithms and Data Structures   *G H Gonnet*
Office Automation: Concepts, Technologies and Issues   *R A Hirschheim*
Microcomputers in Engineering and Science   *J F Craine and G R Martin*
UNIX for Super-Users   *E Foxley*
Software Specification Techniques   *N Gehani and A D McGettrick* (eds.)
Data Communications for Programmers   *M Purser*
Local Area Network Design   *A Hopper, S Temple and R C Williamson*
Prolog Programming for Artificial Intelligence   *I Bratko*
Modula-2: Discipline & Design   *A H J Sale*
Introduction to Expert Systems   *P Jackson*
Prolog   *F Giannesini, H, Kanovi, R Pasero and M van Caneghem*
Programming Language Translation: A Practical Approach   *P D Terry*
System Simulation: Programming Styles and Languages   *W Kreutzer*
Data Abstraction in Programming Languages   *J M Bishop*
The UNIX System v Environment   *S R Bourne*
UNIX^{TM} is a trademark of AT&T Bell Laboratories.

THE CRAFT OF SOFTWARE ENGINEERING

Allen Macro
Independent Consultant

John Buxton
King's College London

ADDISON-WESLEY
PUBLISHING
COMPANY

Wokingham, England · Reading, Massachusetts · Menlo Park, California
Don Mills, Ontario · Amsterdam · Bonn · Sydney · Singapore
Tokyo · Madrid · Bogota · Santiago ·San Juan

© 1987 Addison-Wesley Publishers Limited.
© 1987 Addison-Wesley Publishing Company, Inc.

All rights reserved. No part of this publication may be
reproduced, stored in a retrieval system, or transmitted
in any form or by any means, electronic, mechanical,
photocopying, recording or otherwise, without prior
written permission of the publisher.

Cover graphic by kind permission of Apollo Computer, Inc.
Typeset in 10/12 pt Times by Columns, Reading.
Printed and bound in Great Britain by TJ Press (Padstow) Ltd, Cornwall.

British Library Cataloguing in Publication Data

Macro, Allen
   The craft of software engineering.–
   (International computer science series)
   1. Electronic digital computers –
   Programming   2. Computer engineering
   I. Title   II. Buxton, John   III. Series
   005.1'2   QA76.6
   ISBN 0–201–18488–5

Library of Congress Cataloguing in Publication Data

Macro, Allen
   The craft of software engineering.
   (International computer science series)
   Includes index.
   1. Computer software – Development.   2. Electronic
digital computers – Programming.   I. Buxton, J.N.
II. Title.   III. Series.
QA76.76.D47M33   1987   005.1   86–32076
ISBN 0–201–18488–5

74545

Allen Macro (BSc.; FBCS), the main author, has over 28 years of practical experience in software engineering and its management. He is sometime employee of the UK Atomic Energy Authority, founder and director of CEIR NV (now part of Scicon) and LOGICA BV, and consultant to major international companies including Philips Electronics and Royal Dutch Shell. He is a specialist in continuing education in software engineering and can be contacted at:

Serend (BV)
Valerius Rondeel 215
2902 CG Capelle a/d Ijssel
Nederland
Tel: 010 4507519

John Buxton (MA; FBCS), Professor of Information Technology at King's College London University, is a specialist in software development environments and languages. He was formerly Professor of Computer Science at the University of Warwick, and has been consultant to major international organisations including Philips Electronics and others; as advisor for the 'Stoneman' initiative of the US Department of Defense he was main author of the 'Stoneman' report on requirements for an Ada language support environment.

AUGUSTANA UNIVERSITY COLLEGE
LIBRARY

Preface

To most people, including a surprising number who program computers, software engineering is a mystery. Many adopt the attitude of the orchestra conductor who, when asked if he had ever performed work by a certain composer, replied: 'No, but I once nearly trod in some of it!' As Sir Thomas Beecham might well have agreed, such freedom of comment is often based on ignorance.

Software engineering has become, in fact, well known as a most difficult, costly and hazardous part of information technology. Some would say it is the most problematical technology of all, so many and severe have been the problems of software quality and adherence to estimates.

This book is for people who need and want to know what software engineering is, and how to do it. As well as practising software engineers and some more intermittent practitioners, we envisage amongst its readers a wide variety of people who are not specialists in the subject but who affect the software engineering process in one way or another. For instance, users who specify requirements; commercial and legal staff who may decide timescale and cost limitations on a software development; hardware engineers determining and working to a subsystem interface with software engineers; quality assurance departments and field support groups involved with software maintenance; personnel officers recruiting and helping to retain 'rare resources'; and so on down an extensive list.

Information Technology (IT) is now a major factor in everyday life. Governments see it as 'the sunrise sector' compensating for declining industries and, through its products, rejuvenating some whose means and methods are obsolete. Competition is fierce for a share in, or even domination of, its lucrative markets and, in view of the strategic issues involved, both economic and military, no industrialized society wants to become a large and permanent net importer of IT systems.

Thus, major national and international research and development policies are set, and the education sector is reformed and selectively financed in some countries as a palliative for supposed shortages in skills. For many practitioners and their managers, this is 'jam tomorrow'. In the meantime, IT developments go on, and – within them – so does software engineering, still beset by many of its old problems. For, in many cases, they are old problems – over three decades old in fact – now exacerbated by the expansion rate of IT applications and product innovation.

Some day – no one quite knows when, of course – the research initiatives now undertaken – such as the Strategic Defense Initiative in the USA, Japan's 'Fifth Generation' projects, the EEC's Esprit and Eureka programmes, the work of the Alvey Directorate in the UK and similar ones elsewhere – may further revolutionize IT and cure some (if not all) of the problems of making complex software. Until then software engineers, along with their managers, commercial and technical colleagues, will have to make software systems as best possible. That 'best' must not be as poor as it has been to date in many places, if IT is to have its beneficial effect.

For software engineering to be improved at this time, even within the known limitations of technical means and methods currently applying (and likely to do so for some time yet), it is imperative that the process of software engineering is understood between its exponents and the other populations involved. This book is intended as a bridge between people of different backgrounds, who are active parties to making software systems. Software engineering is not intrinsically unmanageable, but it may be made so. Software developments are not inevitably of questionable or poor quality, nor do they always over-run by 400% or more on cost budget – but these things may, all too easily, occur.

The problems of shared understanding and a shared vocabulary for expressing it are at the root of mismanagement and misdirected effort in software engineering, and are major causes in our view of the somewhat traumatic history of the subject. The problems are illustrated in the well known sketch:

Two deaf men are on a train as it approaches a London suburb:
  'Is this Wembley?'
  'I thought it was Thursday.'
  'So am I!'

We submit this work to its readers and critics in the modest hope that it helps to alleviate deafness.

Acknowledgements

The whole of this text was prepared by one lady only; she has put up with highly volatile source material and the sort of behaviour one might expect to go with it, shameful handwriting from both authors (not to mention accompanying attitudes), under-estimated timescales, and a word processor whose software clearly had been written by amateur programmers. Naturally, having typed Section 6.3 on team structure, the lady (in the best spirit of teamwork) wished to remain anonymous. But we are most grateful to this honorary software engineer.

A. MACRO
Capelle a/d IJssel,
The Netherlands

J.N. BUXTON
Kings College, London

The Publishers wish to thank the following for permission to reproduce extracts from published material:

Professor F.L. Bauer, for a quotation from *Software Engineering* (Amsterdam: North-Holland, 1972).

Barry W. Boehm, for quotations from *Software Engineering Economics*, pp. 75, 118, 374, 460, adapted by permission of Prentice-Hall, Inc., Englewood Cliffs, New Jersey.

Professor M.M. Lehman, for permission to adapt definitions given in *Programs, Programming and the Software Lifecycle*, Dept. of Computing and Control, Imperial College, London.

G.J. Myers, for a quotation from *Reliable Software Through Composite Design* (New York, Van Nostrand Reinhold, 1975).

C.H. Smedema, *et al.*, for a passage adapted from *The Programming Languages Pascal, Modula, Chill, Ada* (London, Prentice-Hall, 1985).

T.A. Thayer, *et al.*, for a quotation from *Software Reliability* (Amsterdam, North-Holland, 1978).

The *IBM Systems Journal*, for permission to reproduce a table from the article by Walston and Felix, 'A method of program measurements and estimation'.

Professor A.I. Wasserman, for a quotation from *Towards Improving Software Engineering Education* (New York, Springer Verlag, 1976).

Contents

Preface   vii

1. Introduction   1

  1.1 Definitions: IT, software engineering, and programmers   1
  1.2 A short history of software engineering   5
  1.3 Current problems in software development   9
  1.4 The authors' approach   10

2. Software engineering   14

  2.1 An extended definition and description   14
  2.2 The software engineering process; complexity   15
  2.3 Software system types   19
  2.4 The software competence audit   25

3. Managing software development: fundamental issues   26

  3.1 Comprehension   26
  3.2 A software 'lifecycle' model   28
  3.3 Visibility; archiving   33
  3.4 Active management and the practice of
     structured walkthrough   36
  3.5 Controlling specification change   40
  3.6 Prototyping and single-author tasks   42
  3.7 Coda   44

4. Specification and feasibility   45

  4.1 An overview of specification issues   45
  4.2 Conceptualizing requirements, and feasibility   51
  4.3 The User Requirement Specification (URS)   52
  4.4 The Functional Specification (FS)   65
  4.5 The Outline Systems Design (OSD)   82
  4.6 Variations on the lifecycle model   96
  4.7 The outcome of the specification and feasibility stage   98

5. Estimating effort and timescale   99

  5.1 An overview of estimating   99
  5.2 Estimating practices   102

5.3 Pitfalls   102
5.4 The 'OSD/activities plan' method   107
5.5 Research into parametric cost models   113
5.6 Lifecycle phasing and person dependency   130
5.7 The effort–timescale relationship   131
5.8 Estimating prototype development   135

6. Organizing and controlling software development   137

6.1 Task planning and control   137
6.2 Necessary documentation   139
6.3 Team structure: The 'peer group Chief Programmer Team'   147
6.4 Managing transformation   156

7. Systems and software design   163

7.1 Principles of good design   163
7.2 Some design approaches   171
7.3 Design practices and notations   180

8. Implementation   210

8.1 Low-level implementation   210
8.2 Choice of programming languages   215
8.3 Programming Support Environments (PSE)   219
8.4 Programming Language trends   226

9. Software quality   228

9.1 Basic issues   228
9.2 Definitions: Verification, Validation, Certification   231
9.3 The quality process   233
9.4 Criteria for software quality   235
9.5 Quality demonstration by testing   246
9.6 Quality Control, Inspection and Assurance practice   256

10. Additional management issues   261

10.1 Deliverable documentation   261
10.2 Maintenance, new versions, and configuration management   272
10.3 Personnel issues   280
10.4 Software engineering education   285
10.5 Contracting   296
10.6 A checklist for good software engineering practice   302

11. Casestudy: extracts from an archive   305

Index   379

Chapter 1   Introduction

Synopsis

Definitions are given for information technology and software engineering.

An account is given of the problems experienced in computer programming over the past three and a half decades, and how software engineering became Big and Bothersome.

The adverse factors currently affecting software engineering are summarized.

The approach adopted in this book is described and explained. The authors offer some advice to different types of readers on how to use this work.

It is taken for granted that the reader will be familiar with basic terms in computer technology (such as 'bit', 'byte', 'compiler', 'high-level language', and so on), or will have access to a lexicon of these terms such as the *Dictionary of Computer Science* (Glaser et al. 1983). Other terms more to do with software engineering as a process (e.g. 'lifecycle', 'functional specification', 'outline systems design', and a variety of others) will be defined and described in the appropriate chapters of this book.

1.1   Definitions: IT, software engineering, and programmers

To begin with, the terms 'information technology' and 'software engineering' need to be clarified. They are often used in the most imprecise fashion and their meanings thought to be common knowledge when, in fact, they are not. For instance, Information Technology (IT), Informatique, Informatica and (no doubt) many other variants, are apparently synonyms with only a loosely defined, generic meaning as they are commonly used. Given the scope and importance of the activities they seem to include, this state of affairs is unsatisfactory.

Recently, a working group in the United Kingdom – under Mr John

Butcher, MP – produced a definition of IT in the course of reporting on its 'skills shortages'. This definition (Butcher *et al.*, 1984) comprised

- Electronic systems and consumer electronics
- Telecommunication and radio frequency engineering
- Computing (software and hardware)
- Computing services
- Artificial intelligence
- Communication between electronic data processors
- Design and production of manufacturing systems (as distinct from their applications)

Classification can be difficult, particularly when categories overlap, are contiguous with unclear demarcation, or are cognate. The Butcher committee's definition is, with all its defects, a useful and succinct indication of the scope of IT. In the process it also makes clear the central importance of computers (essential to all eight components of the taxonomy) and, in doing so, highlights the central rôle of software engineering.

If, as is the case, software engineering is a 'problem subject', then that matter is as central to the interests of a company or country as is IT itself. If we must innovate to thrive economically, then we must solve the problems of software engineering with some urgency.

What then is 'software engineering'? In fact the term is more often used to denote programming – or even just the coding part of programming – than anything more extensive. The reasons for this are historical. Getting computer hardware to solve particular problems by executing sequences of commands was known as 'programming' and its exponents were known, therefore, as 'programmers'. As the first programmers were the problem solvers anyway (applied scientists and engineers) there were no problems with the definition. When, later, a tendency developed for the problem formulators to have programs written (often in a high-level language) by others, this task became known as 'coding' in some places. The inevitable confusion between two not explicitly defined terms was not helped when, around 1968 or so, the term 'software engineering' took on widespread use to denote a set of activities including 'programming' and 'coding'.

Nowadays, it should be taken that 'coding' is that part of programming that has to do with producing the sequence of instructions in a computer language to get the hardware to do whatever is required; 'programming', on the other hand, is the design of computer programs, their coding and testing by their authors as single programs or in combination with others as necessary.

Software engineering itself is the whole set of activities needed to produce high-quality software systems (programs or suites of programs), within known limitations of resources such as time, effort, money, equipment, etc. These activities include specifications and feasibility (including prototyping if necessary), programming as defined above, quality control and assurance, and documentation.

As long ago as 1972 Bauer defined software engineering as:

The establishment and use of sound engineering principles in order to obtain, economically, software that is reliable and works on real machines.

No doubt 'sound engineering principles' include management consider-ations, but there is a definite need to make that explicit. Also, the Bauer definition is less than clear on the need for adequate 'tools' to support the craft, as distinct from 'engineering principles'.

An extension of Bauer's definition in the current epoch might reasonably be that software engineering is:

The establishment and use of sound engineering principles and good management practice, and the evolution of applicable tools and methods and their use as appropriate, in order to obtain – within known and adequate resource provisions – software that is of high quality in an explicitly defined sense.

A more detailed description of software engineering, including its main perceived properties as a process, is given in Chapter 2, along with a definition of software systems types resulting from the software engineering process.

Software engineers are people of sufficient relevant aptitude and ability who perform software engineering (in the sense in which it is defined above) as the whole or a major part of their vocation.

The 'relevant aptitude' attributes are far from easy to define, but are generally agreed to include literacy as well as numeracy, and mental characteristics such as associative abilities, capability in abstract thought, good memory and painstaking precision. As temperamental stability is a desideratum too, the unlikelihood of the combination is one reason why there is a shortage of good software engineers.

The 'ability' of software engineers, given the aptitude factors, is very much dependent on the variety and difficulty of software engineering tasks with which they are confronted, and the environment in which they make software (i.e. whether it has a strong 'culture' in good software engineering practice, as defined, at all levels; where it lacks such a strong culture it may be said to be a 'weak' software engineering environment).

Ability also concerns the stage that software engineers have reached in consolidating their subject knowledge into a framework of practice sufficient for most eventualities, yet flexible enough to be extended and modified when necessary. A career trajectory of increasing ability in this sense begins with an apprenticeship, and proceeds through junior and senior software engineer levels to that of 'master' in the craft. This latter status is quite widely known as 'chief programmer' for historical reasons; properly the term should be 'chief software engineer', or even 'master software engineer'.

The topics of career development and subject education for software engineers are taken further in Sections 10.3 and 10.4. One major problem, due for passing comment here, is that the 'consolidation' of acquired knowledge may be inordinately delayed or even prevented altogether in weak software engineering environments. When this happens the 'software engineers' may more properly be categorized as 'amateur programmers'.

Not all computer programs are written by people whose main job it is to do software engineering. Many hardware engineers, whose main vocation is electronics, are intermittent programmers spending in the range of 10–40% of their time programming.

As with software engineers in weak environments, intermittent programmers are unlikely to have the strong background of experience, means and methods to permit the consolidation of acquired knowledge into a viable and practical conceptual framework. Merely knowing how to program in ABC language on an XYZ computer, having done it for a few weeks last year and the year before, is not enough – even if the results seemed to 'work'. The result is not software developed as a strong process of software engineering, by what may reasonably be viewed as software engineers, but programs written by 'amateurs' – people whose vocational specialization is, in many cases, in another subject altogether. As a result, its exponents are known as 'amateur programmers' – a category that contains a wide variety of people including some 'software engineers' and computer scientists, and many hardware (electronic) engineers.

The growth rate of the IT sector has led, ineluctably, to a very rapid growth in amateur programming. This is, of course, a major factor within the so-called 'software engineering crisis' one reads and hears about. For, whereas software engineering will be likely to produce software of requisite quality within the limits of resources provided (so long as these are adequate), amateur programming will be unlikely to do either on a consistent basis.

A third category of people who write computer programs is that of hobbyists. Whereas software engineers and amateur programmers write programs as part of their job of work, hobbyists do it for instruction or entertainment. Typically, a hobbyist will learn to program in BASIC on a Personal Computer (PC).

One major positive use of hobbyism is for managers and others who are not specialists in software engineering, as a part of an orientation in the subject. One negative effect of hobbyism is when it leads to amateur programming. 'Give the job to Fred – he knows all about computers' is a grave mistake if the problem is large and complex, and all Fred has ever done is to write a couple of 20 statement programs in BASIC on his PC. Hobbyism has received a great boost in recent years through the policy of governments, enthusiastically supported by equipment manufacturers of course, to popularize computer technology. Putting a PC in every classroom, or a terminal on every desk, is a great idea for encouraging the development of some basic aptitudes and subject interest in secondary-school students. If, as it may, it leads to more and more amateur programming in a few years' time, it will have been rather counter-productive.

There is a software engineering 'crisis' at the present time. A summary of contributory reasons for it is set out in Section 1.3. Some of them are evident from what has already been said. What is not always realized, or admitted by those who know, is that there has always been a crisis in software engineering since the inception of computing as a wide-scale activity from about 1950 onwards. In some periods it was recognized; in others it was the object of comment and endeavour; in some epochs it was believed (or asserted) to be solved.

1.2   A short history of software engineering

The programming of non-trivial applications is, without doubt, an extremely complicated and difficult affair. The fact that a child can program its PC in something like BASIC does not confute that point – it confuses it. The control program in the washing machine that has just flooded the kitchen floor is a few thousand instructions of assembler code, but it took people a year and a half to develop. The SDI 'Starwars' research will require a software system of anything between 10 million and 100 million source statements of code and must work right (or at least adequately) first time – unless it is to be tested on a spare planet. Nor will it be done in BASIC, or at least it is to be hoped not.

What is it that makes programming difficult? The *Dictionary of Computer Science* (Glaser *et al.*, 1983) defines a computer and its programs as:

> *A device that is capable of carrying out a sequence of operations in a distinctly and explicitly defined manner. The operations are frequently numerical computations or data manipulations but also include input/output; the operations within the sequence may depend on data values. The definition of the sequence is called the program.*

By this definition computers and programming are of some antiquity. For example, Leibnitz in the seventeenth century; Jacquard, Babbage and

Hollerith in the nineteenth century; Turing and von Neumann in the mid-twentieth century, all made substantial contributions to computers as we know them.

In the period 1939–45 computers, incorporating electrical components as distinct from mechanical ones, were developed in the United Kingdom for applications in decryption, and in the United States of America mainly for computing gunnery tables. By about 1950, computers were becoming available from several commercial sources, and wide-scale use of computers – programming in fact – dates effectively from that period. In the following three and a half decades, computers and their usage went through many major evolutions. Looked at solely from the viewpoint of programming and programmers, the history divides into four epochs correlated with major developments of one kind or another (but not synonymous with so-called hardware 'generations').

Epoch 1 (*circa* **1950–58**)   This was the period during which the first amateur programmers acted as users, programmers and even hardware engineers, for problem solving in the field of applied science and engineering. They used large and expensive 'mainframe' computers and programmed them in number code or simple mnemonic assembler code. This programming was often looked on as a fine intellectual sport for physicists, chemists, mathematicians and engineers of various kinds. It was certainly a lot of fun, and these (we!) first 'amateur programmers' produced a lot of very clever programs which were for the writer's own use, and were then either thrown away or left until needed again by their author.

Epoch 2 (*circa* **1959–67**)   This was the period during which high-level languages were first introduced and then extensively used, and operating systems were evolved to make the use of facilities more efficient. Off-line input/output (character) orientated machines were brought out to delimit the processors from these functions, and as a result the world of business data processing (DP) was added to that of applied science and engineering computations. Formal career structures began to be seen for operators, coders, designers and systems analysts in this period, and the user (the amateur programmers from Epoch 1 and new users in the DP sector), became removed at several stages from the equipment and its programs. The motive for developing high-level languages, such as FORTRAN, ALGOL and COBOL, at that time was to make the task of programming easier for the users themselves. Thus instead of having to write something like:

0 00000001010 101 000000001010100011101

in binary number code, or

+ 21, 5, 5405

in decimal number code, or

ADD B, 5

in mnemonic assembler, one could write statements such as

D = (A + B(I))*C

in a high-level language, and this would be translated by a compiler in the computer operating system software into something like:

CLA A
ADD B, 5 (which is the 'instruction' given earlier in different forms)
MPY C
STO D

This assembler code would then be further translated into binary machine code and executed on the computer (i.e. it would regulate the operations of hardware circuitry in a prescribed manner). Coders tended to use high-level languages increasingly. Users faced with learning several languages and the increasing complexities of operating systems began to specify the problems to be solved rather than to be simply the programmers and computer operators themselves. Around this time the 'virtual machine' concept was developed, in which the computer was seen as being defined by the procedures of the operating systems software and its programming languages. The extension of these facilities progressively cocooned the hardware within increasingly large and complex software regimes.

IBM brought out a range of computers in this epoch – the '360 series' – intended to be modular (i.e. compatible at the software level, from the small and cheap level of the range upwards); to have 'time sharing' facilities for simultaneous multi-user operations; and to possess a full set of virtual-machine features of the operating system and several high-level languages such as COBOL, FORTRAN, PL/I etc. The 360 was an immense commercial success but its operating software – OS 360 – was something of a mess. It had taken 5000–6000 person years to develop and cost $50 million per annum during its development (source: E.E. David in Naur and Randell, 1968).

The first general appreciation of a crisis in programming resulted. If the world's most prominent manufacturer couldn't get it right, who could? The first NATO-sponsored conference on 'Software Engineering' was held (in 1968) as a result. The proceedings of these conferences make salutary reading, there being much of value for the present epoch in the questions raised and the answers given; they may be found in Buxton et al. (1969); and Naur and Randell (1968).

Epoch 3 (*circa* **1968–78**) This was the period during which the minicomputer was invented and became widely used. For the first time the computer could be taken to the problem. Attempts to understand and evolve methods in software engineering (such as the NATO-sponsored conferences and work in computer science), tended to get obscured by the rapid expansion of computers used in the 'classical' areas of DP and Applied Science etc., and more novel uses of minicomputers as electronic components. The world of 'embedded systems' saw the re-invention of amateur programming, this time not just a few thousand applied scientists and engineers but tens of thousands of electronic 'systems' engineers.

The lack of virtual-machine software facilities on the new mini-computers of that time, was as great an attraction to amateur programmers in the early 1970s as the relative smallness and cheapness of the equipment compared with the still large and costly mainframes cocooned in their software. By around 1975–76, however, minicomputers were themselves becoming furnished with better operating software (such as Digital Equipment Corporation's RSX-11 regime for the DEC 11 series), and high-level languages such as FORTRAN, ALGOL, COBOL, and so on.

Epoch 4 (*circa* 1978 to present)   This was the period in which the microprocessor, and its more elaborate relative the microcomputer, were invented and became widely used. This, in fact, added a powerful impetus to the Epoch 3 trend towards embedded systems (IT in general, in fact), and the growth of amateur programming.

As with the minicomputer, the microcomputer was (and still is) for the most part 'naked', in the sense of not being a virtual machine with the hardware buried under many levels of operating software. The virtue of this for some real-time applications is undoubted. It does, however, lead to 'dirty' amateur programming on very primitive development ('host') systems, or on the nearly naked target equipment itself. The tens of thousands of amateur programmers created by the Epoch 3 evolution has now become hundreds of thousands, because of the smallness, cheapness and latent power of the micro. For a few dollars only, one can have literally a pocket-sized version of an Epoch 2 mainframe so far as simple processing power is concerned.

Mainframes and minicomputers are still manufactured and used, the larger ones for major multiple concurrent access systems with extensive archival storage and retrieval capabilities. Increasingly they incorporate micro-circuitry themselves, and the distinction between small mainframes and large minicomputers is progressively blurred, as is that between small minis and large micros. The reader interested in hardware architecture will find much of this detailed in Healey (1976).

It is still the case, however, that mainframe and minicomputer installations tend to be virtual-machine configurations for large-scale DP and computation-orientated applications, and to act as program-development (host) environments for other applications such as embedded microcomputer systems. These program-development systems, or programming support environments (PSE) as they are generally called, are often more costly than can be afforded by medium-sized and small IT companies, and software engineers and amateur programmers in these cases must, of necessity, develop software systems on the target equipment itself – often, as already said, virtually devoid of software facilities. The subject of PSEs is discussed further in Section 8.3.

Nor has the development of high-level languages kept pace with Epoch 4 IT applications of microcomputers. The reader interested in the history of computer-language development may find an account in Wexelblat *et al.* (1981). At the present time, there is no really satisfactory high-level language for software systems containing extreme time-criticality, concurrency, etc. (The most satisfactory solution for many at this time – the C language – can hardly be said to be 'high level'.)

Virtually at the outset of this epoch, Professor E.W. Dijkstra – an eminent computer scientist – warned against the likely effects of cheap and small devices, primitive in software development facilities, used by amateur programmers for complex applications. He said, in effect, that it would put software engineering back 25 years (Dijkstra, 1979) – in fact to Epoch 1 in our terms. In our view the past years have justified Dijkstra's view. The amateur programmer has been re-invented with a vengeance. But this time, unlike Epoch 1 when 'users' wrote their own programs to solve their problems in applied science or mechanical-engineering computation, the results of today's amateur programming may be a major component in some widely distributed product that may have severely detrimental effects if it fails.

1.3   Current problems in software development

The foregoing is a synoptic account of how the current crisis in software engineering arose, whilst the following is an account of the six main problems applying at the present time.

1. The competence (and confidence) of managers and others, if they are not familiar with software engineering and yet affect the process, is often insufficient. This problem has already been commented on, and is often referred to as the 'generation gap' syndrome, as it affects people who did not grow up with terminals on the school-desk and PCs in the home.

2. There is a shortage, at quantitative and qualitative levels, of software engineers. In some IT application sectors, notably embedded real-time systems, and at some levels of experience (Chief Programmer particularly) the shortfall is acute.

3. Faced with a rapidly increasing need to create software systems of

one sort or another, and the difficulties of recruiting and retaining software engineers that follow from point 2, many managers – particularly if lacking competence/confidence themselves – allow amateur programming to be undertaken.

4. Software tools, such as PSEs and configuration management systems, are still in the process of evolution. Those available are either of limited use, for instance PSEs without features for diagrammatic design of software in notations such as those described in Chapter 7, or are expensive at the hardware and PSE software levels.

5. Software engineering methods are still being developed. Research is continuing into specification and design 'languages', program proving by formal methods, 'languages' for rapid prototyping, and so on.

   A tendency to make premature claims for this research, as has been the case in some instances (e.g. 'algorithmic' methods for estimating, program proving, etc.), does not help software engineering and can create an unnecessary division between computer scientists and practising software engineers.

6. Education means and methods in software engineering are usually inadequate, both in the formal education systems of countries and as 'training programmes' in companies; the provisions for 'generation gap' staff to orientate with the subject sufficiently are virtually non-existent.

This book was developed in order to reduce problems 1 to 3, and to help meet the requirements of point 6. In the following section we offer some advice to readers, based on the practical use we have already made of its contents in educating software engineers and orientating their managers and other colleagues.

The fundamental issue of subject education to primary skill, secondary skill and orientation levels is set out in Section 10.4. Briefly, the crucial relationship between point 6 above and the current situation of crisis in software engineering is depicted (after Baber, 1982) in Figure 1.1.

1.4   The authors' approach

This book does not contain hard-and-fast prescriptions or 'standards' for software engineering. The reasons for this are basic to a proper understanding of the subject, and are twofold:

1. The application set for software engineering is so diverse that it is extremely difficult to envisage a prescription of methods that would be equally appropriate under all circumstances. What may suit design of a small DP application will probably be of little use for a large

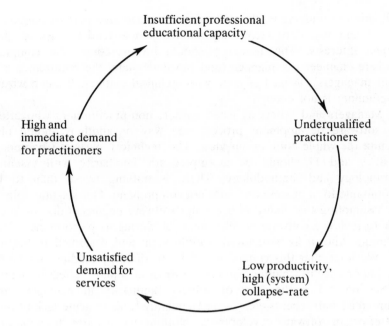

Figure 1.1   Information technology's vicious circle.

real-time system; the programming language appropriate for a numerical computation may be of limited use for a file-handling application.

2. It follows from points 4 and 5 of Section 1.3 that the subject is in a highly dynamic phase, with much continuing research into means and methods, and the development of cheap and powerful tools.

Our approach is that of providing guidelines more than standards. We are aware that many people would prefer definitive methods, and a crystal-clear recommendation of what to do in different circumstances. A 'cookery-book', in fact, which this most certainly is not. Our aim is to provoke thought as the best possible means for understanding.

Some readers may find it a drawback that we present little research material in detail; where such material is relevant we refer to it of course, but many books on software engineering concentrate on future trends at the expense of more mundane (but useful) techniques. We do not want our approach to be misunderstood; software engineers should be aware both of the subject as it is now and its possible future developments, but neither one of these should exclude the other. Where we think it appropriate, we state our opinions on current issues.

Practitioners, software engineers and amateur programmers should see all topics in this work as equally important. There may be some inclination to undervalue the 'management' orientated parts (Chapters 1, 3, 5, 6 and 10), since technically minded people tend to stick to their subject interests. This tendency should be overcome; the complete software engineer can manage (and can understand the requirements of other managers), as well as cope with technical matters. Being a wizard programmer is not enough.

Managers and others as listed earlier, non-practitioners who affect the software development process one way or another, should also attempt the whole book in our view. The 'technical' parts of Chapters 4, 7, 8, 9 and 11 should be attempted for familiarity with essential terminology and methodology. There is nothing worse than to be accountable for a process one does not comprehend. Our starting-point is the assumption that many who are not software engineers do not know how to review a software development job during its performance – the technique known as 'structured walkthrough' and described in Section 3.4. We hope that this condition will be rectified by reading this book. The importance of Chapter 5 should be stressed; a major effect of point 1 in Section 1.3 – the lack of subject familiarity in managers and commercial staff, clients etc. – very frequently leads to acute lack of time and effort in software development. Nothing has a more dramatic and deleterious effect on the quality of the outcome.

The examples in Chapters 4 and 7 are from the same source and are thus harmonized. They do not constitute a case-study, however, being neither complete nor consolidated in one part of the text. To compensate for this, we have included a case-study as Chapter 11, although, for reasons of space, this comprises extracts from an Archive to design level only.

We are proposing guidelines for good software engineering practice. Some organizations making IT products containing software already have well developed methods for system and software development; many others have not. Overall, whereas the improvement in computer processing power since 1955 has been in the order of one millionfold – measured as millions of instructions per second ('MIPS') per unit cost – the improvement in programmer productivity (delivered source statements of code, per unit of time) has been about threefold only (source, Dolotta, 1976).

There is evidence, set out in Boehm (1981) and Walston and Felix (1977), that when practitioners with adequate experience and education in the subject operate guidelines for good software engineering practice in an environment having suitable development tools, then the productivity in terms of high-quality software (not just delivered source statements of code) is substantially improved. We have found that, under the much less ideal circumstances of a master class in software engineering, such as the one described in Section 10.4, productivity can be improved by a factor of two to three over previous 'norms'. For example, in the case of a non-trivial example such as that set out in Chapter 11, a previously assumed 'norm' amongst practitioners of 10–15 source statements per programmer-day was more than doubled, and the code produced was of most respectable quality.

In one sense, however, the case for guidelines in good software engineering practice is better made as a default argument. There are well-known difficulties in establishing the quantitative effects of different factors operating within (or upon) the software engineering process, and these difficulties are discussed in Chapter 5. The fact remains, as in other aspects of engineering, that good practices (and tools) are preferable to the converse; Evelyn Waugh is said to have replied, when asked why his religious faith had not made him a nicer man, that without it he would have been even nastier.

Chapter 2 **Software engineering**

Synopsis

An extended definition of the software engineering process is given.

A description of some properties of the process is offered, based in part on the work of Weinberg and Schulman (1974).

Software systems, the outcome of the software engineering process, are categorized in several ways including definitions of products, projects and prototypes. The S-type, P-type and E-type characteristics of software systems are explained (after Lehman, 1980). Software engineering is further defined as a team-based activity, a matter of fundamental importance to an understanding of what follows.

The problems of software engineering are summarized again – this time in perspective.

2.1 An extended definition and description

A brief, generic definition of software engineering is given in Section 1.1, in which some distinction is made between coding, programming, and software engineering as an all-embracing term for the complete set of activities to achieve the object of 'good' software systems. The aim of this chapter is to extend that definition, and in doing so describe some of the particularities (and peculiarities) of software engineering seen as a process. As a starting-point we take the definition of software engineering given earlier and based on that by Bauer (1972).

> *Software engineering is the establishment and use of sound engineering principles and good management practice, and the evolution of applicable tools and methods and their use as appropriate, in order to obtain – within known but adequate resource limitations – software that is of high quality in an explicitly defined sense.*

At a less general level of definition, software engineering is:

1. Making and maintaining software systems. The activity generally understood to include requirement specification; software system definition; software design, coding, and program testing; software system integration testing, and verification/validation/certification; and software maintenance and emendation for new versions. Subsumed within this definition are the essential issues of documentation and testing strategies.

2. Devising tools and methods for making and maintaining software systems, and using them appropriately. For example (*inter alia*), special approaches and methods for specification; notations and languages for representing design ideas; software tools and utilities – language/debug facilities, editors and the like – to aid coding and testing; configuration management systems to assist in documentation and version control.

3. Managing the whole process, within economic constraints of cost and timescale. For the process of software engineering to be manageable it must be, so far as possible, a visible set of recognizable activities.

    For this state of affairs to occur, both managers and software engineers who are party to the process must be competent in their fields of endeavour; this includes sufficient understanding of software engineering on both sides, and the possibility to communicate that understanding.

2.2   The software engineering process; complexity

Software engineering is widely recognized as being a particular, often very troublesome species of engineering. The question is often asked: Is it really engineering at all; is it not an art or a science?

Insofar as conjectures like this are meaningful, we tend to the view that software engineering is an acquired craft, having strong affinity with engineering in general, approaching an art form in the sense of an intuitive process at the design level, and being very similar to the formal logic branch of mathematics at the coding and testing stages.

As a result of the evident crisis in the subject towards the end of Epoch 2 as we have defined it, much attention was given to understanding the process of software engineering as a means to improving it and its object, software systems. Weinberg (1971) published a seminal work on the psychological aspects of computer programming and, in a joint paper with Schulman (1974), set out the findings – in summary form – from experiments involving software engineering teams. We acknowledge this work as informing the list of software engineering properties given below, which is – in the main – a summary of our personal experiences in the subject.

Some of the following properties of software engineering are inherent attributes of the process, whilst others are widespread defective practices that can, and should, be remedied.

2.2.1 Properties of the software engineering process

Amorphousness

As implied above, there is no clear view in academic, practical (business/industrial), or lay circles about the scope and subject matter of software engineering. Indeed, beyond a general level of definition as given in Section 2.1, there has been much difficulty in recent years in describing the process of software engineering sufficiently to determine whether people can be educated in it and, if so, how. The matter of subject education is taken further in Section 10.4.

Complexity

Weinberg and Schulman (1974) have pointed out that programming, the part of software engineering concerned with program design, coding and testing, concerns complexity at two levels, the compound of which can be extreme or excessive complexity. In the first place there is the inherent complexity present as a result of requirements. The tendency to add dramatically to inherent complexity by apparently simple statements of requirement is dealt with in Chapter 4.

In addition, the programming itself offers 'an almost infinite number of choices' to the software engineer. Bad programming practice, in the sense of program design and coding, leads ineluctably to excessive complexity of software systems and consequential problems in their testing, certification, maintenance, emendation, etc. This is the subject of Chapters 7 and 8.

The general matter of complexity, as affecting software engineering as a process, is the subject of further comment below.

Indeterminacy

Whereas it is obvious that no task (excepting some research and prototyping exercises) should be undertaken without explicit, unambiguous and coherent specifications, the feasibility of implementing these in software may not be determinable until a relatively late stage in the software engineering process. Whilst it is fairly rare for unfeasibility to appear as late in the process as (say) the testing phase, it is not entirely unknown.

The basic cause of this is, of course, the problem of comprehending the complexity involved sufficiently enough to be certain that it can be achieved in software within other constraints which may apply.

Some of the main factors whose impact may be imponderable until late in the day are those of optimality, allowed time, underconfiguration, prematurity, and insufficiency.

1. Optimality in requirements, such as that concerning program size or execution time, often dominates design and coding practice to the detriment of both. The impact on software quality is a subject in Chapter 9.

2. The time allowed to complete a software job is not a critical issue if it is reasonably determined (Weinberg and Schulman). Experience shows, however, that if the required timescale is compressed beyond a certain point, it places severe constraints on the job. Firstly, on its feasibility and, secondly, on the quality of the resulting software system. This point is dealt with in Chapter 5.

3. Underconfiguration of computer equipment can invalidate a software engineering endeavour late in its development. Avoiding this hazard is the subject in part of Section 4.5.

4. Prematurity is the tendency of software engineers (so-called) to dash straight from an early stage of specification into the coding stage. This should not be confused with prototyping, which is the subject of Section 2.3.1 and elsewhere (notably, Chapter 4).

5. Insufficiency is the general lack of means, methods and tools available to software engineers, or their inability or unwillingness to use them.

Invisibility

Earlier the point was made that software engineering must be a visible process. This matter of visibility is the subject of Sections 3.3 and 6.4.

It is frequently said that parts of the software engineering process are 'invisible', such as the coding stage, when what is meant is that either the outcome of a thought process is not yet evident (e.g. as code), or that it is evident but incomprehensible (i.e. in a 'foreign' language such as Pascal, or C, or assembler code). In fact, software engineering as a process is not intrinsically invisible, although its practitioners may make it so, and this supposed property is – like others – curable.

2.2.2 Complexity

As a matter of experience, most practising software engineers, and many of their managers and other associates, know and respect the problems of complexity in software engineering. Nonetheless, there is often a feeling that the difficulties are exaggerated, and questions are raised such as: 'Why should software engineering be any more difficult than (say) hardware electronic engineering – that too can be complex can't it?'

Of course, there is no absolute and universal answer to this kind of question. One could give examples of software that are far less complex than some electronic (hardware) systems, and vice versa. The fact remains that software systems most frequently turn out to be extremely complex constructions – so much so that even with the best practices and procedures the systems are not easy to maintain and emend, even by their authors. This factor alone is sufficient to distinguish software engineering as a process from many others which might be taken as a basis for simile. In fact, the nearest example one can find is the game of chess, where the full understanding of a game or position can take an immense intellectual effort even for the players.

The problem of complexity in software is, in the first place, that specifications are transformed into an intellectual construct or set of constructions to deliver the features and functions required. Furthermore, there may be no immediately obvious relationship between the representation of this construct (the program) and the real world of requirements.

The same is not generally true in hardware engineering. Even the author of a program, returning to it only a short time later (two or three weeks may suffice), may find the code difficult to follow, however well created and documented. Like the chess player, the programmer will say, in effect, I understand the instructions (moves) but I do not yet comprehend the purpose (strategy).

In the field of electronics itself, the closest known application area similar in complexity to software engineering is that of very large-scale integrated circuitry, where one may be dealing with the design of hundreds of thousands of logical features. This fact was pointed out by Mayo (1982), at which time it was a matter of conjecture how close the simile could be drawn between software engineering and 'chip' design, construction and testing. The thesis, effectively that 'chip' design can be made more of a science than an art and that hardware and software design should become part of one and the same process, is eminently reasonable as a statement of aims. It is our view that for reasons of dissimilarity between the two fields of endeavour, these aims are likely to remain unfulfilled at the present time and for the foreseeable future. The greatest of these is that, after three decades of software engineering (or amateur programming for that matter), the expectations of users and potential users are almost unlimited. Perhaps to its detriment, software engineering is seen as including 'flexibility' within a system; after all it is a trivial matter to change a few instructions isn't it? Consequently, the scope of applications for software engineering (particularly in IT products) and the expectations for flexibility are very great indeed, and convenient analogies tend to break down.

Within the matter of complexity, as affecting software engineering, this expectation of flexibility is a distinct and worrying problem. Software is not flexible! In fact the name 'software' is a distinctly misleading one because of its first particle. Software is not 'soft' in the sense of being easily malleable – it is more nearly 'crystalline', given to shattering and the unpredictable propagation of fractures. Of course it is, on the surface, easy to change. For ADD X substitute SUB Y; what could be easier or more flexible? When, several months or years later, an odd and apparently unrelated software failure occurs, the relative inflexibility of the software becomes evident. The more complex the software, by requirement and construction, the less flexible it will be. An aim of software design and coding is to contain and if possible reduce the complexity of construction.

There have been, over the past years, many attempts to address software complexity on a seemingly scientific basis, in order to improve the process of software engineering. Amongst the positive results have been the principles established for good design and programming (coding) practice that are the subjects, in part, of Chapters 7 and 8. Other researchers have attempted to measure and calibrate software complexity in some formula-based or algorithmic fashion. At the present time, there is no definitive and generally accepted 'best method' for measuring software complexity. Amongst several authors in the field, the reader is referred (if interested in the matter at this inconclusive stage of research) to DeMarco (1982) and Boehm (1981) for general accounts; and to Halstead (1977), McCabe (1976) and Thayer *et al.* (1978), for specific complexity models. The reader may get some feel for the abstruse nature of much of this work when reading Chapter 5 on estimating, where the McCabe and Halstead models are quoted on the basis of the claims made for them as correlated with effort to make a software system. The model due to Thayer *et al.* is referred to in Section 9.4.3.

However, at the present time, the matter of complexity as a measurable property of a software system is not established. For the most part, the formulae advanced refer only to retrospective computation of complexity for a particular software system, using parameters such as the number of operators and operands in the program (Halstead), or the number of logic statements, I/O commands, executable statements, etc. (Thayer *et al.*).

2.3 Software system types

For subsequent use as terminology within this text, we define the following basic properties of software systems other than their application type:

1. *The version.* That is, whether the software system is a substantive version, for release as a 'production engineered' entity, or whether it is a prototype as defined in Section 2.3.1.

2. *The end market type.* In particular, for a substantive (release) version

of software, whether the object is a project or a product as defined in Section 2.3.2.

3. *The specification and implementation characteristics.* The so-called S-type, P-type or E-type features of a software system, as defined (after Lehman, 1980) in Section 2.3.3.

4. *The authorship.* In particular, whether a software system is the result of a team or single person endeavour. This matter is discussed in Section 2.3.4.

2.3.1 Prototypes

A prototype is an artefact whose principal purpose is to furnish information, either about what to make or how to make it. In this sense, prototyping is the act of buying information. As this is usually done under severe limitations of timescale and other resources (staff, money, etc.) the outcome – even if satisfactory in the sense of the information it provides – is seldom sufficiently well made for incorporation within a substantive (release) version. These characteristics of prototyping are as true in systems engineering in general as in software engineering in particular. Nevertheless, whereas the limitations of prototyping are fully known and their consequences recognized in other forms of engineering, the same cannot be said for software engineering.

The purposes of prototyping in software engineering are clear enough. Firstly, the process of specification may be enhanced by a tangible system incorporating some of the requirements. The special topic of rapid prototyping as a specification method, a subject of considerable importance currently at and somewhat beyond the research status, is discussed in Section 4.4. Secondly, a decision about the technical feasibility and implementation of a software system might more easily be reached if parts of the software (and perhaps hardware also) are made. This is the subject of specific comment in Section 4.5.

Still, in software engineering there is a danger of misclassifying prototypes and incorporating them in substantive, release-level versions of a system. This is evidently misguided and potentially extremely dangerous, depending on the application. We strongly recommend, and this is reiterated elsewhere, that all prototypes for whatever purpose are clearly designated as prototypes and then when their dominant purpose of buying information has been achieved, they are either properly engineered for incorporation within a release version (see Section 4.6), saved under the proper designation for future prototype use, or thrown away.

2.3.2 End market types

Excepting prototypes and some software systems as the object of research, software engineering is concerned with the development of computer programs for one of two basic purposes:

- *Projects*, which are software developments contracted for a single, identified end client.

- *Products*, which are software developments for a multiplicity of, as yet, unsecured (and maybe unknown) clients.

For a project, the end client should act as the source of requirements, and either effect or participate in their formal specification. The client should also authorize the baseline specification, monitor the implementation directly (or indirectly by other contract), and establish an acceptance procedure of the software system and its documentation. In addition to a warranty arrangement with the supplier of the software, the client for a project should also arrange for the continuing maintenance of the software.

For a product, someone should undertake the same rôle as played by a client for a project, but the issues of who this should be and how it should be done are seldom evident. In this case, the best course of action is to nominate a 'user surrogate' – usually a multi-disciplinary group – from the commercial (marketing/sales) and technical sectors of the firm undertaking a product. This user surrogate should act, pseudo-contractually, exactly in the fashion specified for the client in a contractual relationship for a project. As well as other rôles analogous to those of an external client, the user surrogate should define and instigate a product field-maintenance organization for the system concerned. All of this is, of course, easier said than done, the argument being that the personnel concerned are all in the same company/department/building/room, and that the requirements of the 'users' are unrealistic, too costly, against company policy and so on.

However, the lack of a user-surrogate philosophy for a product development does lead to great confusion of rôles, and problems of demarcation and authority in the matter of product specification, management and acceptance.

Although there is a fundamental distinction between projects and products according to the definition of terms given above, this distinction causes no difference in the scope or quality of deliverables.

2.3.3 Specification and implementation characteristics

The terminology S-type, P-type and E-type software systems was introduced several years ago by Lehman, to classify software systems by some characteristics of specification or implementation. We acknowledge Lehman's original paper (1980) as the source of this terminology, and of our adapted definitions given below. The terms in the classification are:

- Specifiable (S-type) systems
- Programmable (P-type) systems
- Evolutionary (E-type) systems

In S-type systems, the requirement can be precisely specified, is invariant with time, and an exact (provable) implementation can be achieved. Consequently, such systems are, in general, small in software terms (see Section 2.3.4) and therefore often within the capabilities of a single person to achieve within reasonable limits of effort and timescale. Thus, S-type software systems are likely to include the sort of programs written (by hobbyists) on home computers; they are also most often the level of system with which computer scientists work to demonstrate axioms and developed methods in design and programming.

In the case of P-type systems, a complete and precise specification of requirements can be given, for which only an approximate implementation exists at the software level. Thus, P-type software systems include mathematical programming, some games-playing problems (such as chess), meteorological systems and so forth. Apart from improvements to algorithms in the implementation domain, P-type systems remain invariant with time as their requirements do not change. Thus, many P-type software systems are exceedingly large suites of programs existing in relatively unaltered form for many years.

E-type systems are those whose requirements will, inevitably, change with time, either because real-world requirements change (as in the case of organizational evolution and its effect on an information system), or because the existence of the system changes the real world environment in some way. Thus, an E-type system can be said to be one whose requirements can be specified, possibly as precisely as for an S-type system, but that the specification must be seen as valid only temporarily. E-type software systems can vary in size from the very small to the exceedingly large and elaborate (see Section 2.3.4). Their principal property is that requirements change, necessitating emendation of the software system, perhaps in a relatively short timescale. These changes are known as 'new versions' of the software, and may be caused by changes of technology as well as evolution of requirements. E-type systems, more than either of the other two types, establish the need for good engineering practice in making the software in the first place; badly made software prevents its evolution and re-use for new versions, as well as affecting its maintainability. For these reasons, software engineering is generally taken to refer to E-type systems (which greatly predominate in the world of applications anyway), although it is clear that the same general guidelines for good software engineering practice should apply to P-type systems, which may also require emendation, albeit probably over a longer timescale. Lehman (1981) refers to any non-S-type software system (i.e. an E- or P-type) as an A-type system.

2.3.4 Authorship and team size

Software engineering is generally understood to be a team-based activity. The reason for this is that, although software systems exist in many different sizes, by far the most usual case is that in which the size of the software system-to-be is too large for a single author to complete within a reasonable timescale.

The usual measurement of software size is that of source-code statements. Thus we might speak of a system comprising, say, 10 000 FORTRAN statements. That this may translate (compile) into, say, 45 000 lines of object (assembler) code is not significant in the matter of how much software has actually been written. (Nor, incidentally, is the fact that this assembler code may occupy in the order of 90 000 bytes of store for a given computer.) It is generally accepted that small software systems are those of less than about 2000 source-code statements, irrespective of programming language, and that above this level medium-sized, large and super-large software systems are in the range 2000 to 100 000, 100 000 to 1 000 000, and over 1 000 000 source-code statements respectively.

Small software systems can usually be made by a single author 'team', whereas larger ones cannot within normally applying timescales. The multi-person team attribute applies, therefore, to virtually all medium, large and super-large software systems whatever their other properties as prototypes, products or projects, and whether they are S-type, P-type or E-type systems. Having said that, it is unusual to find small S-type systems done by teams, and not unusual to find small P- and E-type systems done by single authors.

The multi-person team property of most software developments calls for special consideration. The organization of software teams is the subject of Section 6.3, and any special provisions needed for single-person 'teams' are commented on, where appropriate, as footnotes to the chapters describing the part of software engineering affected.

Single-author software development is generally for small S-type systems (by hobbyists for self-instruction and by some computer scientists for research), and for small E-type systems that require a few hundred source-code statements, probably in assembler, on a small microprocessor. (Generally it is the sort of IT application needed for a control program for a washing machine, station-search feature in a car radio, and so on.) The result, for E-type systems in the IT sector at least, is most often an exercise in amateur programming. However apparently 'successful' the

Table 2.1 A software competences audit. (Y = yes; N = no; (?) = perhaps; ? = don't know.)

	Practitioner		Manager or other (non-practitioner)
	Software engineer	Amateur programmer	
1. What was the largest program you personally wrote in the last 5 years expressed as source-code size in whatever language?	20KPASCAL	1K assembler	1K FORTRAN (?)
* Was it S, P or E?	E	?	S
* Did it involve prototyping?	Y	?	N
* Was it for a product or project?	Prod.	Prod.	Proj.
* Was it part of a team-based development?	Y	N	N
* Have you ever been part of a software engineering team?	Y	N	N
2. If you were the manager accountable could you:-			
* Do a structured walkthrough of a software development?	Y(?)	?	N
* Know what information is needed to manage it?	N	N	Y(?)
* Do you recognise : a good functional specification?	Y	?	N
: a software design?	Y	N	N
: a test strategy?	Y	N	N
3. Could you estimate a software development job (± 25%)?	Y(?)	N	N
4. Do you think you need much, some or a little more knowledge of software engineering?	Much	Little	Some
5. Are your software development tools adequate or inadequate?	Inadeq.	Adeq.	?

outcome, it may not be a properly engineered software system in the sense that its E-type system properties of evolution can reasonably be achieved by making new versions. Nor are excursions such as these good paradigms for future software engineering practice – neither for the practitioner concerned nor the management involved.

2.4   The software competence audit

At this stage it would be possible in any IT organization to do an appraisal of practitioners, and their managers and other parties directly affecting the software engineering process, along the following lines.

Table 2.1 depicts a checklist of questions based on the terminology already discussed, and indicates some possible ('specimen') responses depending on the nature of the organization concerned. These 'specimens' are by no means uncommon, however, and account for some part of the 'crisis' in software engineering and its poor reputation. The checklist is indicative not definitive; many more questions could be included on both technical and managerial aspects. In effect, this is the sort of audit that managers should undertake in IT companies. (Don't wait for it to be done by others; remember – the line between leading people and being pursued by them is a very fine one!)

Once again let us stress that the entries are 'specimen' only, although not unrepresentative. Where the picture is one of dramatic imbalance (say all the managers and 'others' with little or no subject knowledge; lots of amateur programming; a weak culture for software engineers), the remedy needs to be radical and urgently undertaken.

From the following chapter onwards we set about rectifying some of the possible shortcomings depicted in the hypothetical (but plausible) checklist shown above. This culminates, in Chapter 10, with a definitive checklist for good software engineering practice – at which point the issues and appropriate guidelines for dealing with them should be entirely clear.

Chapter 3 Managing software development: fundamental issues

Synopsis

The basic problem between dialogue partners lacking shared conceptual models and vocabulary is discussed, along with the dangers of substituting simile and analogy for real experience and legitimate paradigm.

A software 'lifecycle' model is identified as the basis of a shared, conceptual framework between dialogue partners in software engineering.

The need is asserted for pro-active management of the software engineering process. The 'archive' is described as the necessary means for visibility.

The method of structured walkthrough is outlined for pro-active management.

The dangers of informal specification change are identified, and the change control committee construction is described as a means of dealing with it.

3.1 Comprehension

As already remarked, the problems of software engineering do not stem only from its inherent complexity as a process, but also from an inevitable lack of comprehension between non-specialists and software engineers. This condition can apply in any subject – mechanical engineering, law, physics, accountancy, and so on. As a result of various factors listed in Section 1.3, its effects are particularly noticeable in software engineering and can often be seen among different groups of people needing (and trying) to comprehend each other:

1. Users (or others who specify requirements) and implementation staff.

2. Subproject staff from different technological disciplines, working on a composite system.

3. Managers and commercial staff with little or no subject knowledge, and practitioners who may be either software engineers or amateur programmers.

The rôle of natural language is clearly central to the problems of comprehension as they beset the various parties to the process. The point has been well summarized, in general, by Eco, who advances the view that:

All forms of communication, interpretation and understanding are tentative acts of influence.

This should be borne in mind by all parties involved in creating software systems. As authors, we too have this condition to deal with. Whilst Eco's aphorism has commonplace application, it is particularly important in software engineering for two fundamental reasons:

1. There is an inherent problem in specifying complex requirements in a totally unambiguous and coherent fashion (see Chapter 4).

2. A very major difficulty arises from transformation out of natural language at the specification stage, via progressive steps of increasing detail and abstract form, into the language of program execution – binary bit patterns.

In these circumstances, 'tentative acts of influence' is a most apposite description of human communication within the software engineering process.

Comprehension involves the creation and use of conceptual models for which the two prerequisites are language (vocabulary, syntax, grammar) and paradigms (exact or sufficiently similar examples). In software engineering, those who are not specialists in the subject but are part of the process lack both a shared language and serviceable paradigms with practitioners and each other. Thus adequate comprehension of the process is disabled, and its management (at least) is an inevitable casualty as a result.

We have noticed a tendency to adopt, as a means of compensating for a basic lack of comprehension, a variety of similes and analogies to account for the characteristics of different steps and stages in the software engineering process. The argument usually goes: 'Software engineering is, after all, just like such-and-such a field of engineering (mechanical or electronic), and so we are justified in thinking so-and-so about this part of it!' Simile in this form is a trap for the unwary. Up to a point it may hold good; for example that planning a software job must be just as possible as (say) planning a bridge-building construction job. Controlling the activities in one must be just as possible as in the other, and so forth.

Where simile breaks down is below this high level of generalization, where the particularities and peculiarities of software engineering become extremely significant. That is not to deny that much in software engineering is similar to systems engineering in general, but the residue – which is considerable – is the essence, the uniqueness of software engineering as a process. In the matter of comprehension we have found that simile can be exceedingly dangerous, and that it is no adequate substitute (when direct comprehension is lacking) for paradigm.

In the following chapter, therefore, we suggest a model of the software engineering process to act as both a shared language and a paradigm between people of disparate backgrounds using this book.

3.2   A software 'lifecycle' model

The notion of software engineering as a cyclic process is consistent with the E-type system property of most software developments, as defined in the previous chapter. The exceptions are S-type systems, 'throw away' prototypes and some categories of software as the object of research. In practice, it is safest to regard all software developments as being of the E-type, whether it is evident that they are so or not. The effects of this will be software systems designed and constructed to be more easily modifiable by their authors, and others, than would be the case otherwise.

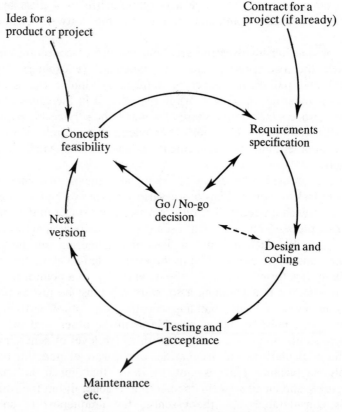

Fig. 3.1   A simple systems lifecycle.

At its simplest level of diagrammatic representation, software engineering, incorporating the E-type loop property, has an appearance of the form shown in Figure 3.1. This schematic depicts the E-type loop as 'Next Version', and also shows the initiation of the cyclic process for products and projects, feedback between main generic activities, and major decision points. (*Note.* The possibility of 'go/no-go' decisions during the implementation activities of design and coding is held to be unlikely but not impossible; as was said in Section 2.2.1, the feasibility of some software systems is undecidable until late in their implementation.)

Some lifecycle schemes favour what is known as 'the cascade' form of representation, as depicted in Figure 3.2. In general we have found either

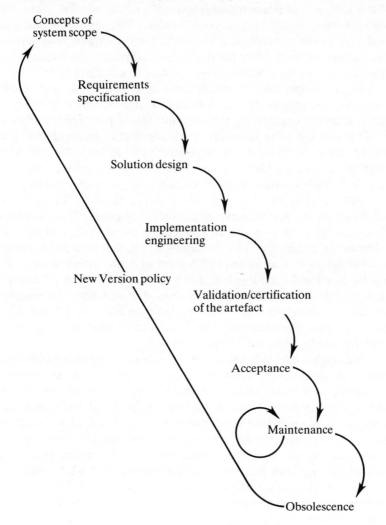

Fig. 3.2   A cascade depiction of the lifecycle.

that these representations are excessively simple or that, being more elaborate, they need to be decomposed into several pages of 'cascades'. Figure 3.1, being an extremely simple representation of a software 'lifecycle', is not quite of the right level of detail to act as a practical paradigm for the full process of software engineering. A more detailed model is given in Figure 3.3. In this schematic, essential activities are logically ordered and represented in arrow diagram form to indicate the sequences and interrelationships between them.

Most companies active in software engineering have a lifecycle model of some sort. Some are over-simplistic, like that depicted in Figure 3.1. Some are excessively elaborate, and it could be argued that Figure 3.3 is of this sort, in that it incorporates too many of the possibilities of real-life software engineering and its complexities. This approach destroys the model as a clear conceptual framework. Others employ non-self-evident terminology or even codes for the generic activities and thereby lose the opportunity to coin a usable language that is self-descriptive.

As a compromise between excessive simplicity and confusing complexity we propose to use a subset of Figure 3.3 as the working model of the software engineering process, and this is portrayed in Figure 3.4.

Our aim has been to create a scheme that is an acceptable level of simplification expressed in an auto-descriptive fashion. Nonetheless, the lifecycle model is an idealized and somewhat simplified representation of generic activities within software engineering. Its usefulness depends on an understanding of that fact. It is not a formula for standardized behaviour on the part of software engineers or others. It (and others like it) should be used as a shared conceptual framework, and as a strong guideline on the essential subprocesses within software engineering.

Insofar as it is an oversimplification in some specific cases, the fact will be noted and a modified version given in the chapters following when such specifics come under consideration. For instance, the complexities introduced when prototypes are needed (see Sections 4.3 and 4.5) may make the lifecycle schematic representation of what is going on almost unrecognizable. Figure 4.12 illustrates this.

Although a lifecycle model of the software engineering process can never be an invariant formula for doing software development, it is invaluable as a basic, shared vocabulary for making the process visible and comprehensible between all parties involved such as users (or surrogates), clients, managers, commercial staff, software engineers and hardware engineers, quality departments, field maintenance and support groups, and so on. Instead of a manager asking a software engineer some amorphous question like 'How is it going on the XYZ project?', the sharper question 'What lifecycle stage are we at on XYZ?' can be asked, so long as a shared framework of understanding exists for the question and its answer.

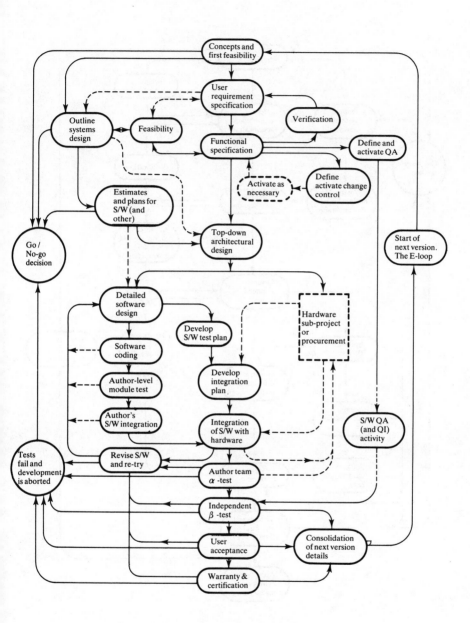

Fig. 3.3   A complex systems lifecycle.

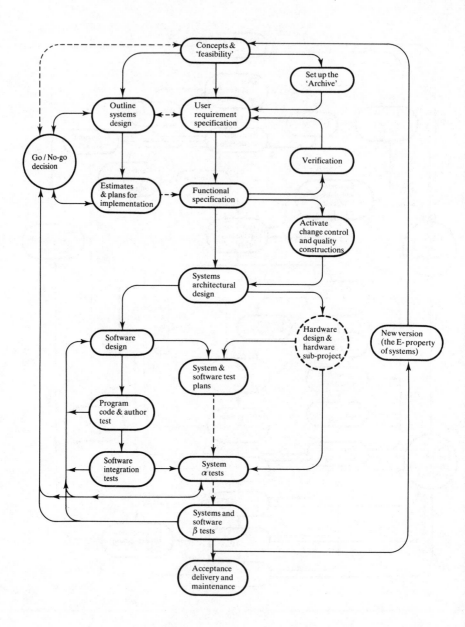

Fig. 3.4 A lifecycle model of the software engineering process.

3.3   Visibility; archiving

The principal vehicle for visibility of a software development, as in systems engineering in general, is the 'archive' of activities. Without an archive (or something equivalent), the process is very difficult to inspect and therefore effectively impossible to manage properly. One can ask a software engineer the question: 'What lifecycle stage are you at on the XYZ project', and – unless the process is visible – the person can answer any way without fear of contradiction. Neither can a manager simply prescribe visibility in some vague way nor, for that matter, try to have visibility created retro-actively. The prescription must be specific; the archive or whatever it is to be called (the terminology is less important than the content) must be created at the start of the lifecycle, and it must be continually updated.

It is, in our experience, worthwhile spending some time and effort in clarifying what is meant by an 'archive'. Managers frequently have a surprisingly poor grasp of what archiving should comprise, and many software engineers (who should have to make and maintain the archive) more often than not regard the whole notion as a complete novelty. There are two basic and exceedingly simple guidelines for archiving.

1. Format the archive.
2. Select material for the archive, and be prepared to discard some of it from the document.

Whilst, on the face of it, an archive is simply an historical record of all activities and correspondence comprising a software engineering task, it will be unreadable if it is in a state of disorder. We have found archives that resemble geological formations with a paleolithic deposit, a neolithic layer and so on. The simple, chronological format is unhelpful. Other formats may be little better. We have seen archives structured on the basis of team membership, e.g. 'Fred's section, Bill's bit, Mary's work' and so on. That too is unhelpful.

Tables 3.1 and 3.2 offer suggestions for formatting the archive in two sections – technical and management materials. We have found the most useful approach is to divide the technical section on the basis of major lifecycle stages. Chapters 4 and 7–9 define and discuss in full the various terms used in Table 3.1. The terms and issues involved in the management section are covered in the current chapter in part, and also in Chapters 5, 6 and 10.

The state of affairs at any stage of the software lifecycle can be extremely volatile, with many aspects of requirement or implementation changing rapidly. This dynamism should of course be controlled, but in any event it may make the matter of documentary records difficult to

Table 3.1   Technical contents of an archive.

Section 1	*Contents*
1.1	Overall contents list for the Archive (both sections)
1.2	Early requirements and solution feasibility ideas
1.3	User Requirements Specifications
1.4	Functional Specifications
1.5	Outline Systems Designs (Hardware & Software taxonomies)
1.6	Architectural Design, and definition of the software task
1.7	Detailed Software Designs (Top level . . . module designs)
1.8	Program Code Listings (names consistent with 1.7)
1.9	Software Test Plans (Individual, Integration, Alpha-test, etc)
1.10	Deliverable Documentation (User, Maintenance, Operators manuals)
1.11	Client (or surrogate) technical correspondence

Table 3.2   Management control contents of an archive.

Section 2	*Contents*
2.1	Overall contents list for the Archive (both sections)
2.2	Definition of organization structure and management methods (including quality)
2.3	Definition of task (contract if an external project)
2.4	Timescale and effort estimates, original and subsequent
2.5	Activities plan and progress status matrices
2.6	Cost (or effort) control documents; actual versus estimates
2.7	Change control requests, decisions etc.
2.8	Minutes of team meetings, design and code review, etc.
2.9	Minutes of structured walkthrough with management
2.10	Client (or surrogate) contractual/non-technical correspondence
2.11	Any standards for documentation or quality factors applying

arrange. As a matter of course, requirements documents will be added to or subtracted from during specification. At later stages of the software engineering process, design and code will be highly dynamic affairs as implementation ideas are put into practice, and both modified and corrected as an exercise in convergence towards the desired system. Testing a system may develop into a highly volatile (and anarchic) scramble against a deadline.

If all and everything pertaining to these stages and their documentation is saved indiscriminately, then the archive will be a difficult record to maintain, and possibly unusable as a result. As a guideline on what to archive and what to discard (or 'purge') we offer the view that one should begin by archiving every lifecycle category of document and thereafter use the following scheme for discarding. To begin with, there are two basic status categories in technical and management archives – 'formal' and 'informal' documents. No version of any formal document should be discarded, whereas only the current and immediately previous versions of informal documents need be retained at any time during a software development. Thus one should save all versions of the Functional Specification (see Section 4.4), Change Control transactions (see Section 3.5) and – for a project – all contract and client transactions, including every version of estimates and project plans (see Chapters 5 and 6). These documents may all have a bearing on any contentions arising about the scope of a software system and its realized implementation. Apart from these documents all else in the technical part should only be archived in its currently valid version, plus the one immediately preceding it, with clear version designation and dating. This applies, therefore, to user requirement specifications, architectural and detailed software designs, code listings, and authors' test-plans and results.

As for the management part of the archive, it is best to save all versions of all documents, to maintain a complete record of the project or product development from the viewpoint of its planning and control.

The organization of archiving and its physical enactment is a specific task within a software team, and this is described in Section 6.3. The overlaps and distinctions between archiving and documentation for other purposes are dealt with in Section 10.1.

Notwithstanding the guidelines given above for selecting and purging material, the archive can become extremely voluminous. As a result it is a frequently heard argument that the whole business is too intrusive into the creative parts of software engineering, too much of a burdensome bureaucracy to justify any real archiving at all. It is true that, in the past, there was little alternative but to maintain archives (and other documentation) manually, and that this was particularly difficult for things like diagrammatic designs and exceedingly volatile documents such as code listings. In recent times, facilities for computer-based software development and configuration control environments have mitigated the archiving (and other documentation) problems in most, but not all, respects. See Sections 8.3 and 10.2.

Today, there is no excuse at all for unarchived software development work. Nor is it an insupportably high overhead on the software engineering process, so long as the practice of archiving is a part of 'good practices' that software engineers adopt at the start of the lifecycle and maintain properly thereafter. It becomes insupportably difficult if it is attempted at the wrong stage or allowed to lapse. Managers should require archiving to be done as a part of 'good software engineering practice', and software engineers should appreciate its value from their own point of view. The visibility thus achieved should then be used as part of a mutual process of management involving the parties to the software engineering process. Not least of its virtues, the archive will also act as some 'insurance policy' against staffing problems on a project – for instance, if software engineers leave or are transferred, then at least their work to date should be in an available form to be taken over by others.

3.4   Active management and the practice of structured walkthrough

The history of software engineering is full of examples of software developments for which the accountable level of management has been powerless to define and control objectives and activities. In some cases the process has been truly 'invisible' through lack of any tangible record of activities; in some cases the process has been visible but incomprehensible because of a combination of subject unfamiliarity on the part of managers, and the use of specialist jargon by the software staff. The result has been, generally, a horrifying mess with the accountable management adopting a strongly defensive posture. The terms 'default' and 'crisis' management have been invented, and may indeed have some application in subjects other than software engineering, where 'default' management usually means no management at all, and even delegation becomes abdication.

It is in the nature of software engineering, no doubt due to the difficulty and abstract nature of its language and terminology, that accountable managers not skilled in the subject lose confidence very rapidly in their ability to manage its practitioners. The resulting 'default' management is generally little more than a lame excuse for doing nothing when, indeed, nothing can be done.

The first step in redressing this condition is for accountable managers to become sufficiently aware of the process of software engineering to enable them to see it as a potentially manageable activity. The second step is to ensure that projects are visible, via a form of archiving such as that described in Section 3.3. The third step is to have the confidence to manage the software engineering process pro-actively, as distinct from re-actively. The generally accepted technique for pro-active management is an ordered and critical inspection of what is going on, in order to anticipate exigencies in the process. In software engineering, this is called 'structured walkthrough' of a software project or product development. Of all management practices in software engineering, the structured walkthrough is fundamentally important if problems are to be anticipated and circumvented. Other factors, such as archiving (as already described) and change control procedures (see Section 3.5), are necessary means to the successful ends, and contribute to the technique of structured walkthrough of a software development. A clear understanding of the technique is, therefore, essential.

Management styles differ from place to place and person to person, but the following elements of a structured walkthrough should be fully provided for irrespective of these differences.

1. The form of the walkthrough must be decided by the manager, otherwise the method will degenerate into a vague review. Along with the form, which should be based on the software lifecycle schematic in Figure 3.4, the wherewithal for the walkthrough must be the archive, which must contain documents for the lifecycle stages undertaken, as well as management-control information as described in Section 6.2.

2. The frequency of walkthrough must be decided by the manager. This will probably be done on a 'best-case' basis (i.e. once a fortnight, or once a month or whatever is deemed suitable in a particular circumstance), and will be varied in the case of necessity if, for instance, something goes badly wrong in the interim.

3. The participants and their rôles must be decided. The manager will clearly require the principal software engineer to attend and explain the current status of the software, in detail and according to the 'form' decided, and the 'principal' will co-opt colleagues as need be.

4. Structured walkthroughs of software development tasks are so fundamentally important that their outcome should be formalized. The manager should, for this purpose, require a check-point procedure to be undertaken and recorded. For this, a checklist of essential provisions and achievements for good software engineering practice should be drawn up for use in structured walkthrough, and an action list should be produced as and if appropriate, in which all actions are assigned to appropriate people and completion times specified.

As well as these four basic guidelines on structured walkthrough as a management technique, several other observations and embellishments are appropriate for a proper understanding of it. These are set out below in paragraph form corresponding to the four indented points above.

Some managers, as a matter of personal style, do not favour a form of structured walkthrough in which technical matters of design and implementation are reviewed in detail, even if these factors are problematical. This inhibition, or downright inability in many cases, is perfectly understandable and has been discussed elsewhere.

To some extent, as described in Chapters 6 and 9, good software engineering practices within a development team – particularly peer-group design review and code reading – should obviate the need for detailed technical exposition at walkthroughs, unless particularly severe problems are being experienced. In these cases, a manager who is not a subject expert (being perhaps a hardware engineer for instance on a large, composite system development), may co-opt a surrogate for the more technology-intensive parts of a walkthrough. Typical sources of such 'surrogates' are independent quality assurance departments, so long as they are competent in software engineering or, otherwise, external software engineering suppliers on contract for the purpose.

If the software implementation team's quality control activities are sufficient, and if software designs and code are independently reviewed as a part of quality assurance, a structured walkthrough is unlikely to involve detailed technical exposition and argument. Otherwise, if severe technical problems do arise, special measures may be called for. These are discussed further below.

The issue of frequency for structured walkthroughs is somewhat a matter of personal style on behalf of the manager accountable for a software development. Some favour a known and fixed schedule, whilst others prefer to spring structured walkthroughs on the software development team at irregular intervals.

So long as the frequency is adequate for the purpose of anticipating and circumventing problems, we hold no strong feelings on this matter of management style – although it must be admitted that a method involving the element of surprise has many attractions. Not least, it tends to keep the issues of archiving very much in software engineers' minds. Otherwise, given (say) a known monthly frequency for walkthroughs, there may be a sudden dash to update an archive just before the meeting. Such practice does, of course, disable the archive as an 'insurance policy' against staffing problems, and must be avoided.

There is no fixed prescription for walkthrough frequency. Nevertheless, for all but shortest, smallest and simplest software jobs the best frequency will be between two and four weeks. A useful method for deciding frequency is to define key milestones, in lifecycle terms, at which something visible should be available. For example, a functional specification, a definition of the software to be developed (part of the architectural design – see Chapter 7), a detailed software design, coded program modules, completed stages of a testing regime, deliverable documentation, and so forth. On the basis of the estimated time to reach milestones, the interregnum may be divided into reasonable review periods such as two, three or four weeks, and walkthroughs scheduled accordingly. Thus, if it is supposed to take six months to do a functional specification, one may decide to have walkthroughs on a monthly basis. Walkthroughs early in the lifecycle will tend to be rather amorphous affairs, as the activities concerned will be ones of specification, and rather difficult to say much about other than that things are generally going well or not. Consequently, the frequency is likely to be lower than at later stages of the lifecycle. Whether this is a good thing or not depends entirely on the nature and difficulty of the task. It must not be overlooked that, at the early stages of specification, the questions of basic feasibility will (or should) also occur. As a result, prototypes may be required, and these decisions will most likely result from structured walkthroughs early in the lifecycle, and will themselves require management by structured walkthrough if undertaken.

Later in the lifecycle, from design onwards, there may be a resistance to structured walkthroughs by a software team striving to get a job done, under trying circumstances perhaps. Nonetheless, structured walkthrough at these stages is just as important as at other times – possibly more so if a variety of problems are applying simultaneously, as is frequently the case.

As to participants at a walkthrough, and their rôles, the situation is usually quite straightforward. The highest level of directly accountable management, such as the overall project or product development manager for a particular system – perhaps comprising several technical subprojects – should determine the frequency and form of structured walkthroughs, and convene and direct them. Higher levels of management may have their own review and reporting procedures also, but these should not replace or diminish the active management provisions for anticipating and circumventing problems. Similarly, development teams themselves may have progress review meetings, and these too should not replace the managers' structured walkthrough.

Software development team leaders must attend a structured walkthrough concerning a software task of which they are a part. It is they, supported by co-opted colleagues if need be, who must present the current status to the managers. This is usually an oral presentation with reference to the archive, activities plans, status matrices and cost-control information (for a description of these terms, see Section 6.2). Depending on the lifecycle stage reached, the manager can use a checklist (or relevant parts of it) such as defined in Section 10.6.

At the stage of functional specification, and thereafter to the 'bottom' of the lifecycle (beta-testing etc.), independent quality assurance staff should also attend structured walkthroughs and are often appointed as 'meeting secretaries'. They may be from an internal but independent quality assurance group, or from an externally contracted source. The rôles of quality assurance groups are discussed more fully in Sections 9.2 and 9.6.

When a particularly severe problem of design or detailed implementation occurs, the development may effectively stop for a time, whilst a very extended and extensive special structured walkthrough is undertaken. This may be by a totally independent, externally contracted agency with particular management reporting provisions. For severe problems the usual walkthrough form and rôles are emended whilst days, weeks or even months are given over to forensic review of specifications, designs and implemented parts of the system in question. When the problems have been remedied, the development should revert to its normal management form.

The usual output from a structured walkthrough is a minute to the manager and the team leader(s) noting progress, slippages, problems, changes and so forth, and attributing remedial actions and due dates for their accomplishment. These minutes should be archived, and therefore available for all implementation team members to see. Where an external client for a project is concerned, the output from structured walkthroughs (whether or not instigated and controlled by the client) may take on extreme contractual significance.

In the event of problems becoming so severe that a full review (say of design) is commissioned, the output may be in the form of a report 'auditing' a part or the whole of the system in question.

Structured walkthrough by management or its appointees is an essential part of good software engineering practice and, as such, it should be established at the start and maintained throughout the lifecycle of software engineering development activities, whatever the scale or nature of the application. Even a software task to make a few hundred source statements of code by a single author needs to be managed in this way, although the process will probably be a much simpler 'special case' of that described above.

A trace of paranoia is no bad thing in a manager, or at least a healthy apprehension of what might easily go wrong in software engineering. Asking 'Fred' how things are going in a vague way on bumping into him at the coffee machine is hardly good management practice.

3.5 Controlling specification change

One of the most virulent problems afflicting software engineering and its practitioners is that of unstable specification, particularly when changes are introduced informally. More often than not this concerns the casual and informal addition of requirements by users or user surrogates and their adoption – also at an informal level – by the implementation team.

Initiatives such as: 'What a pity it is that the real-time process-control system you are making won't do the payroll too', are not unknown. And responses of the type: 'No problem! I know the software backwards (I wrote it backwards). A patch or two here and there and you've got payroll – clever aren't I?', have a tendency to happen.

In an ideal world no one would need to initiate changes because all requirements would have been specified perfectly in the first place. However, the real world of requirement specification is far from perfect (see Chapter 4), and implementation teams will seldom be in a position to refuse changes emanating from clients or their own management.

The result can be chaos. There are many instances of software jobs ending in catastrophic failure as a result of casual attitudes to specification during the post-specification stages of the lifecycle. The effects of informal change to the scope of a software system can be utterly disastrous to the quality of designs and the software code itself.

In fact, the notions of 'fixing' or 'patching' software as a means of changing it – either for new specification or correction – should be prohibited by 'good practice' in strong software engineering environments. The way to effect change is to implement it properly at design and, thereafter, at code level, with as much regard to good design and programming practice as should have gone into it in the first place; then it should be fully and competently documented.

The solution to the problem of informal change is not to 'freeze' the specification but to formalize the process of change. One does not fix the (otherwise) moving target of specification, one manages its change in an orderly fashion.

This requires an organizational construction known as the 'change control' mechanism to be in place from the functional specification stage of the lifecycle onwards, and this construction can be determined from case to case on the basis of the following guidelines:

1. The change-control organization is usually a committee and, as such, has no prescriptive powers – only advisory ones.

2. The change-control committee usually comprises members from both the requirement domain (users/clients or their surrogates) and the technical implementation domain.

3. The change committee should be kept as small as need be – it is the more effective for it. At the very outside, for really enormous software systems involving many users and supplier agencies, the committee size should not exceed a dozen or so people, and may be organized into levels to consider changes of different categories of importance. For more modest applications, four or five people usually suffice.

4. The committee need not meet on a scheduled basis. It should be event-driven, the events being requests for change to the scope and detail of requirements from whatever source.

5. A crucial rôle of management will be to ensure that specification-change requests are made formally. A simple change-request form can be devised for this purpose. In the case of a project the agency ensuring this formality should be the contracting party itself, as a contractual matter. Often, due to the inexperience of clients, the supplier has to initiate the change-control mechanism.

6. All that a change-control committee will do is to evaluate, and report, the consequences of proposed changes to the scope or detail of specifications. This must occur before any change is commissioned.

Thereafter, the accountable management parties must explicitly agree to the changes and authorize all the requisite emendations to baseline specifications, contracts, archives, documents, and acceptance/ quality criteria.

7. The provisions for a change-control mechanism, its procedures and nominees, and its *modus operandi* in general, should be entirely evident as part of the project (or product) management definition, and this should be clear to the software engineers by incorporation in the archive.

   Similarly, all the formal change-control transactions should be archived, whether authorized and therefore acted upon or not.

3.6   Prototyping and single-author tasks

Whereas we view the situation in software engineering as requiring a widespread knowledge and acceptance of good practices in the subject, certain provisions and dispensations are needed for special cases when these legitimately occur. Prototypes and single-author software teams are two such special cases in software engineering.

So far as the contents of Chapter 3 are concerned up to this point, we have dealt with the conceptual model (or lifecycle) approach to software engineering and the good management practices of archiving, structured walkthrough, and managing specification change. How applicable are these precepts in the event of special cases such as prototyping on the one hand and single-author teams on the other hand (software engineering being, in general, a team-based activity)?

3.6.1   Managing prototype development

There is an undoubted tendency for the main objective of prototyping, to 'buy' information as quickly and cheaply as possible, to undermine good engineering and management practice. For that reason we have recommended the very clear designation of prototypes, and the disposal of them once they have served their primary purpose. However, the fact remains that prototyping will involve specification, design, coding and testing, however 'quick and dirty' these phases may be. Prototyping cannot be exempted from management just because it does not directly concern substantive (release) versions. Our recommendation for proto-typing is that all the facets of good management practice identified up to now should be applied.

Firstly, prototyping should involve a logical sequence of activities in specification, design, coding and testing, although in the nature of things this will be a highly complex, 'feedback'-based variant of the simple schematic in Figure 3.4. An example of this complexity is shown in Section 4.6 (Figure 4.12). Although the lifecycle form for a prototype cannot be prescribed in advance it should be evident, as matters progress, in the sense that at any time during prototyping the lifecycle activities up to that point should be possible to schematize in the same terms as those utilized in Figure 3.4.

Secondly, for a prototype to serve its purposes in providing information about requirements or implementation technology, its positive and negative achievements must be fully recorded. The simple adoption of archiving techniques, such as those outlined in Section 3.3 and the technique of structured walkthrough discussed in Section 3.4, may be sufficient for this purpose. In some cases, however, a very detailed de-briefing of the team(s) doing prototypes will be needed to convey thoroughly all the information 'bought' by the exercise.

As to the issue of change control in the case of a prototype, the last thing wanted is for any mechanism or approach to slow down or stop the process of innovation for which the exercise is intended. Thus, the notion of a formal change-control mechanism is not appropriate for prototypes. On the other hand, the changes to specification and prototype implementation (which can be extremely rapid) should be recorded in the archive, along with their contribution to knowledge (positive or negative) if known. The extreme mutability of most prototypes leads to a predominance of 'change' information in the archive, but as 'change assertions', not 'change requests'. When the prototyping exercise has served its purpose, its archive should contribute to the specification or design parts of a full lifecycle to make a properly engineered project or product unless, that is, the prototyping has led to a 'no-go' decision.

3.6.2 Managing single-author teams

There is nothing intrinsic to single-author software development, excepting S-type systems done for casual purposes by hobbyists or for research by computer scientists, that exempts it from the good software engineering and management practices of lifecycle management, archiving, structured walkthrough and formal change control. On the contrary, it is worthwhile emphasizing these needs, since authors of small E-type software systems (particularly as part of composite IT products) are often, simultaneously, the user surrogates and managers of the endeavour as well as its amateur programmer.

Naturally, when this is the case, one cannot expect a person to do structured walkthrough and formal change control within his or her own software-development activity. On the other hand, the correct sequencing of lifecycle activities should be preserved and this, along with their competent achievement, should be evident from an archive. This document should be in no way different from that described in Section

3.3, and should include both management control information such as estimates and plans, and specifications of changes as these occur. This will serve the purpose that, if things go wrong with the development, it will be possible to assess why this is the case and, perhaps, even recover from the problem.

Managers of single-author software developments should ensure adherence to good software engineering practice just as for more extensive, team-based systems. When the software developer is manager and user surrogate at the same time, it is wise for that person to arrange for some independent assessment of methods and achievements. This may be in the form of independent quality assurance as described in Section 9.6.

3.7 Coda

Software engineering concerns issues that are complex enough, and potentially incomprehensible enough, without compounding the problem through inept management of the process. All too often the following kind of scenario is enacted at largely accidental meetings:

Manager: Ah! you must be . . . er . . . Fred? Aren't you working on the . . . , how are things going?

Fred: Fine. We've got expansion-factor problems with the language, and a bug in the PSE has just wiped version two of the screen management software off the disk. Apart from that, and deadly embrace between two of the processors . . . Where's he off to in such a hurry? Was it something I said?

Chapter 4 Specification and feasibility

Synopsis

A general explanation is given of specification, its properties and difficulties.

The first steps in specification are described, and early notions, concepts and preliminary feasibility assessments are discussed.

The next step in specification is described including: the user requirements specification (URS) along with its necessity but probable insufficiency as a baseline for implementation; processes of extracting and systematizing requirement information; and the rôle of prototyping at this lifecycle stage.

The Functional Specification (FS) is defined as the necessary and sufficient statement of requirements to act as the baseline for implementation and acceptance; authorization of the FS; general scope and content of the FS; language and format; the rôle of 'formal' languages.

The Outline Systems Design (OSD) is described as repository for design and feasibility information; the use of software taxonomies as early, non-binding assessments of the possible scope of software to be made and as cross-check on possible hardware; the issues of OSD and detailed software designs are discussed.

Elaboration of the software lifecycle for prototyping in the URS and OSD stages is depicted, along with some variant lifecycle forms that can arise from commercial circumstances.

A summary is given of the outputs from the specification stage.

4.1 An overview of specification issues

Self-evidently, no systems-engineering development of whatever type can be undertaken without some understanding of objectives, however dimly apprehended. Even research and prototyping tasks have goals, expectations or aspirations. For systems development in general, however, the aim must be to specify the requirements adequately, before the substantive version of the system is developed as distinct from any trial attempts, prototypes, or pilot versions. In software engineering, it is especially important to specify requirements adequately, because of the additional difficulties in a process that becomes progressively more abstract in form. For example, it may be difficult to distinguish between errors of formulation, solution and demonstration. This is not special pleading for software engineers over other categories of system developer; it is a fact of life.

In general, the process of requirements specification at the system engineering level is seldom easy, and its outcome (as 'specifications') seldom adequate.

In former epochs, programming computers was thought of as nothing more than writing code in some suitable computer language (if, indeed, a choice existed), followed by the author of the program debugging it as well as possible. Thus, in Epochs 1 and 2 as defined elsewhere, specification might be by word of mouth or on the proverbial 'back of an envelope'. Similarly, design was either absent altogether, or a matter of a few scrappy flow diagrams (sometimes done retro-actively after the coding). Nowadays it is generally understood that the proportions of work involved in the principal phases of the software lifecycle are (approximately):

- Specification: 15%
- Design: 35%
- Coding: 15%
- Testing: 35%

The reader should be aware that these indications, and others similar (e.g. Wolverton, 1974), are indicative of general properties of the process and cannot be laid down as hard and fast rules; the proportions do vary according to circumstances. For instance, product specification involving extensive prototyping may 'front-load' the proportion assigned to specification, whilst prototyping for technical feasibility of a system to meet a set of requirements might 'mid-load' the element assigned to 'design'. Similarly, testing a system whose failure could have catastrophic consequences would 'end-load' the proportion of work due to validation (see Chapter 9). On the whole, however, the effort distribution over main lifecycle stages as quoted can stand as an indication of the non-trivial nature of activities other than coding and debugging code.

The present chapter deals with the process of specification. In software lifecycle terms, this concerns activities towards the top of the schematic of Figure 3.4, as indicated in Figure 4.1.

Henceforth, throughout the text, the following abbreviations are used: URS = User Requirement Specification; FS = Functional Specification; OSD = Outline System Design.

Furthermore, a set of examples is given to highlight different parts of

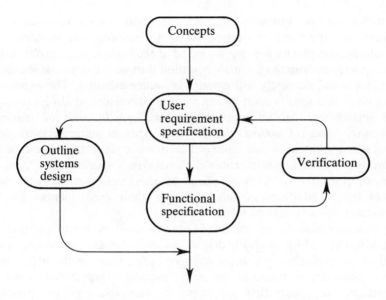

Fig. 4.1 Lifecycle subset: requirements and feasibility.

the specification process. These are chosen from a practical example of a
hospital patient and general alarm-monitoring system. For the sake of
consistency the same source is used for the example set in Chapter 7 (to
illustrate the use of different design notations), and elsewhere. This
harmonization of examples inevitably falls short of being a comprehensive
case-study or 'worked example'. Nor, in our view, is it possible to provide
one that highlights the main points in the text, and yet is not too
voluminous.

However, insofar as a single collection of specification and design
examples is possible and desirable, the collection of 'Extracts from an
Archive' in Chapter 11 is intended to serve in addition to the thematic
examples given here, in Chapters 5–7, and elsewhere.

Specifying systems requirements is often great fun and wonderfully
easy to do – far too easy in fact if not done properly. All one has to do is
say (or write) 'Do this!' 'Do that!' 'And, of course, so-and-so!' and a
requirements specification quickly exists. Like Topsy in the children's
story, these wish-lists of needs and wants can grow outrageously. If we
are to have a computer for the alarm-monitoring system, then it can do
the payroll too, and play grandmaster-level chess for the entertainment of
off-duty staff, and forecast the weather. What could be easier than
specification? Or more fun?

The problem is, of course, that imperatives like 'Do this!' and 'Do
that!' are almost always at a very high level. As general statements of
scope they are fine; as definitions of detail within this scope they are

virtually useless. Furthermore, the ease with which very high-level generic specifications of scope are made obscures the problem that inordinate complexity is being imported at the same time, a problem that may emerge in later stages of specification if these are done (as should be the case), and definitely will emerge in implementation. The expression 'of course' in a specification document at any level almost always presages the introduction of an afterthought, and usually one of fearsome difficulty. 'And, of course, payroll' as a coda to some severely time-critical requirement is not unknown in practice. Another hazard of the same type is the unimplementable etcetera in a specification. 'And, of course, payroll etc.' Clearly, adequate specification procedures must avoid casual additions of this sort, and their consequences for the complexity of a system to satisfy them.

Another hazard, and one not so easy to avoid, is that of ambiguity in specifications. Much of this is due to muddled thought on the one hand, and to the evolutionary process of specification itself on the other hand. Some ambiguity is, however, due to the use and interpretation of natural language. The reason that 'All forms of communication, interpretation and understanding are tentative acts of influence' (Eco) is that 'Language disguises thought' (Wittgenstein). In no instance can this be more clear than that of software engineering.

There are two distinct approaches to this problem of ambiguity through use of natural language. Theoreticians and some software engineers advocate the use of rigorous specification methods based on specially developed 'formal' languages for the purpose. In our experience this approach is 'user unfriendly', except in relatively rare cases where the user who is to specify requirements is also a computer scientist or at least 'literate' in these formal methods. Furthermore, we hold the view that removing the user from the software engineering process is highly undesirable from all viewpoints.

The alternative approach, and the one adopted mainly up to now despite its manifest imperfections, is that of progressive requirements specification in natural language, enhanced by 'user friendly' notations where possible. The object of this is to obtain an adequate specification, and a knowledge of its feasible implementation, before commencing software development. The term 'adequate' is crucial in this context. Its connotations include both the user's interest (i.e. 'truth' of the specification as a complete statement of real requirements), and the needs of whoever is to implement a system on the basis of it (i.e. the unambiguity of the specification to technicians who are not necessarily specialists in the application). We proceed in the following sections to describe this as a tripartite convergent process.

Reference is made at relevant parts of the text to research into the use of formal (i.e. 'rigorous') specification and design languages, inferential logic and proof theory. At the present time, however, this work is mainly of research status or of limited use in some places for investigation, rather than in everyday use as a normal approach. Above all, its major drawback of making software engineering a 'black box' subject to users who should specify systems and ensure their adequacy in full, has not yet been solved in our view. As there is an undoubted tendency to confuse 'formal' specification methods with other issues that are apparently similar but really different, we include a subsection on this subject as a whole in order to clarify categories of system analysis method, formal specification, and rapid prototyping – all of which have a contribution to make to this part of the software engineering process (see Section 4.4.3).

There is, in fact, considerable scope for confusion as regards how to represent different stages of the specification and design process. Whereas, in the following subsection of this chapter and in Chapter 7, we offer some guidelines in these matters, it is useful at this point to set out a glossary of some common terms and acronyms. It is then possible to map the approaches and methods concerned, up to a point, with lifecycle stages. The main representational forms and techniques in use at the present time are:

- Relatively free-form, essay style natural language (NL)
- Structured natural language (SNL)
- Entity relationship analysis (ERA)
- Jackson's system development (JSD)
- Hierarchical input, output (HIPO)
- Structured analysis and design techniques (SADT)
- De Wolf's process identification approach (De Wolf)
- Petri's process and event dependency networks (Petri nets)
- Modular approach to software construction, operation and test (MASCOT)
- Dataflow mapping (Dataflow)
- The system definition language of the Comité Consultatif International Télégraphique et Téléphonique (CCITT-SDL)
- The syntax of a high-level language (Pseudocode)
- Nassi–Schneiderman charts (N–S)
- Structured flowcharts (SFC)
- British Standards Institution Design Structure Diagram (BS 6224-DSD)

All of these, and many others, are representational notations. In some cases they have accompanying methodologies which, in a few instances, are implemented on Programming Support Environments (PSE). The confusion is increased by a plethora of programming languages for use at lifecycle stages below that of software design; e.g. (to name but a few of the better-known ones): Ada, ALGOL, BASIC, CHILL, COBOL, FORTRAN, LISP, Modula, Occam, Pascal, PL/M, RTL-2, and a very wide variety of assembler-level languages.

Setting this extensive list of languages into the context of lifecycle stages and application-types for which they are particularly suited is an extremely difficult and highly judgemental task. To attempt it in any form implying absolute authority and prescription would, in our view, be counter-productive. However, certain indications can be made, with reservation, about what are useful approaches at different lifecycle stages for specification and design. With this overall stricture that the reader should treat this as an indication only, we offer the 'map' in Figure 4.2.

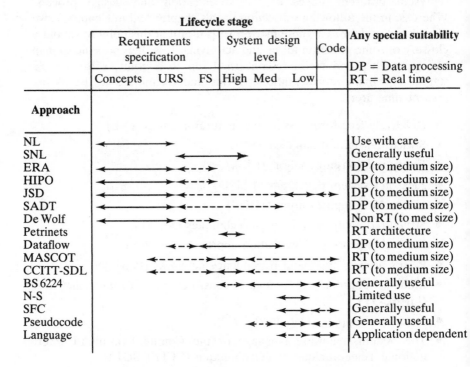

Key :   The unbroken line indicates main area of usefulness; a broken line indicates usefulness in some cases.
The concepts 'DP' and 'RT' are very imprecise; in this case they imply the following:
DP   Orientated to file or array processing with little concurrency or time criticality
RT   Involving concurrency / synchronicity of processes, and time criticality.

Fig. 4.2   Languages, notations and their use.

Some amplification of this table is given in Chapters 7 (Systems and Software Design) and 8 (Implementation), but further advice must be given here on two aspects. Firstly, there is a distinct danger that structured natural language (being most often in the form: subject – imperative verb – object) will simply become pseudocode, and that this will lead to premature coding of systems. Secondly, that techniques implemented down to code-generation level may (whatever their other usefulness) not produce high-quality software systems in the sense defined in Chapter 9. The 'methodologies' of JSD, MASCOT and SDL are 'implemented' in this fashion, and their use for rapid prototyping and reconfiguration of complex systems is growing.

4.2 Conceptualizing requirements, and feasibility

The process of systems engineering, of which software development may or may not turn out to be a part in a particular case, usually starts in the manner already described: a free association of ideas from interested parties, expressed at a generically high level of definition (i.e. the opposite of high degree of detail), and in a disorderly fashion. For example:

'We need a better alarm-monitoring system in this hospital. It's no good a sensor showing a critical state if there's no one looking at it.'

'Let's have a computer-controlled system, with VDU screens to show alarm messages and some bells and whistles; the noise will kill the patients!'

'And a central control point with an operator who can monitor whether alarms are dealt with, particularly the noise!'

'And we'll need VDU screens in all the wards, as well as in the doctors' and nurses' recreation rooms, and alarm messages will need to show what's wrong, where and who's responsible if a patient is involved . . .'

'How will it work? Will the computer ask for the *status* of sensors or get it when the *state* changes?'

'What will it cost? How long will it take?'

Several things should be noted about this informal process. First of all, requirements get mixed up with possible solutions and questions of resource such as time or money. This is pretty well inevitable, and does not matter much so long as it is clearly understood that the process, at this stage, is informal. However, the question of resources may have a significance not recognized or admitted. Great care must be taken at this early lifecycle stage, not to attempt binding estimates of timescale and effort to implement a system for requirements still being envisaged and articulated. We have known many instances of overspending by 400%

and more, merely because the 'budget' was fixed on the basis of 'estimates' (guesses really) at this lifecycle stage. The whole problem of premature estimating is taken up in Chapter 5 below. Apart from that, the informal process of making up wish-lists of requirements, and admixing questions and ideas about possible technical solutions, is largely inevitable if spontaneous conceptualization is to go ahead unconstrained. So long as it is clearly realized that other specification steps will be required to detail and order the material, there is nothing against this state of affairs.

Nevertheless, informal though the process is at this early stage, early concepts and ideas about feasibility should be archived. This serves the dual purpose of causing the archive to come into being at the start, and ensuring that its contents are a complete record. It would be strange for instance, and a fact of material interest that should be visible, if a payroll system were implemented when the original notion had been for a patient-monitoring system.

The form of early ideas, concepts and feasibility assessments will most likely be that of short notes of meetings, block diagrams of ideas, sketches of functional components of a system-to-be, and so forth. In other words, highly informal and based on natural language. Feasibility assessments at this stage are unlikely to involve elaborate investigations of possibilities or prototyping, as generally too little is known of requirements. Any 'go/no-go' decisions are more acts of belief or disbelief than informed assessment, and as often as not represent loss of interest or altered priorities.

Above all else, this early stage should be clearly seen as the precursor to other steps and stages in the specification process; a necessary 'getting started' but not an activity resulting in definitive statements of requirement detail or feasibility appraisal.

4.3 The User Requirement Specification (URS)

The URS activity is an irreplaceable step early in the lifecycle and its outcome is a necessary artefact in the process of specification. As its name suggests it should involve 'users', or their surrogates as described in Chapter 2, whether or not the earlier stage had involved them. Furthermore, whereas the early concepts step may have tended to make an informal and somewhat disordered 'wish-list' of requirements features, and even possible solutions – all described at very high generic level – the URS activity must seek to detail the real requirements. In this undertaking the URS process frequently encounters the following problems:

1. How best to extract (from whatever sources) the necessary detail about real requirements?

2. What to do with information emerging about design or detail of a technical system to fulfill the requirements?

3. How to order the requirements information to avoid error, ambiguity, omission, redundancy and contradiction?

In a perfect world these problems would all be solved, however complex the application and however many people involved in its specification, by a properly sequenced and logically correct enunciation of real requirements, at precisely the necessary level of detail for the purposes of implementation within a system. In practice the process is very different indeed; users are (thank goodness) human, so there it is! It is best to realize this when doing the URS, and not to attempt simultaneous optimization of the processes of information extraction, selection and ordering. There is a tendency for these objectives to interfere with each other, and a typical result is for one to get a reasonably well-ordered and unambiguous subset of real requirements instead of a total statement of them. As with the 'concept' level of specification, it should be realized that another step in the process will see to the problems of discrimination (e.g. of solution or implementation design material), and those of ambiguity and error. Then the detailing of URS information can proceed as a 'stream of consciousness' activity within a loosely (not rigorously) logical framework of enquiry.

4.3.1 Compiling the URS

As a general rule, the URS process is one of information extraction and compilation. Sometimes the users or their surrogates compile their own URS directly, sometimes it is done by others (consultants or systems analysts, or some such).

A URS should be undertaken in the knowledge that it will not be the direct basis for an implementation. It will be the source document for a more comprehensive form of requirement specification which will be the definitive baseline for all further work. Reasonable attempts at keeping URS information relevant, clear, complete and non-contradictory should be made, and the document as it is compiled should categorize information around generic subject headings, corresponding to the main features of the application being described.

With the best of intentions, however, the result may turn out to be a muddle. A user may begin by detailing features A, B, C, D etc. at a fairly high generic level and, in doing so, presume a general understanding of details and subtleties within them. Then, typically, the realization sets in (or is caused by whoever is compiling the URS), that there may have been a misapprehension on the part of the reader, or even loss of essential material, and so the process changes. Suddenly, requirement G is seen to be very complex; so much that it might be best to detail it.

There then follows an exposition of how G really comprises G1, G2, G3, G4, and so on, during which it is realized that the reader (or compiler of a URS) cannot be expected to understand that G7 is closely related to requirement B – or rather a detail of it, B6 in fact. At this point backtracking occurs to define requirement B properly as B1, B2, B3 etc. and the URS is becoming a glorious jumble.

Some authors of techniques to assist the process of systems analysis claim that their methods overcome this incoherency. For some relatively small and non-complex systems that may be true. They certainly tend to slow down the URS process and that may be a good thing up to a point. But beyond this, any claim other than that of helping to record URS information is – in effect – a claim to cure a human condition.

Nonetheless, information extraction and recording at the URS level may be improved in some cases – certainly in the clarity of its representation as a URS (but not necessarily as the FS, or a design, as these are described further below) – by the use of an analysis methodology. Some of the better known of these are Entity Relationship Analysis (for a description of which see Veryard (1984)), SADT (described as a design notation in Section 7.3, but comprising a full methodology for systems analysis), IBM's HIPO approach (hierarchical input/output analysis), and an approach due to De Wolf at the Charles Stark Draper Labs and described in Weitzmann (1980). An example of this latter is given in Section 4.3.4 below. HIPO is described in Yourdon (1979), but is now seen as a limited and dated approach.

As a brief example of systematic approach at a high level of the lifecycle, for systems analysis, the categorization of a requirement by data analysis is instructive as it underlies several of the techniques already listed, such as HIPO, Entity Relationship Analysis, and Jackson's System Development method. In ERA, for instance, data analysis is done by classifying entities and their relationships, and representing them in a simple schematic form. In the case of the hospital alarm-monitoring system, mentioned in Section 4.2 above, and defined more fully below, one can classify such things as buildings, wards, patient beds, doctors, nurses and so on. The ERA notation for representing these is a simple box and connecting line form, as shown in Figure 4.3.

The JSD method contains an entity relationship analysis. Birrell and Ould (1985) describe the method as comprising six steps from systems analysis to implementation:

1. Entities are listed and the actions they cause (or suffer) are listed also.

2. An entity structure is modelled by ordering the actions caused (or suffered) by entities on the basis of its life-span.

3. A real-world model is constructed comprising 'model processes' of

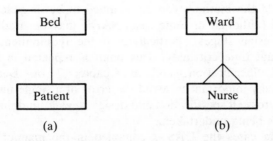

Fig. 4.3 Entity relationship: (a) a one to one relationship; (b) a one to many relationship.

actions in the entity structure. Time ordering is maintained from the previous step.

4. Function processes are inserted into the model, and outputs are represented in it, to make the model a fully representative one of a solution for the entity/model process requirement.

5. Any timing constraints are added to what is now basically a solution model that reflects the requirements.

6. A 'semi-mechanical' transformation is performed to realize the solution model on a target system (computer, operating system, language, etc.).

As already remarked, this approach works well in the area of classical data processing (large-scale file handling, I/O, etc.), even down to code generation in some cases. Its application for highly complex systems containing concurrency, priority interrupts, synchrony, etc., is less clear – certainly below step 3.

The reader should be careful of claims made by their authors (and other enthusiasts) for these methodologies. All of them are of some use in some circumstances; for instance HIPO for classifications in strongly hierarchical business organizations where the methodology can follow the organization structure of the firm. Beyond the references already given, and the descriptions and examples of SADT and the De Wolf approaches elsewhere in this text, we do not feel that these – or other – systems analysis methods warrant extensive comment at this lifecycle stage. SADT has a useful 'author–reader–reviewer' procedure which helps to eliminate ambiguity and error but (as with E–R diagrams in entity relationships), tends towards profuse URS documents not altogether easy to follow for a user lacking extensive experience with the technique. Some (SADT in particular) have a diagrammatic notation rather appealing to engineers, being superficially somewhat like a circuit diagram.

None of the methods can be assumed to be of general use beyond URS level (although in some cases SADT may be used in the FS and software design stages), particularly if the requirements contain concurrency and time criticality. This point is repeated in Section 4.4 on Functional Specification, and in Chapter 7 on Design, as it is fundamentally important to avoid the error of a single methodology and notation across all specification and design steps if, in doing so, one limits the process being undertaken.

In most cases the URS is compiled in the manner described and emerges as a highly imperfect document. It is almost always in natural language and contains a large amount of application-specific terminology. Furthermore, it may contain too great a level of detail for some items, and too little for others. The problems of ambiguity, redundancy, incompleteness and downright wrongness cannot be assumed absent at this stage, and the document may trespass beyond the requirements domain into that of a technical implementation.

In short, most URS documents are a mess – however careful users or their representatives have been. An example of the URS for a patient-monitoring and hospital alarm system is set out in Section 4.3.3.

4.3.2 Prototyping at the URS stage: URS for prototypes

Prototyping to clarify requirements must be distinguished from that to establish technical feasibility. This latter is dealt with in Section 4.5 (Outline Systems Design).

In many cases of new applications, requirements emerge if there exists a system of sorts for the users to get used to. Typically, one would see a subset of known application features, one that could be implemented in a quick-and-dirty (and cheap) fashion, and one would program it in order to provoke users into saying 'Not that, but this' at least.

A case in point, almost inevitably encountered in software engineering applications concerning human users, is that of the justifiably feared requirement to make the system 'user friendly'. Just who is the user, and what might he or she deem friendly, unfriendly, or downright hostile? The answer can usually only be found by trial and error, using prototypes. This is better done at the URS stage than later, as it may also serve to make the user(s) enthusiastic and lead to an increase in the scope of requirements, a development better known about as early as possible. The positive information acquired ('bought') in this way should be embodied in the URS and later documents; where the human factors issues such as 'user friendliness' are concerned, the prototype may act as the basis for the users' manual (see Section 10.1).

The URS for this kind of prototype will most likely be rudimentary, self-evidently as the purpose of the prototype in this case is to extend understanding of the URS. For prototypes to clarify technical feasibility on the other hand, the URS may be extensive. This is further referred to and remarked upon in Section 4.5.

So far as the URS for a research project is concerned one should distinguish between systems involving software as the object of research itself, and systems (including software) that are research tools or parts of research apparatus in some way.

In the first case, nothing categorical can be said about the URS or any other lifecycle stage (nor about good software engineering or management practice), if the object of research concerns these factors directly. In this case, the research method – whatever it is – must supervene. Otherwise, software as a part of research apparatus should be fully specified – including the URS and any prototypes required – and should follow the lifecycle form of development, and 'good practices' in general. It is an unfortunate fact – and the main reason for this comment on our part – that many research staff in all fields of endeavour tend to be very slipshod in the observance of 'good software engineering practice', treating the matter rather like a bit of 'do-it-yourself glassblowing' in the laboratory. They are, in fact, amateur programmers when acting like this.

4.3.3 Example: URS for a hospital

Example 1 is a URS, compiled by 'users' or their representatives, showing many of the defects pointed out in Section 4.3.1. A brief comment on these characteristics is given in Section 4.3.4. Arguments that it should have been done in such-and-such a notation, or by so-and-so method, are not appropriate. The way it is presented is precisely the way in which the users thought it best to express their requirements, in the full knowledge that an FS stage would follow. From that point of view it is a small but very typical example of what happens in 'real life'. However, having said that, a development (a cleaning-up, short of functional specification) of this URS is shown, in 'De Wolf–Weitzman' form, in Section 4.3.4.

EXAMPLE 1

1. General statement of requirements

We wish to use our central computer in the hospital's main administration and control centre to process warning messages from two sensor monitoring systems, already installed, to check certain medical conditions in patients and some general alarm circumstances in the building complex, and to display suitable warning messages on VDU screens at key points throughout the hospital complex.

2. Description of the hospital and its currently installed sensor equipment

The hospital comprises 5 wards each containing 70 beds, and 150 private rooms each containing one bed. The normal convention of one patient per bed is preserved. Each ward is on one floor of one wing of the hospital complex and has an administration office attached to it.

The private rooms are in groups of 30, on each of five floors of another wing of the hospital complex. Each floor has an administration office attached to it. Scheduling and procedures are arranged to minimize the possibility of a floor being unattended at any time.

Medical staff comprise 10 doctors and 50 nurses. Administrative staff comprise 5 secretarial and registrar staff, one porter per ward and one porter per 25 private rooms. There are three guards who work shifts. The medical staff have computer-readable ID cards, each with a personal number on it.

Apart from the wards and private rooms there are several facilities such as waiting rooms, operating theatres, administration offices, storerooms, etc. Also:

- A central room in which the telephone switchboard is located, along with a computer facility for medical staff schedules and administration (all fully implemented). Medical staff information contains the ID number on the computer-readable card held by each of these staff.

- A common room for medical and administration/registrar staff.

- A canteen for all staff.

Each patient has three nominated nurses (one for each shift) and at least one nominated doctor. Procedures operate to change these nominations if and when necessary (e.g. a change in staff schedule, a contingency, a change in treatment); the allocation of medical staff to patients is a function of staff schedules for the nurses, and the patient's location (ward/section/bed, or room number) is correlated with staff schedules in the central control room administration computer; the allocation of doctors to patients is performed on the basis of original diagnosis by the registrar on patient registration (the procedure ensures that no doctor is overloaded).

Each ward is divided into 14 sections each comprising five adjacent beds. We have two control systems in the process of installation.

- A Patient Care Control System (PCCS).

- An Environmental Control System (ECS).

There are two kinds of apparatus purchased for the PCCS, namely the PCCS Mark I and the PCCS Mark II. Both of these devices measure patient pulse rate, blood pressure, temperature, encephalographic (brain) activity, and involuntary muscular spasm. Any of these factors which go out of range (the ranges are preset in the devices) will cause a warning light to be activated on the PCCS. There are five such warning lights on the Mark I and 25 on the Mark II.

The Mark I is a device for connecting to one patient only; the Mark II is a device for connecting to up to five patients. We have purchased 150 of the Mark I devices and 70 of the Mark II devices.

Each PCCS contains a microcomputer which can be programmed; the messages warning of medical factors out of range are presented to the microcomputer by the medical telemetry equipment. In both cases (Mark I and Mark II devices) this message comprises a single-digit number in the range 1–5 corresponding with the diagnostic types listed above. This is presented to the microcomputer as a three-bit binary number (001, 010, 011, 101, corresponding to out-of-range warning on pulse rate, blood pressure, temperature, etc.).

Each device also presents one binary bit per factor (i.e. five binary bits in all are allocated) to indicate if the deviation from a range is serious (the bit set at zero) or critical (the bit set at 1). The warning light is activated at 'Serious', and no further external sign is given if the deviation goes to 'Critical'. The Mark II device also indicates to the microcomputer the bed number (again 1–5 as a 3-bit binary number).

The ECS system measures local environmental temperature, humidity, smoke, noise and glare. Out-of-range values will be signalled by a warning light on the device (there are five such warning lights on each device). Each ECS contains a microcomputer which can be programmed, and the telemetry information for out-of-range values is presented as a three-bit binary number to the microcomputer representing the preset code for the value concerned (001 for temperature, 010 for humidity, etc.).

We have purchased one ECS for each of the private patients' rooms, and one ECS for each of the ward sectors (i.e. 220 ECS devices in total). All PCCS and all ECS equipment is currently delivered and installed.

Bed numbers, sector numbers, ward numbers and floor numbers can be set in the microcomputers of each device as they can be programmed. These simple parameters can be set to any convention desired.

3. A general description of what the required system must do

We have found that the method of signalling used by PCCS and ECS

AUGUSTANA UNIVERSITY COLLEGE
LIBRARY

devices is too limited for our purposes. A warning light is of little use if there is no one around to see it. In addition to the built-in facilities of the control devices we now wish to implement a system which has a keyboard VDU screen in each of the following places:

- The central control room.
- The common room.
- The canteen.
- Each ward administration room.
- Each private patient floor administration room.

We have purchased the 13 keyboard VDU devices which have been delivered already. Each of those in ward or private patient floor administration rooms has a special ID card reader attached.

Basically we wish to have a warning message displayed whenever anything on a PCCS or on an ECS goes out of range. For PCCSs, the warning message should be simultaneously displayed at the VDUs in the central control room, the common room, the canteen, and either the ward administration room on the floor concerned or the private patient administration room on the floor concerned. The message should indicate floor, section (if a ward) or room (if private patient area), patient name and responsible nurses'/doctor(s) names, factors(s) out of range and whether 'Serious' or 'Critical'. Warning messages will only be removed from the screen by insertion of the ID card of a responsible person (nurse or doctor) into a special card reader at the VDU on the floor (administration room) concerned. Unprocessed warning messages will remain on all the screens, unless a screen becomes filled with messages (a maximum of 10 PCCS + ECS messages is allowed at any instant on a screen). If a screen is full, then warning messages must be saved on a floor basis, and a summary count shown on all screens of the number of unprocessed warning messages per floor. This summary count will be on all screens permanently so that even if a screen is full of warning messages for one floor (say) it will show that unprocessed warning messages for that or another floor still exist.

All unprocessed warning messages should be accessible by a simple command 'SEE FLOOR . . .' (nominating a floor as W1–5, private patient, or by PP1, PP2, etc.). This command should result in any warning messages on the screen being saved, and the unprocessed messages for the floor concerned being displayed. There should be a timeout on this feature to avoid the system staying in this mode once it is activated. A time constant of 60 seconds is suggested. Alternatively the display feature of unprocessed messages can (and should) be discontinued by entry of a command 'EXIT' at a terminal. All terminals may be used for this feature, and the special display will be at the terminal used to invoke the feature only (i.e. the original screen messages will remain on the other terminals, and will be returned to the screen from which the special display is invoked after either 'EXIT' or the timeout).

The patient name and responsible medical staff names for warning messages will be accessed directly from the central administration computer.

4. Notes on a preferred solution

We wish to utilize our central computer in the hospital control centre to process warning messages, execute the messages at the VDUs and remove messages in the manner described in (3) above, and enable the special display.

All the microcomputers in PCCS and ECS equipments are now connected to the main computer. This electrical connection is currently passive. It can either be activated by the central computer interrogating the microcomputer in the control devices, or by the control devices interrupting the central computer when an emergency occurs. It does not matter which approach is used.

If the first approach is used, then software will be needed in the central computer to interrogate the control device's microcomputers, and these will require some software to show that some emergency has arisen. In the case of interrupting, the microcomputer in the devices will need some software to send the requisite signals to the main computer.

The main computer is reasonably heavily loaded with staff and patient administration systems, but none of these are highly time critical. Warning messages, on the other hand, are, and whichever implementation philosophy is adopted must treat them as top priority. A warning message which is responded to (see (3) above) should be removed from the screens (and from any floor totals on the summary messages); the control device (PCCS and ECS) should be informed that the message is being dealt with (or this knowledge should be signified in some other way), so that an activated device (e.g. an ECS activated by smoke) does not keep sending the same warning signals when a response to the message has been made (even if the smoke is still there and the device is 'active' as a consequence).

An archive must be kept in the main computer of all warning messages received, and all 'clear message' signals – with the times of these occurrences attached to each part of such a message pair. This history should be accumulated in a small buffer in the main store of the central computer and permanently stored on disk when the buffer is full. History records on the disk must contain calendar date, and this must be changed by the clock in the central computer at 24.00 hours each day.

The operating system in the central computer allows both for a highest-level priority program to exist (and none of the current programs are assigned to this level), and for interruption by external devices. Great care must be taken in designing the system to ensure that:

- Use by systems at the ordinary level of priority does not interface with the highest-priority activities.

- Multiple warnings are processed properly.

- Writing messages on screens does not interfere ' with the occurrence and processing of warnings within the central system.

- Cancelling messages on screens occurs even if other warnings are arriving, and cancelling messages does not interfere with the arrival of other warnings.

In any system description or schematic, the following simple conventions can be used.

OSX   = Operating System in the Central Computer.
SCHED   = Staff Schedules program in the Central Computer.
PATREG = Patient Register program in the Central Computer.
PATREC = Patient Medical Records program in the Central Computer.

The three applications systems (SCHED, PATREG and PATREC) should be shown in relation to the priority *WARN*ing system to be made.

Note also that PCCS messages will access information from the PATREG system (i.e. responsible nurses/doctors for a patient). ECS will access SCHED for nurses' floor assignments.

4.3.4   The move from URS to FS

This example of a URS displays many of the defects often found in these documents (although, it must be said, not in their most aggravated form in this case). For instance:

1. The document wavers uncertainly between a statement of features to be incorporated and the method to achieve them.

2. Requirements are difficult to categorize as mandatory, desirable, optional and so forth. This is particularly clear in the use of 'will', 'should', 'may', etc., a most common feature of the URS process and one to be avoided.

3. The example demonstrates a very well-known tendency to spurious detail at this level. Section 1, in describing sensor equipment, goes overboard (in a small way) on the bit structure of messages. We have seen this tendency taken to extremes in some URSs – frequently giving details irrelevant to the purpose of the document, however necessary at a later stage they may be.

4. Above all, the URS demonstrates the problem of ambiguity, nowhere better than in the part of Section 3 on deletion of message and screen overflow. Most interpretations placed on this text highlight defects at the 'system' thinking level. Is it sensible to have requirements exactly as these are described? In a real-life case, this part (and others) of the URS would lead to a system engineering dialogue with users about how the system should really work in the interests of the hospital staff and patients.

5. The authors of the document clearly set out with good intentions to keep material in its appropriate categories. This intention begins to break down fairly early and, by the end, the authors are putting in anything they think might be relevant almost as a set of afterthoughts.

As already remarked, these problems are endemic in most URS documents. The example given is by no means the worst we have seen.

Dealing with a document such as this is to take a step towards doing a functional specification, but that is not necessarily the same as doing the FS as the first step itself, nor does it imply that a URS can always be cast into its FS form as a single, non-iterative step. Such are the imperfections of most URS documents that this transition is by no means an easy one.

First of all, the URS should be cleaned up in the sense of expunging from it the major defects such as those in points 1–5 above. One method is to read through a URS, marking for attention only those features that are strictly necessary for understanding requirements detail at this level, and omitting redundancy and irrelevancies. The summary document – still a URS and not yet the FS – may then be rewritten and used for dialogue with users to clarify obscure points, and (most important) for evolution of requirements in terms of good system engineering.

This summary URS, containing all the essential features of the requirement in the language of the application, is often used as a preface to the FS. This has the twofold merit of ensuring that the URS is cleaned up before being transformed into the FS, and acting as an introduction and context for that document.

The summary URS may, with advantage, be based on one of several procedural approaches as already mentioned – Entity Relationship Analysis, SADT, JSD – depending on the application size and type. Weitzman (1980) recommends the method (due to De Wolf at Charles Stark Draper Laboratories) known as 'process characterization'. In this approach a table is compiled by a method called 'process identification', not dissimilar to that described above for summarizing the URS in that it employs a method of identifying 'abstract' processes. This notion has much to recommend it at the stage of summarizing a URS, although we would hesitate to recommend its use *a priori* in the URS process, for the same reasons as attach to the use of other methods such as E–R diagrams, SADT, HIPO, etc. On the other hand this approach has many attractions for representing a URS summary of an essay-form document, as Example 2 attests. (We omit the full tabular form of this 'notation' as it is not strictly necessary and tends to waste space).

EXAMPLE 2

Patient Monitoring and Hospital Alarm System

Description of Requirements

1. A patient monitoring and environmental alarm system is required for the two wings of the hospital.

2. Each patient is monitored by analogue devices that measure factors such as heart rate, blood pressure, temperature, brain activity and muscular spasms. Out-of-range considerations are supplied to local microprocessors with individual factors such as patient identity and an alarm (e.g. 'serious', 'critical'). Warning lamps are also activated locally. As well as alarm status information, sensor faults are transmitted.

3. Environment conditions local to the patient are supplied to other local microprocessors. Out-of-range conditions are registered with the local identity for the following factors: temperature, humidity, smoke, noise and glare.

4. Safe ranges for all factors mentioned in 2 and 3 are built into the sensors.

5. If a factor is outside a specified safe range, messages are to be displayed on VDUs in the central control room, common room, and in the administration room related to the patient sensor or environmental sensor concerned.

6. Warning messages can only be cleared by the medical staff nominated as responsible for a patient or area, by means of an identity card and use of a keyboard in the ward and on the floor concerned.

7. A maximum of 10 messages may be displayed on a VDU screen, and any unprocessed message that is not displayed because of screen overflow shall be saved along with its floor identification. A summary count of these overflow messages will be displayed at all times on the floor concerned (as in the case of (6)).

8. All alarm messages and their remedial processing will be saved as a history record, in a form suitable for subsequent retrieval and analysis, in the central computer system's archival store (see (9) below).

9. Use shall be made of the following equipment already installed:

   1 off central computer (undefined make and characteristics)
   150 off PCCSs – microcomputer-controlled and
   programmable; 1 per patient
   70 off PCCSs – microcomputer-controlled and
   programmable
   220 off ECSs – microcomputer-controlled and
   programmable

   An electrical connection system, currently passive but otherwise entirely intact, linking all devices to the central computer.

   The binary format of all alarm messages in PCCSs and ECSs is fixed and known.

10. The central computer is heavily loaded with routine administration tasks. The operating system of this computer will allow programs to operate at higher priority than these, and the alarm messages must be given that highest priority

11. All local microcomputers may either be interrogated for status information or may be programmed to interrupt the central computer when status changes.

At the stage when a reasonably clear URS is available, either as a cleaned-up essay form or in some tabular fashion as depicted (or SADT notation and annotation if that method is adopted, or E–R diagram form, JSD, HIPO or whatever), the task of transforming this from its inevitably user/application-orientated language into a functional specification can begin.

4.4   The Functional Specification (FS)

Earlier lifecycle stages, such as Concepts/First Feasibility and the URS, produce informal documents that should be archived, of course, but that are insufficient to act as a basis for implementation. This is because the process is dominated until quite late in the URS stage by the need to get sufficient detail of all the real requirements, and may require many iterations with users, and prototypes perhaps, to do so.

Whereas a URS produced in this fashion may not be a basis for a definitive implementation (and could not, therefore, be part of an exacting legal contract for example), it is the only basis possible for a better level of specification – for the FS in fact.

In the following section we discuss the general properties of the FS: its likely authorship, structure and form; the use of methodologies, formal notations, and application-dependent rapid prototyping languages. Apart from an example of the FS in the case-study in Chapter 12, a functional specification is given in Section 4.4.4 that corresponds with the URS for a patient-monitoring system in Section 4.3.3. Section 4.4.5 comments on the 'next step' in the lifecycle, the transition between the FS and the Design.

4.4.1   General properties of the FS

The following five points summarize the main properties of any functional specification. Other authors, notably Birrell and Ould (1985), offer an extensive definition of FS contents down to a great level of detail; in our view that is useful as a checklist reminder of what, perhaps, should have been included.

Basically, however, the FS should have the following characteristics.

1. The object of the FS is that it must act as the indisputable baseline for implementation of a system to deliver the features described in it. Thus it must be a true representation of real requirements, expressed in an unambiguous form from the user's (client's) and implementation (supplier's) viewpoints. A succinct statement of this is that the FS must be 'The necessary and sufficient information from the URS, unambiguously expressed.'

2. The status of the FS as 'baseline' must be formally signified, for any product or project development but not necessarily for a prototype, by 'signing-off' the document in its entirety, i.e. including any appendices and material to which it refers. The FS should thus be mutually authorized by the user/user surrogate representatives, and the agency of implementation (if they happen to be one and the same, as can be the case for some small systems, then the FS is 'signed-off' by its authors anyway).

   Also, such is the significance of the FS for software validation, certification and 'quality' in general (as described in Chapter 9), that it should be the subject of independent quality assurance (or at least a 'QA' review), if only to ensure that it adheres to the basic principles of specification at this level, and that it is unambiguous.

3. As the definition that has acted as baseline for the implementation the FS will, as a result, play a crucial rôle in determining the quality of the resulting system and its acceptability – perhaps as laid down in a legal contract of supply. These issues are taken up fully elsewhere – e.g. in Chapter 9 and Section 10.5.

The contents of the FS must be a fully comprehensive and totally clear representation of real requirements comprising, in general, the following:

- A detailed description of all features and functions required including any concerning system security, integrity or performance. A checklist of what this might comprise is given in Section 4.4.2 and a similar one (much extended) can be found in Birrell and Ould (1985).

- Any requirements for system portability at a precise level of definition of the 'target' equipment.

As the FS must be signed-off by users, and as they will be neither will nor, in some cases, competent to authorize implementation features, the FS must exclude systems design information. There are two exceptions to this:

- Design of the 'user interface'. Prototyping should be used within the URS to fix the issues of user friendliness. The outcome, format designs, should be incorporated in the FS and signed-off.

- Existing equipment to be used. A detail of any fixed resources of this type should be attached as an appendix to the FS with the clear indication that this is an inherited 'fact of life', and not necessarily a best (or even feasible) solution to requirements. Particularly important, any severe space constraints (such as 'the job must be done on that 2-kilobyte microprocessor that will just fit into the device'), must be indicated as a system constraint on the scope of the FS, and that scope must – in turn – not exceed what is feasible to implement within the known limitation. This is not the same as defining the system's performance, which generally concerns response times from the system or within subsystems.

4. As baseline for an implementation, and in view of its significance in determining the quality and acceptability of a software system, the FS must be put under formal 'change control' when it is signed-off. Changes to the FS made under 'change control' must be accompanied by collateral changes in timescale, effort (cost) and code size estimates.

5. The FS will be the document referred to by the first (i.e. earliest in lifecycle terms) estimates of timescale and effort for implementation. It is clearly unreasonable to attach undue importance to estimates made before the specification is fixed, and the consequences of doing so are described in Chapter 5. The process of estimating at the FS stage involves that of the Outline Systems Design also. The correspondence between the FS and the OSD (see Section 4.5) is, therefore, crucial.

Of all issues concerned with the FS, the one of getting it signed-off by authorized parties from both the user and implementation domains can be the most difficult. Even in the best-regulated environments, where there are clearly attributed authorities of unimpeachable competence in user requirements and implementation technology, there can be formidable difficulties in agreeing.

In these cases the problem usually contains elements of both 'prematurity' and 'indeterminacy', as these are described as properties of many software engineering tasks in Section 2.2. How does one sign-off a document, perhaps in the process committing the error of prematurity, if the outcome (implementation) is not fully determinable? The answer is largely a matter of specification procedures and (in parallel) evaluation of technical feasibility.

The adequacy of specification will depend on the sufficiency of the URS/FS procedure and may involve prototyping as a means of clarifying users' real needs. However, the development of a URS into the FS does represent a transition of the form described in Section 4.4.2 below. That it may introduce errors of omission or interpretation is obvious, and is protected against by the 'verification loop' shown on the lifecycle schematic in Figure 3.4. In short, the FS must be done in close collaboration with the users, not in isolation from them.

So far we have considered the process of specification and not the feasibility of its implementation other than for very rudimentary considerations at the start. In fact it is essential that technical feasibility is undertaken in parallel with specification, as shown in the subset lifecycle schematic Figure 4.1.

This activity, known as the Outline Systems Design, is fully described below; its adequacy (along with the continuing verification of the FS as isomorphic with the essential information content of the URS) should serve, in the vast majority of cases, to enable the FS to be signed-off. If, however, the FS still cannot be authorized, then it should be realized that either the requirements are still volatile, or their implementation is imponderable, or both. Any resulting activity, other than further URS/FS (and OSD) work, must be seen as prototyping or research.

The significance of the FS for quality determination and software acceptance is dealt with at some length in Chapter 9. At the present stage it is sufficient to point out two facts of life that are often completely overlooked and, consequently, are a source of great tribulation at later lifecycle stages, including those of quality determination and acceptance:

1. However good the FS is, and however meticulous the processes of verification and feasibility, for all non-trivial and non-S-type systems its status as a true representation of real requirements will most likely be a contingent rather than categorical matter. C.S. Peirce defined 'truth' as that opinion fated to be agreed by all those who investigate; nowhere is this more true than for the FS.

The consequences are that, however good the implementation, the resulting software system may fall somewhat short of the users' real expectations once the result is evident. Determining whether the specification or the implementation itself, or some combination of both, is the reason for disappointment is often a far more complex issue in software engineering than in other subjects.

2. Immeasurable quality or acceptance criteria may be included in a statement of user requirements; expressions such as 'the software must be efficient, reliable, portable, testable, modifiable, maintainable, modular, well structured, secure, fail-safe,' and so on.

Anything of this or any other sort that cannot be demonstrated conclusively, so that there is no meaningful metric for the requirement concerned, must be excluded from the FS. However understandable the users' wishes are (e.g. for 'testable' and 'modifiable' software say), it will only cause contention if they are incorporated in the FS.

These matters, along with the special case of 'correctness', are discussed at length in Chapter 9.

It should be clear by now just how fundamentally important the FS is, and how difficult it may be to make it adequate for all parties who have to authenticate it. The FS is a transition document between the specification and implementation stages and, as such, has to look back 'up' the lifecycle for the users' verification, and forwards 'down' the lifecycle to design and subsequent stages.

Care and attention paid at the FS stage, even in the face of clamouring clients or disappearing market windows, will be amply worthwhile. Better to miss a market window than to 'lose your shirt' through it.

4.4.2 Authorship, structure and form

Usually the FS is best done by a combination of 'solution' specialists likely to be involved in the implementation, and users of the system-to-be. This last provision is particularly important if the 'solution' specialists are not strongly conversant with the application, its terminology and nuances. The combination simplifies the task of verifying that the FS is isomorphic in its information content with the essential content and intended meaning of the URS. It also ensures a sufficient familiarity with the FS in the implementation staff. This notion is taken further by having the same implementation 'specialists' do the technical feasibility as a parallel exercise during functional specification by a process – Outline Systems Design – described fully below. The OSD culminates in a substantive estimating exercise, and the plansibility fo these estimates is thus associated with the FS and OSD scope, and with the competence of the authors of the system-to-be. It follows that unnecessary ascription of tasks to diffuse or only partly relevant sources should be avoided, if possible, as it tends to dislocate activities that should be mutually associated. In some types of project supply (eg. the so-called 'Fixed Price' contracting practices) great care must be taken when 'users' do the FS but fail to do an associated OSD. Advice to suppliers required to bid for such contracts is given in Section 10.5 below.

As to the structure and form of the FS, as distinct from its purpose and content as already described, there will naturally be great diversity over the whole spectrum of computer applications. No two FS documents look alike, even when produced by different authors from the same URS (although it is likely there will be much shared terminology). However, it is possible to offer two very simple guidelines on structure and form of the FS, summarized as follows:

1. Structuring the FS by categorizing essential URS contents as inputs, features (or functions) and output is an extremely useful way of dealing with voluminous and complex application details. The result is a formatted FS, the format being known as 'IFO' (not to be confused with IBM's HIPO for systems analysis).

   'Inputs' and 'outputs' may refer to traffic across a human–user interface and will, in this case, comprise screen and keyboard formats that have been determined in the URS stage, possibly by prototyping. Otherwise, 'inputs' and 'outputs' may equally refer to subsystem features at an entirely electronic level – in which case they will comprise bit patterns.

   Typical entries in I, F and O categories of the FS are indicated in Figure 4.4.

   An advantage of the IFO format, other than the clarity accruing from good classification techniques applied to essential URS information, is that of traceability between the categories. The input set should be related in some logical way (i.e. 'traceable') to the output set via the features set. Even a cursory inspection of a well-formatted FS can indicate its degree of coherence. A non-coherent FS is categorically incorrect (examples are any I entries without connection to an F or directly to an O; any O entries without connection to an F or directly to an I; any F entries unconnected with either an I or an O). It should be noted that a coherent FS is not necessarily a correct one.

2. If the FS is to stand a chance of being signed off by users who may not be 'literate' in special notations and languages, it should be done in natural language. As well as the IFO format already described, structured natural language (such as the simple syntax of a high-level language) may be used up to a point, as may diagrammatic notations to describe information flow or logical connections between IFO elements. In this category of useful notations for embellishing the

Inputs	Agency (eg from human or electro/mechanical)
	Media (eg VDU, Sensor/transducer/communication subsystem)
	Form (eg digital alphanumeric or bit pattern, voice recognition, analogue)
	Arrival rate profile, with clearly discriminated peaks
	Formats
	Input error diagnostic (including time out for erroneous discontinuity), and system security features
Features and Functions	All application-dependent features, functions and processes to be provided
	All system-performance requirements such as (eg):-
	* Minimal acceptable throughput under different load conditions
	* Maximal acceptable response time under different load conditions
	* Provisions for system failure, eg cold, warm or hot standby, and any paramount data security/integrity features (unauthorised access/accidental corruption or loss)
	* Any self-checking features, collection of operation statistics etc. required
	Any software portability called for, specifying target equipment in detail
Outputs	Agency (eg to human or electro/mechanical)
	Media (eg VDU, sensor/transducer/communication subsystem)
	Form (eg digital alphanumeric or bit pattern, voice synthesizer, analogue signal)
	Output rate profile, with clearly discriminated maxima and minima
	Formats, indicating priority messages and/or signals

Fig. 4.4   An IFO checklist.

natural language of the FS, SADT, Myers Dataflow representation, MASCOT, and CCITT-SDL may be used as appropriate for a particular application. These are described in some detail in Chapter 7, to which other notations, with which they are compared, belong.

It must be stressed, however, that neither structured language such as pseudocode, nor diagrammatic design notations used in the FS must violate the principles of user comprehension and the exclusion of design; it is a well-known tendency – and defective practice – to start out in natural language, incorporate some simple diagrams to illustrate the text (in, say, SADT), and find oneself merrily designing away instead of defining the requirements. One must never lose sight of the fact that, when doing the FS, one is operating in the requirements domain and not the 'solution' domain.

These two fairly simple guidelines can be encapsulated in a single statement: 'The FS should be "IFO" formatted and in "natural language plus".'

Some theoreticians, and many software engineers too, regret that the FS cannot be improved by moving its form further away from natural language with all its ambiguities. The theoretician's interest is, more often than not, to provide a formal definition of requirements that can be transformed by 'correctness preserving' steps into a computably correct program. The software engineer's interest is, most often, to get the FS into a 'technologist-friendly' form such as pseudocode, MASCOT or whatever.

We maintain our view that, for the FS to be the fully authorized baseline document, signed off by users and implementation technologists, it will have to be in a commonly understood form such as 'natural language plus' – with all the reservations about which 'plus' notations are comprehensible to users, and the dangers of importing design into the FS.

4.4.3   FS representation: notations, formal methods, and rapid prototyping languages

To solve the inherent problems of functional specification, such as how to ensure that it is a complete and correct representation of real requirements in an unambiguous form, various approaches have been suggested. These may be summarized as:

1. The use of procedural methodologies for both URS and FS. A typical example (that of SADT) is described in Chapter 7 because its notation is also widely used for representing software design for some applications.

2. The use of formal or 'abstract' notations.

3. The use of rapid prototyping by writing the FS in a machine-

executable language, and using this as a simulation for demonstrating/ revising the FS to and with users.

There is some confusion possible between these categories, so we offer the following short paragraphs on each.

Procedural methodologies such as entity relationship analysis, SADT and HIPO have been commented on in Section 4.3 for their suitability at URS level; as this usefulness is somewhat limited even for URS, the methodologies are similarly limited at the FS stage – although SADT diagrams for embellishing text in a 'natural language plus' FS can be of use at that level. Figure 7.8 gives such a depiction from the patient-monitoring example.

Many users of IBM equipment have become used to HIPO charts at the systems-analysis stage of URS, and some organizations have used SADT extensively – both as a notation and a full methodology. Where these practices are possible and desirable, they tend to enhance the quality of the URS and FS by introducing an orderly method into information extraction and recording. But they cannot be regarded as universals for all application types. Their usefulness tends to decrease for applications outside the batch/on-line DP sector, such as systems with real-time and concurrency features.

Formal, or abstract, languages have also been commented on at the end of Section 4.4.2. It is noticeable that, in contrast with methodologies such as E–R analysis, SADT, etc., the object of formal languages is less that of information extraction from users and agreement with them of its incorporation in the FS, than the representation of requirements in a form suitable for progressive transformation culminating in a formally 'proved' program. The interests of some theoreticians in formal representation, and the software engineer's urge to make everything 'technologist friendly', should not be confused, although they undoubtedly overlap.

Formal (or abstract) languages for specification or design are currently an important area of research. There are, in fact, several problems as we see it in this area of research. One that seems insuperable at the present time is that the more a representational language is intended for statements of requirement to act as operands in a logically inferrable 'correct' transformation towards a 'correct' program, the more abstract the language becomes. Hence our comment on 'user unfriend-liness'. Another problem is that abstract notations are not necessarily good at the software design level. This is commented on further in Chapter 7, where the design process is described at some length.

A third problem is the unnecessary confusion between abstraction as a process and abstraction of form. Jonkers (1982) correctly identifies the process of abstraction with that of discarding inessentials. That is precisely what should go on in the FS process, whatever representational form is involved. It may not be inferred, however, that the process of abstraction requires an abstract notation; nor – as is sometimes the case – should it be inferred that a rigorous process of abstraction requires *mathematical* rigour if that, in turn, leads to an abstract notation and the problems of user unfriendliness.

A further problem is that the apparatus for computing the correctness of transformations, over a sequence of steps in specification, design and coding, will be a formidably complex program in its own right; so not only may errors of formulation occur but also errors of demonstration.

Given these known limitations at the specification level, and some others at the software design stage too, it is difficult to see how a general use of formal languages from FS to acceptance stages of the lifecycle can be of wide-scale use (beyond the scope of S-systems, for instance) in software engineering. The answer to the problem of amateur programming with poor tools – correctly diagnosed by Dijkstra almost a decade ago – is not necessarily more theoretical approaches, but better software engineering, towards which, of course, computer science will make a substantial but not prescriptive contribution. We are aware that this view may be taken as a polemic against research into formal methods in general, but it is not. We believe that apart from formal languages for use at the FS stage, their cognate subject, formal proof methods, may be somewhat more likely to make a contribution by improving testing techniques. For instance, it is possible to envisage that a software design at its lowest level above that of code itself could be represented as modules specified as S-type systems, and 'proved' at the code level (see Section 9.5). Whether the approach can be taken further 'up' the lifecycle whilst still allowing 'user' participation at the FS level, and good design practice thereafter, is the subject of ongoing research (See Section 8.3.2).

Another approach to the undoubted problems at the FS stage is that of writing the FS in a machine-executable language, using this as a simulator, and producing an evolved FS on the basis of this 'prototype'.

Hoare (1984) has made the interesting suggestion that, in future, specifications may be replaced by a process analogous to that between an architect and the person commissioning a building, and incorporating the sort of prototyping done by production engineers before a consumer product is released. In such a scheme, 'formal' (i.e. authorized) specifications would be a set of users' and operators' manuals based on mathematical models of requirements whose use as simulators will be – in effect – prototypes of the whole specification. This is undoubtedly an attractive proposition, and already some application-dependent languages (e.g. for telephony systems) are becoming available.

Given the probable costs in computer capacity required and the likely expense of developing a language suitable for a particular application, and the potential problems arising for project contracts of supply (how can manuals and models be signed off as baseline?), the most likely areas of application for prototyping will be for extremely large-scale product developments by substantially sized IT firms able to support the investment. In all, this is a promising area for research and application along application-sector lines for large-scale IT-product development companies. (Examples brought to our attention include a growing use of the Ada language for this purpose, as well as products like RAPID and FLAIR in use at the US Department of Defense and TRW.)

Above all these approaches hovers the tendency to claim the invention of a 'philosopher's stone' for software engineering. Each of the three specification ('representational') approaches has a contribution to make, at some level, for some applications. None of them contains a standard method for specifying a software system, let alone one for other lifecycle stages as well.

4.4.4 Example: FS for a hospital monitoring system

In Example 3 below, the FS begins at the point in Section 4.3.3 where the essay-form URS exists; the implementation technologists (*note*: not necessarily software engineers only) start by summarizing that highly imperfect document. In the case given, this is done by reference only, whereas in real life the summary URS would be fully incorporated in the FS as the 'Introduction'. Likewise, some schematic of the alarm-system requirements (such as an information flow diagram, SADT, etc.) are only referred to in the FS and depicted in Chapter 7 at the point where their notations are described.

A different example of a functional specification can be found also in the case-study in Chapter 11.

Example 3, and the one in Chapter 11, are illustrations only and are not given as prescriptions of how to do the FS in all cases; the one below may even contain errors of omission or interpretation, not having been through a 'verification loop' with users and therefore not yet having been signed off. (The one in Chapter 11 was, in fact, fully implemented.)

EXAMPLE 3

Functional Specification

Section	Contents	Page
1.	Introduction; the nature and scope of requirements (summary)	000
2.	Schematic of how the new alarm system will work	000
3.	Assumptions (clarification of the URS) and disclaimers	000
4.	System inputs, features and outputs	000
5.	Appendix A: Existing equipment	000
6.	Authority	000

1. Introduction; the nature and scope of requirements (summary)

(See Section 4.3.4 above)

2. Schematic of how the new alarm system will work

The diagrammatic representation below is intended to show the main features of the future alarm system. In this respect it is intended only as a clarification of our understanding of requirements and is in no way a design of the system to fulfil these requirements.

(Of many possible schematic notations two, 'Information Flow' and SADT, are given in Section 7.3.2 as part of the description of these notations. Either one could appear here.)

3. Assumptions (clarifications of the URS) and disclaimers

To compile this FS we have had to make interpretations and assumptions from the URS document. These are summarized as follows and must either be authenticated by the user or revised and used as the basis for FS revision before this document is signed off.

3.1 That a file exists in the Central Computer System (CCS) containing all identification references (name and number) for authorized persons having identification cards and access the special readers.

3.2 That the same convention is to be adopted for displaying ECS warning messages as for PCCS, i.e. that they are displayed at VDUs in the central control room, common room, canteen, and the ward administration room and/or private patient porter's location for the floor concerned.

3.4 That removal of warning messages can only be done via the identification card procedure, and that both insertion and removal of an identification will cause a message to be sent to the CCS. Identification cards inserted but not removed will cause a special alarm message to be displayed calling the owners to remove the card (or someone else to do it on the owner's behalf).

3.5 That the VDUs provided for the alarm system will not be used for accessing patient records, nor for any other purpose than described in this FS.

3.6 That all CCS, PCCS, ECS, VDU and electrical connection equipment (see Appendix A) is fully installed and operational as described, and that its performances and capacities are fully adequate for the alarm system as required. Of the PCCS equipment it is assumed that Mark I devices are installed in private wards on a one-per-patient basis, and Mark II devices are installed in private patient wings of the hospital on the basis of one device per five patients.

4. Systems inputs, features and outputs

4.1 *Inputs*

- CCS interrogation of PCCS and ECS devices for status information.
- Keyboard input to cancel alarm.
- Keyboard input to page up overflow alarm messages.
- History record input to database.
- Identification reader inputs to CCS.
- CCS to clock enquiry for date/time.
- CCS to PCCS/ECS devices instructing them to desist for processed alarms.

4.2 *Features*

- PCCS and ECS devices respond to CCS enquiry with fixed format status message. Failure to respond within a given time (10 s is suggested as a timeout in the CCS) results in a system-failure alarm message being shown on all VDUs.
- All alarm messages to be recognized by the CCS and messages formatted and routed appropriately. This feature will test for screen overflows, and will administer the overflow counters and saved messages facilities. The history record will be augmented and, if the history buffer is full, it will be saved on archival store.
- Responses to alarm messages will be received and recognized by the CCS from identification readers, alarm messages cancelled as a result, and the history file augmented and administered.
- Requests for overflow messages will be received and recognized by the CCS, and a new page and overflow count displayed at the VDU concerned. The displayed messages will be saved as 'overflow'. If more overflows are requested they will be displayed, and so on, treating the file of these messages for a screen as a circular organization of records.
- All identification input messages to the CCS will be checked on a timeout basis; if no identification output message has been received after five minutes a special warning message will be displayed on the appropriate screen for the doctor/ nurse concerned (i.e. at ward or patient level) and in the central control room, common room and canteen.

- Processed alarm messages will cause the CCS to send a 'desist' message to the PCCS/ECS device(s) concerned.
- PCCS/ECS devices will recognize the CCS desist message. It will activate a timeout of five minutes at the device concerned (i.e. within its micro) during which that particular message will not be re-sent.

4.3 *Outputs*

- PCCS/ECS status signals to the CCS.
- The CCS will output alarm messages (patient condition, environmental factors, equipment failure, identification card warnings) at VDUs. Each of these messages will comprise one or two screen lines, and a screen will be 'full' when ten lines (alarm messages) are displayed. An agreed screen format is shown in Figure 4.5.

4.4 *Load and throughput on the system; safety and system integrity considerations*

The adequacy of currently installed equipment will be the crucial determinant in whether the performance of the system degrades unacceptably in some circumstances. It is not certain that the

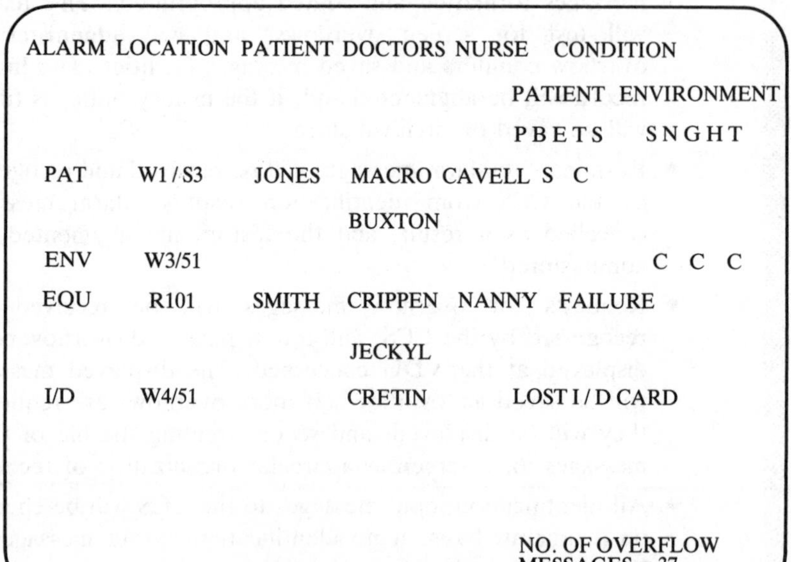

ALARM	LOCATION	PATIENT	DOCTORS	NURSE	CONDITION							
					PATIENT					ENVIRONMENT		
					P	B	E	T	S	S N	G	H T
PAT	W1 / S3	JONES	MACRO CAVELL		S	C						
			BUXTON									
ENV	W3/51									C	C	C
EQU	R101	SMITH	CRIPPEN	NANNY	FAILURE							
			JECKYL									
I/D	W4/51		CRETIN		LOST I / D CARD							

NO. OF OVERFLOW
MESSAGES = 37

Fig. 4.5   User interface: screen format in the FS.

central computer system (CCS) or its electrical connection to sensors is adequate for all load conditions; before implementing this FS a thorough feasibility study must be carried out from this point of view.

As to the safety of the system, it should be noted that no redundancy of equipment is provided for; failure of the CCS or a major part of the communication system could therefore cause complete failure of the whole system. Of particular concern is the issue of how devices are connected to the CCS. If they are multidropped on to a concentrator (front end) then this node will be especially vulnerable.

5. Appendix A: Existing equipment

5.1 *The CCS*

A computer of unspecified make, capacity or other characteristics is provided. We assume that it has the following characteristics:

- Adequate programmable store, archival store, processing speed and operating system features for the task specified herein. Minimally, there should be 128 kbytes of available RAM and one 5 Mbyte disk attachment.

- The operating system must be a pre-emptive, real-time multitasking scheduler permitting tasks of at least two priority levels (the highest of which is currently unused) to execute in a pseudo-concurrent fashion, the highest-priority ready task being the running task. It should also allow semaphore and message passing between intercommunicating tasks. Furthermore, the I/O system must allow a high-priority task to access files at all times – even if in use by other priority tasks or ones of lower status.

5.2 *The communication subsystem*

An electrical communication system of unspecified characteristics is provided between sensors and the CCS. We assume that it has adequate line speed for the purposes envisaged and that the issue of whether its inputs are parallel (i.e. via sufficient ports/DMA in the CCS) or concentrated into serial, or partly parallel, is already decided and the necessary equipment (hardware and software) is in place.

5.3 *The sensor subsystem*

It is assumed that the existing PCCS/ECS equipment will act, or be modified to act, outside the scope of this FS, in the following ways.

- All devices will recognize a status request input from the

PCCS and will transmit a binary bit pattern response. These bit patterns are defined in Section 5.4.

- All devices will recognize a 'desist' message from the CCS when an alarm has been serviced, and will not resume transmitting this alarm for 5 minutes after the 'desist'.

- PCCS/ECS equipment will contain its own diagnostic features for malfunction (as distinct from outright failure) and will detect plausible but wrong conditions before sending them. Malfunction will be diagnosed as 'failure' by the CCS in just the same way as failure (no response) on receipt of this message.

5.4 *Fixed format messages from sensors*

- 220-off PCCSs that signal as follows:

001	Pulse rate	010	Blood pressure
011	Temperature	110	No alarm
101	Muscular spasm	100	ECG
111	Malfunction		

  A fourth bit, in the 8 position, indicates serious (0) or critical (1) status. Thus 'ECG serious' would be 0100, 'Pulse rate critical' would be 1001, etc.

- 150 Mark I PCCSs will transmit a unique address locating it with patient–floor/ward.
  70 Mark II PCCSs will transmit a location address plus a three-bit bed indicator (001, 010, etc. for bed 1, 2, . . .).

- 220 ECSs present alarm input as follows for out of range values:

001	Temperature	010	Humidity
011	Smoke	110	No problem
101	Glare	100	Noise
111	Malfunction		

  A device address uniquely identifying ward section or private room is attached to all messages.

- 10-off identification card readers present ASCII BCD numbers and staff names uniquely matched to a file in the CCS.

6. Authority

This document is authorized as being the substantive FS for the alarm system at XYZ hospital, and is signified as such by:

_____   ____(for the users/clients), and

_____   (for the implementors/suppliers), on

_____   (date)

The completion of this section, signatures and date immediately signifies that this FS document comes under formal change control as defined elsewhere.

The FS example highlights several positive features, and some problems experienced in dealing with the URS. The major issues requiring comment are:

1. The overall format is a reasonable example of IFO, and the diagrams in Part 2 (see Chapter 7 below) illustrate the use of 'natural language plus' without becoming design.

2. Interestingly, some design does get into the FS. In order to clarify the working of PCCS/ECS equipment it is revealed that the implementation philosophy will be based on the CCS polling sensor devices, and not change of status of the sensors initiating interrupts. This minimal (but fundamental) excursion into design could have been avoided, but would have led to omission from the lists of inputs and outputs (i.e. the issue would have been ignored, at cost to the completeness of the FS).

3. The authors of the FS raise useful points of systems engineering concerning system performance and safety. Before this FS is signed off, these factors and all the assumptions about installed equipment will have to be clarified.

4. The list of assumptions is a good idea for any FS if there are outstanding issues of interpretation of the URS. Often it is better to attempt the FS and indicate areas of confusion than to iterate (endlessly) with users in discussions about detail and meaning.

5. The technical detail of installed equipment, bit-level stuff in some cases, is tucked away in an Appendix – a much better policy than scattering it through the text.

After some iterations with users the FS, in a form similar to that shown, will no doubt be signed off by all parties and put under formal change control. In parallel with the FS development, an outline system design exercise should have taken place as described below. This OSD will be to establish the feasibility of implementing the FS (either within known constraints of installed equipment as in the example, or on the basis of facilities defined in the OSD); the OSD is also the basis for acceptably accurate estimates of timescale and effort, as described in Chapter 5.

4.4.5 The move from FS to design

The move from FS towards detailed system and software design represents a major transformation best described as follows. The URS is a representation of requirements largely in user/application terms; the FS is a representation of requirements in more neutral (or 'functional') terms, mutually comprehensible to both users and implementation technologists; the design (at system or software level) is a representation of the system to be implemented.

The design process is described in Chapter 7, and its relationship with OSD is discussed in Section 4.5.

What is a distinct danger, to be clarified before moving on, is that apparent structure in the FS is taken as the basis for structure in the design. In some cases such an obvious decomposition into programmable tasks may be allowable and one can get away with it; on other occasions extreme difficulty will arise if programming transpires directly out of the FS stage without an intervening design stage.

The problem here is that one can never tell, frequently until well into the implementation stage of coding and testing, if an 'assumed design' from the FS structure is justified or not. For that reason the structuring of the FS documents, e.g. in IFO format (or any other way for that matter), must be clearly understood as being to enhance the unambiguity of the FS and not to pre-empt the design nor influence it beyond the scope of requirements to be incorporated.

Consequences of this are that 'rapid prototyping' as described in Section 4.4.3 above may not generate a useful 'production' version, the objective being more that of clarifying specification than designing an implementation; also, the use of pseudocode as a formal specification language tends to lead to coding as a next stage without a proper software design at all. These traps should be borne in mind when doing the FS. Creating the baseline for implementation is the imperative at this stage, along with establishing its feasibility (technical and economic) as an implementation. A design stage should then follow as described in full in Chapter 7, the significance of which is indicated to some extent by the effort attribution statistics for software engineering quoted in Section 4.1, i.e. 35% or so of software engineers' effort over the lifecycle (maintenance and new version effort apart).

4.5   The Outline Systems Design (OSD)

It is not natural for specification to proceed to FS level without the occurrence of implementation considerations, and even if it were, it would be inadvisable. Otherwise a specification might emerge that was not feasible – either because of the constraint imposed by existing equipment, or because of the economics of buying or making the necessary equipment, or (in extreme cases) because the specification was not feasible on any equipment at any price.

Therefore, as implementation considerations are being enumerated and evaluated during the FS stage, the question arises of how to keep the resulting design and detail ideas out of the FS so that it may be signed off. The problem is made more difficult by the natural (and correct) tendency to have the FS done by the implementation technologists to make sure that they understand the requirements; they will naturally think of the implementation also and, for the feasibility exercise, this is highly desirable.

A stringent FS procedure that excludes implementation design and technical detail will go far to protect the FS. Another device is to have a separate but contiguous category for technical information – an archive section in fact – called the Outline Systems Design. This OSD will play a significant rôle during specification as:

1. The separate 'pigeonhole' to keep the FS uncorrupted by design and implementation information.

2. The classification of notional hardware and software subsystems required (*note*: 'notional' since they do not yet constitute detailed design – a much more extensive exercise in general).

3. The basis of acceptably accurate timescale and effort estimates for an implementation (detailed design, construction and testing stages for both hardware and software as appropriate).

Whereas the FS is a formal document to be signed off as described, the OSD – like the Concepts and URS stages – results in an informal document, for fundamentally important use as described but informal nonetheless within the archive.

4.5.1 Authorship, form and content

In Section 4.4.2 it was suggested that the same people should do the OSD and the FS to ensure the correspondence of the two, and that these people will normally be implementation technologists, so as to achieve a full understanding of requirements at the implementation level and a technical competence for the OSD. This last point is extremely important and, in effect, determines the time in lifecycle terms at which software engineers should be first involved in the process; quite literally no software engineers in the OSD activity may mean a lack of attention to the scope and feasibility of software required, with potentially catastrophic effects on configuring hardware subsystems, unassessed overall system performance perhaps, and a tendency to underestimate software development timescales and required effort. Software engineers must be actively involved in both the FS and OSD activities for requirements likely to involve software.

The object of the OSD activity is to describe one or more possible systems solutions to the requirements, as these become manifest during the URS/FS stage. To do this a process of categorization should take place comprising, in principle, three taxonomies:

1. a hardware taxonomy;
2. a 'tools' taxonomy;
3. a software taxonomy.

A taxonomy is, in general, a classification of items – very often using a specialized terminology for designating them. In the following paragraphs we describe the taxonomies in general and offer examples of each from the hospital monitoring context already described to URS and FS stages. A further example of a software taxonomy is given in the case history in Chapter 11.

The order in which we present the three kinds of taxonomy (hardware, tools, software) is not representative of the relative importance of the three, so much as a desire to conclude this subsection with the main issue – that of the software taxonomy.

For computer applications involving some freedom of choice about equipment, a hardware taxonomy evolves as OSD authors speculate over the hardware types it might be best to use (computer, communication, special purpose hardware as need be), jotting down the items and their characteristics, and making simple sketches of the connected box-diagram type.

Sometimes the hardware taxonomy stays at a fairly high generic level of component descriptions, such as: 'A 1.024 Mbyte MC68000 operating UNIX, having a 1 × 10 Mbyte disk attachment and a keyboard (full ASCII set)/screen (80 × 24)', or something of the sort. On other occasions an extensive hardware component list may be made. The level to aim at is determined by the essential purposes – feasibility and estimating – to which the OSD will be put; if these can be done plausibly on the basis of a high-level taxonomy then that is the right level, and, if not, then the taxonomy should be detailed until it is at the right level.

An example of a hardware taxonomy for the patient-monitoring system is shown in Table 4.1 and Figure 4.6. As well as a component list, a simple hardware taxonomy may be illustrated by a hardware diagram. This 'possible solution', based on a local area network philosophy, may well have resulted from the further clarification of the FS before it was signed-off.

One feature not clear from these examples is the speculative, notional nature of the taxonomy. In effect, the entries in Table 4.1 are of the form:

'MC 68000 (?) with 1 Mbyte (?) of RAM and 1 × 10 Mbyte(?) disk archival store.'

Hardware taxonomies do not usually have question marks scattered

Table 4.1 Example of a hardware taxonomy.

Component	Description	Quantity
Computer	MC 68000 with 128K RAM and 10 megabyte hard disc	1
PCCS – Mk I	Patient care control-system – single patient	150
– Mk II	– five patients	70
ECS	Environmental control system	220
VDU	XYZ Colour graphic VDU + Keyboard (Qwerty)	13
Card reader	Special PQR personal i/d reader	10
Cables – Type 1	RS232–RS232, 1 metre	453
– Type 2	RS232–RS232, 6 metre	1
– Type 3	600 JC Co-axial, 100 metre roll	8
Gate	Local area network gate	454

around them in practice, but they should be seen nonetheless as speculative outline designs of possible hardware solutions – not definitive designs of the hardware subsystem. We return to this point under the software taxonomy.

The OSD stage is the earliest in the lifecycle at which development tools for software and hardware can be realistically considered if their taxonomies are well defined. In general these tools are known as the programming support environment (PSE) for software development. We would expect a tools taxonomy to include computer facilities for concurrent software development, the language envisaged for the implementation, cross-compilation/assembly tools for generating the software for the target machine(s), editors and debug features, word processing for documentation, and configuration management. A full list of possible PSE tools is suggested in Sections 8.3 and 10.2.

In many cases the tools are already procured and in operation as a part of the software engineering environment, at a sufficient level or otherwise for the purposes. In other cases the OSD 'tools' taxonomy may be essential to list, as its components could comprise a major investment (or development) in their own right. The justification of a PSE as a general part of a software engineer's facilities often arises from an aggregation of OSD tools taxonomies and a cost/benefit analysis over past, present and forecast future requirements. It is well worthwhile, therefore, to make sure for all software engineering jobs that the tools taxonomy is competently done.

In the patient-monitoring example, most program development may be done on the 'central computer provided' unless, that is, it is so loaded that it would prove a major limitation to use it (in which case the alarm

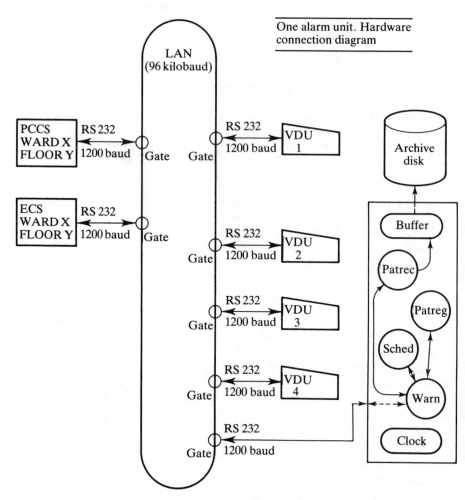

Fig. 4.6   Example of a hardware taxonomy diagram.

system would probably also be questionable). An alternative might be listed in the OSD part of the archive as:

- A host development system for up to five concurrent users and having Pascal to CCS object code, and Pascal to PCCS and ECS object code generators (and other features).

- A PROM programmer and eraser for PCCS and ECS microcomputers.

For the rest of this subsection we concentrate on the software taxonomy.

Like its hardware and tools equivalents, the software taxonomy is a components list of a possible (notional) implementation – in this case of that part of requirements it is thought best (for whatever reasons) to implement in software. As with the hardware taxonomy, it must be stressed that the software part of an OSD is not a proper software design. This matter is discussed further in Section 4.5.4.

The usual way to make a software taxonomy is for competent software engineers to make a connected box diagram of possible features to be implemented in software by a method of progressive definition. Thus, the first-level 'box' may contain a simple statement such as 'The Software' and then the next level boxes may appear containing expressions such as 'Outstanding Warnings Manager', 'PCCS/ECS Input–Output', 'Terminal Output' and so forth (the example is again taken from the patient monitoring system; see Figure 4.9). In this fashion a taxonomy is built up that looks something like Figure 4.7.

The progressive detailing of FS features that might be realized in software goes down the taxonomy to a level at which the software engineers realize that, beyond this point, real software design will be beginning in the sense that common features of different parts of the taxonomy will be appearing as possible program modules. At this point the process stops. As a rough guideline, the bottom level of a taxonomy comprises boxes containing elaborated features of the FS which, if they were to be programmed as they stand, might result in a few hundred source statements of code each.

Small software systems as defined in Section 2.3.4 require very simple, two- or three-level taxonomies usually; these can be easily accommodated in the form shown in Figure 4.7. Larger systems will require many-level taxonomies. For example, a medium-sized system of, say, 100 thousand source statements of code may go down to as many as ten levels and require a decomposition of the taxonomy to represent it reasonably. Extremely large software systems (such as the SDI 'Starwars' application) have – or should have – exceptionally large taxonomies with numerous levels.

There is a natural tendency for smaller systems to have taxonomies down to a level of detail which, if implemented, would result in quite

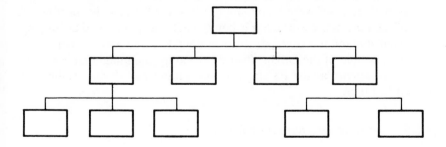

Fig. 4.7   Software taxonomy: hierarchical format.

small amounts of code (about 100 source statements per 'box', say); the taxonomies for larger software systems tend to stop at a level where the definitions in boxes might represent 500–1000 source statements of code.

When decomposition of the taxonomy is necessary because of the system size, taxonomies tend to be represented in an orthogonal form (as depicted in Figure 4.8), and the 'boxes' disappear in favour of indented text. In some cases a taxonomy will start out in the connected box-diagram form, and then devolve into the orthogonal form with indented text at lower levels, so as to get more of it on a page before decomposition of the taxonomy occurs.

A : A1

A2 : A2.1 : A2.1.1

A2.2.1

A2.2

A3

B : B1 : B1.1

Fig. 4.8   Software taxonomy: orthogonal format.

The form shown in Figure 4.8 readily lends itself to representation in pseudocode, and we find that many software engineers eschew the connected box-diagram approach altogether. The only argument against this state of affairs is that the software taxonomy may be confused with a pseudocode representation of low-level software design. The whole issue of OSD and software design is discussed in Section 4.5.4, since the box-diagram notation may itself be confused with a software design (e.g. a calling-sequence diagram; see Section 7.3 for description).

In making a software taxonomy in whatever form, sight must not be lost of the purposes for which it is being made (feasibility and estimating) and what its limitations are; it is not a definitive software design.

An example of the OSD software taxonomy, as it might emerge from a parallel activity at the FS stage of our patient monitoring example, is shown in Figure 4.9.

4.5.2   Software and hardware sizing

The scope of a software development task in terms of its approximate size (in source-code terms) and complexity, can be assessed by competent soft-

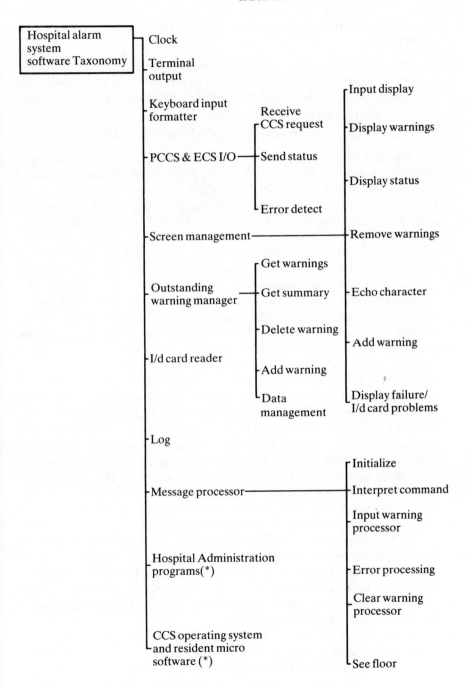

Fig. 4.9 Example of a software taxonomy.

ware engineers from the software taxonomy. This has two fundamentally important uses:

1. For estimating effort and timescale required to do the software development (although a warning must be given that effort estimates should not be made by dividing the estimate of software size by some 'average' programmer productivity).
2. For configuring the hardware on which the software is to operate.

The first of these is dealt with extensively in Chapter 5 and is not further commented on here. As for configuring the hardware, this is essential in many IT applications where the computer is to be a component in an electronic system (small-scale or large-scale – from a car radio to a military on-board command and control system, for example).

The dangers of under-configuration cannot be overstated; nothing is more detrimental to a development task – unless it is an unreasonable timescale constraint – than to discover late in the lifecycle that the equipment is grossly inadequate. All this serves to emphasize the importance of a software taxonomy, and the involvement of software engineers early enough in the lifecycle to influence hardware configuration.

The method of software sizing is basically this. When the software taxonomy exists down to some reasonable definitional level, software engineers can assign notional software size to the entries on the lowest level. These estimates are notional in that they relate to entries in the classification that may not be implemented in the form in which they are described, the taxonomy not being a software design after all.

Although notional, they are, if properly done, good first-order approximations to software size. The attribution of source-code sizes at this stage is entirely judgemental, and based on the software engineers' experience and 'feel' for the possible complexity of this part of the requirements. Thus it is unwise to have this step taken by people who are not software engineers, such as amateur programmers or trainee software engineers not supervised by more experienced staff.

At the same time, as notional source-code sizes are attributed along the bottom line of the software taxonomy, parts of it can be 'flagged' as being best done in either a high-level language or in assembler (e.g. if particularly time or space critical), and so on. Similarly, existing or to-be-purchased software (such as operating systems, database-management packages, etc.) can also be indicated.

Table 4.2 takes the software taxonomy for the hospital alarm-monitoring system and shows how software sizing can be depicted (see Figure 4.9, from which the 'bottom line' has been used).

On the basis of a source-code size estimate of this sort, an object-code size estimate and its associated programmable memory-size calculation can be performed. For instance, to choose a more dramatic example than that above, let us say that a software size estimate results in

Table 4.2 Codesize estimate from a software taxonomy.

Item		Code-size		Exists(*)
		HLL	Assr.	
Clock		100		
Terminal		50		
Keyboard input		75		
PCCS-ECS i/o	CCS request status		300	
	Sensor response status		200	
	Error diagnosis		200	
Screen				
management	Initialise display	50		
	Display warnings	50		
	Display status	50		
	Remove warning	75		
	Echo char.	50		
	Add warning	100		
	Display error etc.	75		
Outstanding				
warnings	Get warnings	100		
	Get summary	100		
	Delete warning	100		
	Add warning	50		
	Data management	150		
Message				
Processor	Intitialise	250		
	Command interpreter	200		
	Input warning	200		
	Error processing	100		
	Clear warning	200		
	See floor	150		
Log		50		
I/d card reader		50		
Hospital admin.				
progs.				*
Operating system				*
TOTALS		2375	700	

75 000 statements of RTL-2 (a high-level language) and 10 000 instructions of assembler code that might have to be written. Also, let us assume that we have 'guessed' at a hardware configuration (within the hardware taxonomy) having 128 kbytes of programmable memory with no overlay, memory management or roll-in/roll-out features for programs (i.e. all the software must fit into this programmable store at one and the same time).

The memory required for programs (excluding their data) is estimated as follows.

First of all, 75 000 RTL-2 statements will compile into $n \times 75\,000$ instructions. This value of n is known as the 'expansion factor' of the high-level language and represents the fact that there is a $1 : n$ relationship (on average) between a statement of high-level language code and assembler code produced by its compiler. An example of this process is given in Section 1.2. A typical average value of the expansion factor from RTL-2 is $n = 4$.

Thus, the 75 000 statements of RTL-2 can be expected to generate about 300 000 instructions of assembler code when compiled. To this must be added the 10 000 assembler instructions to be written for the parts of the taxonomy thought best to be done in this language. Thus we say that the object code size of the software is 310 000 instructions of assembler code as distinct from its source-code size of 75 000 + 10 000 as stated.

To this process must be added a last step of translating the assembler code into bytes of store, since each instruction will require (on average) several bytes of store to contain it. Typically, for a computer of 16-bit architecture, one assembler instruction requires between 1.5 and 2 bytes. If we take this further expansion factor, for this stage of translation, as being 2, the object code of 310 000 instructions will require about 620 000 bytes of store to accommodate and execute it, or 620 kbytes (excluding data space) as we should put it. At this stage it is evident that a 128 kbyte microcomputer is somewhat inadequate for programs that have to be simultaneously store-resident, and are likely to occupy over 600 kbytes of store, excluding any data space required. The hardware taxonomy has under-configured the computer required. The metaphorical '?' in the hardware taxonomy has been justified.

4.5.3   OSD prototyping for technical feasibility

In Section 2.3 a prototype was defined as a pre-production version of a system or subsystem, the object of which was to buy information of some sort. In Section 4.3 one form of prototyping within the URS was described as a useful means of clarifying requirements – particularly on the user–system interface.

Other prototyping requirements occur, particularly concerning technical feasibility. A piece of hardware, previously non-existent, may have to be developed and it may require software features also; an algorithm may be best evolved if an experimental version of it exists in software, and so on. In all these cases, a prototype (or even a whole set of them) is needed. We will refer to these as OSD, as distinct from URS prototypes.

Unlike URS prototypes, OSD prototypes often proceed from a strong (P-type) specification. One knows what one wants to do; one is not sure how to do it. Furthermore, unlike URS prototypes which are manifestly 'quick and dirty mock-ups' and therefore very easy to designate as 'throw-away prototypes', those for technical development and feasibility at the OSD stage often require major innovations, extensive and costly equipment and considerable time and effort to achieve.

A resulting system can, when its result (the information 'bought') is positive, take on an entirely spurious significance – far beyond its engineering merits seen from the production quality viewpoint – just because it has taken x years, and cost y dollars to make. Furthermore, whereas users tend to be gratified and motivated by a URS prototyping process, since it is clearly taking into consideration their interests and needs, it is the implementation technologists, not the users (or, as is more often the case, their surrogates for products), who are enthused by OSD prototypes. In fact, OSD prototyping often causes frustration in management and commercial staff, being seen as 'technical hobbyism', however unfairly.

All this serves to increase the pressure on implementation technologists to 'get the job done', not only at the prototype level but also for the first release versions of a product (or contract due-date for a project). There is an unfortunate tendency, resulting from this pressure, to incorporate OSD prototypes in release versions of a product or project. The results are almost invariably disastrous in a variety of ways – technical (e.g. inordinate maintenance support) and commercial (as in lost reputation and markets). In other aspects of engineering this error is much less often committed. One does not put a prototype aircraft into passenger service, drive a prototype car without a certification of its roadworthiness, and so forth. Nor should one try to sell a 'bread-board' version of a hardware (electronic) engineered item.

Software prototypes at the OSD stage tend to get incorporated in production-engineered versions for a set of reasons, some applying more severely in some cases than in others. Market (or client) pressure is one reason; a lack of visibility of software with the commensurate lack of understanding of its quality criteria and how to achieve them is another. Acute staff shortage in software engineering exacerbates the problem in one of two ways; the pressure to release software staff for other work is often very strong, and the tendency for hardware engineers to act as amateur programmers for OSD prototypes is very marked.

In these circumstances it can be very difficult to go back to management and say: 'Our lovely ABC system, such a knockout at the recent trade exhibition, will take another two years for a release version. You see, the software is a prototype, and we should either throw it away or take it through a proper software-engineering process!'

Difficult though it may be to recognize the prototype status of software, and even more difficult to admit it, a correct designation must be made. Then, for successful prototypes, the results should be incorporated in the OSD (and, if setting hardware policy in some way, as constraints in the FS). The software should then go through a proper lifecycle of definition within an overall architectural design, detailed design, coding, proper documentation, and testing up to the stage of validation and certification of its quality.

This emergence from prototyping status into full lifecycle-based development does not imply that prototype software should not itself be well designed, coded, documented and tested, but that these processes may have suffered from the basic imperative of prototyping – that of 'buying information', usually on a minimum timescale and cost basis. Nor should it be assumed that prototyping is a one-pass process itself; it might be a highly complex process with feedback and re-attempting. A hypothetical instance of this complexity, and how it appears in lifecycle terms, is given in Figure 4.12.

All of this has the most profound effects on management and commercial decision-making for IT products. To whatever 'guesstimates' are made for timescale and cost of OSD prototypes (and these will, in the best regulated environments, be more a matter of 'allowable' than 'expected' values) there must be added a provision for doing a proper version, fit for release after the prototyping exercise.

This is inevitably less a matter of accurate estimating at the start than an allowance of time and budget, the former at least based on considerations of 'market window' and competitors' policy, the latter on product price. The only useful advice we can offer is:

1. To managers and commercial staff: understand that a 'continuing development' that includes OSD prototyping will reach a stage when the development time and cost for a release version can (and must) be estimated.

2. To staff doing OSD software prototyping: recognize the nature of the endeavour and designate it clearly; a prototype of anything is not likely to be a reliable version. Then, at an appropriate stage, undertake a proper software-engineering approach to the development of high-quality software.

We are under no illusions about the difficulty of admitting the prototype status of software, or its commercial consequences. We submit, however, that the clarity of designation we propose is essential.

4.5.4   OSD software taxonomy and software design

The dangers of mistaking a software taxonomy for a software design are very real, as are the dangers of expressing the taxonomy in some pseudocode form and omitting design altogether – trying to go, thereafter, straight from this pseudocode representation into an extended 'code' version (the ailment of 'prematurity').

In the one case, managers and others tend to mistake a connected box-diagram of the taxonomy for a very similar schematic known as a subroutine (or 'module') calling-sequence diagram. Figure 4.10 depicts the two. Whilst both are hierarchical in a sense, it can be seen that in the case of the taxonomy we can speak with reason of 'levels', and in particular a 'bottom level'. In the calling-sequence case we cannot. Also the two are different in the treatment of detail; the taxonomy is a depiction of progressive levels of requirement detail, whereas the calling sequence is a 'flat' depiction of implementation detail.

When software engineers do an OSD software taxonomy in its orthogonal form, with indentation to depict hierarchy, and when they use pseudocode (which is often the technicians' own internal language of discourse anyway), the danger is that an attempt will be made to go straight from the OSD to a code implementation, bypassing the full design stage. As with the fallacy of presuming design on the basis of apparent structure in the FS, this use of the OSD as the design is exceedingly dangerous. In some cases (generally small and non-complex systems) one may get away with it. On the other hand one cannot know if a particular case falls into that category until late in the implementation.

Another error is to take the whole OSD (hardware, software and 'tools' taxonomies) as constituting a fixed and binding architectural design. That is not the purpose of the OSD at all, although in many cases the architectural design will take the OSD taxonomies as its starting-point. One especially prevalent danger, referred to in later chapters, is to define a so-called 'hardware/software interface' to segregate – behind a fixed and immutable barrier – any hardware development tasks from their software counterparts. Defining this HSI, as it is called in places, too

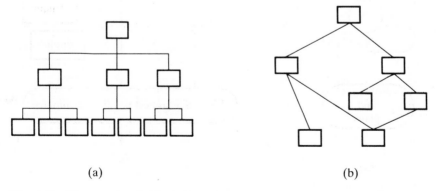

(a)   (b)

Fig. 4.10   Taxonomies and calling sequences: (a) software taxonomy (connected box-diagram form); (b) subroutine calling sequence [design] (connected box-diagram form).

early in the lifecycle (usually as an excuse to get on with hardware development, if that is the more familiar technology) is a very grave error. Defining requirements that may best be done in hardware and software, as hardware and software taxonomies, is a fundamentally useful thing to do to assess feasibility and make accurate estimates. But it is not design of the type which will be used for the implementation. The design process is, on the whole, a very much more extensive exercise (e.g. up to 35% of a software engineer's total effort over a single pass of the lifecycle), and usually cannot be undertaken whilst the FS is still being done. It is commented on, in full, in Chapter 7. The OSD must be seen for what it is and not confused with detailed systems and software design.

4.6   Variations on the lifecycle model

The software lifecycle schematic depicted in Figure 3.4 is for an ideal, project-form software development. It takes only limited account of many real-life instances in contracted software project work and product developments involving software prototypes.

Take the case of a client submitting a specification to potential suppliers and requiring their fixed and binding estimates to do the job. Often the state of the specification is that of a fairly early URS; and the injunction is to bid for the complete implementation by Tuesday of next

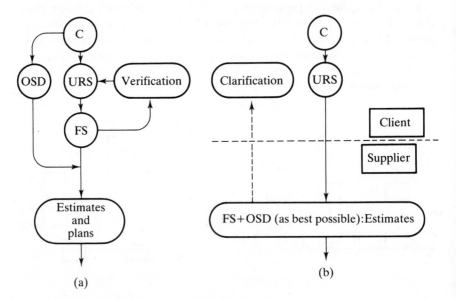

Fig. 4.11   Lifecycle depiction of the premature bid: (a) the ideal Lifecycle; (b) the effective, real-life Lifecycle.

week, and a users' meeting to discuss the specification is refused! The contrast between the ideal lifecycle and reality is depicted in Figure 4.11.

This problem in general is dealt with in Section 10.5 and need not concern us further here, other than to note the alteration to the lifecycle from that as previously depicted.

For projects and products requiring prototypes, the lifecycle can take on an exceedingly elaborate appearance. In the following example, the concepts and specifications go through a variety of evolutions before being agreed 'true' and definitive, and in a state sufficient for a first substantive pass through the lifecycle to achieve the proper engineering status for a release version.

In Figure 4.12 the abbreviations C, URS, and FS have their usual meanings whilst F denotes 'Feasibility assessment', and P denotes 'Prototype'.

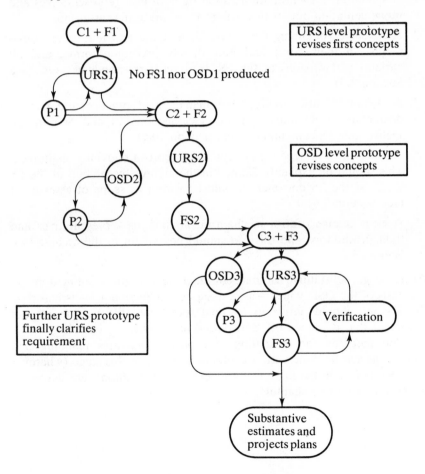

Fig. 4.12 Lifecycle depiction of prototyping.

As can be seen from Figure 4.12, the lifecycle can turn into a whole set of mini-lifecycles, especially during the early specification stages. When this happens, it is exceptionally important to keep track (and to keep archives) of what is going on. The alternative is likely to be an unmanageable mess, particularly if there are several different versions of different types of prototype for various purposes, all proceeding more or less simultaneously.

4.7   The outcome of the specification and feasibility stage

At the end of the specification stage there should be:

1. A signed-off FS with authorization by both user representatives and implementation authorities, where these are different groups.

2. An archive containing Concepts, URS, OSD and feasibility assessments, in their latest and immediately preceding forms, and all variants and versions of the FS, contract correspondence, etc. (see Section 3.3).

3. A definition, also archived, of management practice and control documents for the implementation (see Section 6.2), and the required Deliverable Documentation (see Section 10.1).

4. An identified independent agency for software quality assurance. This should be explicitly defined in the archive by the end of the FS stage, as the FS document should be within its scope of assessment (see Section 9.6).

5. A clear change control mechanism, nominating representatives and their procedures, and this too should be evident in the archive (see Section 3.5).

At this stage, substantive estimates of timescale and effort can be done on the basis of the OSD which – as is described in Section 4.5 – is based on the FS and should derive in its final form from the version of that document that is 'signed off' and placed under change control.

The methods for estimating and project activities planning and control, as can be done with acceptable accuracy at this stage (whatever has gone before in the matter of budgetary appropriation), are described in the following two chapters.

Chapter 5 Estimating effort and timescale

Synopsis

The lamentable history of cost and timescale over-runs in software engineering is described, along with the tendency to premature estimating and the relationship between expected accuracy and lifecycle stages.

Some known methods and practices in software estimating are listed, along with advice on practices to be avoided.

A recommended technique is given for effort and timescale estimating in software development.

Research in parametric cost-estimating models is discussed.

Problems of phasing estimates, and the issue of person dependency in estimating are dealt with.

A view is given on the relationship between effort and allowed time in software engineering.

Estimating for prototype development is described.

5.1 An overview of estimating

Most managers, and many others involved with software engineering, would assert one main characteristic only by which to describe it; it is that (expletive) business that is always late and costs n times the amount anticipated. On the other hand, many software engineers would describe their jobs as being to produce miracles but, like a penny-in-the-slot machine, instantly and cheaply. Not surprisingly, there is truth in both views. It is not unusual to find cost over-runs of 300% and more in software engineering, particularly for tasks above the level of small systems.

The evidence for timescale over-run is somewhat less dramatic, as it is often the attempt to avoid (say) a 50% violation of timescale that may incur an additional effort of many hundreds of percent. When, in addition, timescale over-run is not avoided anyway, the phenomenon is known as 'Brooks' Law': 'Putting more people on a late job makes it later' (Brooks, 1975). The whole subject of effort and allowed timescale, and the relationship between them, is dealt with at some length in Section 5.7.

There are many contributory factors to the poor state of affairs in software engineering, where it is common to find budgetary violations of 300%, 400% and upwards, and developments that are cancelled outright at higher levels of cost over-run.

In this chapter we set out the reasons deriving from defective estimating practice whilst acknowledging that this – although an extremely problematical matter in its own right – is not the only factor involved in over-run. Amongst other reasons causing over-run are lack of management control (see Sections 3.4 and 3.5 and Chapter 6), inadequacy of tools and methods for software development, and the competence and motivation of software engineers (see Section 10.3). Our approach in the following sections presumes these other factors are under control.

Estimating effort and timescale needed for a software engineering task is an extremely difficult and misunderstood matter. The first problem is that estimates are more often than not required and attempted too early in the lifecycle. Quite obviously, for software engineering as for anything else, one can only expect a reasonably accurate estimate of requirements to do a job when sufficient understanding of its scope exists.

Boehm (1981) represents the relationship between estimating accuracy and the lifecycle stage at which an estimate is done as a schematic of the type depicted in Figure 5.1. In this representation, we have used our own lifecycle nomenclature and Boehm's metric for accuracy in which the

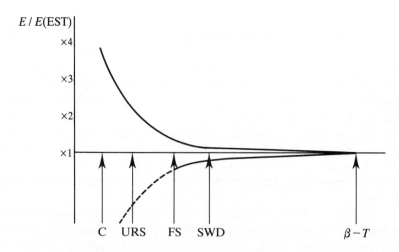

Fig. 5.1 Estimating inaccuracy as a function of lifecycle stage.

terms in the ratio E/E(EST) are: E = the real effort put in to complete the job; and E(EST) = the effort estimated at whatever lifecycle stage it was done.

It is unlikely, in our view, that estimating errors are symmetrically distributed on both sides of the normative E/E(EST) = 1 line for all lifecycle stages at which they may be done. There are three plausible reasons why estimating early in the lifecycle is more likely to lead to underestimating rather than overestimating:

1. Specification is a process, not usually an instantaneous assertion of requirements as though fully revealed. Within this process, the scope of a system will be far more likely to grow than diminish.

2. Complexity is underestimated more often than not. In many cases it is imponderable at the time requirements are defined and agreed.

3. Estimates are very often affected by knowledge (or belief) about acceptable costs and timescales. Such views of what the market (or manager) will bear are generally only loosely, if at all, related to the scope and complexity of requirements. Whereas such notions should be seen as potential constraints on the task to be undertaken, they seldom are.

Some lifecycle stages do allow, given competent methods, symmetrical expectation of estimating error of the form $\pm X\%$. As Figure 5.1 indicates, we regard overestimating as equally likely from the FS stage onwards, but not at earlier lifecycle stages.

Readers are advised to refer to Table 5.1, which shows what we consider to be likely levels of inaccuracy in estimating.

Table 5.1   Tabular depiction of estimating inaccuracy.

LIFECYCLE STAGE	E/E(EST)	NOTES
First concepts	4.0 upwards	
Early URS	3.0 upwards	See note (1) below
Late URS/incomplete FS	2.0 to 4.0	
FS/OSD	1.0 ± 20%	See note (2) below
Late software design	1.0 ± 10%	
Successful β-test	1.0	

1. The degree of inaccuracy early in the lifecycle – likely to be high in any case – will depend upon available analogies, and people competent enough to recognize them. Otherwise any estimate done before the FS/OSD stage is very much a random guess. Practices such as these are the subject of discussion in Section 5.3.

2. The degree of accuracy from the FS stage onwards depends on adequate methods applied by competent people. A method for practical application by software engineers is set out in Section 5.4.

5.2   Estimating practices

There are some eight distinct practices in use for estimating effort and timescale for software development. With acknowledgement to Boehm (1984) who lists seven of them in slightly different nomenclature, we define these practices as follows:

- Analogy involving expert judgement on the basis of known, representative examples.
- Analogy based on more or less representative experience of non-specialists.
- Application of Parkinson's law.
- Bidding 'price-to-win'.
- 'Top down' requirements analysis and rudimentary definition of a 'system'.
- Detailed software design by software engineers, and the derivation of estimates from the 'bottom up' using activities planning techniques based on actual tasks and staff assignment.
- Parametric estimating models.
- Notional activities planning by software engineers based on the software taxonomy of the OSD.

We discuss all eight of these practices in Sections 5.3–5.5 under three classifications, along with their supposed advantages and disadvantages. Table 5.2 indicates the likely 'cost' of the method in terms of percentage of total software engineering effort over the lifecycle (excluding maintenance and new versions) to achieve an estimate of the sort concerned.

5.3   Pitfalls

It is clear from Table 5.2 that the first five listed approaches are likely to be excessively inaccurate whatever their other supposed virtues may be.

Table 5.2 Estimating practice.

ESTIMATING PRACTICE	ACCURACY	COST	PARTICULAR VIRTUES OR DRAWBACKS
1. Analogy (expert)	Probably exceedingly	0–1%	Very poor practices generally for
2. Analogy (inexpert)	poor	0%	quick and dirty guesses
3. Parkinson	Worse than +400% not unknown	0% 0%	Usually done too early in the Lifecycle.
4. Price to win		0%	
5. Top down	+200 to 300%	1–5%	System view but lacking software detail
6. Bottom up	± 10%	30–40%	Motivational, accurate but very costly
7. Parametric model	± 20%(?)	10–15%	Basically at the research stage
8. OSD	± 10% to 20%	10–15%	Motivational, acceptably accurate, quick and cheap.

It is easy to dismiss them all with a blanket condemnation of the form: 'Don't adopt this practice!' but to do that would be to conceal some issues best exposed to view. Consequently, we offer the following explanation of the five approaches, in the hope that in so doing we will help management and commercial staff to avoid some of the pitfalls in estimating that have beset the subject of software engineering to date. In addition to these five, we add below a comment on the defective practice of trying to compute effort required as the ratio of software size estimates and average productivity factors.

On this basis, the six practices to avoid are:

1. Analogy with so-called expert judgement.
2. Analogy without expert judgement.
3. Parkinson's law.
4. Price to win.
5. Top down.
6. Average 'productivity' factors.

5.3.1 Estimating by analogy, and 'Parkinson's law'

Estimating by 'informed' analogy is inaccurate at whatever lifecycle stage it is done for the simple reason that it runs the risk of mistaken analogy, where the complexity of either the system being estimated, or the comparative one, is undervalued. This tendency will be reduced from the FS stage onwards (at least for the complexity of the system being made), but will remain an informed guess, not a real estimate. Earlier than the FS stage, the expected estimating error will be very high – anything above 300% can be the case, because (however 'expert' one is) there is little way of telling whether a generic similarity is a sufficient basis on which to confirm estimates, not to mention the possibility that a specification may grow in scope and complexity. In fact no real expert, such as a practising software engineer, would place much credence on estimating by analogy. The only justification for this practice in any context is that, in its effect within the so-called 'top-down' method, it furnishes a relatively quick and cheap way of doing crude, order of magnitude estimates for first budgetary approximations.

Analogy without expert judgement is the lay-person's best guess on the basis of generic similarity of requirements. Thus a manager or sales representative might say: 'It's a payroll system so it will cost X and take Y months to make, because so-and-so did a payroll and that's what happened.' At whatever lifecycle stage, a practice of this sort is worthless from the estimating point of view.

As in the case of analogy with inexpert judgement it is a sad commentary on the state of affairs in software engineering that the aphoristic 'law' of C. Northcote Parkinson has any adherents at all for estimating. 'Work expands to fill the time available for it' is not a way of estimating but a philosophy of despair.

5.3.2   Price-to-win

On the face of it this is a practice strictly to be avoided also. One determines what the market (client or manager) will bear and then underbids that limit, irrespective of the scope of requirements or the complexity of an implementation to achieve them. In this respect, like Parkinson's law, it is not an estimating method at all. On the other hand it is a frequently encountered commercial necessity for one reason or another, and cannot be dismissed out of hand. A firm may have to 'loss lead' to keep a client or market base, to prevent a competitor getting a toehold, and so on. Or one may underbid to get a job so as to keep a workforce occupied over a temporary slack period.

Whatever the reasons for doing it, establishing effort and timescale budgets on a price-to-win basis is a very perilous practice in software engineering. Generally, the lifecycle stage concerned is that of very early URS or even 'concepts' in some cases, and the commercial imperative requires a quick bid to a client or manager. Just possibly there may be some highly inaccurate impression of effort and timescale requirements based on 'expert judgement', or even the 'top-down' approach described below, and these may be regarded as the best cases for this method. Use of price to win should, in our view, induce a strong collateral imperative to establish the 'cost to do' as accurately and early as possible. The worst of all worlds is achieved when the price to win is taken as the factual estimate of effort and timescale required.

5.3.3 Top-down and bottom-up estimating

In top-down estimates an attempt is made to construct, from the generic features of the concepts and early URS, some notional model of the implementation-to-be. This is then used, so far as feasible, for some sort of 'expert' judgements about the effort and timescale needed for the different systems engineering components, including software. The most obvious disadvantage is that there is far too little definition available of the possible scope and complexity of the software to allow it to be reasonably estimated. The result is a high level of inaccuracy, in the range +200% to +300%. As well as the matter of inaccuracy, another major problem in this method is that it is bound to become unstable as perturbations occur within the URS/FS stage.

On the other hand, and instructively in this case, an advantage of this approach over the other fairly dire practices listed is that – at some expenditure of effort (typically 3–5% of total lifecycle software engineering effort, not counting maintenance and new versions) – the systems features are considered, as distinct from just the software detail. All in all, the top-down method (with expert judgement) is not recommended for substantive estimates, nor is it sufficiently accurate for the cost-to-do evaluations needed in combination with price-to-win. Its principal use is for early, quick and cheap (and inaccurate) budgetary estimates at the outset of a product development (*note*: not project/contract).

In bottom-up estimating, the known modularity of the software at the late design stage and the known assignment of software engineering staff working on the system are used as the basis for detailed activities planning (see Sections 5.4 and 6.2). From these activities plans, very accurate estimates can be done by experienced software engineers (about ±10% in some cases). The method is motivational in that software engineers prefer to do their own estimates rather than inherit resource limits of timescale and effort.

The drawback to the bottom-up method is that it is 'slow' (i.e. done well down the lifecycle) and costly (up to 35% of a software engineer's total effort to get to this stage). Consequently, bottom-up estimating should be used to ratify/emend estimates during the implementation, but not for the first substantive estimates for a software development.

5.3.4 Spurious productivity factors

This is, in effect, an oversimplified variant of the FS/OSD method described (and recommended) in Section 5.4. The basis of the approach is to divide a source-code size estimate for the software by an assumed figure for average 'programmer productivity', expressed as delivered source instructions (DSI) per person-day. For example, in the case cited as part of Section 4.5 a source-code size estimate comprising 75 000 statements of RTL-2 and 10 000 instructions of assembler code may have been made.

Also, perhaps some notion of global or average productivity factors exists in the following form, averaged over applications and all lifecycle activities:

- 20–30 statements of high-level language source code per programmer-day; and

- 5–10 instructions of assembler code per programmer-day.

At this stage an obvious (and wrong) approach is to calculate the required effort as something in the order of $(75\,000/25 = 3000)$ + $(10\,000/10 = 1000)$ = 4000 person-days or about 20 person-years. What could be simpler as a costing method? The problem is that it is too simple, that it assumes productivity is a simple factor whereas it is a complex of several factors.

In Section 5.5 the endeavours of several authors to identify the potential amplifiers of effort (or, conversely, the modifiers of productivity) are mentioned. In particular the tabulated factors due to Boehm (1981), Herd *et al.* (1977), and Walston and Felix (1977) are given. At the current stage we need only consider the following simple, but not too simple, thesis: that so-called programmer productivity is likely to be affected by the following issues:

1. Task scope and complexity.

2. Familiarity of the implementation team with the task type.

3. General competence, as software engineers, of the implementation team.

4. Management factors such as team size, pro-active management, motivation, etc.

5. Relative stability of requirements, and good 'user' contacts.

6. Relative stability of the implementation team.

7. Availability of adequate software development tools, methodology, etc.

8. Competent resources estimates, particularly that of allowed timescale.

Clearly, in one case comprising limiting values (however expressed) of even a subset of these eight factors, productivity will tend to zero. (DSI = 0, or DSI of adequate quality = 0).

Of all these factors, the allowed time to do a software job has a particularly far-reaching effect on estimating effort. In the case cited earlier, that of 75 000 statements of RTL-2 and 10 000 lines of assembler, a true software engineer using a method such as that recommended in Section 5.4 may make the following estimate:

20 person-years of effort in 2 elapsed years of time.

Imagine now the impact of a manager or client saying (in effect): 'Yes, agreed that the job will cost 20 person years of effort, but do it in 1 elapsed year of time!' When the software engineer protests that 20 person-years of effort in 2 elapsed years is in no way equivalent to 20 person-years of effort in 1 elapsed year, the manager (or client) may offer a pro-rata deal of 40 person-years of effort in 1 elapsed year to compensate for the timescale compression. Alternatively the manager (or client) may try pointing out that 20 person-years of effort over 2 elapsed years clearly implies a staffing level of 10 over that time, and that 20 people will be made available for the new timescale of 1 elapsed year. So what is the problem?

The problem is that the 'effort' (like the 'productivity' itself) is not a simple entity in software engineering, as it is probably not a simple entity in other engineering subjects, allowing a straight pro-rata tradeoff with allowed timescale. Thus we cannot simply assume that the product of effort and timescale is unity, or even some other constant. There may be some functional relationship of the general form $F(E,T) = $ constant, but the complexity of the function (F) is to be determined, not assumed.

Thus, for instance, even simple rectangular staffing–time histograms of the form 10 people for 2 years ($= 20$-person years) cannot axiomatically be assumed equivalent to 20 people for 1 year. There is no 'law' of conservation of area under a resource–time graph.

The RTL-2 job is not a 20 person-year job; it may be a 20 person-year job in 2 elapsed years, with either a rectangular or non-rectangular staffing–time histogram as may be. Any method that purports to estimate either effort or timescale independently is basically peddling nonsense, and any 'expert' making such an 'estimate' is talking nonsense.

The whole issue of an effort–time relationship in software development is dealt with in Section 5.5 and also as a special topic in Section 5.7.

5.4 The 'OSD/activities plan' method

By the time a software taxonomy exists of the kind described in Section 4.5 some idea can be gained by the software engineers involved in the OSD about the possible scope and complexity of the software-to-be. As cited in the example, the bottom level of the taxonomy will represent features and functions at a level that, were they to be realized, would result in a few hundred source code statements in each case.

At this stage it is possible to employ a simple activities-planning technique to derive simultaneously both effort and timescale to do the software-engineering task. This derivation of both effort and associated timescale from the single process is, in itself, a convincing feature of the estimating method, if only because it avoids treating the two issues as independent entities and thus avoids the 'productivity factors' fallacy.

The technique of activities planning is often known, generically, as 'PERT' or 'CPM', which are acronyms for 'Project Evaluation and Review Technique' and 'Critical Path Method', respectively. The method of 'PERT planning' has been very well known in engineering in general (mechanical and electronic in particular) since late in the 1950s, and the reader requiring a detailed knowledge of the techniques involved may find an excellent exposition in Staffurth (1969).

Basically, the method (CPM as we shall refer to it) concerns the definition and ordering of activities comprising a task. Thus, for the simple task of getting to work in a morning we may define things like: 'cycle to work', 'dress', 'shower', 'eat boiled egg', 'get up', and so forth, and then (we hope) order them in some more rational way than we have defined them. This produces a logically ordered sequence of activities which may or may not be of particular use, depending on whether the availability of resources needs to be taken into account. Where this needs to be done the result is a 'resources constrained', logically ordered sequence of activities. The representation of activities-plans of this sort is usually graphical, using one of a set of simple notations that are widely known and used. The simplest of these represents an activity as shown in Figure 5.2.

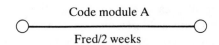

Fig. 5.2   Activity depiction for a single CPM.

This simple convention incorporates three items of information per activity. Further information is incorporated in the scheme of connecting activities. Dependencies are represented by nearly vertical lines between nodes, the inclination indicating the dependency. Furthermore, 'slack' activities (which are really just representations of time elapsing and are incorporated to keep a network schematic from becoming distorted), are represented by null activities using dotted lines between the nodes. Thus Figure 5.2, expressed as a null activity, would be two small circles (nodes) connected by a dotted line, with no activity ascription above the line;

below the line there would be a duration (e.g. '2 weeks') in any event and, if a resource were involved (in doing nothing) that too would be shown (e.g. 'Fred').

Other more elaborate notations exist, such as one incorporating information in the nodes, as shown in Figure 5.3.

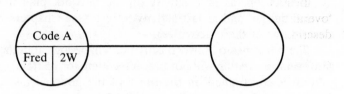

Fig. 5.3 Alternative activity depiction.

In our view, the notation used in activities planning is not very important. We tend to use that represented in Figure 5.2. Furthermore, we advise against the use of computer-based PERT/CPM methods to generate activities-plans in software engineering, as this reduces the personal involvement required of the software engineers.

An example of a network for a software development task is given in Figure 5.5 below, and another one may be found in the case-study in Chapter 11.

The method of notional activities planning for estimating software engineering tasks involves the following steps:

1. Complete the software taxonomy as described elsewhere.

2. Notionally aggregate the items comprising the bottom level of taxonomy into tasks, either for known resources who will be working on the software development, or assumed resources if actual assignments have not been made. An example is shown in Figure 5.4.

   The assignment of code-size estimates to the bottom of the software taxonomy may help in this notional assignment of resources to 'tasks', but this should not descend into the practice of productivity factoring, which is condemned elsewhere.

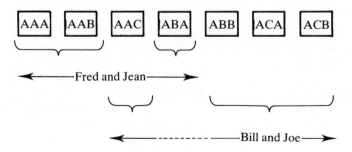

Fig. 5.4 Notional task aggregation.

3. Resources constrained activities planning should now proceed for all items on the bottom level of the software taxonomy. For each item there will be four basic activities to consider, namely the design, coding, module testing and integration testing of software corresponding to that component of the taxonomy.

In addition, as first activity on the network plan there will be 'overall design' and as last activity 'α-test' (see Chapters 7 and 9 for descriptions of these activities).

The relationship between activities will be logical in the first place (for example, testing will not precede coding for an item), and will be 'resources constrained' in the sense of the notional task-assignment done in step 2.

For software systems above the level of 'small scale' as defined in Section 2.3.4, the result of notional activities-planning will most likely be a large but fundamentally simple activities-plan with logical and resources-based dependencies.

It must be understood that this, being based on the informal OSD, is not an activities-plan for the software as it will be designed and coded (hence the term 'notional'). Instead, it is an estimating method providing acceptably accurate estimates of effort and timescale reasonably early in the lifecycle, and doing so plausibly within one process from which the estimates are produced in association with each other.

The matter of finding work content (effort) and timescale from the notional activities-plan is a simple one in both cases. Each activity has a resource assignment of X people and a duration of T. The total work content represented by the network plan is

$$E = \sum_{i=1}^{n} X_i T_i.$$

So far as the timescale is concerned, each path on the network plan has a timescale associated with it, being the sum of all activity times on that path. Paths on which there are no 'slack' activities are known as 'critical paths' on the activities netplan since, being incompressible, any disturbance to the duration of part of such a path disturbs its end point by at least that amount.

In the process of notional activities planning, software engineers discount the main factors likely to affect the software-engineering task. These are listed as items 1–8 in Section 5.3.4 and some idea of the effects of these can be derived from the tables due to Boehm, Herd *et al.* and Walston and Felix given in Section 5.5. Basically, the effect of such factors are dealt with subjectively rather than algorithmically by software engineers, who will be likely to say things like: 'That part will take at least three weeks to design' and 'Better not give that bit to a junior to do, it's far more complex than it seems', and so on. This process is very valuable as it not only enters a high degree of reality into estimating but it also motivates the software engineers, who feel more convinced than otherwise that some of the possible exigencies of software engineering have been accounted for. Weinberg and Schulman (1974) found that software engineers 'pad their estimates'. It is usually with extremely good reason, we must add.

The method of activities-planning as described can (and should) be adopted for even more precise estimating at a later lifecycle stage than that of FS/OSD. Late in the stage of detailed software design, when the definite modular structure is known but before the software modules are designed in detail, a very exact activities plan based on actual activities and staff assignments can be made, and extremely accurate effort and timescale estimates done for the remainder of design, coding and testing. Whereas this bottom-up method is generally far too late for substantive estimates for projects and products (the 'cost' to reach this stage in terms of software engineers' effort over the lifecycle being around 35%), the method should be used for reviewing estimates done at the FS/OSD stage. In both cases of activities-planning based estimates, at the FS/OSD stage and at detailed software design, the outcome will be an estimate effort (in person–weeks, months or years), and its associated 'comfortable' timescale. The effects of altering this comfortable timescale on effort required for a software development are, potentially, severe – as every software engineer knows, even if unable to explain exactly how severe or why. For this reason the matter of effort–timescale relationship, whilst much commented on in the following section, is dealt with separately in Section 5.7.

An example of network plan (CPM) estimating is shown in Figures 5.5 and 5.6. These are derived from the hospital alarm system defined in Section 4.3 (URS) and 4.4 (FS). In fact the terminology is taken from the penultimate line (generic task-descriptors in this case) of the software taxonomy depicted in Figure 4.10. The fact that the penultimate line of this taxonomy is the one used constitutes a 'special case', and is due only to the fact that notional tasks are reasonably well described in this way in this case. In other cases, a less obvious way of aggregating notional tasks may be required, as depicted in Figure 5.4.

In the following example, there has been a codification of notional tasks and their notional attribution to software staff. The network plan is presented in encoded form as a result. The reason for this compression is the problem of depiction within a book such as this; in real life, the network plan would be hand-drawn most likely, and have handwritten task, duration and resource ascriptions on the activity lines.

Task assignment

Task \\ Person	Fred	Evelyn	Sarah
PCCS & ECS i/o			A
Message processor	B		
Screen manager		C	
Outstanding warnings		D	
Other: Clock			
:Terminal I/O			
:Keyboard	E		
:Log			
:I/d reader			

Task encoding

Activity \\ Code	
Detailed S/W design	1
Module design	2
Design review	3
Code	4
Code read	5
Author mod. test	6
Integration test	7 e.g. $(X + Y)$
Test plan	8
α-test	9
Documentation	10

Task duration

Task \\ Activity	1	2	3	4	5	6	7	8	9	10
Total system										
A	20							5	5	10
B		20	5	30	7	10	5			
C		10	2	17	2	5	2			
D		10	2	10	2	3	2			
E		10	2	10	2	3	2			
		10	2	5	1	2	2			

For example: A6 means the testing of programs in this module, by its author Sarah. Duration of tasks in the table below is quoted in normal (7-8 hour) working days of time

Fig. 5.5 Task assignment, encoding and duration tables.

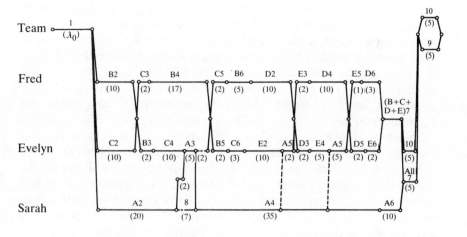

Timescale (minus beta tests): 102 days (20 working weeks + 2 days)
Work content (minus quality): 312 person-days (not including 'slack')
Critical path: Fred

Fig. 5.6   Activities plan example.

5.5   Research into parametric cost models

The object of research in parametric modelling is to find, by empirical means, some plausible relationships between the basic resources of effort and allowed timescale to do a software development, taking into account the prevailing characteristics of the task and the environment in which it is to be done.

Research of this sort has gone on since the early days of Epoch 1 (as defined elsewhere), when programming became an increasingly wide-scale activity. As early as the mid-1950s Benington (1956) indicated some measurement of programmer productivity and its distribution over different tasks, time required for documentation, and computer time needed.

At the present time there exist a dozen or so models, implemented on computers because of the complexity of their calculations and incorporating their authors' empirically derived algorithms. The vast majority of these algorithms derive from statistical investigation and the interpretation of large sample-size data from completed software development jobs. Some of these 'databases' are rather venerable affairs, relating to work from Epochs 2 and (early) 3, and the value of models based on them must be questioned if they exclude or de-emphasize modern factors in software engineering.

Considerable claims have been made over the past decade for some of the models, and the period 1979–84 seems to have been one of particular emphasis. Authors (perhaps not unnaturally) and some users of parametric cost models have, until recently, made considerable claims for the approach in general and some model in particular. In our view readers should take a cautious line in the matter. As Pressman (1982) points out, no one model adequately represents all task types and environmental factors in a totally convincing fashion. This view was endorsed by Boehm as recently as 1984 when, in a paper, he noted that the field of endeavour requires additional research and went on to list major areas in which this is the case. For this reason, we designate the whole of this topic 'research', and our view of it is supported by the fact that no one of the many models developed is conclusively better than others in all circumstances. We will return to this topic in Section 5.5.5, after a synoptic description of the main lines of development to date, so far as these are known (some highly confidential 'research' has gone on in this area in some large organizations, and probably is still going on).

One thing is quite clear, however, and that is that research into parametric cost models – if still falling somewhat short of a definitive technique – has produced many insights into the software engineering process. In no case is this more true than that of the relationship, in software development, between the effort to do a job and the time available for it. So important is this (as every software engineer knows intuitively, and many managers and others discover with discomfort), that we include a special comment on the issue in Section 5.7.

The next four subsections categorize and describe (in the strictest summary form) the various approaches and their best-known examples as developed to date. In a fast-moving area of research a complete list is impossible, and readers should not assume that the omission of a particular model is for any reason other than summary.

5.5.1 Analytical methods

This line of research is based on a plausible mathematical relationship between team-size and the phase of activity in a software development. In theory, such a relationship would cover any and all lifecycle stages, but there is evidence that it is less 'plausible' in the maintenance stage (Weiner-Erlich et al., 1984) and for new versions of existing software.

The foundations of this approach are due to Norden and Bakshi, set out in a paper by the former (1963) in which he describes the derivation of a Rayleigh-type mathematical formula for the statistical properties (i.e. distribution form) of a large sample of completed jobs in systems engineering in general. Essentially, Norden demonstrated the 'Rayleigh' behaviour of the so-called 'manpower utilization curve', during 'cycles' of work on development projects planned and controlled by CPM/PERT techniques at IBM in the late 1950s. This mathematical form is described below.

By plotting the team-size history of systems development projects against elapsed time for a large statistical sample of completed jobs, Norden *et al.* produced a 'noisy' (or 'cluttered'), but quite clearly discernible distribution. In the early 1970s, Putnam applied Norden's conjecture to a very large sample of completed software development tasks and, after considerable refinement of data by classification into application types and sizes, suggested a strong 'Rayleigh'-type behaviour of the manpower–loading curve for software developments. Schematically, Putnam's findings are shown in Figure 5.8, alongside those of Norden *et al.* (Putnam, 1982).

The Rayleigh equation contains terms having the following meaning:

y = manpower utilized in each time period.

k = total cumulative manpower used by the end of the development and maintenance.

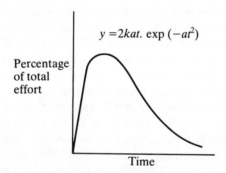

$$y = 2kat. \exp(-at^2)$$

Percentage of total effort

Time

Fig. 5.7 The Rayleigh distribution of teamsize with time.

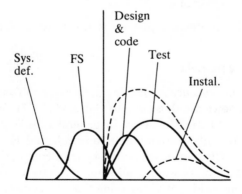

Design & code

Sys. def.

FS

Test

Instal.

Fig. 5.8 Putnam's manpower loading curves.

a = a shape parameter governing the time to peak manpower (t_d) and equals t_d^{-2}.

t = elapsed timescale from the start of the development.

By a series of mathematical operations on the Rayleigh equation, and correlation of the outcome with properties of the software task and environment in which it was done, Putnam (1982) has derived a 'software equation' comprising: $S_s = C_k K^x t_d^y$, where:

S_s = source code size of the software.

C_k = a constant of proportionality correlated with the competence level of the technical environment.

K = effort to make the software.

t_d = time at which the software development team size peaks (to a first approximation, t_d is the development time for the software task, i.e. from specification to β-test).

x = $\frac{1}{3}$; y = $\frac{4}{3}$.

This relationship is the basis for a highly developed model by Putnam and his co-workers (the 'SLIM' system as it is called), incorporating mathematical (linear) programming techniques for determining optimal values of objective functions in the light of known constraints. The model has become well known over the past five years or so, and its principal author has, creditably, made great efforts to explain it in detail. It is the basis of at least one derivative model (see Section 5.5.4).

Perhaps above all, this work (and Putnam in particular) has raised the fundamentally important question in software engineering: 'What is the relationship between effort required and allowed time in which to do a software development?' Putnam's 'software equation' easily reduces to the form (for a given software development and environment): ET^z = constant, where $z = y/x$ and, hence,

effort $\times$ time^4 = constant.

So important is this conjecture that we return to it in Section 5.7.

5.5.2 Complexity models

Of several models in existence purporting to measure software complexity, perhaps the best known are those due to Halstead (1977), McCabe (1976) and Thayer et al. (1978). The work in general is still at the stage of interesting, but not fully substantiated, research and is the subject of further comment in Chapter 9, where the issue of complexity is seen as a major problem affecting software quality and its metrics. DeMarco (1982) points out that some evidence is emerging that the complexity models of Halstead and McCabe may be correlated with the effort to make a software system (naturally there should be some correlation between an adequate metric for measuring complexity and the effort to make systems of different complexity levels on that metric).

Halstead (1977) offers a metric called variously a 'program volume' or 'information volume' V defined by

$$V = (N_1 + N_2) \log_2 (n_1 + n_2)$$

where:

n_1 = number of unique operators in the program

n_2 = number of unique operands in the program

N_1 = total number of operator occurrences in the program

N_2 = total number of operand occurrences in the program.

Boehm (1981) gives the formulation of Halstead's hypothesis and cites an extension to this:

Effort = $(n_1 N_2 V)/36 n_2$

In McCabe's approach (1976) a 'cyclomatic complexity metric' $V(G)$ is defined as 'the number of regions in a planar graph' (Pressman, 1982). DeMarco (1982) further defines this as being 'the number of connections minus the number of nodes, plus two', and Boehm (1981) offers the generalized version of this as: $V(G) = e - n + 2p$, where e and n are the first two terms in the DeMarco formulation, and p is the number of connected components (i.e. programs or program modules).

Pressman's definition of the McCabe complexity metric is illustrated in Figure 5.9 by a schematic.

Apart from the obvious differences in approach and resulting form, two other somewhat less obvious differences between the Halstead and McCabe complexity models should be borne in mind. The usefulness of

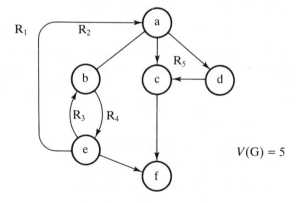

Fig. 5.9 McCabe's cyclomatic complexity model.

these, or any other models, is a function of how late (in lifecycle terms) their inputs are available at a reliable level of measurement or estimate. Thus, in the Putnam 'software equation' one might reasonably ask when a reliable software size estimate can be made, because any attempt to use the model previous to that point would inevitably lead to unreliability in the estimates derived.

With this in mind it is clear that Halstead's model concerns detailed knowledge of (or estimates about) the software at the level of coding. 'Operators' and 'operands' are features of written code. Although Halstead's formulation may be entirely plausible as a complexity metric (and some doubts have been raised on this point), and therefore correlated with development effort in software engineering as established after the event, it is difficult to escape the conclusion that it can have little or no real use as a predictive estimating method.

On the other hand, McCabe's approach seems more suited to application at the design level. Many graphical design notations (as described in Chapter 7) result in a form that could, perhaps, be used as a basis for a graph of the type depicted in Figure 5.9. This holds out some level of possible application if, as claimed, McCabe factors are correlated with software development effort. It should be noted, though, that the lifecycle point at which this may be the case (design) is a very expensive one to reach (about 35% of total effort), and other methods, if adequate, will have been used long before, e.g. the OSD/FS method described in Section 5.4.

5.5.3 Factor analysis models

As with Putnam's so-called 'analytic' model, which had its basis in work done in the late 1950s, an early attempt to define a parametric model for software development effort was due to SDC, around 1960–65. In this, a basic linear equation was formulated of the type:

Effort $= a_0 + a_1x_1 + a_2x_2 + \ldots + a_nx_n$

in which the x-values are properties of the task or environment, and the a-values represent 'weights' derived for each x-value by some form of factor analysis. Thus, the SDC model was formulated according to Boehm (1984) as:

$-$ 33.63   person months

$+$ 9.15 $\times$ lack of requirements (expressed in the range 0–2)

$+$ 10.73 $\times$ stability of design (in the range 0–3)

$+$ 0.51 $\times$ percentage of mathematics instructions

$+$ 0.46 $\times$ percentage of storage and retrieval instructions

$+$ 0.40 $\times$ number of sub-programs

$+$ 7.28 × programming language (expressed in the range 0–1)

$-$ 21.45 × business application (expressed in the range 0–1)

$+$ 13.53 × stand alone programs (expressed in the range 0–1)

$+$ 12.35 × first program on computer (expressed in the range 0–1)

$+$ 58.82 × concurrent hardware development (in the range 0–1)

$+$ 30.61 × random access device used (in the range 0–1)

$+$ 29.55 × different host–target hardware (in the range 0–1)

$-$ 0.54 × number of personnel trips

$-$ 25.20 × developed by military (in the range 0–1)

Apart from some obvious problems of credibility, such as negative effort required for a certain kind of job for which all the factors rate zero or nearly zero, the SDC model provided effort values whose standard deviation from actual values was unacceptably high. However, the method was held to be sufficiently interesting to be taken as a basis for developing other 'linear' models and one such is of particular value for the insight it provided into the significance of parameters. Walston and Felix (1977) proposed a 'Productivity Index' (I):

$$I = \sum W_i X_i$$

where: $X_i = -1$, 0, or $+1$ depending on whether the task rates 'low', 'medium' or 'high' with respect to a certain attribute in a list of such Productivity Variance values (PV_i) and:

$$W = 0.5 \log_{10}(PV_i).$$

The model itself is apparently not widely available, and its further details are not entirely clear. However, the table of PV values has been published and is a valuable insight – particularly for those who are not software engineers – into the factors potentially affecting software development. The table is given (after Pressman, 1982) in Table 5.3. Further comment on these factors is deferred until another sort of model (the 'multiplicative' type) has been described.

With due respect to their adherents, linear models have not proved very convincing over the years, and another general form of parametric relationship was increasingly tried as the object of factor analysis and correlation with real life. The form of these 'multiplicative' models is:

$$\text{Effort} = (a_0)(a_1 x_1)(a_2 x_2) \ldots (a_n x_n)$$

with the same meanings attaching to x-values and their corresponding a factors as previously. Two such models in particular justify definition and comment, those of Herd et al. at the Doty Corporation, and Boehm at TRW. Both can be found extensively described in their authors' own texts, Herd et al. (1977) and Boehm (1981). In essence, models of this sort can be described by the general formula:

Table 5.3   Walston & Felix's productivity variance factors.

Question or variable	Response group mean productivity (DSL/MM)*			Productivity change (DSL/MM)*
Customer interface complexity	<Normal	Normal	>Normal	
	500	295	124	376
User participation in the definition of	None	Some	Much	
requirements	491	267	205	286
Customer originated program design	Few		Many	
changes	297		196	101
Customer experience with the	None	Some	Much	
application area of the project	318	340	206	112
Overall personnel experience and	Low	Average	High	
qualifications	132	257	410	278
Percentage of programmers doing	<25%	25–50%	>50%	
development who participated in	153	242	391	238
design of functional specifications				
Previous experience with operational	Minimal	Average	Extensive	
computer	146	270	312	166
Previous experience with	Minimal	Average	Extensive	
programming languages	122	225	385	263
Previous experience with application	Minimal	Average	Extensive	
of similar or greater size and	146	221	410	264
complexity				
Ratio of average staff size to duration	<0.5	0.5–0.9	>0.9	
(people/month)	305	310	173	132
Hardware under concurrent	No		Yes	
development	297		177	120
Development computer access, open	0%	1–25%	>25%	
under special request	226	274	357	131
Development computer access, closed	0–10%	11–85%	>85%	
	303	251	170	133
Classified security environment for	No		Yes	
computer and 25% of programs and	289		156	133
data				
Structured programming	0–33%	34–66%	>66%	
	169	–	301	132
Design and code inspections	0–33%	34–66%	>66%	
	220	300	339	119
Top-down development	0–33%	34–66%	>66%	
	196	237	321	125
Chief programmer team usage	0–33%	34–66%	>66%	
	219	–	408	189
Overall complexity of code developed	<Average		>Average	
	314		185	129
Complexity of application processing	<Average	Average	>Average	
	349	345	168	181
Complexity of program flow	<Average	Average	>Average	
	289	299	209	80
Overall constraints on program design	Minimal	Average	Severe	
	293	286	166	107

Table 5.3 *continued*

Question or variable	Response group mean productivity (DSL/MM)*			Productivity change (DSL/MM)*
Program design constraints on main	Minimal	Average	Severe	
storage	391	277	193	198
Program design constraints on timing	Minimal	Average	Severe	
	303	317	171	132
Code for real-time or interactive	<10%	10–40%	>40%	
operation, or executing under severe	279	337	203	76
timing constraint				
Percentage of code for delivery	0–90%	91–99%	100%	
	159	327	265	106
Code classified as nonmathematical	0–33%	33-66%	67–100%	
application and I/O formatting	188	311	267	79
programs				
Number of classes of items in the data	0–15	16–80	>80	
base per 1000 lines of code	334	243	193	141
Number of pages of delivered	0–32	33–88	>88	
documentation per 1000 lines of	320	252	195	125
delivered code				

*DSL/MM = delivered source lines/man-month

$$E = S^a M_i,$$

where E is effort, S is software size and each M_i is, generally, one of a set of product-form factors. In the so-called Doty model, two basic formulae are given:

$$E = 5.288S^a \quad \text{and} \quad E = 2.02S^a \, \Pi \, (f)_j,$$

where in both cases $a = 1.047$. The first of these is used for software systems of over 10K source-code size, i.e. medium, large and super-large in our terms, and the second is applicable for 'small' software systems of less than 10K source-code. The product-form factors in the second formulation are well known in the area of parametric cost modelling as the 'Doty factors'. There are fifteen of these 'effort amplifiers' or, seen conversely, productivity modifiers, and they are depicted in full – for four different application types and the general case – in Table 5.4.

The purpose of showing Table 5.4, as with that of Walston and Felix, is to give the reader an idea of the parameter-types used in models of this sort, and the significance and sensitivity of the factors. It is dangerous though to try to read too much into them, as it is by no means clear how they are determined in isolation, or whether combinations of some have a

Table 5.4 The 'Doty factors' for productivity attenuation.

Factor	Application type									
	All		Common & Control		Scientific		Business		Utility	
$E = cS^a \prod_{j=1}^{n} (f)_j$	a = 1.047		1.263		1.019		0.781		0.811	
	c = 2.060		2.501		2.011		3.742		1.744	
	Yes	*No*	*Yes*	*No*	*Yes*	*No*	*Yes*	*No*	*Yes*	*No*
(t$_1$) Special Display	1.11	1.00	1.11	1.00	1.11	1.00	*1.43*	1.00	1.00	1.00
(t$_2$) Detailed URS	1.00	1.11	1.00	*1.54*	1.00	*2.00*	1.00	1.00	1.00	1.00
(t$_3$) Volatile URS	1.05	1.00	1.05	1.00	1.05	1.00	1.05	1.00	1.05	1.00
(t$_4$) Real Time	1.33	1.00	1.33	1.00	*1.67*	1.00	1.00	1.00	*1.43*	1.00
(t$_5$) CPU constraint	1.43	1.00	*1.25*	1.00	*1.25*	1.00	*1.00*	1.00	*1.18*	1.00
(t$_6$) Time constraint	1.33	1.00	*1.51*	1.00	*1.67*	1.00	*1.00*	1.00	2.32	1.00
(t$_7$) New H/W	1.92	1.00	1.92	1.00	1.92	1.00	1.92	1.00	1.92	1.00
(t$_8$) Parallel H/W development	1.82	1.00	*1.67*	1.00	2.22	1.00	1.33	1.00	*1.25*	1.00
(t$_9$) Remote dev.	1.43	1.00	1.43	1.00	1.43	1.00	1.43	1.00	1.43	1.00
(t$_{10}$) Site dev.	1.39	1.00	1.39	1.00	1.39	1.00	1.39	1.00	1.39	1.00
(t$_{11}$) Host dev.	1.25	1.00	2.22	1.00	*1.11*	1.00	*1.00*	1.00	*1.43*	1.00
(t$_{12}$) Multi site dev.	1.25	1.00	1.25	1.00	*1.75*	1.00	1.25	1.00	1.21	1.00
(t$_{13}$) New lang.	1.80	1.00	1.80	1.00	1.80	1.00	1.80	1.00	1.80	1.00
(t$_{14}$) Interactive dev.	0.83	1.00	0.83	1.00	0.83	1.00	0.83	1.00	0.83	1.00
(t$_{15}$) S/W eng. access	0.90	1.00	1.00	1.00	0.67	1.00	0.90	1.00	0.67	1.00

markedly more virulent effect than might appear for example through mutual reinforcement.

Boehm's model, 'COCOMO', is extensively described in his own source-work (1981). We offer only the most cursory description compared with that exegesis. In his formulation there are two basic relationships:

$$E = C_1 S^a \quad \text{and} \quad T = C_2 E^b$$

where E, S and T are – respectively – effort, software (source-code size), and time required. The factor C_1 is a composite comprising a scaling factor for system type, and an effort multiplier computed as a product-form from up to fifteen 'cost drivers' (analogues in type to the productivity variance factors of Walton and Felix, and the Doty effort amplifiers). The COCOMO scaling factors, along with values for the exponents a and b, are shown for one of the forms in which the model may be used, in Table 5.5. The factor $c_2 = 2.5$.

The terms 'Organic', 'Semidetached' and 'Embedded' – as applying to software systems – are defined, but their meaning is nonetheless somewhat imprecise and the use of the terms must be strongly subjective in some cases. The values of a and b will, like the exponent in Putnam's effort–time relationship, take on some significance when the question of

Table 5.5   Values in the COCOMO model.

	Scaling factor in C_1	$a=$	$b=$
"Organic" systems	2.4	1.05	0.38
"Semidetached" systems	3.0	1.12	0.35
"Embedded" systems	3.6	1.20	0.32

Table 5.6   'Cost drivers' in the COCOMO model.

	Very low	Low	Nominal	High	Very high	Extra high
Required software reliability	0.75	0.88	1.00	1.15	1.40	
Database size		0.94	1.00	1.08	1.18	
Product complexity	0.70	0.85	1.00	1.15	1.30	1.85
Execution time constraints			1.00	1.11	1.30	1.66
Main storage constraints			1.00	1.06	1.21	1.56
Virtual machine volatility		0.87	1.00	1.15	1.30	
Computer turnaround time		0.87	1.00	1.07	1.15	
Analyst capability	1.46	1.19	1.00	0.86	0.71	
Application experience	1.29	1.13	1.00	0.91	0.82	
Programmer capability	1.42	1.17	1.00	0.86	0.70	
Virtual machine experience	1.21	1.10	1.00	0.90		
Prog. Lang. experience	1.14	1.07	1.00	0.95		
Use of modern prog. practice	1.24	1.10	1.00	0.91	0.82	
Use of software tools	1.24	1.10	1.00	0.91	0.83	
Required development schedule	1.23	1.08	1.00	1.04	1.10	

how these issues are related in software engineering is raised in Section 5.7. The 'cost drivers' in the COCOMO model are shown in Table 5.6, once more for purposes of comparison in the matter of identified parameters by which productivity may be modified, and their relative significance and sensitivity within a model.

There are two essential questions arising from work with models of this sort. Firstly, what are the most potentially significant factors affecting effort and timescale required to do a software development and just how significant may they be? Secondly (reinforced, if not initiated, by the rather extreme derivation from Putnam's model), what is the relationship between effort and allowed time for a software development job? The second of these is treated at some length in Section 5.7 as already mentioned. As to the first question, a cursory inspection of Tables 5.3, 5.4 and 5.6 show some interesting features. Although, for the reason we have already given concerning factor analysis, too much significance should not be placed on the values attaching to parameters outside the context of their application, it is possible to rank factors from the different tables according to their apparent significance. In Table 5.7 we list the most significant four (apparently) from each source.

There is much to agree with in all three lists, and a little – it must be said – with which to disagree (e.g. the 'host development' for a command and control application entry is possibly a bit dated now in the light of modern PSE development). Without placing too much emphasis on the outcome from such a rough and ready method, and taking as read the fairly self-evident need to have competent software and management staff, the lists show several interesting insights. In particular:

1. The 'customer interface complexity' factor from the Walston and Felix list. This is a comment on the vitally important issues of specification and feasibility as described in the previous chapter, and the desirability of URS prototyping.

2. The 'time constraint' factor which can be added to the growing number of references to the effort–time relationship (Boehm treats the issue within the model by $T = C_2E^b$; it is interesting that there is no clear reference to the effect on PV of constrained timescales for a software development in the Walston and Felix list).

3. Boehm's factors highlight the impact of optimization considerations,

Table 5.7   Significant factors from different models.

Walston and Felix	Doty factors (any application)	Boehm's COCOMO model
Consumer interface complexity	Time constraint for a software utility development	Extra high product complexity
Overall personal experience and qualifications	Parallel hardware development for a scientific application	Extra high execution time constraint
Extensive previous application-type experience	Host development for a 'command and control' application	Extra high main storage constraint
Experience of programming language	New hardware for any type of development	Extra low 'analyst' capability

run-time 'efficiency' and object code-size constraint. The effects of these have already been observed by Weinberg and Schulman (1974).

For the rest, the 'insights' from this class of model tend to confirm the list of main potential modifiers of productivity, given in Section 5.3.4. Having said that, we caution once more against reading too much into factors used in parametric modelling, although management staff particularly are bound to find the Walston and Felix research of great interest so far as it goes.

Of far greater importance than their supposed quantitative effects, the lists do depict a set of truisms not always completely evident to practitioners, managers and others – i.e. that task properties and environmental characteristics do have an effect (a most marked effect in some circumstances) on productivity. It should also be clear that the concept of productivity itself must be more than just 'delivered source code statements' and must, to have any real significance, subsume the quality of 'delivered' code.

5.5.4 Other models

Boehm (1985) and Reiffer (1982) identify between them thirteen distinct systems for parametric cost estimating. These are: SDC (1965), TRW (1972), Putnam (1977), Doty Corp. (1977), RCA (1979), IBM (1977), Boeing (1977), GRC (1979), TWR (1980), Telecote, Sofcost, DSN and Hughes Aircraft (*circa* 1982).

We have already given brief descriptions of some of this work such as that at SDC; Putnam's SLIM; the Doty model of Herd *et al.*; the IBM research of Walston and Felix; and Boehm's COCOMO model at TRW.

Some models and their underlying research are extensively described by their authors, particularly conspicuous in this respect being Boehm (1981), Jensen (1984) at Hughes Aircraft, and Putnam (1982). Other research is less readily available, being the proprietary development of the company (or author) concerned. Noticeable in this category are the IBM and RCA (PRICE) models.

Of those on the list of which something more can be revealed, that of Jensen at Hughes Aircraft is a recent and somewhat novel development. Basically it is a hybrid of Putnam's model (with some adjustments) and the Doty factors (revised also). Jensen (1984) formulates his basic software equation as in Table 5.8, the Putnam formulation being shown for comparison.

One model not yet referred to here differs from others in its scope. As Pressman (1982) points out, the microscopic work-characteristics model of Esterling purports to provide a means of estimating the proportion of useful working time over a person's working day. The factors defined include such things as 'average duration of interruptions to

Table 5.8   Jensen's and Putnam's software equations.

Jensen	*Putnam*
$S_s = C_t.K^z t^y_d$	$S_s = C_k.K^x t^y_d$
where: $X = \frac{1}{2}$; $y = 1$	where: $x = \frac{1}{3}$; $y = \frac{4}{3}$
$\quad\quad C_t = C_{bt}$	$\quad\quad C_k$ is a 'technology factor' correlated with application types and environment characteristics. A set of C_k ranges is provided
$\displaystyle\prod_{j=1}^{15} (f)^*j$	
The $(f)^*j$ are revised Doty factors	

work', and 'average time to recover from interruptions to work'. We have not found the methods of work study, as required for this type of data, particularly appropriate to highly creative endeavours such as software engineering.

5.5.5 Footnote on the status of parametric modelling

We have designated the whole area of this work as 'research' in spite of the claims by some authors (and some users) of developed models, and their commercial exploitation by their authors. In one sense this under-represents the case for parametric models. Several large organizations and major developers of software systems have produced or adopted models, and are using them in some way or another.

On the other hand, the research nature of the whole field of endeavour is manifest and has been set out as such quite recently by a major author in the area (Boehm, 1984). There are clearly some major questions lacking answers at this time. These include the following principal matters for concern:

1. No one model has, as yet, proved conclusively to be the most consistently accurate predictor of effort and timescale requirements for software development. To quote a not uncommon view; one user of two of the models described in outline above recently remarked that one of them was the best of a bad bunch, and 'if I can get within 50% to 100% of cost I'm doing well'.

2. An obvious area for major research effort is that of significance and categorization in the databases of completed software tasks. Not all organizations producing models have the same job mix, objectives (products, projects, research), environments (equipment, staff competence, 'culture') and so on. It is hardly surprising that disparate approaches have occurred; an interesting comparison of input-data

requirements for five of the models is given in Table 5.9, after Boehm (1984).

3. The manner of treating effort–timescale relationships very clearly differs from model to model. This is discussed separately (Section 5.7), but Figure 5.10 in that section gives a clear indication of the nature of this problem.

4. As will be seen from Table 5.9, the input data required by models are such as cannot realistically be available before the FS/OSD lifecycle stage anyway. Few authors make this clear. It means that the lifecycle cost of using a model is not less than that of the CPM method recommended in Section 5.4.

We would endorse the view that major software development organizations should monitor this research work most closely. Perhaps the best way of doing this is to adopt two commercially available models on an experimental basis. At the present time (no offence intended to others) the best choices would seem to be Boehm's COCOMO and the Jensen model from Hughes Aircraft. Firms already trying one other model (e.g. RCA's PRICE-S or Putnam's SLIM) could choose either the Boehm or Jensen for comparison. It is impossible in a book of this sort to detail any model completely; the reader will have got some general idea from the foregoing about the approach taken in some of this work. One major problem is that so much of the work is 'black box'. For example (and it is only one example of several), the detailed workings of RCA's PRICE-S system are not generally available for scrutiny – although the model may be used under lease. This black-box approach is, generally, an unsatisfactory state of affairs and may lead to little more in the matter of benefits derived than an enhanced awareness, in management and commercial staff, of the factors potentially affecting software estimates. Compiling databases of completed software jobs, and experimenting with the sensitivity aspect of models, may achieve that much. Some practising software engineers, on the other hand, seem disinclined to use parametric cost models, and this reluctance is not helped if the issue they are dealing with is presented as a 'phenomenological' black box, and needs extensive calibration into the bargain. In this context, 'phenomenological' means 'non-causal' and, although a perfectly correct description of the empirical methods of modellers, does not induce confidence in software engineers who usually know all too well the causes (and their effects) of poor estimating. The calibration of a model for a particular environment can also be a lengthy affair – we have known it, for one model, take 1–2 years to do.

For those inclined to experiment with this approach – as we in fact recommended for large software development organizations who are likely to be able to make a database of completed software project histories – Table 5.9 sets out (after Boehm, 1984) the input requirements for five of the models described in summary.

Table 5.9 Some required inputs to parametric models.

Group Attributes	Factor	Putnam/SLIM	Doty	RCA/PRICE-S	COCOMO	Jensen
1. Size	Source instructions	x	x		x	x
	Object instructions					
	No. of routines			x		
	No. of data items			x		
	No. of o/p formats					
	Documentation		x			x
	No. of personnel	x				x
2. Program	Type	x	x	x		
	Complexity	x		x	x	
	Language	x				
	Re-use	x		x	x	x
	Reg. Reliability	x		x	x	x
	Display req.		x			x
3. Computer	Time constraint	x	x	x	x	x
	Space constraint	x	x	x	x	x
	H/W configuration			x		
	// H/W Dev.		x	x	x	x

Category	Factor					
4. Personnel	Capability	X		X	X	X
	Continuity	X		X	X	X
	H/W experience	X		X	X	X
	Appr. experience	X		X	X	X
	Lang. experience	X		X	X	X
5. Project	Tools & techniques	X		X	X	X
	Customer i/f		X			
	Req. definition			X		
	Req. volatility	X		X	X	
	Schedule	X				X
	Security		X			
	Computer access	X		X	X	X
	Travel/Multisite	X	X			X
	Support S/W qual			X		
6. Calibration	yes/no	X		X		X

5.6   Lifecycle phasing and person dependency

The FS/OSD stage is the earliest at which acceptably accurate estimates can be made for effort and timescale requirements in software engineering, whether a CPM technique or a parametric model is used. In cases requiring estimates to be done earlier than that, there is no alternative but to do the best possible (such as 'top-down' with 'expert judgement' based on the URS) and – as with 'price to win' – qualify the estimates accordingly. Typically, this is done by designating them 'budgetary estimates only' as distinct from substantive and possibly binding estimates. The budgetary estimates should then be reviewed (and most probably changed) at the FS/OSD stage by the method described in Section 5.4. This is also the time and method for determining the 'cost to do' for a software task bid (and won) on a 'price-to-win' basis.

Finally, the FS/OSD-based estimates should themselves be reviewed at the late stages of software design (e.g. a CPM-based 'bottom-up' derivation when the details of software design, such as modularity, are known).

In some places there is a practice of factoring an early 'estimate' by, say, 1.5 or 2 and so on, to compensate for expected inaccuracy. Thus, for example, an effort estimate of 20 person-years, derived by an analogy of some sort based on 'top down', might be bid to a client (or manager) as 30 person years, or 40, and so forth depending on the degree of pessimism prevailing about the estimate's likely inaccuracy.

There are two things to be said about this practice. Firstly, it is reasonably harmless (perhaps in some cases even helpful) in budgetary estimating. Secondly, it is no substitute for proper estimating and unfortunately, where we have found it practised, this rule-of-thumb contingency factoring has tended to be seen as some clever form of real estimating. It is not; it is the product of two extremely uncertain numbers – no more and no less.

Sometimes confused with this issue of inaccuracy in estimating at early lifecycle stages is the question of the person dependency of estimates, however they are done. Some authors recommend using several sources for estimates and then using statistical averaging techniques. The example usually given, however, concerns software size estimates and can be summarized as in Table 5.10.

This technique, known as the Delphi method of multi-source estimating, is perfectly valid for the sort of cross check on hardware taxonomies done at the OSD stage (see Section 4.5). Also it undoubtedly has value for input to parametric models where these are used (see Table 5.9). Unfortunately its use for effort and timescale estimating cannot be inferred from its use for source-code size estimating. Firstly, the elements in a table such as that above would be dyads, not single entities, estimates

Table 5.10   The 'Delphi' technique for codesize estimating.

| Source | Source code estimate in Kilostatements | | |
	Best	Expected	Worst
A	12.5	16	21.5
B	15.0	17.5	24.0
C	8.0	13	18.5
Selected Values	X = Min	Y = Av	Z = Max
	= 8.0	= 15.5	= 24.0

Expected source code size $= \dfrac{X+4Y+Z}{6} = \dfrac{94.0}{6} = 15.7$ kilostatements

of effort and associated timescale. To use a 'delphic' method in these circumstances is effectively meaningless. Secondly, the concepts of 'best', 'worst', and 'expected' estimates do not really apply in activities-planning methods.

Confronted with an estimate one wishes to check, it is perfectly reasonable to have another source produce estimates from the same premises, e.g. the OSD. The results may be something like the following:

'20 person-years in 2 elapsed years'
'32 person-years in 1.25 elapsed years'.

In such cases it makes little sense to average or admix the estimates (the salesperson would instantly adopt '20 person years in 1.25 elapsed years'!). The recommended course of action is to have the two sources try to reconcile their estimates. In the event that they cannot, then a value judgement between the two has to be made, either by the managers on the basis of previous track record of the sources as estimators, or by a competent third party asked not for a third estimate but to choose between the two on offer. (A third offering is of little use unless it happens to lie within the other two, e.g. '25 person-years in 1.5 elapsed years'). On most occasions we have encountered, similarly competent sources can and do reconcile estimates, and a plausible compromise emerges.

5.7   The effort–timescale relationship

Software engineers know, often in a way they cannot adequately express, that effort and timescale are inextricably linked, and not in any immediately simple or obvious fashion. Managers and clients observe this when trying to fix an effort estimate and at the same time compress the timescale with which it is associated.

Authors have tried to articulate the fact and formulate laws to account for it from Brooks' (1975) famous aphorism:

Putting more people on a late job makes it later.

to Putnam's (1982):

Work and time are not free goods.

Some insight into the question (if not the answer) comes from the research field of parametric cost modelling described in Section 5.5.

Models such as those of Putnam and Jensen give an effort–time relationship directly. $S_s = CK^x T^y$ produces an effort–time relationship of the form:

$$ET^z = \text{constant}, \qquad \text{where } z = y/x.$$

In Putnam's formulation, this relationship is quoted by its author as: $ET^4 = \text{constant}$. (By the same token, Jensen's formulation produces $ET^2 = \text{constant}$, although that author also lists a relationship of the form $T = c_2 E^b$ with $b = 0.33$ as well as his Putnam form relationship quoted earlier).

Models of the general form $E = c_1 S^a$ and $T = c_2 E^b$ should, by simple algebra, produce an effort–timescale relationship of the form:

$$ET^z = \text{constant} \qquad \text{where } z = 1/(1 - b).$$

In these cases, typical values of b (in the range 0.3 to 0.4) seem to imply $ET^z = \text{constant}$, with z in the range 1.4 to 1.7.

What, then, is this effort–time relationship? Is it, as in Putnam's formulation, an exceedingly severe fourth power relationship? If so, then the effects of timescale compression and expansion will indeed be severe. A job estimated to require 20 person-years in 2 elapsed years would require 320 person-years of effort in 1 elapsed year or, alternatively, about 4 person-years of effort in 3 elapsed years. Alternatively, is the relationship less severe, such as $ET^2 = \text{constant}$, or something of the form $T = C_2 E^b$ (where b is approximately 0.3)?

The question is highlighted, within the field of research into parametric modelling, by Boehm (1981), who indicates the somewhat paradoxical nature of the various approaches in a schematic of the type shown in Figure 5.10. In this, the proportional changes in a nominally computed value of effort $E(\text{NOM})$ for changes in its associated nominal timescale $T(\text{NOM})$ are plotted in relative effort $E/E(\text{NOM})$ against $T/T(\text{NOM})$.

Although research into parametric cost modelling has highlighted the question of an effort–timescale relationship it has not, in our view, done much to answer it. Of the very few clear and unequivocal statements on the subject, the ones of Putnam (1982) at least have the virtue of addressing the issue which, in software engineering, causes so much

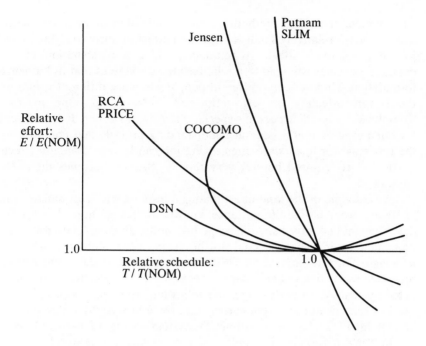

Fig. 5.10   Effort/Timescale relationship in some models.

uncertainty and exasperation – what really happens when one compresses a timescale (as in underbidding a job?).

In our view, an effort–time relationship of the form: ET^z = constant with z greater than 1.0 is a plausible way of representing the sensitivity of effort estimates to changes in the timescale with which they related, with the reservations that:

1. No one value of z is likely to account for all application types and software development environments.
2. Any effort–timescale relationship will only be plausible within limits of possible change to timescale.
3. The effects of timescale compression are likely to be far more severe than their concomitants for timescale relaxation.

In our judgement values of z between 2.0 and 4.0 can be used in the relationship ET^z = constant, with the reservation that this refers to compression of the 'comfortable' timescale up to about -25% of that value only; in most cases compression beyond this amount will make the task infeasible anyway. The severity of this timescale compression effect will depend on the complexity of task (including its adequacy of specification), and the adequacy of resources (software engineers, development tools and methods). One combination of extreme factors will produce a relatively small compression effect (a fairly straightforward job in a relatively ideal environment), whilst a combination of the opposite extremes will lead to a relationship as severe as that in Putnam's formulation. Undoubtedly, different people will place different values on the factors affecting the effort–timescale relationship. One person's 'complexity' is another person's special pleading, no doubt. It is sufficient for our purposes that a general understanding prevails that compressing the timescale for a software engineering job can lead to dramatic effects on the effort required before, very rapidly, the job becomes infeasible anyway.

An example of the kind of estimating questions arising in practice can be taken from a real-life instance known to this author. A software development task of substantial scope but moderate complexity was to be implemented in what seemed to be a perfectly suitable high-level language. On the basis of an OSD (CPM) approach, the 'comfortable' timescale was estimated at 5 elapsed years, with an associated effort of 42 person-years. At an early stage, the following 'accidents' occurred:

1. For reasons not apparent earlier, the whole task could not be done in the high level language without the system ending up 'non-compliant' in a major respect. The only way around this was to develop about one third of the code (as originally envisaged) in assembler code.
2. A reduction in timescale from 5 to 4 years had to be adopted, for some 'force majeure' reasons.

This type of situation makes a good examination question. Given that the commitments outlined were entered into by management (an instance of 'price-to-continue', although Fred was febrile with rage), what was the real cost likely to be? Someone had performed an entirely spurious calculation along the following lines: 'Double the effort for one third of the job for assembler productivity, and that gives a total work content of $2 \times 14 + 28 = 56$ person years, then add a pro-rata 20% for timescale reduction; result = 67 person years. It's a deal!' What should have happened – a new OSD/CPM estimate – would have shown something like a 'comfortable' timescale of 6 years with an associated work content of 61 person years. Then, the timescale compression from 6 to 4 years would have been evaluated from $ET^4 =$ Constant (nb. before the 'accidents' this might well have been $ET^2 =$ Constant, or some such); thus the new effort would have been given by $E = (61 \times 61^4)/4^4$; i.e. about 309 person years. In the real-life example, the company only recognised the 'black hole' facing it during the third year of the development. The result was in gigantic example of 'Brook's Law', with resources being drawn into the task from other projects and, significantly, from many outside sources. After a total of six years and several hundred person-years of effort, the development was terminated, with contractual consequences on top of everything else.

In terms of the activities-planning method of estimating software engineering tasks, the effects of timescale compression are obvious; the assumptions on which the activities plan is based are disturbed, and the whole plan rapidly becomes invalid as a result. The uses of mathematical-programming techniques, specifically integer linear programming for scheduling problems involving CPM planning, is well known in the transportation business (airlines, railways, commodities such as oil, etc.). Investigation of planning software-development activities on this basis is a suitable area for research, if only to set plausible values on z for different types of software task and environment.

5.8 Estimating prototype development

The two cases to consider are those of URS/FS prototyping (i.e. to elicit requirement details), and OSD prototypes (to investigate technical feasibility issues).

Many examples of URS prototyping are 'quick and dirty' programs to give a user something on which to base a preference. Nevertheless, 'quick' might well be weeks or months in some cases and may involve substantial effort. Before such an exercise is undertaken, the prototype software should be defined in terms of what it will do, and a software taxonomy developed. Method 5.4 (CPM at the OSD stage) may then be applied however rudimentary the taxonomy may be.

Prototyping at the FS stage, particularly using a rapid prototyping language for developing an FS simulator, should be based on a proper FS for the prototype (simulator) which is in turn based on the FS of the system required, so far as this is developed. An OSD software taxonomy for the 'prototype' (simulator) can then be made, and estimates duly derived. Extensions to the FS of the system required, as a result of the use of the prototype, should cause an extension of the FS for the prototype (plus additional taxonomies for the prototype and estimates for its extension). At some stage, the prototype will have served its purpose and the FS of the required system will be complete, coherent and representative. At this stage the question may arise: can the prototype be cast into a software system that meets the requirements in all respects of functionality, the known operating constraints (such as object-code size and run-time efficiency), and it is easily modified (for the E-type system property)? In some cases the answer may be affirmative whilst in many others it will not be. In these latter cases, the full FS of the required system must be put under lifecycle management, and OSD taxonomies done, estimates derived, software designed properly and so on.

As to the criteria for deciding whether to generate object code from a prototype, in cases where this is possible (a suitable fast prototyping language, a developed PSE), the matter is highly complex and concerns the possible price to be paid for omitting a software design stage. We do not recommend this as a general principle, since under-design of software leads ineluctably to problems of quality (see Chapter 9). Whilst on the subject though, it is interesting that some implemented design notations (e.g. MASCOT – see Chapter 7) may lead more safely to generated code, as it will then be based on a design.

In the case of OSD prototypes, the requirement will probably be clear at the level of general objectives, and less clear at the level of strategies to be tried so as to achieve them. In fact, the OSD prototype will be a P-type system. Nonetheless, each strategy will be definable (otherwise no prototype work could be done) and, before an attempt is made to investigate an approach, each one must be defined. That, effectively, constitutes the FS for that strategy and an associated OSD/estimating exercise can proceed. The complexity of backtracking (requiring re-estimating) is depicted in Section 4.6 (Figure 4.12).

In both cases of prototyping, therefore, the estimate status is that of the prototyping stage being enacted and may have a fairly high expected inaccuracy level attaching to it. We would judge this to be +50 to 150% but, it must be said, some OSD prototypes lie well outside this estimating range.

The global estimate for a development involving either kind of prototype can be seen as the summation of inaccurate estimates of this sort, plus a final and accurate estimate to engineer a release version properly.

Chapter 6 Organizing and controlling software development

Synopsis

Some general observations are made on planning and controlling software engineering tasks, and the dangers of bureaucracy and over-elaborate procedures are described.

The necessary management control documents for a software engineering development are defined.

Organizing software engineering teams. The basic notions of the Chief Programmer Team, its advantages and disadvantages are explained, and a modern variant of it is defined.

The problems of management with the transition from specification to implementation are discussed, along with the problems of 'visibility with incomprehensibility' and how to face (and deal with) them.

6.1 Task planning and control

In Chapters 2 and 3 we identified some of the major problems of managing the software engineering process. Of these, two major ones are the issue of how to handle the complexity of a software system, and the 'generation-gap' problem of some managers with the concepts and vocabularies of programming (let alone software engineering). In Chapters 4 and 5, we described the requirements specification process and how this can be used to estimate timescale and effort needed to do a software development; in effect this begins the discussion of how to handle the problem of complexity, and Chapter 7 continues that discussion.

Before doing that, we need to add two further categories of management means and methods to those already identified in Chapter 3 (lifecycle-based management; archiving; structured walkthrough; and specification change-control). They are:

- management control documents.

- software team structure.

These are dealt with in Sections 6.2 and 6.3 respectively. In Section 6.4, the matters of visibility and comprehension of the software engineering process are further commented upon in the light of the major transition between requirements specification and design.

The issues of management-control documents and software team structure may be provided for, in an IT company, in one of three ways:

1. Rudimentary, *ad hoc* approaches.

2. A developed set of standard procedures, with a lexicon of terms and a set of formal steps for each lifecycle activity phase. Rules may be included for estimating, documentation and configuration management, walkthrough, change-control, quality reviews, coding practices, testing methods, contracting (or pseudocontracting), maintenance support, and new version policy.

3. Guidelines in all the aspects listed under 2, but falling short of a mandatory 'standard method'.

There is nothing to be said for the first approach, widely found in small companies new to IT. In fact, a main purpose of this book is to act as a corrective to this condition.

As for 'standards', it is undoubtedly true that very large software development agencies, such as departments of defense and their suppliers, have to make and maintain many large software systems with a lifetime of the software in excess of ten years in some cases. Some use of standards, if only to achieve consistency in form and quality of documentation for 'configuration management' (see Section 10.2) is clearly essential in these cases. On the other hand, some 'standards' that start out with limited objectives (such as for configuration control) have tended to grow into standard practices for managing, specifying, designing, coding, testing, and quality assuring software systems. The result (we have seen several) can turn out to be a 'cookery book', and a gigantic one at that. If this is to be used by clerical staff, or computer operators in DP environments, to make changes to 'standard software' that has been and will remain in use for many years, this state of affairs is unexceptional. But for use by software engineers in highly innovative IT product or project firms it is more questionable. The procedures tend to become too intrusive into the creative process; software engineers tend to ignore a cubic metre of 'standard methodology'.

Also, 'doing things by the book' may have a sedative effect on managers; what can possibly go wrong, it's all on page 10 000?

Our approach in the following will be to offer guidelines on minimal provisions and procedures. These may, of course, be developed into 'standards', and we have no further comment to offer than that which we have already given; this is, in summary, to beware 'standards' that are so highly procedural that it becomes a major and intrusive task for software engineers to operate them. This goes equally for hard-copy-based procedures and computer-based ones. Some current research into extended 'virtual machine' environments, to make software development more rigorously procedured, have yet to demonstrate their economic and general usefulness.

Essentially, the management of software development tasks boils down to two issues:

1. Managing for technical quality (the criteria for which are described in Chapter 9).

2. Managing for economic quality (i.e. the adherence to reasonable effort and timescale provisions, competently derived as in Chapter 5).

These axioms (also true enough outside software engineering), follow directly from the definition of software engineering given in Section 2.1. Furthermore, the value of any approach to achieve them – 'standards' or 'guidelines' – depends on:

1. Whether it enhances the objectives in the first place.

2. Whether it enables the prediction of problems in either 'quality' domain, and therefore helps to avoid them.

3. Whether, in the event of failure to predict and avoid problems, it increases the chance of recovery in technical or economic terms (recovery in the one often being at the expense of the other).

It is clear that rudimentary *ad hoc* approaches will be likely to fail on all of these counts. So indeed will standards and guidelines, whichever is the approach adopted, if allowed to lapse into a rudimentary *ad hoc* state. Perhaps the strongest argument for standards is that they militate against this tendency in organizations where they can be, and have been, reasonably fully adopted and are an essential part of the culture. 'Better the standard way than no way at all' is a trite but very true saying. Better still though, in our view, are clear and flexible guidelines that management and software engineers can comprehend, and that are minimally bureaucratic.

6.2 Necessary documentation

Three levels of document are required for a software engineering task to be manageable:

1. A general level of documentation such as provided by the archive. Archives, and their use in pro-active management practice, are discussed in Sections 3.3 and 3.4.

2. Activities planning and control documents. These are discussed further below.

3. Cost (or effort) reporting documents. These are discussed further below.

6.2.1 Activities planning and control documents

As already described above, from the FS/OSD stage onwards, a software engineering task can and should be represented for planning, estimating and control purposes, as a set of activities ordered in accordance with their logical relationship, and any resource constraints applying. The techniques for doing this are those of CPM (or PERT as it is sometimes known).

PERT diagrams for hardware sub-projects within a composite systems engineering task are often done with very great attention to detail. It is not uncommon to see activities to build or buy, and to assemble and test such subsystems, detailed down to component levels.

Somewhat incongruously, the software engineering part of a composite systems engineering task is seldom so well represented, and we have found many occasions in which the ordering of activities has proceeded as in Figure 6.1 below, for no better reason than that the hardware was fully understood and the software not. However risible an example this may seem, and however difficult it may be to believe that such things can happen, the reader can be assured that it is by no means uncommon in hardware (electronic) engineering orientated IT companies.

It should be obvious that software must be as defined, planned and controlled in its development as any other part of a system. This process can and should begin at the FS/OSD level by the creation of notional activities plans as defined in Section 5.4. The activities-plan produced at that stage may, in fact, be 'notional' in two respects. Namely that the

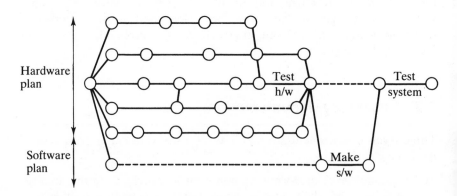

Fig. 6.1 Misplanned system development.

software taxonomy is only a catalogue of possible software items generically expressed, and is therefore not a design of actual software components (modules) to be made; and that staff assignment to notional tasks may itself be notional if real staff assignment has not then been done.

For this reason, the activities plan at the FS/OSD stage should be used for estimating purposes primarily. Its use as a planning and control document beyond the FS/OSD stage will be somewhat limited, until sufficient of the software design (and staff allocation) has been done to allow actual as distinct from notional planning.

A part of the problem that this presents is depicted in Table 6.1, where the percentage of software engineers' total effort over the lifecycle (excluding maintenance and new versions) is shown against the major estimating points.

This should not be taken to mean that a software task cannot be effectively managed until after 20% of the job has been done, but it does indicate that the management of early lifecycle stages will be a somewhat more amorphous matter than will be the case beyond the FS/OSD stage. The specification process and the implementation process are substantially different in that respect. Nonetheless, the same management methods will be used: activities planning (if only by defining milestones), archiving and structured walkthrough, as have already been defined. The inference from Table 6.1 is that activities planning and cost control documents will be less based on accurately determined estimates in the specification stage than they are in the implementation stage.

There is a tendency to mistake activities netplans for resources barcharts and this error should be avoided. A barchart is generally a schematic depicting the assignment of people to tasks, in a fashion such as that in Table 6.2. This is taken from the hospital alarm-monitoring system used as an example elsewhere and, in particular, is related to the activities ascriptions made in Section 5.4 (Figures 5.5 and 5.6).

The purpose of a resources barchart is primarily for staff allocation

Table 6.1 Progression in estimating and controlling tasks.

Cumulative effort	Lifecycle activities
0%	
	* Concepts
	* URS
10–20%	* FS/OSD/Verification: First acceptably accurate estimates; notional plans
	* Architectural design: detailed planning
Up to 35%	* Software design: Ratify estimates

Table 6.2   A barchart depiction of resource allocation.

Person	Weeks					
	36	37	38	39	40	41
	(e.g. Projects, courses, holidays, marketing support, etc.).					
A						
B						
Evelyn	E2	A5,D3	E4	A5	D5,E6	B+C+D+E/7
Fred	D2	E3	D4		E5,E6	B+C+D+E/7
P						
Q						
Sarah			A4			A6
X						
Y						

over a variety of projects and activities, in large technical departments under a single manager. At a glance, the manager can see what resource so-and-so is doing, or scheduled to be doing, during week such-and-such. For a department of a few dozen people or so and a dozen or so projects at any time, resources barcharts are a useful management device. They are, however, no substitute for activities planning covering a whole development. They are particularly poor for showing critical paths.

In some places, activities plans are themselves presented in the form of barcharts with the left-hand column indicating project and phase rather than resource. By and large the use of this form is a matter of personal choice and familiarity, but in general the practice is somewhat less favoured than that of PERT netplans as described.

Updating activities plans is a periodic matter, depending for its frequency on the duration of activities, and the generally expected rate of significant change in the status of activities. For example, if the FS is expected to take 6 months to do, then it makes little sense to update an activity plan for it on, say, a weekly basis. On the other hand, during the design, coding and testing of a lot of software modules, each stage of which takes a matter of days or weeks, then it makes sense to review progress on a short-term basis. Instead of reviewing the whole activities plan in this case, the recommended method is for the software engineers to preserve and archive a 'status matrix', which can be updated on a weekly basis with great effect.

In appearance, a status matrix resembles the barchart form of an activities plan for a software task, and represents the status of individual activities. In the scheme depicted in Table 6.3, a convention is used for activities 'not yet started' $(-)$, 'started but not complete' (0) and 'complete' $(+)$. The 'modules' are taken from our hospital example and

Table 6.3   A status matrix.

Module	Module design	Design review	Code	Code read	Author test	Integration test (1)	(2)	(3)	α-test	Complete and ratify	documentation
PCCS RCS i/o	+	+	0	–	–	–	–	–	–	–	–
Message processor	+	+	+	+	+	–	–	–	–	–	–
Screen manager	+	+	+	+	+	–	–	–	–	–	–
Outstanding messages	+	+	+	0	–	–	–	–	–	–	–
Other: Clock	+	+	+	0	–	–	–	–	–	–	–
Terminal i/o	+	+	+	0	–	–	–	–	–	–	–
Keyboard	+	+	+	0	–	–	–	–	–	–	–
Log	+	+	+	0	–	–	–	–	–	–	–
I/d reader	+	+	+	0	–	–	–	–	–	–	–

the state of affairs depicted is a 'time slice' through the activities plan shown in Figure 5.6.

There are several advantages in indicating the status of a software task in this way.

1. A status matrix, being effectively a snapshot through the software activities plan from design stage onwards, can be a very much easier thing both to update and to read than the full activities plan.

2. The information embodied in a status matrix is essentially binary. The 'state' of a module is either complete (+) or not (0 or −). This avoids, for managers in particular, the problem of the incomprehensible percentage answer to the question of progress: 'How are things progressing on the XYZ software?' 'We're 62.87% complete!'

   Such an answer, dreadfully common in practice, is usually meaningless. It can signify that 62.87% of allowed time has elapsed, or 62.87% of the money has been spent, or that 62.87% of estimated code size has been written, or whatever. It is usually, whether qualified or not, a highly misleading answer.

3. The status matrix can (and should when it occurs) show backtracking. For example, the next update of the status matrix shown in Table 6.3 may appear as shown in Table 6.4. Obviously, something has gone seriously wrong with three modules and this has been picked up at the integration test stage. All three have had to go right back to the design stage (a proper process anyway when things go wrong – far better than trying to patch the code). At a guess, it would be reasonable to suppose that the original task attribution of 'Screen manager' and 'Terminal I/O' to different people had something to do with the problem.

Table 6.4   The status matrix updated.

Module	Module design	Design review	Code	Code read	Author test	Integration test (1)	(2)	(3)	α-test	Complete and ratify	documentation
PCCS RCS i/o	+	+	+	+	0	−	−	−	−	−	−
Message processor	+	+	+	+	+	+	0	−	−	−	−
Screen manager	+	+	+	+	+	+	0	−	−	−	−
Outstanding messages	0	−	−	−	−	−	−	−	−	−	−
Other: Clock	+	+	+	+	+	+	0	−	−	−	−
Terminal i/o	0	−	−	−	−	−	−	−	−	−	−
Keyboard	+	+	+	+	+	+	+	+	−	−	−
Log	+	+	+	+	+	+	+	+	−	−	−
I/d reader	−	−	−	−	−	−	−	−	−	−	−

Sufficiently updated activities plans and status matrices must be available to managers. They will be done by software engineers and will be visible in the archive in their most up-to-date forms and all previous.

Medium-sized and large software tasks, as defined in Section 2.3.4, usually require something in the order of monthly updating of activities plans in the specification stage, becoming fortnightly updating from design onwards. The updating of status matrices is appropriate from design stage onwards, and is usually on a weekly basis for medium-sized and large software tasks. As a status matrix system can only reasonably be established at the late design stage, when the software module structure is known (see Chapter 7), it is very much up to the software engineers to initiate and update it. However, managers should insist that it is done, and that its results are visible – particularly as backtracking is represented so clearly this way.

6.2.2   Cost control documents

Such cost control as exists for software development may be generated by an accounts department, but its source material will have originated in the software implementation team in the form of time reporting records. In many organizations there is no practice of time recording, and one will have to be instituted.

However it is done, cost (or effort) accounting of a software engineering task should comprise four elements of information:

- target or budgetary costs (and an associated timescale);
- actual costs to date;

- an estimate of cost to completion (and an associated time to complete);
- a valued (or weighted) actual cost for progress to date.

The first three of these are often presented in graphical form as in Figure 6.2. In this representation, a very worrying situation is presented at the time of cost review (T_a). The targeted timescale and costs are both expected to be violated by what seems a substantial proportion. Still, the information is incomplete. How, for instance, is the manager to assess progress as well as cost? It might be that the estimates to complete the job are not even plausible, as bad as they seem in this case.

In addition to the three items of information incorporated in Figure 6.2, it is recommended that a weighted, actual-cost histogram is incorporated on the same schematic. To do this, actual costs should only be aggregated when a task is completed. For example in Table 6.3 the work done to complete the design of a module should only be added when the status changes from 0 to + on the status matrix. No effort (or cost) should be included for activities of status − or 0, and any backtracking (+ to − or 0 change) should cause the previously incorporated effort (or cost) for this task to be subtracted, as shown in a deliberately dramatic fashion in Figure 6.3.

A manager now has some view of the real and effective costs to date and is more able to arrive at rational conclusions about such things as the plausibility of estimates to complete (not very high in the example given), the need for contingency planning, re-assessment of go/no-go decisions, and so on.

One of two conventions can be used for re-aggregating work after backtracking. When tasks are re-completed, either the work to re-

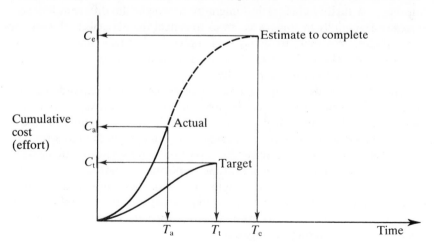

Fig. 6.2 Actual and target cost accretion.

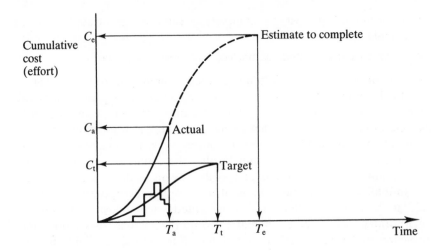

Fig. 6.3   Weighted cost accretion histogram.

complete can be accrued simply, or the work to re-complete plus the previously subtracted work can be accrued. In the first case, the histogram will never coincide at its final points with the real cost curve, whereas in the second case they will coincide on final completion. In the former case, the gap between the histogram and the curve at completion represents the cost of backtracking. Other features have been suggested, such as the incorporation of an ideal 'weighted-cost histogram' for the original targets. This, of course, would show no backtracking (nor for that matter will any extension of the histogram for 'estimates to complete'; backtracking is not an issue that can be scheduled or foreseen). A further elaboration might be to weight the different lifecycle stages differentially in some way, so as to reflect the expected difficulty of some stages. We tend to avoid such practices because they are over-elaborate and clutter the simple schematic form of cost representation needed for unequivocal grasp of the realities.

As with activities plans and status matrices, much depends on the fidelity with which time records are kept by the software engineers themselves. Managers must make clear their requirements for these necessary control documents, and assist software engineers to incorporate the minimal administrative activities as part of 'good software engineering practice' in organizations where time reporting is not a part of the 'culture'. Choice of software engineers, and their organization into effective implementation teams, should be arranged to enable these aspects of good practice as well as any expected virtues of technical design and programming competence.

6.3   Team structure: The 'peer group Chief Programmer Team'

Software engineering is a team activity in the vast majority of cases. An amateur programmer may be able to get away with a few hundred source statements of code, done as a solitary activity in a short timescale, but the application that person meets next will probably be orders of magnitude larger and more complex, and the timescale limitation to achieve it will imply multiple (or 'team') authorship.

Towards the end of Epoch 2 of computing (as defined elsewhere) the realization dawned that the organization and staffing aspects of software engineering were much under-appreciated as factors affecting software engineering, and consequently hardly provided for at all. Expressions were coined such as 'the Chinese army approach' to software staffing, and much levity ensued when large teams of programmers were discovered labouring together in unhappy disunity in some organizations.

From sources such as the NATO conferences on software engineering in the period 1968–69, there emerged a set of initiatives and early ideas about software team size and structure. The early ideas of how to organize software engineers, in the ways best fitted to achieve high-quality software systems in a highly productive (economic) fashion, are thoroughly described in the works of Brooks (1975), Metzger (1981), Mills and Baker (1973) and Yourdon (1979).

The approach became known as the 'Chief Programmer Team' structure, and comprised notions of small team size, charismatic and highly specialized team leadership, powerful task orientation and clear rôle assignment. Mills and others put these precepts into practice in one way or another, and researchers such as Weinberg and Schulman (1974) investigated their behavioural properties.

One approach, described in detail in Brooks (1975) after work by Mills, relates the team structure and behaviour of a software engineering (Chief Programmer) team as being, at its best, analogous to those of a surgical team, where skilled technical assistants provide the instruments to the chief surgeon who performs the specialist work called for. Metzger (1981) cites evidence of highly increased productivity (no doubt presuming collateral quality achievements) through the use of Mills' approach.

Strange to say, given the manifest need and the claims of the authors of the Chief Programmer Team approach, the idea was not quick to become accepted in the world of software engineering. Three reasons account for this:

1. The rapid growth of amateur programming from Epoch 3 onwards obscured this and many other 'good practices'. Not only did this

effect mean that concepts such as the Chief Programmer Team remained at a very low level of usage compared to other practices, but also that amateur programmers in a company could (and did) actually prevent software engineers from trying the ideas out.

2. Whatever attempts were made to quantify the effects of introducing Chief Programmer Team structures and practices, the supposed virtues of the approach could only be discovered by trial.

3. As will already be clear, the basic idea of the Chief Programmer Team seems élitist (small 'surgeon' teams, highly task orientated, etc.). Not all companies can accommodate the consequences of this, neither in their general 'culture' nor in their career structure. Furthermore, when general societal attitudes tend away from notions such as élitism, software engineers themselves may find difficulty in adopting what they may think is an élitist team structure and operating practice.

The fact is, however, that at the present time, some one and a half decades after its inception as a set of ideas, the concept of the Chief Programmer Team is established (although somewhat modified, as we describe), and looks set to become the norm rather than the exception in many companies. In the process, many of the original ideas have been revised and, in the account following, we describe the current practical guidelines for a Chief Programmer Team. The case for a complete change of name from 'Chief Programmer Team' is strong. The expression 'Small Software Engineering Peer Group' is a closer approximation to what is current practice. However, we do not want to increase the problems of proliferating terminology, and so, with some reluctance, we preserve the original designation. Likewise for the Chief Programmer who, as the peer-group team leader, would be better described as 'Master Software Engineer' if the masculine connotation of 'master' could be ignored.

6.3.1 The Chief Programmer Team (CPT)

There are eight basic ideas underlying the concepts of the CPT nowadays:

1. Small team size.
2. Special characteristics of the team leader (chief programmer).
3. Team composition and structure derived from the job, not vice versa.
4. Nomination of a suitable 'deputy' chief programmer.
5. All team members to be active software engineers, even if differing in experience level.
6. Assignment of special tasks to acquire expertise needed by the team as a whole (toolsmiths).
7. Assignment of a team member to do housekeeping tasks such as

maintaining the archive ('librarian task'). Assignment of a 'tester', perhaps.

8. Careful assimilation of trainees into the team.

These points are expanded in the following paragraphs.

Large teams suffer the disability of a general increase in the degree of communication needed between team members, and this effect begins to be noticeable with a team size as small as 6, and unacceptable for 7 or more. Smaller teams (1 or 2 people) tend to lack the perspective – particularly crucial in design – that comes from alternative views of a problem.

The Chief Programmer (CP) must embody several qualifications and, just as importantly, lack several disqualifications. Firstly, a considerable level of relevant technical experience is required. In this case, 'relevant' may mean concerning similar applications and technologies rather than identical experiences. The level for Chief Programmers is usually about 7 years of relevant experience and upwards. Secondly, the person must have some leadership qualities (actual or latent), however these are determined or on what basis they are supposed.

The team leadership style is crucial. Too autocratic a style is highly counter-productive; too democratic a style may lead to 'paralysis by analysis' where no decisions are ever taken without full team consensus, and no leadership is given either for that consensus or in the event of its absence. The right balance is difficult for anyone to find and changes from occasion to occasion as different aspects of personalities within the team are highlighted by different tasks; the best balance inclines to decisive leadership when required, with due care not to alienate other team members by discounting their ideas arbitrarily. (The CP whose attitude is that 'a team effort is a lot of people doing as I say', is a bad CP.)

Teams, their size, structure and composition should be determined by the structure of the job, not vice versa. Usually one (or more) chief programmer, or at least senior level software engineering staff, will have been involved in the OSD/FS stage in order to do the software taxonomies, estimates and notional plans for the task. The job of estimating involves notional task determination and staff assignment, and this is carried forward to determine the composition of the CPT needed for the task. As design proceeds, it may be decided that a CPT should be changed: for example, the greater insight available may change the premises on which the original staffing decisions were taken.

A CPT should have a nominated 'Deputy Chief Programmer' who is to act on that person's behalf when he or she is absent. Generally this is a person with rather less relevant experience (about 3–6 years usually) and, perhaps, not such clearly evident leadership qualities. A particular requirement in such a person is that they do not politicize their job at the expense of the Chief Programmer ('That – fool X! If I was in charge we wouldn't be in this mess . . .'). A divided CPT is a disaster. More than anyone else, the deputy can divide the team.

All team members should be software engineers, however different their background or experience levels, and all should be active software engineers within the team. The old notion of software jobs structured around the career progression of technicians has no place in the CPT. Thus one should not find 'systems analysts', 'designers', 'programmers (or coders)' and so forth, of diminishing technical experience and ability, doing partitioned tasks within a job, and then passing the results on like the baton in a relay race. All too often it gets dropped. The CPT is a 'peer group' of practising software engineers, all of whom do parts of design, coding, testing, etc. Within this general notion and objective there are three natural modifications in practice, but only three: firstly, the more senior staff (certainly the CP) are assigned first and entrusted with the OSD taxonomy for software and the estimates; secondly, the more difficult parts of design may be done by more, rather than less, experienced staff; and thirdly, the CP may become too occupied with collateral technical and administrative tasks, such as sub-project co-ordination, to do major parts of coding and testing.

If this last is not the case, then it must be included in the qualifications of a CP that he or she will not only be able but will wish to write and test programs as a part of the CPT task. The team leader who says 'I haven't programmed for years and don't expect to any more', is not a suitable CP.

Apart from the Chief and Deputy Chief Programmer assignments, there may be a case for other rôle assignment within the CPT. One such rôle, that of 'Librarian', is described below. An early (and now largely outdated) idea required the definition of an extensive list of tasks and their assignment – as rôles – to team members. Yourdon (1979) lists ten such rôles. Nowadays the practice is to identify any special technical expertise that should be available within the team, and to assign tasks to achieve that specialism in the shortest possible time. Such people are called the 'toolsmiths' within the CPT and the determination of these rôles must be based on task necessity and individual ability.

For example, in the hospital alarm system, there is clearly a need to become familiar with the operating system of the CCS, the microcode of the sensors, the high-level language for most of the software (if, for some reason, it is unfamiliar), the PSE facilities if the development is to be done on a 'host' machine, and so forth.

The assignment of 'toolsmith' rôles is not to prevent others from achieving competence in the specialism concerned – they will do that naturally and rapidly during the implementation – but to ensure that everyone does not try to become specialists in everything at the start, in which case no other work would be done. During the CPT task, the need for 'toolsmiths' tends to disappear.

The set of technico-administrative tasks associated with a software engineering development is often assigned as the 'librarian' rôle to a team member to organize and expedite. The scope of this includes project planning and control material, cost (effort) accounting, archiving, keeping and updating status matrices, dealing with change control traffic, monitoring deliverable documentation and so forth.

The librarian rôle is to monitor and expedite these, rather than be their sole agency of production. A now somewhat outdated notion was that the librarian should be a full-time administrator attached to the CPT. Whilst it is sometimes a good idea to have a secretary assigned anyway for very large jobs, the librarian tasks are not entirely administrative as the list shows. Either one team member should be designated to act as librarian along with other tasks, or the rôle should be undertaken by team members in turn (possibly excluding the CP) over some relatively long period like one month.

Another fixed-task assignment may be that of 'tester' within a CPT. Such a person would probably be designated, from design stage onwards, to devise and do integration tests on software components as their authors bring them into being as partly tested code (see Section 9.5).

A policy concerning trainees within the CPT should be determined and adhered to. This has caused some problems in the past. How are new staff to be trained and used, and how are client staff to be incorporated if (as is often the case) the client wishes to take over and maintain a system after delivery?

The whole ethos of the CPT is that of extremely strong task motivation and professionalism about both the technical and economic quality (adherence to timescale and effort estimates). Clearly the competence level of CPT members is crucial.

Nevertheless, it is possible to incorporate 'trainee' or client personnel (whether at trainee level or not) into a CPT. One such person should be assumed to have zero productivity and each additional one should be assumed to make a sharply increasing, negative contribution to productivity. These assumptions should be made in order to account for the supervision and team-interaction time required for a trainee – someone with less than one year's programming experience say. Apart from that, trainees or client staff should be treated as normal team members at their experience level, and an objective should be to ensure that their contribution is positive. In practice, this 'rule-of-thumb' generally means that no more than 2 trainee (or client) staff should be placed on even the largest (6 people) CPT, and this can clearly be seen as a limitation on the growth rate of IT companies through trainee recruitment. Where this limitation has not been observed, quality has suffered. The librarian and tester rôles are particularly suitable for trainees, as that way they become aware of the techniques of good software engineering practice by precept or default. The deliverable documentation part of the librarian's expediting rôle is a most suitable task for client technical personnel attached to a CPT.

6.3.2   Methods and practices of the CPT

There are two highly significant methods associated with the notion of the CPT:

1. design review;
2. code reading.

These are both peer-group based, constructive criticisms at a detailed level of the software design and code respectively. What happens is that the CP will nominate reviewers/readers for each piece of design and code done, including his own designs and code and including the CP as a reviewer/reader (note 'a' not 'the' reviewer/reader). Each piece of design and each piece of code is then 'read' by that benevolent but critical adversary from within the CPT.

The object of these practices is quality control in general (see Section 9.2), and the early detection of errors in particular. A general thesis is held in software engineering, as in other forms of engineering, that the earlier errors are detected, the cheaper they are to correct.

Boehm (1981) points out that the savings involved are large indeed. Figure 6.4 indicates the order of magnitude differences in cost to detect and correct errors at different lifecycle stages (the figure expresses this in a slightly different form from Boehm).

The methods of design review and code reading should be 'formal' within the CPT itself. A process of reviewer/reader 'signing-off' should be instituted for design and code listings. Detailed errors should be listed and flagged by the author when corrected. This may be in the form of a simple, handwritten checklist on the design diagram or code listing during the development, but must be fully incorporated into any documentation versions for maintenance, configuration management, and so on (see Section 10.2).

We have been asked on many occasions whether the methods of design review and code reading really 'work'. Is it not all some internal 'rain dance' gone through by programmers, to demonstrate how difficult it all is and how different they are from mere mortals? The short answer

```
URS           β-Test = 1:100
S/W Design    β-Test = 1: 40
Code          β-Test = 1: 10
```

Fig. 6.4   The economics of error detection and correction.

is that the practice of design review and code reading really does work, if undertaken seriously and by competent people. We have many examples of CPTs, the quality of whose work and the high productivity of whose endeavours have been very largely attributed (by them) to the saving graces of design review and code reading.

Not all CPTs turn out to be successful. Apart from any factors arising from the task or the technology involved, the CPT ethos and methodology contains its own stresses. The practices of design review and code reading establish at a very early stage in the lifecycle of the software whether there are likely to be personality problems in the team. Very few people, confronted with the prospect for the first time, feel entirely comfortable about having their intellectual creations (design, code) criticized, however 'benevolently' or 'constructively'. Equally, some people feel acutely embarrassed at being the reviewer/reader.

Most software engineers get over these feelings quite rapidly and design review/code reading become part of everyday professional life in a highly ideas-orientated job. Some people never do manage to overcome their fears as reviewer or reviewee. This can undoubtedly lead to stress at both the personal level and at team level. Fortunately, in one way, the results are usually evident very early, and perceptive management has a chance to rectify the problem by one of several means.

In some cases, when the personal problems of a team member are really acute, it may be that the person is not really a software engineer in the slightly circular definition of that term as possessing the sort of attributes fitted for team membership.

The reader may have heard of 'ego-less design' and 'ego-less programming' in connection with the recommended behaviour for software engineers working in teams. In our view there is no such thing, nor is it desirable that there should be. Good software engineering is done by highly capable people doing a very difficult job often in less than ideal conditions; they are not 'ego-less' people. What is required of software engineers working in constructions such as the CPT is that they possess a willingness to subjugate their attachment to their own ideas and creations to the aim of getting the job done as a team. When A and B have alternative designs and the chief programmer C finally decides that B's design will prevail, then A must be able to put as much into the adopted design as if it had been his own.

Over the years, practice has brought about an improvement (slow but steady) in the way software engineers understand the realities attaching to their job. Design review and code reading are two such realities.

In the early days of the CPT philosophy, the dangers of a team failing catastrophically through breakdown of the CPT itself were fairly high – two or three out of ten perhaps. Nowadays CPT catastrophes are fairly rare (less than 10% in our own experience) but still not unknown.

Against this there is growing evidence that the modified CPT (peer group) approach, as part of good software engineering practice in general, is the best way of achieving high levels of software engineering performance in the sense of quality and adherence to timescale and budgets. Not all software engineers agree; not all managers have enough authority in the subject to bring CPT structures and philosophy about. We discuss some of these problems below.

6.3.3 Drawbacks to the CPT approach

In summary the four objections to the concepts of CPTs are:

1. The notion of élitism, as in a highly task-orientated professional peer group, may be socially unacceptable in a particular epoch, or counter-cultural in some organizations. Where and when this is true, there will undoubtedly be a high resistance to CPTs and the approach may be disabled as a result.

2. CPT practices of design review/code reading may upset some team members, but this is far less prevalent than a decade ago. The profession of software engineering is growing up. People pathologically incapable of the process of review – whether as reviewer or reviewee – are not really software engineers in the team sense, however brilliant they may be as designers, coders, etc.

3. Successful CPTs want to stay together for the next job too. There is a tendency for the peer-group respect generated in a successful CPT to carry over into attitudes of who will and who will not work together. Rapidly a list of 'goodies' and 'baddies' may come to exist in software engineers' minds. This may prove to be highly unpalatable in any organization, and particularly so in organizations who work largely by consensus. For managers in any event, the notion of a team electing itself is anathema, and this CPT tendency must be educated out of people when it occurs.

4. The CPT is clearly a project or product 'task-force', assembled for a particular job. It may draw in staff from different parts of an organization, particularly if that is a matrix-form construction with product or skill specialization being aggregated into divisions or departments of separate authority/accountability. The operation of CPT structures in organizations of different types (centralized/decentralized hierarchical; or innovative/adaptive) is an issue in organization theory, and somewhat beyond the scope of this work. We submit the following comments nonetheless, presuming in the reader only a basic understanding of organization forms such as 'hierarchical' and 'matrix'. The operation of matrix, and some similar organization forms, militates against the CPT philosophy only in the sense that authority/accountability may be unclear or fragmented for

a particular product or project. Where it is not, that is when there exists a single product or project manager, then the structure of teams for multidisciplinary development involves temporary migration of staff from their department(s) to the team(s). This can cause problems of reporting, but not if simple guidelines are followed. The 'project form' organization for tasks, with a clear hierarchical management structure, is far to be preferred for both projects and the project-like development of substantive versions of a product. This need not disturb a 'matrix' organization, in which project-form developments can go on so long as the accountability issue is clearly assigned to the project/product manager, and the problems of reporting solved for the staff who migrate (temporarily) to the team. The more flexible, less hierarchical organization forms (e.g. matrix or 'innovative' and 'adaptive') are appropriate at early lifecycle stages for product development, particularly if prototyping is to be done, and we should not expect to see a marked CPT orientation above the FS/OSD level in these cases.

In summary, we see no real reason why software engineers and their companies should not adopt the modern variant of the CPT, and many good reasons why they should, with the reservation given in (4) above.

6.3.4 Guidelines for the CPT

Teams of software engineers change from job to job, and it is good that they do so. Occasionally, staff leave the company; sometimes new employees join. The XYZ job last year had four chief programmer teams on it, led by A, B, C and D. Now we have three new jobs that need staffing, and B is working on that big proposal for the bank and D has been seconded for six months to research. New CPTs are formed.

At the outset, however well a CP may know the other team members, the CP must bring the CPT into being as a 'peer group' entity with a strong purpose and clear methods. The recommended way to do this is to have the first team meeting scheduled and chaired by the CP. This team meeting should:

1. Initiate the archiving by setting up a well-structured format for the archive and a simple, explicit set of procedures (to be archived) for its maintenance and updating. This should already be in place if work has proceeded, previous to this point, on a matrix-form basis, e.g. for a product development with considerable OSD prototyping.

2. Appoint a Librarian (or roster of several).

3. Discuss and determine any 'toolsmith' rôles seemingly required.

4. The CP should initiate a full team understanding of the requirements by distributing (if not already done) any URS/FS/OSD material in

existence. The team should begin to evaluate the requirements as a group, by open and 'free-form' discussion of the apparent specifications. Often, the CP has to take an initiative in this, by making presentations on aspects of requirements for team members to respond to.

5. Define the management documents required, other than the archive, and the means and methods to achieve them. This is a CP initiated action for discussion/emendation/adoption at the inaugural meeting. There may be administrative practices needed that are not otherwise present in the organization; these should be kept to a minimum but made to happen. This too is a part of professional practice for software engineers.

6. Define what is, or should be, the deliverable documentation for the task at hand (see Section 10.1). The aim of good, professional software engineers should not be to get away with as quick and dirty a job as possible in this respect, but to see the documentation requirement as the next person's need – possibly not a team member, probably some time hence.

7. Define and assign tasks, and the next meeting date/time.

That should suffice for a first meeting. The whole style of the CPT can be set in this way. It is probably unnecessary (and maybe not even possible) for the CP to nominate a 'deputy' at the first meeting. It should be done early, but not this early.

Other matters will undoubtedly crop up as time goes on: change control issues; interfaces with independent quality assurance staff; design issues; computer resources required for the development; and so on. A well-established, staffed and motivated CPT will cope with them all, however difficult, as a matter of professional commitment.

6.4   Managing transformation

One of the distinguishing features of software engineering is the severity of transformation between the real world of things happening, the classification and specification of requirements to emulate these or react realistically to them, and the processes involved in then making a computer-based software system to achieve these functions and features.

In this respect, the matter is unquestionably an engineering process and is, on the surface, just like any other engineering process in that it seeks to make a representation of a real-world thing, however abstract the processes of specification, design and coding may be.

There are many analogies with mechanical and electronic engineering that occur to one, and that are true and useful up to a point. These analogies break down, as they often do in practice, for various reasons:

1. Software is not tangible like hardware. People with literal and material casts of mind are often not able, with facility, to deal with issues other than in concrete and physically visible terms. That is not a limitation, it is virtue (which we should respect every time we use a bridge, drive a car, live in a house which doesn't collapse around our ears, and so on). Would we had such virtue in software engineering.

2. Most, if not all, engineered artefacts have abstract-level plans (draughtsman's drawings, circuit diagrams, architect's designs), all of which are done at a level above the physical activities of making the artefact. The sombre fact is that in software engineering we have no well developed, standard ways for representing our thoughts, for example, at design level. We may have dozens of them more or less in intermittent use by software engineers.

3. The process of specifying, designing and coding a software system is one of progressive abstraction up to FS stage, and abstractness of form beyond it, ending up with what should be a highly logically structured set of procedural statements within a bounded universe of procedural regulations. These statements will be further transformed into binary bit patterns to activate and be acted upon by electronic hardware. The translation from the real world, via natural language and perhaps pictures, to this state is an exceedingly taxing one to follow through, particularly when the system concerned is formidably complex in its own right.

For most management, these problems are insuperable – or so it would seem. The lifecycle is a 'nice picture' of an ideal world, and it assuredly helps our understanding, and the archive is a great (if obvious) idea for making projects and product developments visible. But, at a certain stage in proceedings when managing a software development, we – the managers – come to a full stop, and all the lifecycles and archives in the world seem unable to help us. The process has gone invisible, or so it seems. As we have pointed out elsewhere, this invisibility is really (if lifecycle activities are done properly and the archive of them is completely maintained) more a matter of incomprehensibility.

In software engineering we speak of lifecycle activities as being 'above the line' or 'below the line' for that reason. The 'line' represents a demarcation between general comprehensibility and specialist comprehensibility.

Figure 6.5 represents a simplified schematic of lifecycle activities, using abbreviations as hitherto. 'The line' is indicated by *----------*. This schematic is for a composite hardware and software development. When the hardware expertise predominates (as is usually the case in IT applications), the problem may disappear very simply and automatically.

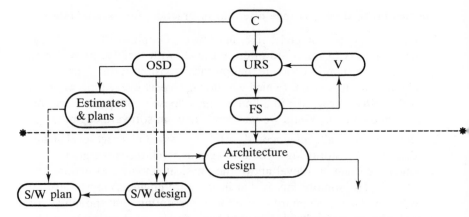

Fig. 6.5   Domains of generalist and specialist comprehension.

Everything becomes hardware in the first place, so there is no OSD, no real architectural design, no software design (after all, is not the software just the 'glue' to stick all this fine hardware together?).

As remarked earlier, this is a dangerous notion. Its connotations include the hardware/software interface (HSI) as a barrier against the uncertainties of software engineering for hardware people. H.L. Menken was reported to have said that every problem has a solution – elegant, simple and wrong. The premature HSI solution is, most often, just that – wrong.

In the more general case, however, the 'line' exists as depicted, and is a fundamental barrier to managing software engineering tasks. Above-the-line activities can be comprehended, controlled and (importantly) increased in value by managers, because these activities are basically in manager (and user) 'friendly' languages and form. Below-the-line activities on the software side of the lifecycle (beginning even at Architectural Design) may be amorphous, abstract, baffling and impossible for managers to comprehend, control or increase in value. That is the general nature of the problem for most managers: 'What does it all mean, I wonder?' is a common reaction below the line.

In Chapters 7 and 8 we deal with some technical issues of software design and implementation, in the software engineer's own terms. The problems for most managers begin immediately, and as abruptly as in real life one may seem to pass from the FS (in natural language, praises be!) to Design (in . . . what? Can that depiction really be in a 'language'? Can it really be saying something about our dear old FS?). Oddly enough it is a fact not fully appreciated by managers that the passage 'across the line' is far from easy for software engineers too. It may help all populations contributing in whatever sense to a software engineering task to realize what is going on as one 'crosses the line'.

What software engineers are trying to do when progressing from a relatively simple OSD software taxonomy stage to one of real design is to make some conceptual model at the abstract level of the features and functionality to be achieved in software as these features and functionalities are set out in the FS. This model will go through progressive steps and stages in which the level of detail is increased, the level of complexity reduced or contained within reasonable limits, and compliance with specification and quality criteria achieved (see Chapter 9). This highly complex process is called, in the first place, 'design' and is a matter about which one can say surprisingly little in general (more is said in particular in the next Chapter), other than that:

1. Design is very much an intuition-based skill which can only in part be developed in a person, and then only if they have a natural aptitude in the first place.

2. The process of design is generally a mass of trade-offs and compromises to achieve a balance between requirements, economical solutions, constraints (such as 'the machine', 'the language', etc.), achievement of quality criteria, and so on.

Design is the closest that software engineering comes to being an art form, although its ends are very utilitarian in most cases. The paradox lies between abstraction and utility, and is a problem that makes the desired attributes of software engineers so difficult to identify and cater for in education (see Section 10.4).

The design of a software system, that first step 'across the line' is often as traumatic for the software engineers as for their managers. Lehman *et al.* (1984) describe the design process as being one of stepwise refinement with enrichment at each step and the possibility to backtrack. Furthermore, the authors identify that at each step two things are required:

1. a *base* (e.g. from the previous step);

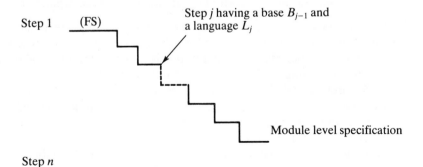

Fig. 6.6   Design as a stepwise process.

2. a *language* in which to express the present step.

Thus design can be represented as a process of the sort shown in Figure 6.6. This very simple pictorial representation enables the following points to be made about software design:

1. The base for one step is the product of the previous step. Thus B_1 is the FS/top-level architectural schematic (OSD) itself, expressed in the language of that step, i.e. natural language plus some diagrammatic notation. Similarly, the bottom level B_n is the detailed module designs, which are the input base for the coding (see Chapter 8).

2. The language (L_j) in which to express the design notions at each step may or may not be identical over all the steps. This is precisely the point made in Chapter 7, namely that the 'languages' or 'notations' of design are neither standard nor singular. One simply uses what is best at a design stage.

3. The endeavours of design are set out in more detail in Chapter 7, but it is clear from the schematic that the issue of 'enrichment' in the terms of Lehman *et al*. is a judgemental one between the peer group of software engineers doing the development. Although the principles of good design are fairly well known, the notion of enrichment (or its converse 'impoverishment') in design is bound up with the trade-offs between delivery of functionality and features, good design practice and quality criteria, and the limitations of the 'virtual machine' (hardware/software) with which one is working. In effect, design may have false starts, wrongly chosen 'languages', backtracking and all sorts of hazards before the module level designs are reached.

    A team may strike out bravely doing designs of increasing detail in (say) SADT as the 'language' (notation) at the top level, and then find several steps down that no real enrichment is occurring. Switching to (say) Myers notation may suddenly reveal all sorts of insights and, before one knows it, we have gone back up the design and begun again, this time doing it in Myers notation. Or we may start in Mascot and proceed via SDL to BS 6224, or whatever.

The design process, its criteria in 'goodness', its objectives, and its 'language' or notations are described below. For managers and those who are not software specialists in general, this is 'crossing the line'. With the simple understanding given above of what software engineers are trying to do themselves and the trepidation with which they cross the line, we advise and recommend the non-specialist to read the following chapter. Otherwise 'the line' becomes a reinforced concrete wall separating the manager from the managed.

    The first step in the transition is, usually, the undertaking of an architectural design after the FS/OSD steps have been completed. This generally takes the form of increasingly detailed designs, using the OSD taxonomies as first-order approximations of hardware and software subsystem scope, but holding out the possibility for an eventual change from one solution approach to another. Both hardware design schematics and those for software design will be done – on this rather flexible and informal basis – until, at some point in this design process it is possible to decide outright what the hardware and software parts of the system will be. At this stage the software developments task can be defined (note how relatively late in the lifecycle this is; premature definition is a great peril).

A danger to be avoided is to take the OSD as being, axiomatically, the only architectural definition done. Not only managers but some software engineers fall into this trap – particularly if the form of the OSD lends itself to coding at an early stage, e.g. if the software taxonomy is done in pseudocode. In some cases (small and relatively simple systems) the OSD may be adequate as the definitive architectural design; in other cases not. Our advice is always to do a full design irrespectively. At most, an OSD should be seen as a first 'base' (probably incorporating 'impoverishment' in the real design sense) for the real design.

It was noted in Section 4.1 that many languages and notations and some fully developed and implemented methodologies exist for specification, design and coding. Some rough, judgemental classification by lifecycle stage at which they are thought most useful was set out there. In Chapter 7, several approaches to design are discussed. In particular, the methods of SADT, Dataflow, MASCOT, CCITT-SDL, Nassi-Schneiderman, BS 6224 and Pseudocode are described. Before embarking on this chapter, the reader should be aware that all of these approaches have some merit for particular circumstances and types of application. So far as their current status as notations, methodologies and implementation (i.e. as part of a PSE) are concerned, the situation is roughly as in Table 6.5.

Table 6.5   Some design methodologies and notations.

'Method'	Notation	Status Methodology	Implementation	Level most appropriate
SADT	***	*****	*?	High/medium
MYERS (DATAFLOW)	**	**	*?	High/medium
MASCOT	****	**	****	High/medium
CCITT–SDL	***	**	***	High/medium
BS 6224	****	*	**?	Medium/low
N–S/SFC	**	*	*?	Low
PSEUDOCODE	***	*	***	Low

Key: Asterisks depict the relative strength of 'methods', at relevant design levels. Thus, there is no real comparison between (eg.) MASCOT and N–S charts at levels above module or program design (see Chapter 7 below).

   With the same stricture to readers that guidelines such as these should not be taken out of context, we proceed now with an exposition of system and software design principles and practical techniques.

Chapter 7 Systems and software design

Synopsis

The principles of good design are described and the complexity of design objectives, methodologies and notations is discussed.

Some types of design approach are defined for different application types.

Some notations for representing software designs are described, with examples of their usage in some cases.

No one methodology or notation is recommended, for the good reason that no one (nor any combination) is universally applicable over all applications and all phases of design.

7.1 Principles of good design

The object of design is to produce an implementable 'model' of a solution to requirements, where 'implementation' connotes coding and the demonstration of quality criteria for the code. The starting point is the FS, which is very largely in the language and form of 'users' as it is a product of the requirements specification domain of lifecycle activities; the OSD is a subset of FS features represented in taxonomies form for estimating purposes, and is not necessarily a representation of anything bearing on design issues other than being a statement of what might be developed in software. Nevertheless, it is frequently the case that the OSD also contains a very high-level representation of the solution to be, in some suitable diagrammatic notation as described below, describing the main hardware and software subsystem features and how they are supposed to work in combination. This will have been done for feasibility assessment in the FS/OSD stage, and is a very high-level architectural design for the 'solution'.

The central problem is to pass from the requirements domain (FS document) to the architectural design stage, and to detail progressively the elements of a system (solution) to fulfill the requirements. The

163

problem is made more severe by the explicit, or at least 'understood', requirement that the outcome must be implementable as a well-organized structure that embodies principles of 'good engineering quality' in the sense that the system can be changed, emended, tested and so forth.

The transformation between FS and design is not of equal severity in terms of unmappable representations between the two for all application types and sizes. For instance, a small DP application may have a design that flows obviously from the format of the FS, and in this case the OSD is a legitimate top-level architectural design and very little more may be needed in the way of adding detail and transforming ('designing') to ensure all requirements are met.

On the other hand, some other systems may require a solution design that is only adequate for implementation after several iterations (or 'steps') in which the implementation features are progressively detailed, functionality is achieved in the sense of all FS features, and general quality criteria are built in. In these cases, design may be an intensely complex and highly intuitive process subject to typical engineering constraints such as the availability of useful approaches and methods, and the adequacy of timescale and cost budgets.

This chapter is concerned with the issue of 'useful approaches and methods', the other matters such as adequate cost and timescale estimates being dealt with elsewhere.

In general, the approaches and methods fall into three categories:

- General principles for good design.
- General approaches to design; for example concerning decomposition with increasing solution detail, for particular application-types.
- Methodologies and notations to assist at design stages and represent the results of these stages.

The complexity of this whole subject is represented by the confusion, obscurity and overlap of issues between these three, and the whole business is worsened by the greater relevance of some principles, approaches and methodologies to different types of application and even different stages in the design process. This is described further below, but it is useful at this stage to indicate that:

1. The general principles for good design, set out in Section 7.1.3, have been investigated for some years by computer scientists, along with the associated issue of good programming practices. The results are of particular use 'low' in the design process – i.e. near to and at the module and program design levels.

2. The general approaches to design (e.g. decomposition) have emerged from practical problems of defining systems for different types of application in a way that is useful for the well-ordered refinement

processes that are to follow. The results, described in Section 7.2, are mostly applicable 'high' in the design process – i.e. at and somewhat below the architectural design level.

3. The methodologies and notations to assist the design process and represent the results, the better known of which are described in Section 7.3, tend to have particular merits for certain application types and parts of the design process (architectural, module/program, and intermediate).

The following sections should be read with those guidelines in mind.

7.1.1 A general approach to design

The best approach to the problem of design is to regard it as an exercise in reducing complexity. A central technique for this is the one of hierarchical decomposition, in which the system is partitioned into subsystems, and the subsystems partitioned in turn, and so on, each level of the hierarchy being of lesser complexity than the one immediately preceding (higher than) it. The process is repeated recursively until the whole system is expressed in terms of a well-formed structure of manageable components. This approach is also known as 'stepwise refinement', 'functional decomposition' and 'top-down design', and variants of it have been put forward by many authors.

The method of hierarchical decomposition is often contrasted with one known as 'bottom-up design'. This approach begins by grouping together elementary functions into more powerful ones which can be seen as relevant to the eventual solution. In computing terms, this may be described as the 'virtual machine' or 'levels of abstraction' approach. The lowest 'machine' level is the hardware, and on this we normally expect to see constructed the first 'abstract machine' – the operating system. To this we add other levels by writing device drivers, macros, general-purpose subroutines and so on, all aimed to produce more powerful and specialized facilities directed towards the problem solution.

In practical situations, the hard and fast choice of one approach over another – top down or bottom up – disappears, as one iterates between the two. The upper levels of design (generally the starting point of the process) are usually best analysed as hierarchic structures, and the lower levels as abstract machines providing services to the upper levels.

Alternation between the two approaches is a common feature of design practice, for example between dataflow representations and calling structures, as one moves down levels of refinement and detail in the design.

A useful and widely applicable general design principle is that originally proposed by Parnas (1972) and known as 'information hiding'. The idea is to separate out the design decisions taken in devising a solution to requirements, and to encapsulate all information – data structures and algorithms – relative to each specific decision, into a separate module. If a decision has to be changed at some later stage, then ideally only one module needs to be changed in consequence as all entities (data and algorithms) are localized. This approach is of particular use at low-level design stages, in module or program design, just prior to coding.

These general comments and approaches apply both at the systems level, and also at lower and more technology-specific levels of design. In general terms they apply in any field of technology, such as in computers or in electronics, at the level of the micro-circuit design of a VLSI chip. Analogies can be quoted from many other areas of engineering, but care should always be taken not to overburden an analogy; for example other fields make more use of re-usable components, whereas in software engineering the issue of re-usability is a topic for research.

We do not, in this work, address ourselves to disciplines other than software engineering. Nevertheless it is, to some extent, helpful to consider them in order more fully to appreciate the specific and unusual problems encountered in software design.

In mechanical or electronic design, for example, we have available well-established methods for design, and widely accepted standard notations for expressing them, such as blueprints and circuit diagrams. In these engineering subjects, the behaviour of the intended system can, to a substantial extent, be determined by study of the design documentation. In other words, the probable behaviour can be reasonably well visualized.

In software engineering, we have no generally accepted notations or approaches to design and, furthermore, the behaviour of a program is in most cases not really determinable by study of the program itself. Whereas the program is a static representation in its visible form, its behaviour is highly dynamic in time. For these reasons, software behaviour may be extremely unpredictable.

In software engineering we have a further general issue to consider – the choice between algorithms and data structures in the design. These are complementary, since the choice of one determines the other. Data structures model entities in the problem area, and algorithms model the activities. The program, when developed, will involve both algorithms and data structures.

Data design is interwoven throughout the process of software design and eventually may lead, via data dictionary and module interface specifications, to a database specification and design.

We can now proceed to raise two central questions in systems and software design:

1. When we proceed to partition a system or subsystem into further levels, how do we choose the partitions and what do we use as the

basis for the choice? As Bergland (1981) says: 'With respect to what do we decompose?' And similarly, when working bottom-up, how does one choose the virtual machine functions?

2. Having carried out or proposed a partitioning, what criteria do we use to assess the quality of the resulting design as compared with all the other choices we might have made?

In subsequent sections we will discuss various approaches to these questions. First, though, we will proceed by providing some definitions and an overview of the material contained in this chapter as a whole.

7.1.2 Terminology and overview

In discussing how to proceed with a systems design, and in particular with its software aspects and components, we will make use of the terms 'module', 'methodology', 'notation', and 'support'.

In software engineering in particular we speak of partitioning into 'modules'. There is no fixed definition of a 'module'; it is a term generally taken to mean a section of program (or data structure, or both), of a small enough size and complexity that can be implemented (coded and author tested), by one person, in a matter of days or weeks. In code-size terms it may amount to a few hundred statements, or less, of source code and data description. To some extent the scope of a module is influenced by overall software size, as modules tend to be larger if they are components of large systems, and smaller if parts of a small system.

Typically, a module may implement a collection of related sub-programs, or it may encapsulate a data structure with its access routines.

A 'methodology' is a collection of procedures, rules, criteria or guidelines, which describe a way of carrying out the process of design from specification phase through to a detailed description of how the system is to be built. These guidelines, as we set them out below and elsewhere in this work, constitute a general methodology for 'good software engineering practice', including software design and construction as in the current chapter. Some methodologies set out to be more than guidelines, and purport to be generally applicable standards. As indicated elsewhere, this is not our approach in software engineering, and we tend to comment on these more under their notations (Section 7.3) than as 'methodologies'.

A 'notation' is a collection of symbols, together with diagrams or other logical descriptions as 'modules' of systems. Notations are often technology specific; for example, the agreed symbols and conventions for representing electronic circuit diagrams are of little use in drawing topographical maps. A further significant issue is that of 'support' for a specific methodology, or notation, by software tools available to the user (software engineer) as a 'programming support environment' (PSE). The existence of software tools, which will aid a software engineer in constructing, maintaining and storing documentation on a support computer, can add considerably to the acceptability of a notation. As text may, typically, be easier to handle for most support computers than diagrams, textual notations may be favoured over diagrammatic ones, irrespective of the other merits of methodologies. PSEs are discussed in Chapter 8 from the programming point of view.

A central problem which arises in discussing software design is the complexity of the interrelationship between general approaches to the issue, good design principles, the methodologies for archiving designs and the notations for recording them.

There is, in fact, a complex mapping between them. For instance one methodology (such as SADT) may use one notation throughout, whereas another may enable a design transition between two levels best described in different notations (e.g. dataflow diagrams for transform-driven design to Myers diagrams – for details of the notations see below). Furthermore, one notation may play a rôle in more than one methodology. One may attempt to categorize the subject first on either the methodology axis or the notation axis; either way round may cause comprehension difficulties on the other axis.

It may be helpful at this stage to outline the material covered in this chapter. Figure 7.1 may be regarded as a schematic representation of chapter subheadings, and is intended to show the complexity in the substructure of this subject. Material on the three issues of principles for design, general approaches, and notations is presented in that order in subsequent sections of this chapter.

The practical complexities involved in choosing methodologies and notations for software design can be formidable. The actual number and value of possible relationships in Figure 7.1 is a measure of the complexity of this subject. Our aim is to describe some 'good design principles', classes of approach to problems of decomposition, and notations. Examples of notations are taken from the FS stage and software design of the hospital alarm system defined earlier.

We have never found it helpful to classify methodologies or notations along application lines (e.g. ABC only for small DP applications; PQR for large, distributed DP applications with on-line response features; XYZ for real-time systems . . .). To us, the design process itself is enriched by selecting what seems to be best, proceeding with it so far as it produces 'enrichment' and then adopting an approach (perhaps with backtracking) as appropriate. We are aware that this view will not find favour in some quarters, where the urge is – no doubt for excellent reasons – for a prescribed way of doing design. In some cases this might be possible, depending on the job mix concerned; in other cases it is a notion that overlooks the essence of the design process – intuition.

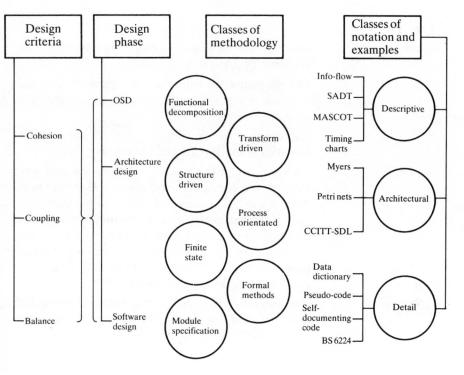

Fig. 7.1 Design criteria, approaches and methodologies.

7.1.3 Criteria for good design

The design criteria we use to help us in assessing the quality of a proposed design are consequences of the central design goal to minimize and control the complexity of the system being made. There are three particular criteria which should be used as objectives for achieving good software design:

1. Maximize the activity and strength (cohesion) within each module.
2. Minimize and simplify the interfaces (coupling) between modules.
3. Aim at a 'balanced' overall control structure.

Criteria in the first two areas, cohesion and coupling, have been proposed by Constantine and Yourdon (1979), and other authors.

Constantine proposed two scales of 'goodness' of cohesion within modules and coupling between them, and these are widely described in the subject literature on software engineering – e.g. Myers (1975) and many others. We give here a modified version of Constantine's two lists.

Cohesion

0 Coincidental: There is no meaningful relationship between the elements of a module.

1 Logical: The elements all relate to an apparent external function – e.g. we might provide, as one module, all input routines.

2 Temporal: The elements relate in time – e.g. all initialization activities could be grouped in one module.

3 Functional: All elements in the module relate to the performance of one function in the system. This expresses Parnas' (1972) principle of 'information hiding' in that, if the implementation of the function has to be changed, only one module is affected due to the deliberate design policy of localizing a particular purpose ('function') in a module, and making its data unavailable to other modules.

4 'Abstract':   The module provides all the services connected with one data structure, and hence can be regarded as an 'abstract data type' module.

Coupling

0 Direct coupled: One module directly references elements in another module, with no privacy or access controls.

1 Common coupled: Two or more modules have free access to elements in common space (cf. FORTRAN).

2 Block coupled: Inner blocks of program may refer to elements defined at higher levels in a block structure (e.g. ALGOL and Pascal).

3 Import–export coupled: Each module lists the names of elements to which it will grant external access and, conversely, names of modules to which it requires access. (Inter-module access control, by specific extension or restriction on the scope of names, is a property of some recent programming languages (e.g. Ada).)

4 Procedure coupled: All inter-module calls are phrased as procedure calls, with transmission of single element parameters only.

Clearly, the best general strategy to adopt is to aim for maximal cohesion and minimal coupling (in both cases, 4 on their value scales).

A further criterion is that of 'balance' in the calling structure of modules or programs. This is really a 'stylistic' feature in which, for

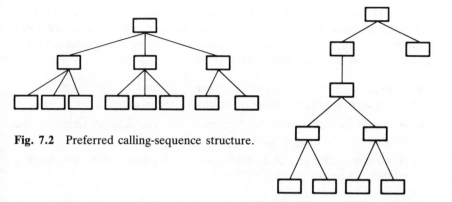

Fig. 7.2   Preferred calling-sequence structure.

Fig. 7.3   Unbalanced calling-sequence structure.

example, the calling-sequence structure depicted in Figure 7.2 is preferable to that in 7.3, all other considerations being equal.

In practice, a design process usually alternates between considering the upper levels top-down and the lower levels as virtual machines, considering at each stage the trade-off between algorithms and data structures.

However one proceeds, as the design begins to coalesce into recognizable modules the three criteria for good design prove helpful. Using them amounts to a process of 'enrichment' in design; if they are not used, then either another design step is needed, or even a backtrack in the design process to overcome the null value or even impoverishment of the design process.

7.2   Some design approaches

Figure 7.1 depicts seven approaches to design. These are defined and described below and should not be confused with methodology-based, procedural systems of one sort or another purporting to aid and support the design process, although some of these may be based on some type of design-methodology approach, in the sense that we understand the term.

Proprietary systems of these kinds are commented on, so far as relevant, together with their notation, in Section 7.3.

7.2.1   Functional decomposition

We have outlined above the general idea of hierarchical decomposition, and introduced the concepts of top-down and bottom-up design. In software engineering it is common practice to proceed with little more in the way of guidelines than those, and to select the actual partitioning into software components on the basis of practice and experience. For example, in designing a compiler program, experience suggests that a good top-level decomposition consists of:

- A lexical phase to analyse the input text into tokens, each one of which represents one linguistic unit, such as an identifier or operator.
- A syntax analysis phase to determine the syntactic structure of the program, producing a 'syntax tree' as output.
- A semantic analysis and code generation phase which produces a module of object program.

Meanwhile, we can establish by bottom-up thinking a collection of useful general functions, e.g. to manipulate a dictionary table of program identifiers and to process syntax trees, and so on; this will be a first level of 'abstract' (or virtual) machine.

The analysis can then proceed to greater detail, both top-down and bottom-up, with the choice of partitioning determined at each stage essentially by the experience of having done it (rightly or wrongly) before, or having spoken to someone else who has done it, read a book on it, attended a course of lectures on the subject, or something of the sort.

This approach is generally described as 'functional decomposition', which means decomposition directly into components implementing required functions in the system. Partitioning choices are derived from those features and functions of the FS visualized by the user, and then modified and further partitioned on the basis of experience. It is a technique widely used in familiar fields, but much less useful on a new problem or with inexperienced staff.

An alternative to functional decomposition in design is an approach known as 'object-orientated' classification of the solution system under consideration. This approach, being rather recent, is currently of somewhat limited (but growing) application, and some of the claims made for it need a more complete demonstration. It is, nonetheless, very probably to be evolved and adopted on a wide scale compared with other useful approaches to design.

Object classification within 'object-orientated design' embodies Parnas' principle of information hiding. This has already been referred to (Section 7.1.1) as being of particular importance for good design at the module/program design level when the complex admixtures of data structure and algorithms are being defined in a way suitable for implementation. The application of information hiding at higher levels of the design process (starting at architectural design level) is accompanied, in object-orientated design, by the use of abstract data types and careful use of structured natural language.

In one strategy (detailed in Sommerville, 1985) a very high-level solution description to the FS requirements is developed in natural language first – basically a statement of approach to the solution in which requirements and technical means and methods may be admixed. Then a set of abstract data types is defined using the noun occurrences in this textual description as the means of classification. The verb and adverb structure is then used as the basis to define operators (on the 'objects' expressed as abstract data types), and attributes of objects. These are then related as sets of objects, operators and attributes.

At this stage a depiction of the structure can be drawn, using a simple 'bubble and arrow' convention to relate objects and operators, the latter being seen as the basis for defining message passing within the system.

There are still many open questions in the approach of object orientated design, such as how really distinct it is from other existing approaches (e.g. entity relationship at the higher, systems analysis stage), how useful it is for large and complex systems incorporating concurrency, and whether it has adequate graphical notations (as distinct from textual ones plus bubble and arrow diagrams).

Nonetheless its advantages, as it develops, will include a useful correspondence between design/implementation structure and the structure of the requirements, and that will be of advantage for systems maintenance. At the present time, its advocates are principally workers in the area of Ada language/PSE developments, and those in a research field concerning possible applications of an object-oriented paradigm (derived from Simula-67) at the programming level, where the language Smalltalk is an instance (see McDermid, 1985).

7.2.2 Transform-driven design

This is perhaps the most well-established and most widely used approach in 'classical' (i.e. Epoch 2 onwards) data-processing environments. It has been developed by many authors, amongst the most widely read of which are Constantine and Yourdon (1979), Myers (1975) and Yourdon (1979).

The approach starts from an information-flow analysis of the problem, so as to establish the flow of data and the 'transforms' or 'processes' which take place on the data. This is shown as one or more data-flow diagrams of which we show examples in Section 7.3. The transition to a structure of modules is then performed by determining the 'central transform' – that is, the transform or process whose input data are in their most abstract and remote form from the original raw inputs and, similarly, where the output produced is the most abstract manifestation of the eventual delivered outputs.

The first stage in partitioning the module structure is essentially obtained by 'picking up' the data-flow graph at the central transform, and establishing a three-module partitioning into what are called 'afferent' (i.e. input-related), central-transform, and 'efferent' (i.e. output-related) partitions. This process of partitioning into input, transform and output modules is then repeated recursively on each component until a level of partitioning is reached which is judged sufficient. The eventual result will be a program structure chart in, for example, the notation recommended by Myers (1975) amongst others.

The process is relatively simple and reasonably consistent, in that different designers are likely to produce similar designs for the same problem. It is at its best in logically simple cases, where the input/transform/output model is a reasonably good approximation to the actual problem structure.

7.2.3 Structure-driven design

This is an alternative approach developed by Jackson and Warnier. The basis is to establish as an early design activity the data structure by which the system communicates with the real world. These structures model the entities in the part of the world which is embodied in the system.

Paraphrasing Jackson's words, the approach is to make the entities in the public domain determine the matching data structures in the program. These data structures then determine the program structures which build and manipulate them. Thus sequences, repeats or alternatives in the data description lead directly to corresponding sequences, loops or choice statements in the code.

The method ensures a close relationship between the problem structures and the system structure, and so is particularly helpful in producing readily modifiable systems. When the environment changes in some detailed area, that change should only affect the corresponding program structures, and should not have a wider impact. Recently Jackson (1983) has proposed a composite methodology called Jackson System Development/Jackson Structured Programming (JSD/JSP) for casting an entity relationship model of requirements into executable programs, by a series of steps in definition followed by a 'semi-mechanical' process of code generation. These steps have been already defined (after Birrell and Ould, 1985) in Section 4.3, and the simple notation for depicting the models is commented on further in Section 7.3.3.

This approach has found widespread favour in the area of business data processing, where such a method is most appropriate for data-flow and transformation types of application.

7.2.4 Process-orientated design

The design of concurrent systems is a particularly difficult and developing area where useful guidelines are hard to find. Of various possible lines to follow, that of top-down process analysis is possibly the one in most widespread use. This approach is described in Allworth (1981) and we give a short summary of its main points below.

Top-down process analysis begins by partitioning the system into modules, on the basis that each represents a function that can usefully be performed independently in time from others. We term such a function a 'process' and, therefore, this decomposition of the system is said to comprise a network of such processes operating independently in time (possibly concurrently).

Such processes will, of course, communicate and it is convenient to postulate two ways in which they may do so:

1. Directly, by transmission of messages that represent transitory data.
2. By reference to more permanent collections of data (called 'pools' in the MASCOT notation – see Section 7.3), where indirect communication results from access to the pool by more than one process.

When synchronization is required between processes, it can be achieved by the use of messages. Locking mechanisms are assumed on the pools to avoid access conflicts from concurrent processes. Such a system may be visualized, in current hardware terms, as ideally implemented on a network of micros, one per process, with communications lines and with some multi-accessible stores or data.

The outcome from a top-down, process-orientated analysis is generally (a) a description of the processes, (b) a description of the pools of system-wide and persistent data, and (c) descriptions of the inter-process interfaces such as a network diagram of processes, channels, and pool accesses.

Whilst this general approach has much to commend it, there are three areas of conspicuous difficulty in concurrent systems design. These can be conveniently formulated as key questions thus:

1. How to treat problems where processes have different priorities?
2. How to avoid deadlocks between communicating processes?
3. How to achieve safe and consistent use of shared data pools?

Question 1 can be handled as being the responsibility of implementation. It will help to construct a timing diagram of the entire system, on which one can indicate real-time stimuli, their frequency and interconnected pattern relationships, and the time limits on required responses. An example of a timing-diagram notation is shown in Section 7.3.

In an ideal situation, each real-time signal could be handled by one process on a fast enough processor. In practice, it is more probable that processes will be packaged into fewer processors (in the limit only one), and will be run in quasi-concurrency by a real-time operating system which will provide priority levels and interrupt handling.

The classical design approach is to establish a mapping of processes to interrupt levels such that, given maximal stimulus rate, all processes can complete their responses within the allowed times. In situations of high demand on minimally sized hardware (e.g. in constrained military applications), this requirement will determine the partitioning.

It is worth noting that, within each process, interrupts are 'transparent' – i.e. if this process is interrupted by one of a higher priority, the operating system guarantees no visible effect except a reduction in real speed. However, concealed effects arise if data are shared between processes on different priority levels and – in such cases – lock-out protection schemes may be required.

Question 2, the avoidance of deadlocks, has been of central interest to computer scientists for many years. A basic concept, that of a semaphore introduced by Dijkstra some twenty years ago, has been much used in the study of deadlock strategies. Semaphores are non-interruptable signalling devices to regulate inter-process communication, and the reader will find a good account of current work in this area in Ben Ari (1982). In summary, apart from its being created, set and abolished, a semaphore is a data item that can be in one of two states: the 'wait' or P state (sometimes referred to as the 'down' state), and the 'signal' or V state (sometimes known as the 'up' state). The values of the data it uses are such that they can never be negative. In the V state it is increased by one and indicates that the resource to which it refers is now accessible; conversely in the P state it is reduced by one and indicates that the resource is in use.

It is a quite widespread misapprehension that the use of semaphores at the implementation level avoids deadlocks, or other conditions of this type. In an incorrectly designed or implemented system, deadlocks are signified as a result of the use of semaphores. Figure 7.4 represents a simple case of deadlock in which processes A and B operating concurrently and requiring both of two resources in the order P, Q and Q, P respectively have each acquired the first of these.

A generally useful way to check the design of a concurrent system is based on Petri nets. The reader will find an account of this technique in Birrell and Ould (1985) and the notation is described in Section 7.3.

Deadlocks, and their special cases of 'deadly embrace' (or unproductive looping) and inaccessible topography, can often be detected quite straightforwardly for small concurrent systems by using Petri nets. It can be of formidable complexity for larger problems, and the matter becomes one of simulating the Petri net and exploring its behaviour.

Question 3 (how to achieve safe use of shared data) is particularly difficult in the case of distributed multiprocessor systems, where strategies may have to be devised to update data whilst avoiding inconsistent system states, and despite the risk of communication failure between components

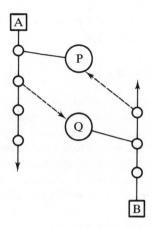

Fig. 7.4   Contention for resources: deadlock.

of the system. Such strategies may work in two phases: firstly to signal that a change is to be made to users of the data, and secondly to complete the update and restore access. The problem, and methods to deal with it, are further discussed in Ullman (1982).

Once the system design has proceeded to the state where a set of concurrent processes is described, further work can proceed on the design of each process – viewed as a single program – by any of the approaches described for ordinary processes, e.g. by functional decomposition into smaller modules as appropriate. The fact remains, as we said at the start, that the area of concurrent systems design offers little in the matter of guidelines on how to proceed, other than with extreme care.

7.2.5   Finite-state transition design

For some systems, such as interactive menu-driven systems or message-processing systems as in the case of telephony, the concept of the finite-state machine provides an appropriate and helpful way to model the system. The basic idea is that the system is regarded as being able to exist in any one of a number of states where it waits for the receipt of input messages. On receiving a message, the system performs a series of actions – typically, it runs a sequential program on conclusion of which control is transferred to the same or another waiting state.

In a menu-driven system, each menu constitutes a 'state' in which certain commands are valid, i.e. they represent messages which can be sent in this state. Each command level leads to a sequence of actions terminated by a return to the 'wait' state with a menu.

Finite-state transition design can be applied both at the system level (as for the examples cited), and at more detailed design level, as in the case of describing the behaviour of a process in a multi-process orientated system as discussed in Section 7.2.4.

7.2.6   Design by formal methods

Much current work in computer science is concerned with the search for methods of 'proving the correctness' of programs. The most promising approach seems to be to establish the proof constructively; that is, to develop the proof whilst the implementation is proceeding as a parallel activity. The starting-point is a 'formal specification' stated in a formal (or 'abstract' or 'mathematically rigorous') language, which is either predicate calculus or some close derivative of it. This is a formal statement of the desired result, or postcondition, for the program.

Implementation steps are regarded as predicate transforms under sets of pre- and postconditions and the design task, and the proof consists of developing a series of steps for each of which the precondition is the postcondition of the previous step, such that the final step yields (by correctness preservation) the required result.

We regard this work as of little real application in software engineering at the present time, for the following reasons:

1. It is exceedingly time consuming and difficult to perform for other than small problems, and requires a very high level of staff training, making it economically viable only in rare and extreme cases such as (perhaps) the critical routines in larger systems.

2. As observed elsewhere, a 'formal specification' done in predicate calculus, or a variant of it, will almost certainly be totally opaque to the real user, and will so fail in its primary purpose – to establish and record mutual agreement on the systems requirement. Some current research work seeks to minimize this problem (e.g. the PSE development endeavours based on formal techniques, such as the 'meta-IPSE' project 'ASPECT' in the UK).

3. Any mathematical proof method, other than at a trivial level, is a process that is, itself, liable to error and as such cannot in any absolute sense guarantee ultimate 'correctness'.

4. The primary purpose (correctness preservation and, ultimately, program proof), may require a 'language' that is not 'enriching' in the design sense. Thus the approach may only be effective, given other factors, after design.

We therefore take the view, as expressed elsewhere in this work, that formal correctness proofs of programs are at present an interesting research area, with limited current application in software engineering. As formal methods become more developed, however, we would expect their use to be of increasing importance in future years, especially for systems where high reliability is a critical requirement. First, though, the objections listed above (not least that in 4 as concerns this section) must be overcome.

Another class of formal methods, those concerning machine-executable formulations not primarily for program proving, are of possibly even greater interest. Fast prototyping methods for the FS stage have already been commented on elsewhere in this text, and the point has been made that these may not be cast into programs for substantive release versions without running the risks associated with omitting (or under-emphasizing) the design stage. Machine-executable formulations in specifically design-orientated notations (such as an implemented MASCOT within a PSE) are not, in our view, 'formal' methods; they are highly useful in some design circumstances and are commented on under their notations in Section 7.3.

7.2.7 Module specification

The output from final stages of a software design is, in general terms:

1. A description of the system structure as a network of control and data relationships between the components.
2. For each component a description of the function it performs within the system.
3. For each component a detailed description of all its interfaces.

If we now concentrate on the software aspects we expect, in effect, to see FS-like descriptions of each module specification, and its interfaces, as a final product of the software design. The module specification represents an important link between the teamwork on the software design and the individual work on module implementation.

The definition of a 'module' is naturally rather imprecise and has already been mentioned above. It may encapsulate code, or data, or both. In size terms it may be anything from 50 to 500 source-code statements though, as a design principle, overall complexity is less if module size is smaller (see the theoretical work of McCabe as quoted in Chapter 5).

In some situations one must distinguish between 'design modules' in the sense intended here, and 'load modules' which are sets of programs packaged together for implementation convenience (such as the subset of a system resident and operational in a computer at any one time).

A large system may amount to hundreds of modules. At the other extreme, such as a small system carrying out a limited set of functions on a 2 kbyte microcomputer, the single module may be the entire system (and this may be represented also in the OSD as a single-item taxonomy). What is said here, and below, about modules applies as much to such single, small programs as it does to their combination into larger systems, and these guidelines are as much for the authors of small systems as for software teams making extensive software systems.

The notations appropriate for representing module level design are dealt with below.

7.3   Design practices and notations

As the reader will now be aware, and as we pointed out earlier, design is a highly multivariate subject. There are no clear and watertight rules or methods leading inevitably to the required outcome. We have identified the principles and criteria for good design at low levels in the process and the approaches to design that are appropriate for some types of application and at some stages of the design. We now go on to describe some of the better-known practical methods (methodologies/notations) indicating so far as possible what their particular merits are and in what circumstances, application-type/design level, they may best be considered for use. The notations are illustrated by examples from the hospital monitoring system, depicting at the same time some of the approaches listed above, e.g. transform-driven (Dataflow/Myers, SADT) and process-orientated decomposition (MASCOT, CCITT-SDL). Other notations are described (e.g. Petri nets) and one, BS 6224 DSD, shows a low-level program design for the hospital system.

First we find it helpful to make some rather loose and overlapping distinctions into three kinds of notation:

- Descriptive
- Architectural
- Detail

In Figure 7.1, and in the following section, notations are loosely categorized as follows:

Descriptive: Information flow; SADT; MASCOT; Timing charts.

Architectural: Myers; Petri nets; CCITT-SDL.

Detail: Data dictionary; Pseudocode; Self documenting code; Graphical notations (e.g. BS 6224).

Furthermore, we associate these categories (again only loosely) with lifecycle activities including the different stages of design, thus:

Descriptive: Specification/OSD; Topmost level of Architectural design.

Architectural: Architectural design/Higher levels of detailed software design.

Detail: Lower levels of software design/Module level design.

The reader must be very careful not to impute to this approach too much in the way of 'system' or 'method' for design. The classifications are intended to be guidelines only as to what is likely to be of use at the different stages of design. The choice of the most useful notation depends largely on the application type, size and complexity. For instance, for some applications MASCOT would appear at Architectural and Detail level also, and SDL might appear as both a descriptive and detail notation.

Some authors of notations and their 'methodologies' (i.e. procedures for standard practice), assert the view that a single, prescriptive method/notation is possible in all instances and for all lifecycle stages. Our own experiences indicate otherwise, and we submit the following as guidelines only. The reader will find a 'best mix' of these approaches for the particular circumstances of an application.

7.3.1 Notations and design phases

Notations which we would characterize as 'descriptive' are used for illustrative diagrams describing, for example, information flow or process relationship. Such diagrams are probably understandable to the user and may appear in the dialogue phase of establishing the FS. They may well also be used in the OSD. This is all as set out in Chapter 4.

Other notations are more directly applicable to the architectural representation of, for example, the control structure within a system or of intermodule interface specifications. Such notations are more used within the system designer's area of activity; they describe the 'how' of the system rather than the 'what' of the requirement; they are not likely to be readily understandable to the non-expert user (or manager – this is, in fact, 'crossing the line' as referred to elsewhere).

These notations, such as 'calling-structure' diagrams as depicted below, are likely to be used in the architectural design and in the upper levels of detailed software design.

Yet other notations are suitable for detail description of the software design at the module or program level. Historically, this was done by flowcharts (a most abused and, in fact, somewhat wrongly maligned approach). Later came the structured flowcharts notion and the works of Nassi and Schneiderman, and others.

Nowadays, as well as flowcharts (still!) and N–S diagrams, low-level software designs are often done in Pseudocode and the British Standard Design Structure Diagrams notation, both of which are described below.

We have used above, and also naturally elsewhere, the terms Outline Systems Design, Architectural Design, and (Detailed) Software Design. The OSD represents the first attempts to construct a notional 'design', for feasibility and estimating purposes only, by hierarchical decomposition into taxonomical diagrams and component lists. The OSD is produced in parallel with the FS, and depends entirely upon its contents (unless it contains 'given' or 'inherited' solution components, in which case the OSD bears on the FS rather as a constraint).

The design proper of the system-to-be is then undertaken on the basis of the agreed (signed-off) FS, and begins by transforming (and maybe amending) the components lists and taxonomies of the OSD into a first approximation to the real architectural structure of a system, with its major parts and subsystems.

In general, the architectural design is the central activity of the development team as a whole, involving all disciplines and technologies apposite to the implementation. In particular, if the system is to contain software, it will be disastrous to omit the software engineers from the architectural design phase.

The notations used in this phase are 'architectural'. In the upper levels, block diagrams of subsystems and their interface specifications appear, together with diagrams in notations appropriate to the range of disciplines involved – blueprints, circuit diagrams, etc. The architectural design phase is likely to include the upper levels of the software design, based for instance on 'information flow analysis' of the requirements. In simple cases it may be possible to treat the software as one component only, and one can then possibly speak of 'the hardware/software interface (HSI)' – the notion referred to in Section 6.4 as a hazardous outcome of imbalanced technologies. For most cases, the premature determination of HSI in the architectural design represents an incorrect oversimplification of the situation. A system of more than trivial size containing software usually has several software components and subsystems; indeed the software content is often the dominant constituent and its interaction with hardware is highly complex. The best course of action is not to conceal this fact behind an artificially constructed HSI but to decompose the system properly to meet the design criteria. In ideal circumstances one can use this functional decomposition to decide hardware and software subsystems on cost and performance criteria.

In very many large and medium-sized systems, software is the dominant technology at the system level. The user interface in such systems is software driven, and so the majority of features and functions seen by the user are provided ('delivered') by the software. It may be appropriate in such cases to see the architectural design as being the upper levels of the software design, with hardware components entering at a lower level and providing services to the software. We note that this is not a point of view readily accepted by hardware (electronic) engineers.

As we move into software design both at architectural and software design stages, and as we move down the steps of detailed design whatever these comprise in a given case, the 'visibility' of the design becomes an increasingly severe problem. Elsewhere, we have commented on 'invisibility' (e.g. for users and managers) being synonymous with 'incomprehensibility'. Now we have another concern, that of evident relationship or 'mapping'. At lower levels of software design we are dealing with software structures – both algorithms and data – that we can only represent statically. It is very hard, given such a description, really to foresee what the program will do as it functions over time. The dynamic nature of software behaviour is a central cause of difficulties in software engineering. Eventual products of the architectural and software design phases are diagrams describing the proposed structure. For the software components these are calling-structure diagrams of modules, and module interface and function descriptions.

In the case of many simple systems, the eventual components visible in the design (or the description of how the system works), has a clear one-to-one relationship or 'mapping' with the features and functions described in the FS; in other words each specific user feature (or function) is implemented by a specific (software) system component. This may well be the case in, for example, a transform-orientated data-processing system, where each data transformation required is recognizably carried out by a specific hardware or software component.

In some places it is relatively common practice, especially concerning cases such as the one just cited, to confuse the concepts of specification and design in the following way. The FS gets partitioned into 'component design specifications' or 'mini-specifications'. Each of these contains, in effect, the FS content relevant to the function performed by this component, together with the specification of the interfaces to other components and with some level of detail of the component design.

This procedure is often justified on the grounds that it provides an effective and simple way of partitioning the entire specification and design activity, and gives good control of resulting documentation. We have already warned against this simplistic notion in Chapter 4. In some specific cases of small and exceedingly straightforward systems, the approach may turn out all right, but in general we must advise strongly against it.

In most systems the mapping from functionality to design is exceedingly complex, and an assumption of the mini-specification approach has major disadvantages. For example, it assumes aspects of design that should be specific, and it conceals the fact that major decisions underlying the partitioning have been made from, perhaps, false design premises. As a result the perspective of good systems structure may be entirely lost. Each 'mini-spec' becomes a substantial subset of both FS and design information, much of which is repeated in other 'component design specifications'. Control is lost and the consequences of specification or design changes become very difficult to trace.

For larger systems another problem arises. In such cases, it may be necessary to undertake an overall specification and design activity intended specifically to break down the system-to-be into major sub-systems, each of manageable size. For these very large systems there may be multiple levels of architectural design. The mapping of 'visibility' will remain, however, and should not be 'solved' by the sort of artificial partitioning referred to.

The best way to demonstrate this problem of visibility is by trying to generate a design upwards out of code – effectively going up the design steps instead of down. As every software engineer knows, this is at best difficult to do, and often downright impossible. The transformations at each step (down) involve more conceptual design than is immediately evident through the notational representation.

In the general case, the bottom level (module designs) are not mappable with the FS, although they will achieve its features and functions.

The use of notations in the various steps of design may help or hinder the design process, and may or may not assist in the issue of 'visibility' or mapping. An essential consideration – that of software modification – will require that the design is visible. Equally, the requirements of a complex application may require that design is done at any step in the notation most suitable for enriching that step of the process. With these considerations in mind we submit the following notes on some of the design notations in widespread use at the present time. This is not by any means a complete list, nor is it a prescription. Our own view is that notations are like engineers' tools – to be used as and when appropriate, by software engineers skilled in their use.

7.3.2 Descriptive notations

In this section we describe the following:

- Information flow diagrams
- SADT
- MASCOT
- Timing charts

(A) Information flow diagrams

These, or 'data-flow diagrams' as they are sometimes called, are typically used as the first illustrations of a system as the notation is particularly intuitively simple and relatively informal. They may be used for description in the OSD phase, text embellishment in the FS (so long as it is clearly designated such), or for some applications further on in the architectural design and detailed software design stages if the approach is particularly suitable. The method has been widely used for many years and is associated with the work of DeMarco, Yourdon and some others.

Data-flow diagrams are used as the starting-point in transform-driven designs, and the symbols used in the original notation, and their simple rules of use, are set out in Figure 7.5. (The symbols and rules of usage of a notation are simple forms of vocabulary and grammar of a language.)

It is important in this or any other notation to make a meaningful choice of names. Function names are often best in imperative–verb–predicate form. In other words, say what is done to what. Data flows and stores have brief, descriptive names and these should be amplified by full descriptions in the data dictionary (see Section 7.3.4 (H)). Names such as 'FRED' do not add clarity to a program despite their widespread and historical usage. A data-flow diagram makes no presumptions as to time – the functions may be regarded as all working together, or some of them may, or none of them; the diagram gives no indication. They have been used in relatively straightforward data-processing work for many years now. They are of use at the FS stage, as the 'plus' of 'natural language +', and for relatively simple systems at the logical level such a diagram may well be a sufficient architectural description. The detailed design may be, in effect, the data dictionary to describe data, together with the process internal designs in, say, pseudocode (q.v.).

Figure 7.6 depicts a data-flow diagram for the hospital patient-monitoring system as previously described. The reader may note, in this and other examples in this chapter, that design diagrams concern an interrupt system and not – as in the FS – a polling system. Either the FS has changed for some reason, or these are OSD 'ideas' (feasibility) diagrams.

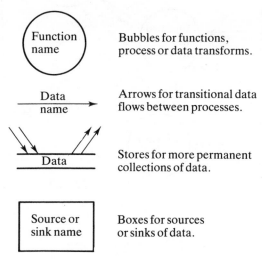

Fig. 7.5 Dataflow notation.

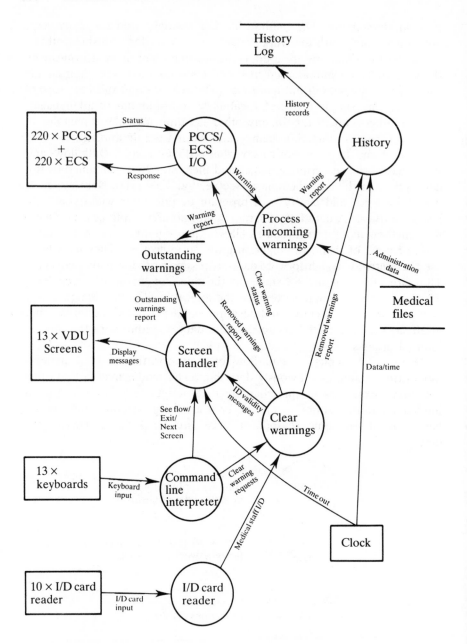

Fig. 7.6 Dataflow example.

(B) Systems analysis and design technique (SADT)

The SADT methodology and notation was published some years ago by D.T. Ross as an approach to preparing 'engineering blueprints' of systems. There is a strong and detailed methodology for the SADT approach emphasizing an author–reviewer–reader cycle for producing diagrams and establishing the importance of the viewpoint or viewpoints adopted. The notation consists of dual forms known as actigrams and datagrams. Here we briefly summarize the datagram use of the notation, which is used quite widely, and without the full 'methodology' (procedures, etc. in the full SADT), as a slightly more formal way of drawing data-flow diagrams. Figure 7.7 depicts the notation as based on boxes used in a stylized format.

The typical SADT diagram normally consists of about seven such boxes with interconnections on a single page. Diagrams tend to start at the upper left of a page and proceed diagonally across and downwards to the right. The notation is hierarchical in that any box may be expanded, with matching interconnections and decimal numbering, into a further diagram. The notation essentially provides a rather weak syntax for stylized data flow; the problem with constructing an SADT picture is in expressing the semantics of the problem. The names on the data flows and the actions in the boxes are the user's problem, and the SADT methodology is intended to help in the systems analysis. As with data flow, SADT has nothing to say about time dependence and does not help for real-time systems design.

The SADT approach is claimed to be applicable throughout the design process down to fine levels of design detail, presuming a rather strict top-down approach. We think this is too wide a claim and find SADT useful primarily at the URS stage for systems analysis ideas, and FS/OSD for top-level representation of information flow over features and functions in the requirement.

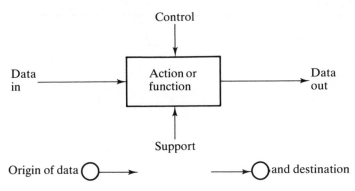

Fig. 7.7   SADT (Datagram) notation.

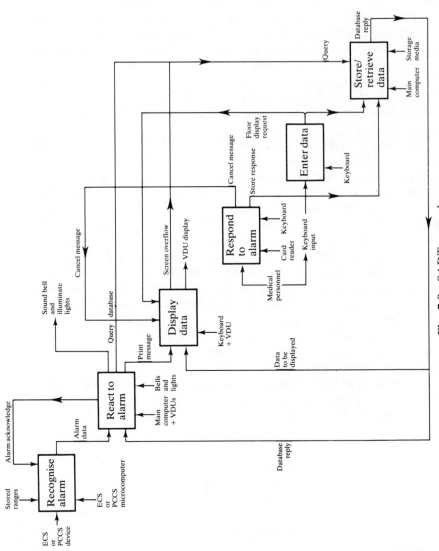

Fig. 7.8 SADT example.

The method has been published quite widely and so SADT diagrams are useful for communication purposes. Many engineers, electronic and mechanical, find the SADT notation a 'friendly' one, as its depictions of requirements look a bit like circuit diagrams. As to support tools, the notation's detailed features has in the past posed some difficulty to its being supported on computer graphics configurations, though some proprietary systems supporting SADT now exist and are in use.

Figure 7.8 shows a depiction in SADT of the hospital alarm system requirements, as may be found in the FS.

(C) MASCOT

This was produced by the Royal Signals Research Establishment in the United Kingdom as a software production system, with graphical and textual design notations and with strong software tools support, for the design and implementation of real-time systems – in particular for military use.

The method starts with a process-orientated analysis of the system. This is represented by what is called an 'activity–channel–pool', or ACP diagram. The symbols used in an ACP diagram are depicted in Figure 7.9.

A channel models message transmission between concurrent processes, but at the ACP diagram level detail as to message format or queuing is not shown. A pool models a store of non-transient data. It is assumed that access conflict is prevented by suitable access-control mechanisms.

The method gives some quasi-hierarchical ability to partition the system, and subsystem boundaries are shown by dotted lines connecting the channels bounding the subsystem.

As an example of the use of MASCOT, Figure 7.10 shows the previously quoted hospital alarm system as an ACP diagram at the level of FS/OSD.

The MASCOT system offers support all the way to on-line testing and reconfiguration, and provides most helpful facilities at all stages. The system is, however, not cheap to re-implement for a new host or target and, short of its availability as fully implemented, its notation is mainly of use at the FS/OSD and top level of architectural design stages.

At first glance there is considerable similarity between a data-flow

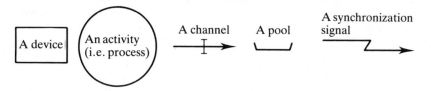

Fig. 7.9   MASCOT ACP notation.

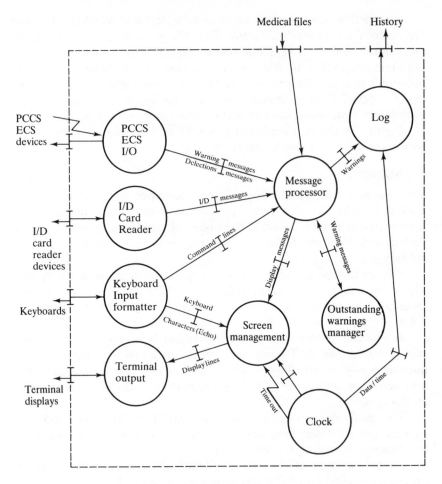

Fig. 7.10 MASCOT example.

diagram and an ACP diagram. The essential difference is that ACP bubbles express activities that may run concurrently in time, whereas a data-flow picture says nothing of concurrency. Thus, data-flow and MASCOT-ACP pictures of the same system may look much the same but be conveying quite different aspects of a part of the design. We return to discuss this in Section 7.3.5, where the subject of combined notations is dealt with.

(D) Systems timing diagrams

Systems containing time dependency require that fact to be manifest in the FS, with as much detail as possible defining the requirements. Similarly, the feasibility of an implementation requires the OSD to

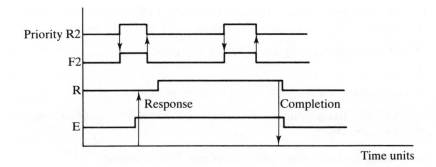

Fig. 7.11   Timing chart example.

contain and consider these timing requirements lest the system-to-be is undertaken at too great a risk of failure.

The usual practice in representing time dependency is to adopt a diagrammatic representation; that is the convention for timing diagrams in electronics. Figure 7.11 depicts this convention, showing a time axis travelling from left to right, with state changes or response periods shown by level changes and events marked by cross lines or arrows. The vertical axis is often used to indicate priority – the highest-priority activities being shown as the topmost timing lines in the diagram.

7.3.3   Architectural notations

It is worth noting as a revision point at this stage that the notations so far described (information or data-flow, SADT, MASCOT-ACP and timing diagrams) are all examples – widely used ones at that – of descriptive notations. Their use is, in our view, primarily as descriptive notations, as the two with purportedly strong 'methodologies' (SADT and MASCOT) have some disadvantages for use throughout the lifecycle.

They are all potentially helpful in the early stages of the lifecycle and may well appear in the FS (to clarify meaning) and OSD (as requirements and quasi-systems 'design' diagrams). These representations may appear (and be rapidly amended in many cases) as the top-level architectural design document. The choice of which descriptive notation to use will be based on experience, personal predilection, and the characteristics of the requirement. There is no universal 'best' notation at this (or any other) level, and it is a mistake to spend too much time on choosing a notation; it is better to get on and use a notation of some sort. Literally, any notation is probably better than none at all, although one can find oneself in a notation that is unhelpful at times. In that case, backtrack.

The notations we next describe are more useful at the architectural design stage of the lifecycle and the top level of detailed software design.

They describe system and software construction rather than functionality, and the following three, in quite widespread use, are of this type:

- Calling-structure diagrams (Myers notation)
- Petri nets
- State-transition diagrams (CCITT-SDL notation)

We continue the alphabetic sequencing of notations as begun in the previous subsection.

(E) Calling-structure diagrams (Myers and JSD notations)

This notation for showing the calling structure of a software system has been used in various forms for many years. We illustrate the variant described by Myers (1975) in summary form, as for previously cited notations. The symbols used are as shown in Figure 7.12.

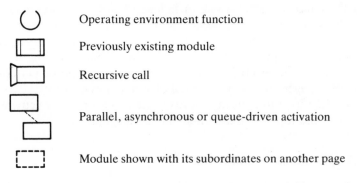

Fig. 7.12   Myers dataflow notation.

A typical usage of these symbols might be as shown in Figure 7.13. The notation shows the control structure of one sequential program. It may be used at the software design level to show module interconnections or at a more detailed level to show subroutine structure within a module.

Data transfer is shown either by numbered reference to a table, as in Figure 7.13, or as simply depicted in Figure 7.14. A characteristic feature of such diagrams is that the lower levels tend to be shown as a nest of connections to frequently called service routines, as illustrated in Figure 7.15. When this occurs it is an indication that design might be better represented as an abstract or virtual machine at the lower levels.

In the Myers notation as depicted in Figure 7.12, the dotted-line box is provided to allow some degree of hierarchical programming. On the other hand, the Myers notation provides an inadequate, almost non-existent means of showing concurrent operations and we recommend that the notation is used, therefore, exclusively for sequential programs. These may well themselves be components of larger systems with

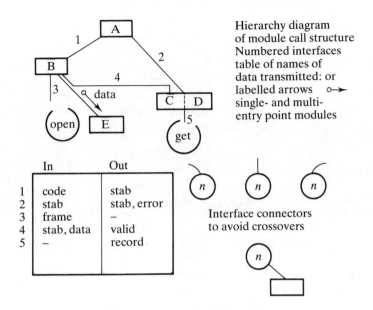

Hierarchy diagram
of module call structure
Numbered interfaces
table of names of
data transmitted: or
labelled arrows ○─►
single- and multi-
entry point modules

	In	Out
1	code	stab
2	stab	stab, error
3	frame	–
4	stab, data	valid
5	–	record

Interface connectors
to avoid crossovers

Fig. 7.13   Myers notation example.

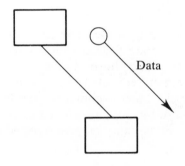

Data

Fig. 7.14   Dataflow depiction in Myers notation.

concurrent aspects – in which case the upper levels will be shown in a more appropriate notation, such as MASCOT (ACP) diagrams.

The method of calling-structure diagrams is generally used to display the design of a single sequential program or module. Such diagrams are usually the output of design methods such as transform analysis.

The form of calling-structure diagrams is exceedingly close to that for the Jackson JSD/JSP method referred to earlier which, for transform-driven applications of the data-processing type, can act as both a descriptive and architectural notation. Boxes contain entity descriptors and the box and line structure models the entities, their relationship, and the data flow in the system. An asterisked box means that it is an iterated

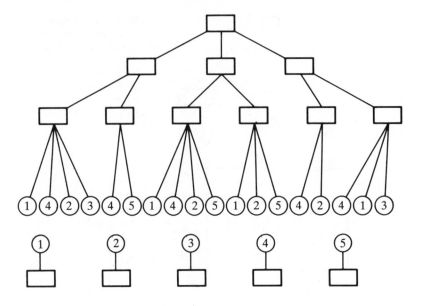

Fig. 7.15   Calling structure in Myers notation.

feature, and boxes occurring at the same level and related to the same source node (peer boxes) are flagged with a small circle if only one of them may be selected. Peer boxes lacking this flag are said to be unselected, and represent sequential parts of a system which will be executed in left-to-right order within the peer-box family. There is, therefore, an element of time ordering in a JSD representation, and the duration (or lifetime) of an entity may be signified too.

(F) Petri nets

The design of process-orientated systems with concurrent features is not a well-served area at the present time in terms of notations. Some tend to extend the use of MASCOT–ACP diagrams from specification, through architectural design into detailed software design, and find limitations in doing so – even though an implemented MASCOT at the software-development level may have many desirable features as stated already. Others tend to finite-state representations (see Section (G)) with similar results. One of the main problems is to design a multi-process system, having concurrency features, well enough to avoid the problems listed in Section 7.2.4.

A Petri net, based on original work over twenty years ago by Carl Petri, is a graphical representation of a multi-process system employing a special notation. The simple elements of this notation are defined in Figure 7.16.

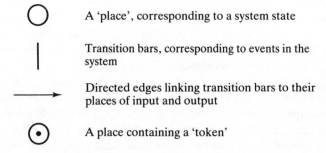

Fig. 7.16 Petrinet notation (simple 'atomic' form).

A typical Petri net is shown in Figure 7.17, and this – lacking tokens – is said to be 'unmarked'. An example of a 'marked' Petri net (i.e. containing tokens) is shown in Figure 7.18. These schematics are given, amongst many others on the subject of Petri nets, in Birrell and Ould (1985).

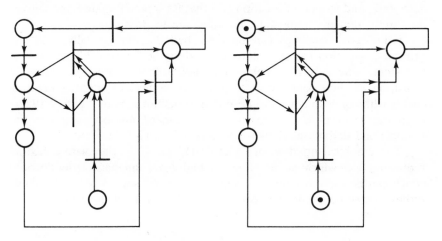

Fig. 7.17 'Unmarked' petrinet.   Fig. 7.18 'Marked' petrinet.

In this notation, a change of state is said to occur when a transition bar 'fires'. A transition fires by removing a token from its input places and putting a token into each of its output places. Places and transition bars can be connected by more than one directed edge, so firing may require the simultaneous removal/addition of several tokens as appropriate. A transition bar can only fire if all its input places contain tokens.

Petri nets are useful for high-level architectural design involving relatively few 'places' whose states may change asynchronously. At greater levels of detail the complexity of the network may increase, and the problems of analysing it rise very steeply also.

A further property of Petri nets tends to inhibit their use at lower levels of design. Whereas the notation and its rules are useful for modelling concurrent, asynchronous processes so as to determine questions of the boundedness of a system, its safeness (in terms of deadlock) and so on, the notation is not one that progresses the matter of software design as such towards the module level of specification and the code. For this reason, Petri nets are a tool at the architectural design stage for a special class of system; they may assist in design in the sense of avoiding fundamental architectural errors (see Nelson *et al.*, 1985). Rather like timing diagrams at the specification phase, their usage is quite specific and quite limited.

(G) State-transition diagrams and the CCITT-SDL notations

State-transition diagrams are based on the notion of finite-state 'machines' that comprise a set of inputs (I), a set of outputs (O), a set of states (S), a 'next state' function (F) that for a given I and S produces the next state, and an output function (G) that for a penultimate I and S gives the output that the finite-state machines are to produce.

Finite-state machines can be described diagrammatically, and the general convention has been adopted to describe the control structure of a system. There is no single, generally accepted notation for state transition at the system level. Most often states are simply drawn as circles with connecting arcs representing transitions, as in Figure 7.19. At a greater level of detail, the CCITT standard notation contains the symbols and definitions shown in Figure 7.20 and Table 7.1.

The graphical notation of CCITT-SDL goes together with a textual representation which is, in effect, a high-level language (pseudocode) which can be used as input to a support software system for SDL. Thus, rather like some versions of MASCOT, SDL is 'implemented' down to

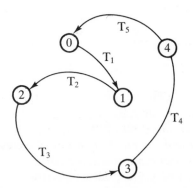

Fig. 7.19 State transition.

code level. The examples in Figures 7.21 and 7.22 show a detail of the process from the hospital alarm-monitoring system. Once again individual preference will play a part in determining the usefulness of SDL, but software engineers will find that it 'enriches' many design processes.

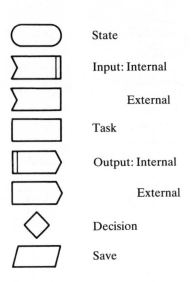

State

Input: Internal

External

Task

Output: Internal

External

Decision

Save

Fig. 7.20 CCITT–SDL symbols.

Table 7.1 CCITT–SDL definitions.

Term	*Definition*
Process	A serial logic function; either in a status awaiting input or in a transition.
Signal	A data flow between processes, input to one / output from another (internal if processes within the same 'function block' or module).
State	A condition of a process suspended awaiting an input signal.
Save	Postpone recognition of a signal unacceptable in current state.
Transition	A sequence of actions between states.
Output	An action within a transition which generates a signal.
Task	Any action which is neither input nor decision.
Decision	Selection of a criterion from a choice of continuation transition paths.

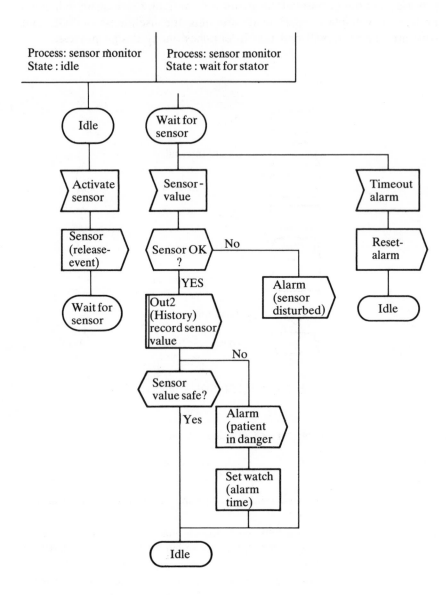

Fig. 7.21   Detail of hospital alarm-monitoring system.

7.3.4   Detail design notations

In Sections 7.3.2 and 7.3.3 we have discussed the process of descriptive formulation of requirements and that of architectural and top-level software design in which the basic structuring of the system and the software is done. The final stages of architectural design will result in module specifications taking the form, at the lowest level of detail, of 'mini-functional specifications' in that the inter-module communication inputs and outputs are described, together with the purpose of the module and the functions and features it encapsulates.

For medium-sized and large systems the 'module' definition at this stage is still at a fairly high level of design definition, comprising fairly (or very) large functional blocks, or process decompositions, or transform partitions, or whatever. Also, it should be noted that these 'mini specs' as we have called them, are in no way the same as those condemned as an approach in an earlier section; these, in the case of architectural design, having emerged from a proper – if still quite high-level – design process.

```
PROCESS SENSOR-MONITOR

STATE IDLE

INPUT ACTIVATE-SENSOR
OUTPUT SENSOR (RELEASE-EVENT)
EXIT WAIT-FOR-SENSOR

STATEND IDLE

STATE WAIT-FOR-SENSOR

INPUT SENSOR-VALUE
IF SENSOR-OK
    THEN OUTIPC OUT2 (HISTORY, RECORD-SENSOR-VALUE)
        IF SENSOR-VALUE-SAFE
            THEN
            ELSE OUTPUT ALARM (PATIENT-IN-DANGER)
                TIMESTART SET-WATCH (ALARM-TIME)
        FI
    ELSE OUTPUT ALARM (SENSOR-DISTURBED)
FI
EXIT IDLE

INPUT TIMEOUT-ALARM
OUTPUT RESET-ALARM
EXIT IDLE

STATEND WAIT-FOR-SENSOR

PROCEND SENSOR-MONITOR
```

Fig. 7.22   Detail of hospital alarm-monitoring system.

For small systems of a few hundred source statements of code only, the process has effectively terminated at the architectural design stage and the single module design (in whatever notation) is the program design.

In the more usual case, the first stage of a detailed (or within-module) design will continue to be a further hierarchical decomposition into data structures and/or program structures, such as subroutines or procedures. Generally speaking, this is done by informal functional decomposition. A set of data structures and procedures is defined so as to deliver the defined module functions.

The detail choices are much influenced by practice and experience and, at this now quite low level of design in particular, it is worth emphasizing that the process of design is largely intuitive; in their use of experience and other forms of acquired knowledge, plus such tools and notations as exist, software engineers are practising a craft. One cannot be specific as to, for example, the best trade-off between choice of data structures and choice of related algorithms; all one can say is that the two are intimately related and the choice must be made by experimentation and experience – any attempt to predetermine or to prescribe these choices puts the designer in a straitjacket and prejudices the outcome. We continue this point in Section 7.3.5.

Traditionally, the 'design' of a module of code (perhaps part of a far larger architectural design 'module') was described by comments in the code listings. Even for simple logic modules (programs) written in assembler code, this is not a satisfactory approach. For anything more complicated it is likely to be disastrous (see Chapter 9). Part of the problem is that comments on code listings tend to refer to the statements of code rather than the design notions underlying them; rather like the chess player who, after 1. e2–e4, solemnly writes down: 'White plays the king's pawn opening'.

Code should not be written before its detailed design is fully developed, and this should then be an essential level of its documentation for modifiability/maintenance purposes.

In general, the detailed design emerging at the end of the software design stage will produce a data dictionary, and a set of program-module specifications which may be in one of several 'notations'. These are described in the following subsections (H) to (K).

(H) Data dictionary

It is important to remember that, at each stage of a software design, the data structures used to model the problem domain and the functions manipulating them are considered together. Notationally, data items in the early phases are shown diagrammatically as pictures of data records and structures, probably in tabular form, and this is easier to conceptualize than the dynamic complexities of the algorithms.

It is helpful in doing the design process to build up one consistent record of data definitions and descriptions for the entire system, in the form of a 'data dictionary'. Entries are arranged systematically, for example alphabetically within a module, and some or all of the following are present:

- Name of data element, and owner of module.
- Aliases if applicable – i.e. different names in other modules.
- Related elements – abbreviations, pointers.
- Ranges and meanings of values.
- Access rights and usage information.
- Storage details.

A data structure will be described by giving its syntactic descriptions, with optional structures or variants, alternatives and iterations. The elements will then be described as above. In many systems, the physical handling of the data will be done by a Database Management System of some sort – which we treat as a part of the low-level, abstract machine. The data dictionary will then develop into a database schema acting as the interface to the 'DBMS'.

(I) Pseudocode

This approach can be summarized as the use of a programming-language statement syntax, combined with informal semantics in the language of the specific problem domain. Some attempts have been made to recommend standardized pseudocode, but in general the tendency is to use the syntax of the favourite locally supported language (and to use it rather informally at that).

The structures needed in a typical pseudocode are based on those recommended for use in 'structured programming' – that is sequence, choice and iteration, with some customary extensions. A possible set is as shown in Figure 7.23.

Yourdon (1979) recommends the use of a form of pseudocode at the architectural design stage, essentially by presenting a form of 'structured English' using a restricted grammar (as indicated above) containing only the main structured constructs, clear imperative sentences and clauses, names defined in a data dictionary, and simple verbs such as 'print', 'compute' and so on. This provides a simple but not very powerful approach and is confined in its usage to describing rather limited and straightforward systems.

A further limitation for its use, and that of pseudocode in general in the design stage and above (in lifecycle terms), is that it tends to be one-dimensional, representing things in strings of textual statements. Indenting makes the notation 'one-and-a-half-dimensional' in those terms, and

sequencing: *A;B;C*

choice: **if** *B* **then** *a* **else** *B*

                if *B* **then** *A*

                case x *of* x_1:*A*

                      x_2:*B*

                      x_3:*C*

                      else : *D*

repetition: **while** *B* **do** *A*

                repeat *A* **until** *B*

repetition

with break: **while** *b* **do**

                   A

                if *b* **then break**

                 B

                end while

Fig. 7.23 Pseudocode.

subscripting makes it multidimensional but in a very mathematical way for high-level design.

Against this must be set the great popularity of pseudocode deriving from the fact that, being textual and of the programming-language syntax, it is readily supported by software tools at the level of text editors and filing systems; furthermore, it is relatively easy to produce even more powerful tools such as syntax checkers.

At the lowest levels of software design it is no bad thing to employ pseudocode for all the good reasons given. These 'good reasons' become a very mixed blessing, however, if the notation is taken 'up' the lifecycle into higher levels of design, where its limitations soon become very apparent indeed.

(J) Self-documenting code

Pseudocode was presented above as a combination of the relatively formal use of the syntax of a structured programming language with the relatively informal, problem-orientated semantic components.

If one uses for implementation a well-structured language, of which Pascal is a widely accepted example, together with careful use of good and meaningful names and helpful layout on the page, then it may well be possible to write programs in sufficiently good style that a higher-level pseudocode representation of them would add nothing to their clarity or the ability of a person modifying/maintaining the code to understand it. It requires considerable attention to style to write code of sufficient clarity to be entirely self-documenting. Even though careful layout can help, code is essentially linear in nature and this is inevitably less rich than two-dimensional, graphical representations – at any rate to the eyes of an engineer.

A substantial advantage of self-documenting code as its own design notation is, of course, the strongest possible tool support! We recommend the greatest attention to programming style at this level, as well as the sufficiency of higher-level designs in whatever notations are deemed appropriate. Ledgard (1986) has spent much time working with the authors and his guidelines on good programming practice are most warmly recommended. We do not, however, recommend self-documenting code as the only design practice undertaken, except for a closed community of software engineers who make and maintain only relatively small systems.

(K) Graphical notations for module-level (program) designs; BS 6224 DSD

Graphical notation has been used, in the form of flowcharts, since the earliest days of Epoch 1 computing as defined elsewhere.

At the time of the great revision of ideas towards the end of Epoch 2 (circa 1965–68 or thereabouts), flowcharts fell into extreme disrepute in academic circles. It was widely supposed that flowcharts and unstructured code, 'spaghetti' stuff littered with unconditional transfer instructions such as **goto** statements, were unavoidably linked (and wicked!).

In fact, flowcharting is entirely neutral, but the older fashions did allow control of transfer without restriction to be diagrammed, if the designer so wished. Structured flowcharts, allowing only the constructs of structured programming (see Chapter 8) saw some vogue in the 1970s, as did a notation due to Nassi and Schneiderman. This latter is simply depicted in Figure 7.24 and represents linear flow in a simple sequential fashion, and tests with branches as a diagonally divided box.

This notation had, and has, some adherents whose applications are relatively small and not logically complex. Otherwise the proliferation of 'N–S' diagrams and their readability rapidly becomes problematical. However, for small and medium-sized data-processing applications N–S diagrams are useful. As with many notations at higher levels of lifecycle use, N–S diagrams lack all reference to time, concurrency, etc.

Alternative notations have been researched and developed, with the intention of combining the basic expressiveness of a flowchart with more control over the structure, and at the same time to be appropriate for process- and time-orientated applications if possible. A recent and good example is the Design Structure Diagram (DSD) notation described in British Standard No. 6224.

Control flow in DSD is described essentially as a binary tree walk; proceeding from the start symbol, control proceeds to a node and then – to explore the tree structure – the left branch of a node is explored first, followed by the right branch (with 'left' and 'right' viewed as a traveller

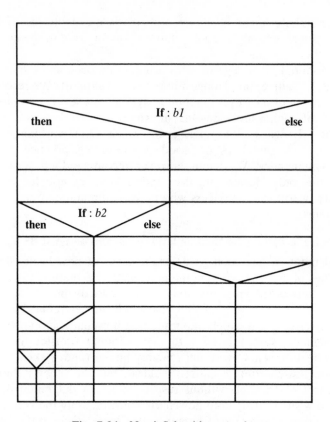

Fig. 7.24   Nassi–Schneiderman chart.

down the path from the start – the reader's view of the design will be the mirror image of this). The DSD diagram is, by convention, laid out with the main flow of control as right-hand branches (to the viewer/designer) from top to bottom of the page, and nested structures shown as left-hand branches across the page.

The notation shows some influence from the CCITT notation described above, and in particular it has symbols showing messages passing between processes as well as showing sequential logic within individual processes. Its scope is, therefore, wider than for single program modules only, and we have seen it used with effect at higher levels of software design, and even – for medium-sized systems containing concurrency – as high in the lifecycle process as architectural design.

The essential features of this useful notation are summarized in Figures 7.25–27, as well as being excellently described in the British Standards Institution's own document. Figure 7.28 gives an example (an interrupt-handler routine) from the detailed software design of the hospital system. More examples of BS 6224 at this level will be found in Chapter 11, in the example used there as a case study.

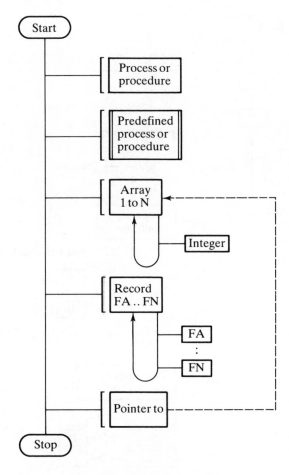

Fig. 7.25 BS 6224 definition.

7.3.5 Mixed notations

The area of notations for software design is not conspicuous for its adherence to standards. In this respect it resembles the field of musical composition before, say, 1800.

Some notations such as Myers' version of dataflow and SADT have achieved a certain degree of consistency in use, but the general practice is for notations to be used rather freely and with local variants. We see nothing against this state of affairs – indeed in such an early stage of the development of software engineering it seems quite natural. Others may disagree, but we would point out that those authors claiming universality for their methodologies have yet to make their point to the level of a fully

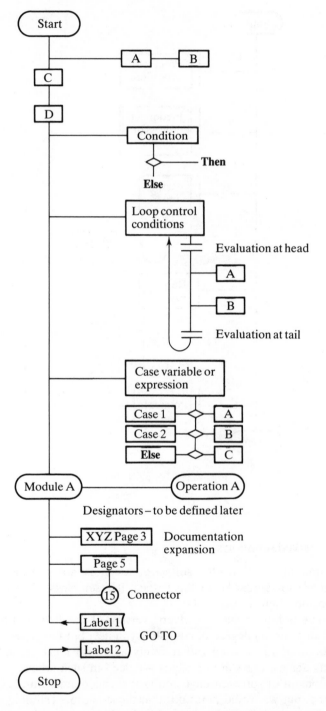

Fig. 7.26 BS 6224 definition: sequential control flowchart symbols.

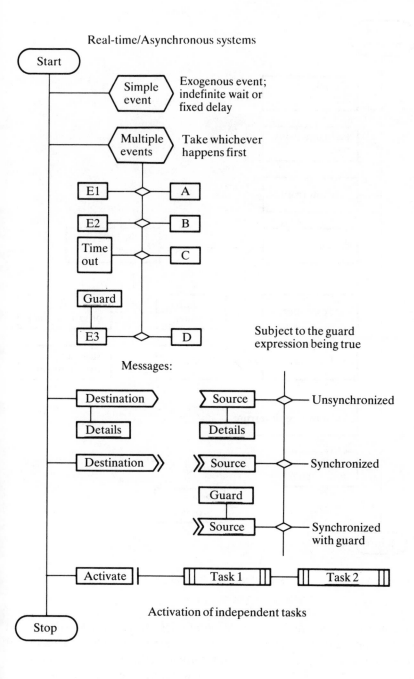

Fig. 7.27   BS 6224 definition: real-time/asynchronous systems.

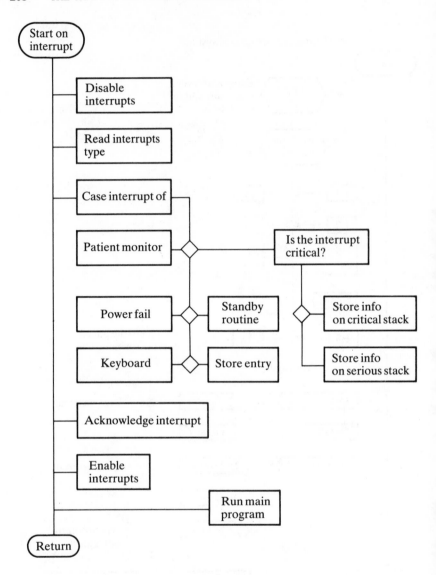

Fig. 7.28 BS 6224 example.

implemented, generally applicable notation with strong procedures and useful tools. Equally, another school seeking the standardization of software engineering practice around 'formal methods' has yet to make its point in a fashion likely to benefit practical software engineering.

The 'amateur engineer' is sometimes viewed as the person botching a system, driving screws with a hammer, using a chisel to withdraw a nail and so forth. We do not advocate the equivalent practice in software engineering. But as matters stand, and for the foreseeable future in our view, software engineers will be making do with a whole variety of tools and methods, not least in design, some of which are inferior for their purpose.

In addition to the free use of single notations, we observe considerable use of compound or mixed notations. A system may, for example, be mainly represented in data flow with some time-critical features on the same diagram, using MASCOT-like symbols.

On the whole we think it preferable in such cases to draw separate diagrams of the system in different notations, in order to emphasize different viewpoints of the same system. Thus, the overall functionality may be shown (or emphasized) using SADT, with Myers or Dataflow used to highlight the information-processing aspects, and MASCOT to emphasize some concurrent equipment-handling features; lower down the design (in this hypothetical case) we may encounter BS 6224 detail designs and, finally, above code level a specification of programs in pseudocode.

The so-called difficulties of operating in a variety of notational 'languages', can be greatly overdone; few such 'languages' amount to more than basic symbols and simple rules. Good software engineers should be literate in several design notations (able to design in them and read other designs fluently) just as with coding languages. We prefer to see notations used rather freely as to style also, rather than the designers being put in a straitjacket because so-and-so isn't allowed (by whom, may one ask?).

The use of various notations, in our experience, leads to an enrichment over steps of the design process when it naturally occurs; one should not, for example, backtrack on purpose just to use another notation, but when that has happened, the additional perspective has nearly always been fundamentally revealing about hidden complexities to be dealt with in design. Some care should be taken when admixing design notations, however. It is important not to admix them on single diagrams, and to give reference to what notation is being used, for what purpose, and with what (if any) local variant or 'dialect'.

Chapter 8 Implementation

Synopsis

Guidelines on good programming practice are offered. Whereas these will be known to many practising software engineers and all computer scientists, they are intended to introduce the amateur programmer and the manager to such concepts.

Likewise, some notes in choice of programming languages are given, and trends in this topic are discussed briefly.

The present state of affairs in development environments for software engineers is briefly discussed.

It is generally unwise to begin any coding until design has proceeded properly at the various levels, and is complete down to the program-module level. The chapter assumes that software design has proceeded in the manner recommended previously, and has reached program-module level as represented by a set of design diagrams in either BS 6224, structured flowcharts, Nassi–Schneiderman tables, or pseudocode.

In the following notes and guidelines, it is not our intention to provide a textbook for learning how to program; there are enough of those in existence already – excellent books at the introductory level and many providing details of specific languages. What we assume is some familiarity with programming in the reader.

8.1 Low-level implementation

The term 'implementation' is rather loosely used to denote the activities 'below the line' in the software lifecycle. It commences at a very high (and informal) level of conceptualization in the OSD, and takes on substantive significance at the design level described in the previous chapter.

There is some degree of overlap and merging of issues between design and coding in software engineering. In particular, one style of module design (or of complete program design in the case of a suitably small part of the system), is to produce 'self-documenting code' by using a good, well-structured language in a style intended to ensure that the structure of the design is clear, and can be seen easily from the code listing itself. The virtues of this are emphasized in Chapter 9 when the software quality aspects of modifiability and reliability of code are discussed. The reader should not overlook 'cosmetic' aspects of coding just because they may seem subjective and stylistic; code should be developed not only for its author, but for others who may have to maintain and amend it. Again, the reader is recommended to assimilate the guidelines of Ledgard (1987) on this point.

An alternative style – that of design in pseudocode – produces documentation that is itself relatively close to the programming level. The difference is that pseudocode, as well as using the syntax of a programming language, describes the program (or module) in the open, or informal, semantics of the problem domain. Pseudocode can therefore be used at higher levels than self-documenting code; at module as distinct from program level, for instance, where this distinction applies. Indeed, in academically orientated computer-science environments, the use of pseudocode is often advocated, together with some form of top-down functional decomposition, for the entire design process. The whole matter tends to get confused with 'formal methods' for specification and design and a general blurring of issues occurs, against which we have cautioned. However one arrives there in design-process terms, and in whatever notation the intentions at this level are expressed (BS 6224, structured flowcharts, Nassi–Schneiderman tables or pseudocode), one finally arrives at the point where the code is to be written in the form in which it will be presented to the virtual machine. The procedure at this point concerns the practices for good programming, beginning with the design approach to the details of the code itself.

Since the early days of computing in Epoch 1 the programming stage – comprising good (low-level) design practice, coding and code testing – has been a major area of study, with the result that these lifecycle activities are by far the most widely provided with good, established methods and tools for software engineers to use in and around the coding stage. Moreover, much current research is directed towards the improvement of programming support environments (PSEs) and the tools for an even wider support – such as a fully integrated project support environment (IPSE). This work is commented on further in Section 8.3.

At the present time there exist a number of fundamental and widely known principles for good programming practice, of equal application at low levels of design and at the coding stage; these are discussed further below. The main purpose in presenting this material is to assist those who are neither software engineers nor computer scientists (in particular, amateur programmers) to organize the structure of programs so as to facilitate the demonstration of functional compliance (e.g. with the FS baseline) and other aspects of software quality. We take it for granted that all computer scientists and *bona fide* software engineers already know and are practised in these techniques.

8.1.1 Structured programming

The best current design approach at the program level is to use, with discretion, the well-established principles of 'structured programming'. These basic principles of good program structure were enunciated in the 1960s as a result of theoretical and experimental work in computer science by Dijkstra, Jackson and others. The fundamental ideas can be indicated in flowchart form, annotated in a generalized programming-language fashion as in Figure 8.1.

In any specific programming language, one or more statements may be provided offering these facilities or their effective alternatives. The basic features of these constructs are:

1. They are all single-entry, single-exit statements as regards flow of control. This is essential to limit logical complexity of a program to a manageable level, linear with program size. For this reason, **goto** statements are discouraged.
2. Each structure is hierarchical; that is, within any box a lower-level construct of any of the three types may be introduced.

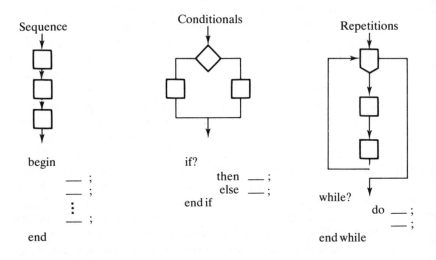

Fig. 8.1 Basic constructs in structured programming.

3. These three constructs are sufficient to program any sequential problem. (In fact, logically, they are more than sufficient; however, the three are more convenient than any two alone.)

For some programming tasks, the set depicted in Figure 8.1 is, perhaps, slightly over-restrictive. A well-known example is the requirement to exit from a repetition if a criterion is satisfied in the process of repetition – e.g. on a successful lookup as in the flow diagram for a table search shown in Figure 8.2.

One can take the view that a classical **goto** is the best solution to the requirement to exit from the body at a loop, though some recent languages provide a loop exit statement for this purpose. Another important example arises in the programming of systems based on the finite-state machine model discussed in Section 7.2. On completion of a series of transitions, represented by a single program sequence, a transfer of control must take place to the correct subsequent state; this is most naturally effected by a **goto**.

For these reasons amongst others, the **goto** statement is not regarded with the rooted antipathy of former years, though its careless and

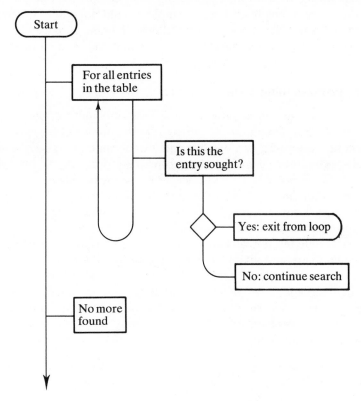

Fig. 8.2 'Goto' exit from a table lookup.

indiscriminate use leads to 'spaghetti code' and is definitely not advised.

Good program design should begin from the 'structured programming' point of view, and should only be relaxed when necessary as the foregoing examples show. This intent for a high degree of structuring is based on very good theoretical principles. Even used informally (i.e. not as a rigid formula for program design), and even if this is achieved by deliberate restraints in the assembler language, the use of structured-programming constructs has the effect of reducing the complexity of a program to a level approximately linearly proportional to its overall size, thereby materially aiding its correct construction, testing and subsequent maintenance. More formally, it is the essential basis for any attempt to prove assertions about the behaviour of the program.

Most importantly, a lack of structured approach to the design of a program very likely leads to the exact converse of these virtues. The program becomes more complex (very non-linearly increasing with program size), and hence more likely to be incorrectly constructed as well as more difficult to test (testing may be difficult enough anyway, for other reasons). The maintenance of gratuitously complex programs is a particular trial in software engineering, and comprises a major cost of software. The principle of 'keep it simple' should operate at the program design and coding level, and structured programming practice can then be violated if necessary (but only if necessary), knowingly and from strength.

8.1.2   Programming style

Much can be said about programming style and, indeed, some authors expound at great length on the subject. On the one hand this is a difficult subject because 'style' is subjective and also because many people tend to trivialize what they deem to be the 'cosmetic' aspects of a highly exacting and innovative process; a typical reaction of software engineers (let alone 'amateur programmers' who are usually more extreme still in their reaction) is: 'Look, it's cost me an arm and a leg to get this thing working – don't start criticizing its appearance!' Such reactions are entirely understandable but not very constructive, as the issues concerned bear on the modifiability and maintainability of code by others than its authors.

In Section 7.3 (J) we make some comments on the concept of 'self-documenting code', as being an ultimate aim of good style at the programming level. Here we give a checklist of some considerations leading to improvements in style and, thereby, in program comprehensibility and modifiability.

1. Choose data names to give a clear indication of the content and purpose of the data.

2. Choose names of program subsections such as procedures to describe

the action performed. The name will normally be a verb or verb-predicate form such as *get-record*, *sort-items*, etc.

3. Pay attention to the indentation of code lines. Ideally the start and end symbols of each construct should be equally indented, with the contents indented further to the right.

4. Use one statement per line and line them up vertically, for example, with all assignment signs in one column position, thus:

while *b* **do**
    namefield: = *item*
    tag   : = 15

end

5. There should be little or no need for documents within a section of code, if the code is really self-documenting.

6. Use comments at the start of each program section to give a clear informal description of the purpose of the section.

7. If the language does not itself require full interface descriptions, describe all links to other sections in the opening comment.

Further than these guidelines on style we recommend the reader to pay attention to the readability of code as it might affect other software engineers.

8.2 Choice of programming languages

Software engineers and their managers are frequently confronted with the problem of choosing a programming language for an implementation. Often the managers are subjected to manufacturers' advertising material ('Our new XYZ machine has extended GRUNT, the wonder-language'); on the other hand some software engineers tend to become fascinated by obscure developments, and want to try out new ideas from authors of languages – most often in academic environments – generally before these ideas are fully developed. The matter of choice can, on the face of it, be far from easy.

The basic design of a programming language (for which software engineers and others act as users/user surrogates – although their input to requirements specification is diffuse and indirect by and large) has been a central matter for study and development for many years. Although languages proliferate, there probably being hundreds (or even thousands if dialects are included) in active or semi-active existence at the present time, the state of affairs can hardly be said to be satisfactory.

The set may be stratified by application types for which they are more or less suitable, and this reflects the purpose usually for which a language was developed. Thus, for small-scale engineering computations, BASIC may be an adequate language; for large-scale file-handling applications, COBOL. Even with such a loose stratification, errors of language choice are not uncommon and one area of application in particular – process-orientated systems with concurrency, synchrony and other time-critical features – is singularly poorly served at the level of compiler- and interpreter-based high-level languages. As a result, much programming in this application-set is in low-level assembler language or the semi-high-level 'C'. As for compiler-based high-level languages, they have tended to be somewhat inefficient for system reconfiguration after change, compared with interpreter-based languages, since the whole of a suite of modules may have to be compiled before execution, and changes may cause considerable recompilation and reconfiguration of the software. On the other hand they tend to be more efficient as run-time systems than interpreter-based programs, in which the translation and execution of statements occur as part of the same step of the translation process.

As well as the problem of suiting a language-choice to the particular application type, there is the risk that a language may be poorly designed itself in one of several ways. Smedema *et al.* (1985) define the criteria for language design as follows (slightly paraphrased in our version):

- The facilities of a language must be simple to understand in all situations where they can be used, and free from unexpected interactions when they are combined. These are known as the requirements of clarity and orthogonality.

- The notation (syntax) of the language must be easy to understand and use, and the language shall aid the software engineer in the design of programs. This is known as the requirement of writeability.

- The meaning of a program must be easily deducible from its text, without the excessive use of comments or other documentation. This is the requirement of readability.

- It must be difficult to misuse the language deliberately. This is the requirement of orthodoxy (and is to prevent the use of 'clever' programming tricks).

- Modular design approaches (as discussed in Section 7.2) must be facilitated by providing suitable abstraction mechanisms in the language (e.g. procedure, module) and allowing the proper control over the visibility of names.

- The language must be secure, i.e. all rules of the language shall be verifiable either by the compiler or during the execution of programs.

For long-term policy, involving the choice of a few appropriate languages for an application set as it is likely to develop over a period of years, the best way is to gain experience with the main competitors' languages and make some rational choice based on ease of use, maintenance, efficiency of object code (possibly using benchmarking techniques), and so on.

In the more general case, the issues to be considered in choosing a programming language in which to implement a system include the following:

1. Availability of support in the working environment in which the system is to be implemented. In particular, a serviceable compiler of adequate quality is a necessity, together with further tools of adequate scope and coverage for the problem area. The general issues of tool sets are discussed in Section 8.3.

2. Applicability to the general problem area; COBOL would not be an obvious choice for writing a fast matrix-inversion program, for example. The problem area may itself require a mixed-language approach; for performance reasons, for example, it may be necessary to write some sections in assembler code.

3. Generality of use – in that a language in relatively wide use can be expected to be the subject of courses and textbooks, and centres of advice and expert support may be assumed to exist. The use of obscure languages or local dialects is likely to be restrictive.

4. And finally there are the issues of portability and the related subject of standardization. We do not take a strong position on portability of applications-program code. In general terms the important requirement is not code portability but visibility, and hence portability, of design.

In a specific user environment such as a major industrial concern, these issues generally lead to a *de facto* establishment of a 'short list' of available languages. A typical example would include:

COBOL, BASIC, FORTRAN, Pascal, C, and, of course, the relevant assembler language on the target equipment, for high-performance applications in terms of execution speed of code.

Such a short-list is not entirely static. Five years ago, for instance, one might have found ALGOL on some lists, but not Pascal. In five years' time we might have Modula-2 and Ada.

The inclusion of a relatively new language such as Ada on the list is, we suggest, primarily determined by the availability of support software at a stable and suitable level. We do not propose to embark here on a discussion of the merits or demerits of Ada; we merely remark that full user acceptance of a new language does not usually take place until, typically, some ten years have passed since the first publication, and acceptance is crucially dependent on widely available and satisfactory compilers and other necessary tools (see Section 8.3).

It may well be that, within a specific environment, we do indeed find some few languages available for use in the sense that effective software support and centres of advice do exist. For a specific problem we then need to choose a suitable language, and we will need criteria for that choice. This is the issue of 2 above.

One will need to look at the data and program structures available in a language in order to assess how well they match the structure of the problem area. If, for instance, the problem data can be modelled adequately in terms of numerical vectors, then the data structure of FORTRAN may well be most suitable; if on the other hand the data are large in volume and tabular in format, with mixed types of data in table entries, then COBOL may be a better match.

Differences in statement structure in languages are normally of much less significance than the differences in data structures when it comes to choosing a language. It is essential to know what basic data types are available in the language and whether they are structured into arrays, records, or both.

As to statement structure, however, almost all languages offer statements for assignment, choice and iteration in similar ways. There is generally little to choose in this respect between a variety of contenders. A more interesting and important area of comparison is in the facilities for structuring the code into subprogram sections. One wishes to assess the language facilities offered in this respect at two levels, which we now proceed to discuss.

At the lower level, we wish to see an adequate set of facilities for the specification of subroutines, procedures, functions (or whatever is the lowest level of code) into subprogram sections. This is generally available in any current language, though the quality of the mechanism differs considerably between, for example, the relatively crude approach in BASIC or even COBOL, and that of more advanced languages such as Pascal. At the next level up in program structuring, we would like to see provision of facilities in the language to support the concepts of modularization of software as described in this work and elsewhere. Thus, we would like to be able to package related collections of data, subprogram definitions and code into modules, and to have some support for separate compilation and long-term maintenance.

We have to say that such facilities are not yet widely available; we discuss this matter further in Section 8.4. So far as current choices are concerned, the best available and currently implemented set of facilities are offered, historically, by FORTRAN and, more recently and effectively, by Modula-2. Several relatively modern languages (Pascal, Modula, CHILL and Ada) are discussed in a most useful little work by Smedema *et al.* (1985), and interested readers in this aspect of language-choice are recommended to view that work for a basic description of the four (the language CHILL is, incidentally, the CCITT-defined grammar and syntax for use in the telephony/telegraphy application subset of transaction-orientated systems).

8.3   Programming Support Environments (PSE)

The programming, testing and version (or configuration) management parts of software engineering are made unnecessarily difficult – however good the chosen language for implementation might be – unless software engineers have a set of appropriate tools including the language. Such a set of tools is known as a programming support environment.

Some years ago, towards the start of the Ada programming language development, much interest arose in the subject of programming support environments (PSEs) in general, and one concept in particular – the notion of an environment for Ada language program development itself – the Apse.

Circa 1978–80, at roughly the same time as the 'Stoneman' definition of the scope of an Apse requirement (Buxton *et al.*, 1980), Boehm (1981) offered a definition of possible levels of support environment required by different user-types, and their likely development costs (in thousands of US dollars, at 1980 values). Boehm's definitions (with some abridgement) are given in Tables 8.1 and 8.2. These notional development costs will now undoubtedly be conservative estimates only. Nor do they include the cost of hardware on which a PSE is based.

8.3.1   Current practice

Since that time, the area of PSE development has seen some large-scale development endeavours (mainly in large users such as the US Department of Defense and its main suppliers, such as aerospace companies). More recently, some other government- and multi-government-funded research initiatives have occurred for more general PSEs than the Apse. These have included support tools for the wider scope of IPSEs Integrated Project Support Environment for the full lifecycle, as well as for multilingual support in the sense of several design

Table 8.1   PSE development cost (circa 1980).

Level	Likely development cost	Cumulative cost
1. Very low	$ 365K	
2. Low	$ 2420K	$ 2758 for 1+2
3. High	$ 8930K	$ 11715 for 1+2+3
4. Very high	$ 1470K	$ 18565 for 1+2+3+4

Table 8.2   Levels of a PSE.

Level	*Software tool*
1. Very low (typically the basic facilities on self-hosted micro-computers)	Assembler, Basic linker, Batch debug aids, Langugae-dependent monitor
2. Low (typically as provided as basic facilities on a mini-computer)	Macro asembler, simple overlay linker, High-level language compiler, Language-independent monitor, Batch source editor, Basic library aids, Basic database aids
3. Nominal (typically as provided on a well-furnished mini or a moderately equipped 'mainframe')	Real time or timesharing operating system, database-management system Extended overlay linker, Interactive debug aids, Simple programming support library, Interactive source editor
4. High (as in a Stoneman MAPSE on a well equipped 'mainframe')	Virtual memory operating system, Database design aid, Simple program design language, Performance measurement and analysis aids, Programming support library with basic aids, Set use analyser, Program flow and test case analyser, Basic test editor and manager
5. Very high (full Stoneman APSE on an advanced 'mainframe')	Full programming support library, Integrated documentation system, Project control system, Requirements specification language and analyser, Extended design tools, Automated verification system, Special purpose tools (i.e. cross-compilers, instruction set similators, display formatters, communications processing tools, data-entry control tools, conversion aids, etc.)

notations and programming languages. In this section we try to strike a balance between depicting the situation as it is in this rapidly moving field, and as it might imminently become through the continuing research. We identify the following practices prevalent at the present time:

1. *Self-hosted practice*
   The traditional approach to developing software is to carry it out on the machine on which the application itself is to run. The tools available are likely to be an assembler, compilers for one or more programming languages, a link loader and some operating system. A run-time debug package is sometimes available, and in many cases there are separate operating systems for development and for run-time support.

   This approach has the advantage of administrative and technical simplicity. It allows direct contact with the machine for the team, with hands-on debugging, patching of the object code at assembler level and so on. The disadvantages are that in many cases the actual requirements for the operational system are not the same as those for development support. Nevertheless the approach is widely and often correctly used, especially on medium-sized to large applications where the 'target' equipment is more likely to have reasonable PSE features.

2. *Microprocessor development systems (MDS)*
   The self-hosted approach is inapplicable for the development of software for the relatively small, embedded microprocessor and microcomputer applications which have arisen in the last decade. The microcomputer suppliers met this problem by the provision of micro development systems for their product lines. These are often desk-top personal-computer-style machines, providing rather modest development and download facilities.

   The tools normally include a text editor, filing system based on floppy disks, assembler, compiler for BASIC, PL/M or more recently Pascal, down-line loader, and perhaps some emulation features.

3. *Word processors for documentation*
   The tendency has been to prepare the system documentation, when possible, on a machine rather than by hand. Word processor systems have come into use to support documentation, together with similar facilities on larger support computers.

4. *Recent MDS developments*
   In the last few years there have been three perceptible trends in MDS support. The first has been away from the single-user, desk-top approach to multi-terminal systems. These offer better services to the bigger projects – in particular to multi-person teams. The second is the evolution of systems to support development in environments

where several micro 'chip' types are in use. The third trend is towards cross-development systems. Typically, a host system on a mainframe or large minicomputer is used for development with cross compilers, cross assemblers, and possibly target-machine emulators added as tools. The host operating system and tools are used to develop and file the source text, followed by cross translation and emulation or down-loading to the target. Such systems are often based on VAX (or similar equipment), with VMS or UNIX as the host system. This approach can offer economies of scale, and the more powerful tools and services appropriate for larger projects.

Frequently, however, there are problems in that the new cross-machine tools may not be well unified into the basic support toolset. This can lead to overheads in use and the need for much manual intervention to get work through the system.

5. *Methodology-based systems*
In a few areas more special-purpose systems of tools have been provided for a narrow application area, but supporting the software process at more stages in the lifecycle – for example, in design and in version ('configuration') control as well as implementation. One such system is MASCOT, designed for embedded real-time military systems in the UK and mentioned elsewhere in this work.

So far, such approaches have been only moderately successful.

8.3.2   Developments in PSEs

There is a strong current trend towards supporting software design and production by larger, more extensive and integrated sets of tools as presaged in the work of Boehm and others (see Table 8.2). These may be expected to offer computer-based support to the software engineering activity throughout the lifecycle, and across many projects in diverse areas of applications, and should enable version control of documentation and configuration management features as well as the tools for software development. Work in this field has, to some extent, been associated with certain specific project areas, notably by the Ada programming support environment (Apse) activity by the United States Department of Defense, the IPSE initiative supported by the United Kingdom Alvey Directorate, and similar activities in the 'Esprit' initiative of the EEC.

As Boehm's cost estimates to develop such things show (see Table 8.1) such initiatives are hardly trivial undertakings.

At the present time, the basic characteristics of a PSE are held to be as follows:

1. The host–target model of development is normally adopted. The support system resides in a host computer which is usually large, with multiple access terminals and substantial file store and processing

capability. Systems are developed, emulated, tested to a large extent and maintained on the host. Operating versions are down-loaded to target configurations with minimal further software support.

2. One class of systems (in use or currently planned) supports, in general, one modern segmental language such as Pascal, Modula 2 or Ada, with a tool set which is likely to include text editor, compiler, linker, loader, debugger, configuration controller, and command-language interpreter, all communicating via a database.

3. Another class of system represents a different approach to the problem, adopted principally by the community of workers in the field of artificial intelligence (AI). In this approach separate tools may not be distinguishable, and the process of building a system may be a more integrated and interactive one of incremental development and transformation. This is typified by the INTERLISP system based on LISP, a functional language much used in AI and by object-orientated systems such as Smalltalk.

4. A requirement behind either of the former two approaches is for the support of more than one project. This requires version and configuration control of multiple versions for long lifetimes, for systems which may share components with other similar systems.

The central importance of more software support than the mere provision of a language compiler is now widely appreciated. We contend that BASIC, for example, became widely accepted not because of its virtues as a language but because, from the first implementation onwards, it came as an integrated support system with text editing, filing and even a degree of on-line debugging built into the package.

At the professional level of software engineering, UNIX with SCCS and MAKE represents the current state of practice, and there are several analogous systems; e.g. VAX/VMS with CMS and a cross-development package.

Though the advantages are clear, we have to admit that the development of PSEs is still a relatively new and difficult area. Most development is still at the research stage (subject to large-scale government or multi-governmental funding), or the proprietary development of very large-scale users who have extremely large mainframes and communications-based networks. Reiffer (1982) lists seven PSEs in development *circa* 1982, all in major user environments such as Bell Laboratories (UNIX), Boeing (Argus), Hughes (Aides), ICL (Cades) and so on. Apart from UNIX (and its look-alikes) the others are largely experimental systems on very large facilities. One, for example, has a CDC-Cyber-based network; another has a VAX 11/780-based network with HP 2647A interactive graphics workstations, etc.

Any expectation that computer manufacturers will produce advanced, cheap PSEs is likely to be misplaced, as their research endeavours are directed over many different fields; they are not, themselves, the largest and most diverse users of computers; and the investments required are very high for a full PSE.

The current state of affairs in PSE/IPSE research was well represented recently at the conferences in York, England (see McDermid, 1985). From this, and other sources, it is evident that there is an intense level of activity in the USA and Europe (nor must one overlook the Japanese 'fifth generation' research). The main lines of this activity may be categorized as follows:

1. In the USA there are many versions of Apse (of various levels of quality) coming to use already. All, of course, support Ada – although that language is not by any means in the sort of widespread use one might expect, given the commitment to it by the Department of Defense in the USA. Current research is centred on the extension of the basic Apse concept into the requirements domain, and the definition of a common Apse interface set (CAIS) with approaches to improving the means of accessing and recording specifications.

    Another approach is the development described by L.P. Deutsch of Xerox Corporation (see McDermid, 1985) which involves the evolution of an environment to exploit the power of bit-mapped workstations and an 'open' system (including languages such as APL, LISP, BASIC) based on the facilities of Smalltalk-80, in which there is no distinction between operating system, run-time support system, library, application and user code. The user interface is extremely 'friendly', including overlapping windows and pop-up menus, a bit-mapped display controlled by a 'mouse' and such state-of-the-art display technology at the work station.

    This latter area of research is tending to emphasize the 'object-orientated' paradigm for description and implementation stages.

2. In the UK there are several IPSE development projects, and other lines of research (such as for rapid prototype development), mainly supported by funding from the Alvey Directorate. Of these, the IPSE developments ECLIPSE and ASPECT, and the contract-model-based ISTAR seem most interesting and are described in the briefest summary below.

    ECLIPSE is a joint development between system/software companies (CAP, Software Sciences, Learmouth & Burchett) and Universities (Lancaster, Strathclyde, UC Wales Aberystwyth), and currently comprises a tool set that can be demonstrated by its Jackson JSP/JSD implementation. A work station for overall development management, design edit, forms editing, text processing, and directory browsing exist. Jt supports LSDM and Mascot 3 tools.

Future developments intend to develop more tools to assist in transformation between representations.

ASPECT is another Alvey-sponsored joint industry/university project (*inter alia* System Designers, GEC, MARI, Universities of Newcastle and York, ICL). The approach is to develop a 'meta-IPSE' based on a distributed host architecture, operating UNIX, for distributed host target systems. The work incorporates recent developments in relational database theory such as that due to Codd (ACM Transactions on database systems) and a formal ('Z') language for specification. The intent is to support specification and design (in graphical and textual form) and programming in several languages.

ISTAR is a joint IST (Imperial College and industrial partners) and British Telecommunications development. It is based on the very interesting and practical notion of contract modelling for the full lifecycle process (in which the approach is not dissimilar to a main feature of this book). The software engineers' tasks will be negotiated and monitored via a lifecycle paradigm, pseudocontracting, a large-scale IPSE database and an extensive and highly distributed display system suitable for both representation and development in all phases, i.e. multi-notation and language support, full PSE tool set and configuration management systems.

3. The main initiatives in the EEC are a joint development between equipment manufacturers (Bull, GEC, ICL, Nixdorf, Olivetti and Siemens) within the ESPRIT initiative of the EEC, for a portable common tools environment (PCTE), and a French version for more specific industrial application (Emeraude). There is considerable interaction between these and the UK initiatives funded by the Alvey Directorate.

Prediction is a perilous business, and we will not presume to comment on the likelihood of these ventures with respect to each other. The impression remains however that within a fairly short timescale, perhaps three to five years, major developments will accrue in one or more areas. Perhaps (dare we guess) a CAIS-based system or a system using the object-orientated design/implementation paradigm in the USA, and ECLIPSE or the unusual and promising ISTAR in the UK? But that is not to demean all the rest; the forefront of knowledge in the PSE/IPSE area is now being taken ahead at an increasing pace.

Within ten years extended PSE facilities on the cheaper ranges of equipment will very probably be the norm, and full IPSEs on larger and more expensive configurations may be by no means rare.

The circumstances under which amateur programmers try to model the universe on a notched stick will be passing, or will have already passed.

8.4 Programming language trends

The principal concern, shown in the design of programming languages in recent years, has been the requirement for modularization.

It is necessary, especially for very large software systems, to be able to construct a program from separate components representing a low level of decomposition in the design. These components must be separately compiled and maintained in the database of the PSE under version and configuration control (see Section 10.2), so that new versions of the complete system can be assembled without unacceptable recompilation loads.

The conflicting demands of separate compilation and of inter-module linking are a central issue in language design. In the classical example of FORTRAN, subroutines are linked mainly by shared data areas in COMMON. This lends itself readily to separate compilation, but with maximum insecurity. The members of the Algol family of languages use block structure as the model of modularization and thereby make separable compilation an intractable problem. As a consequence, in the case of Pascal, different user groups have produced incompatible extensions for modularization.

Newer developments, and in particular the Ada language, use more specific techniques to describe inter-module linkage by specifying for each module those contents that it makes visible or available to others. This enables a more controlled network of accesses to be built up between modules. Furthermore, interface specifications of modules may be presented to the PSE as documents separate from the relevant module bodies. This in turn allows the replacement of a module body by a new version meeting the same interface specification, without re-compilation of the entire system.

The Ada language project has acted as a considerable stimulus to the development of computer programming, and the language itself is a major intellectual achievement. It introduces many new or unfamiliar concepts, and it covers a wide field of applications. Perhaps unavoidably, however, it is large (the reference manual occupies some 190 pages, plus appendices), and in our view it will not be easy to learn for the average programmer of today, working in industry and without a strong basic education in computer science. It may be that a language of this complexity will require the support of a high-quality Apse in order to become an effective tool in the hands of a typical programmer. The present indications are that the development of Ada support software is turning out to be a slow and expensive process, which may limit the inputs of Ada in highly cost-conscious environments.

However, some Ada support systems now exist and are coming into use for some applications, and the language is also being adopted in some areas as a program design notation. Meanwhile, Modula-2 has won a measure of acceptance, by providing a Pascal-like language with serviceable facilities for the specification of systems in modules and, in some areas, it may be a viable alternative to Ada with less overhead costs.

Current research into other areas of computer types and languages, particularly the field of AI, may produce generally usable languages based on, say, object-orientated design and programming approaches – but this and its like are still at the research, experimental and trial stages rather than currently and widely available within the craft of software engineering.

Chapter 9 Software quality

Synopsis

Some general remarks are offered on the subject-status of software quality, and its unclear terminology. Achieving software quality is described as a process, culminating in the need to demonstrate mandatory criteria concerning the software system.

Terms in 'VV&C' and Quality Control, Inspection and Assurance are defined.

The quality process in software engineering is described.

Mandatory criteria of compliance and modifiability are defined and discussed, along with the issue of reliability.

Program-proving and software-testing approaches are discussed, and guidelines on the latter practice are offered.

Some notes on organization issues affecting software quality are introduced, including the special case of software quality control and assurance in the case of single-author teams. Finally, a note is appended on the issue of 'quality cost' and, as relevant, the possible 'price' for poor quality.

9.1 Basic issues

In general, the subject of software quality has not been well served to date.

As several commentators have said: 'Quality is nobody's favourite subject.' Well, not to put too fine a point on matters, that state of affairs should be vigorously challenged – software quality must become everybody's favourite subject. Managers and their staff, software engineers, computer scientists must all take up this concern, because any endeavours in and around the software engineering process which do not have software quality as a priority can be of no more than academic interest. If the modalities of the subject are boring to some, then all the more reason for concentration lest they go by default, to the detriment of quality.

In the past, specialist books have tended to concentrate on testing techniques for programs, or mensuration methods of one sort or another. On the other hand, some major developers of software systems have evolved large-scale quality methodologies, alongside their general management practice for software tasks, PSEs and configuration management systems. Not all of these approaches are either available or suitable for other 'cultures'.

One major problem concerns an agreed definition of the term 'software quality' itself. Different authors identify somewhat different properties of software to characterize its 'quality'. For example Cho (1980), Glass (1979) and Reiffer (1982) propose criteria that are in part identical and, in part, interestingly different. This is shown in Table 9.1, where the degree of mutual agreement is indicated; figures in parentheses indicate the shortfall in agreement.

Alternatively, Myers (1976) defines 'software goals' within a set of product objectives, as:

User Definition, Functional Objectives, Publications (e.g. Documentation), Efficiency, Compatibility, Security, Service-ability, Installation and Reliability.

In the *Dictionary of Computing* (Glaser *et al.*, 1983), there are definitions for several aspects or properties of software quality – e.g. 'software reliability', 'software quality assurance' and so on – but no definition of the term itself under that designation.

As may be seen from these examples, there is some tendency to admix what should be mandatory criteria with what are clearly optional ones for a given system. Thus, 'correctness' and 'reliability' (both mandatory for any non-prototype or research systems), and 'efficiency', 'portability' and the like (options at requirement specification time). Also, there is a confusion between objectives (e.g. 'modifiability'), and the means to achieve them ('structuredness', 'understandability'). This state of affairs is not conducive to a clear understanding of software quality and how to achieve it.

Table 9.1 Ill-conditioned quality criteria, methods, etc.

Agreement	Characteristic
Complete	Reliability, efficiency, maintainability, portability
Partial (2)	Consistency, understandability, human engineering (usability), modifiability
Singular (1)	Conciseness, structuredness, robustness, testability, correctness, integrity

In part, the problem is historical. In Epochs 2 and 3 as we have defined them, little attention was given to the subject of software quality, as there remained the notion that software should be made rather in the fashion that early amateur programmers had made systems for their own use as problem-solvers. The question was raised at the time of OS 360 with its very visible imperfections, and a particular slant was given to the issue when (in Epoch 3) computers became widely used as components in electronic systems. At that time hardware engineers, some of whom had clearer notions about the quality of electronic systems, began enquiring, with some frustration, why software was not the same.

Attempts were made to form similes between hardware and software engineering, not too successfully it must be said, and any attempt by software engineers working on a composite systems development to refute these similes was viewed by their colleagues from other disciplines as 'special pleading'.

As it is our stated intention to identify and clarify essential issues (as distinct, say, from promulgating a particular 'method' or 'system' for dealing with the issues), we proceed below to categorize the properties of a software system that comprise its 'quality', and the approaches needed in software engineering to achieve this. These are summarized as follows:

1. The two critical properties of a software system determining its quality (prototypes and research software possibly excepted), are its compliance with requirements as expressed in the FS, and its modifiability for maintenance and new versions. The reliability of the software will have bearing on both of these issues and can be said to comprise aspects of the two.

   Compliance and modifiability are treated as mandatory criteria and described more fully in Section 9.4, along with the question of metrics for them and means to achieve them. Reliability is also discussed there.

2. The achievement of high quality in a software system is a process, not an event, and one that concerns all parties to a software development including users (or surrogates), managers and commercial staff, implementation technologists, and quality operatives. Each major lifecycle step having a tangible outcome should have its quality demonstrated as well as possible, and this will lead to considerations of FS quality, Design quality, Code quality and Documentation quality. The mandatory criteria of compliance and modifiability in 1 above are generally taken to apply to the quality of code and documentation, and are achieved by this overall quality process.

   The quality process is described more fully in Section 9.3.

3. The sufficiency of a quality process requires it to be verified, and the adequacy of a software system with respect to its mandatory criteria

requires it to be validated and certified. These states (**verified, validated** and **certified**) are known as 'VV&C'.

The quality process itself comprises three subprocesses known as Quality Control (QC), and independent Quality Inspection (QI) and Assurance (QA). The terminology of VV&C and that of Q(C,I and A) are described in Section 9.2.

Finally some guidelines are offered on the main issues in software testing (9.5), organizing for software quality (9.6), and the special case of single-author teams.

9.2   Definitions: verification, validation, certification

There are several different and somewhat overlapping terminologies in use for quality aspects of a software system, and the process whereby that system was made and authenticated. For instance, Deutsch (1982) quotes both Miller (1972) and Reiffer (1974) as providing somewhat variant uses of the terms 'verification', 'validation' and 'certification', and suggests a further variant as a compromise. The *Dictionary of Computing* (Glaser *et al.*, 1983) defines 'verification' and 'validation' but not 'certification'. The reasons for this are not hard to find. Difficult though it is to establish standard terms at a national level, it is virtually impossible internationally in some subjects; software quality is such a subject. There is, however, a basic mapping between the terminologies in most widespread currency, and we define this below for our further use. Again, our intention is to classify and clarify rather than to promulgate a 'norm' of some sort.

The issues of VV&C are all to be determined objectively (i.e. by independent sources from the implementation team). In the following definitions, we use the same convention ($-$, 0 and $+$) as in the status matrix notation in Section 6.2 to depict the states 'not yet begun', 'started but not complete', and 'complete'.

The acceptance of a software system by clients, user/user-surrogates or whoever may be authorized to do so, follows from it being in (minimally) the first two of the following three states:

Verified: This concerns the objective determination that the software engineering process, as undertaken, has been adequate up to the point at which the implementation team declare that the system is compliant on the basis of their own tests, culminating in an α-test of the software (see Section 9.5).

Validated: This concerns the objective determination that the mandatory criteria of compliance and modifiability have been achieved. It takes the form of an independent β-test of the software and its documentation (see Section 9.5).

Certified: In some cases it is necessary, but not sufficient, that the software process is verified and the software itself validated as described. In such circumstances, the software behaviour (and that of other systems components), needs to be evaluated in real-life circumstances. Then the system is exposed to its real operating environment for a determined period (typically three or six months) and, if successful during that time, it is 'certified'.

Looked at in lifecycle terms, the process of verification should begin (status 0) at the FS stage, and conclude (status +) when the author's α-tests have been concluded apparently satisfactorily. However this 'verified status' (+) should only be accorded if all major aspects of the lifecycle required have been competently undertaken (e.g. prototyping and its correct designation, specification, feasibility other than by prototyping, design, estimating, and so an – including all aspects of 'good management practice'). Whilst the overall status of verification is '0' the states attaching to different parts of the lifecycle may be +, 0 or +, and backtracking (eg + to – or 0) may occur. This kind of of backtracking on the verification status may not be directly correlated with actual backtracking in workterms on the status matrix. For example, poor design may be allowed to remain (however unjustified) although coding level problems have revealed it as inferior. In such cases the verification status of the design step should indicate the matter by being set to 0 (or even –), although the coding part of the lifecycle may proceed impeccably and be positively verified. Then, even a successful α-test would not justify an overall verification status of +, as all substates must be in that condition as prerequisite. It would then be clear that an explicit decision was needed to proceed (or not) to validate the system.

Sometimes, as well as an independent quality source (department or external agency) determining V&V, there is a superior organization of some sort to authenticate the whole process. In this case, the method is one of superior verification, and the object of it is the totality of other VV&C activities. This level of verification, rare except for very large, potentially hazardous implementations, will begin (status 0) at the FS stage and conclude (status +) on either successful validation or certification – usually the latter in these cases.

The independent testing of software and its documentation, to determine whether it is to be classified as 'validated', is initiated by the verification state being changed from 0 to +. The validation state is changed at this point from – to 0 and, when independent tests are successfully completed, to +. In the same way certification (if required) begins (status changed from – to 0) when the validation state becomes +, and, if successfully concluded, results in the system being certified (+). At this stage all states of VV&C should be + in terms of our status matrix notation.

The quality process, of which VV&C is a part, is usually described in terms of Quality Control (QC), Inspection (QI) and Assurance (QA). The mapping of these terms with those of VV&C is as follows.

QC: This consists of the activities of the internal team of authors to ensure, at a subjective level at least, the quality of work at the Lifecycle stages; specifically the CPT (or similar) techniques of design review/code reading (see Section 6.3), and author testing at individual module, integration and α-test levels (see Section 9.5).

QC is the object of independent verification as described above, and normally ends when that is concluded. If, as is often the case, the validation process highlights defects in the software and/or documentation, then QC may resume when backtracking up the lifecycle occurs to remedy the defects (the 'verified' status also changes from + to − or 0 in this case too).

QI: This is a verification of the software engineering process by an independent agency; specifically the participation in (and perhaps scheduling of) design reviews/code reading; the inspection of the team of authors' test plans, and the observance (and perhaps determination) of tests up to and including the α-test.

QA: This is independent determination of whether or not mandatory criteria for software quality have been met (including its document-ation in the definition of software – see Section 10.1).

This is done by the same agency as QI normally, and culminates in either an independent β-test of the software (see Section 9.5), or that plus a period of certification by operating in its real environment.

In summary, QI is the process of verification and the author team (or other) QC is its object along with overall management practice QA is Validation and, dF need be, certification of the system.

9.3 The quality process

Point 2 in Section 9.1 asserts that the achievement of high quality in a software artefact is strongly associated with the lifecycle process itself. In particular this means that quality aspects of the system-to-be must be defined, where possible, as early as possible in the lifecycle, and must be an ongoing part of achieving requirements at every stage.

Thus, to use our hospital alarm system as an example; if the software in the central control computer (CCS) has to be portable, then that must be stated at the URS/FS level, clearly expressed in the FS (in greater detail concerning the 'target' equipment), then reflected in the OSD/ estimates, the detailed design, code, and testing strategy.

With this clarification it will be seen that the continuing process of achieving quality (in general terms) can be associated with major lifecycle stages at which some evident artefact (or 'deliverable' as these are called) is produced. Thus we may speak of:

- FS quality and the quality of estimates
- Design quality
- Code quality
- Documentation quality
- Management quality, and the quality of V,V & C itself

To achieve all of these one should have the following provisions:

1. Competent management to do structured walkthroughs, general management planning and control, and Specification Change Control. All of these are dealt with in earlier chapters. Each major lifecycle stage should be subject to a major quality review of its output.

2. Competent software engineers in the implementation team, specifically to undertake QC of design and coding stages. (*Note.* The quality control of the FS is a dual issue between implementation and user/user-surrogate staff in many cases, and the signing off of the FS is both QC and – in part – QA of that document.)

3. Competent software engineers and application specialists in the independent QI/QA team. All aspects of quality must be addressed by this team (or person). Thus the QC aspects of FS, Design and Coding must be inspected, and the QA aspects of compliance and modifiability undertaken, as already described (and further detailed in Section 9.5). The 'quality of management' determination and reporting can be particularly fraught.

Given these fourfold quality issues, and threefold resource levels to deal with them, a quality plan can be produced (at about late FS/OSD stage) in which the whole development-to-be is seen from the quality viewpoint. For example, using the activities netplan in Section 5.4 – the implementation plan for the hospital alarm-monitoring system – we might find an initial quality plan of the form (units in project-days) shown in Table 9.2. This schematic signifies events not activities; for example, the QA β-test will have required substantial planning (and software development work perhaps) prior to 'project day 102'.

Quality must be a strongly managed issue; it is not enough to leave it to the technical 'wizards'. Nor is it an item that can be 'bolted on' at the end. Thus, however elaborate a quality system may exist (with a cubic metre of written rules and procedures for its observance), adhering to it in the hope that all will be well may turn out to be counter-productive, like the man on a stricken ship clutching the anchor for safety.

Table 9.2 A quality plan.

Quality plan (Project days)		Management walkthrough	Team (QC) activity	Independent Quality Team
FS		0		0
Design Review:	Overall	21	1–20	15–20
	A	48	43–47	47
	B		31–32	32
	C		31–32	32
	D		67–68	68
	E		67–68	68
Code Read	A	66	83–84	83–84
	B		50–51	51
	C		50–51	51
	D		79–80	79–80
	E		80–81	81
Test Plan				28
Author test:	A	92		82–91
	B			
	C			
	D			
	E			
	All(–A)			82–91
Author team-				
α-test		102		97–
β-test (Software)				102–106
β-test (Documentation)				102–106

Having said that, we repeat the point we made earlier, that some strong practices, and informed management, implementation teams and quality staff are essential. Our mild polemic against over proceduralization is for companies yet to evolve 'standards' (or adopt them from elsewhere), and is because – beyond a certain point – bureaucracy and software engineering do not mix, except to the detriment of the creative process; on the other hand unregulated software development is usually a catastrophe. The matter is one of balance, as the tightrope walker said as he hit the pavement.

9.4   Criteria for software quality

A cursory glance at Table 9.1 and the accompanying comments reveals some confusion over mandatory and optional objectives, and an equivalent confusion between some objectives and the means to achieve them. We have asserted in point 1 of Section 9.1 that the crucial aspects of software quality, the essential criteria in fact, comprise compliance and modifiability, with the understanding that a part of each consideration comprises the reliability of the system in question. In fact, the reliability issues concern:

- categorical error as affecting compliance; and
- inherent instability in the construction of the software, rendering it vulnerable to disturbance (change, hardware error, other software errors and so on).

These two concepts are strongly related, each one leading in some circumstances to the other. The subject of software reliability is discussed in more detail later.

The two mandatory criteria for software quality are further defined as follows:

1. *Compliance.* The software must 'deliver' the features and functions specified in the FS, and must go on doing so; this last property is the specific reliability of the software.
2. *Modifiability.* The software must be capable of amendment, either for corrective maintenance (failure of compliance), or for new versions, and any such amendments must not adversely affect its previously determined status as regards the two mandatory criteria; i.e. a modification must reduce neither the degree of compliance plus its reliability, nor the modifiability itself. This last property is the stability of a system.

We discuss these two further in the following subsections.

9.4.1 Compliance

The compliance of a software system is evaluated against the requirements as detailed in the FS. Thus there is a direct relationship between the quality of that document and one's ability to determine the compliance component of quality in the software artefact.

The basic categories of information to be embodied in the FS are described in Section 4.4, and the mutual process between users (or surrogates) and implementation staff to verify this content is the quality control of the FS. In addition, the FS activity and its outcome should be quality assured (as far as possible), by inspection from an independent QA agency. This will inevitably fall short of full QA since the quality of the FS will, in effect, be demonstrated by the implementation. For example, its basic feasibility will become evident and – although this is not usually a problem – it is possible for the FS to have infeasibilities incorporated in it.

Other aspects of FS quality will become evident during implementation. Such things as its 'truth' as a representation of real requirements, and its unequivocal clarity in representing them will be manifest in the change control mechanism and mainly corrected by it. Nevertheless, the partial QA of the functional specification, early in the lifecycle (i.e. before the FS is signed off) can be highly illuminating. Table 9.3 shows the independent QA checklist review of a version of the FS (clearly inadequate) done during the hospital monitoring example. It will be

Table 9.3   A quality audit of the FS.

QA(FS) FS Version 1 Result	Checklist issue	Reference to detailed points and criticisms
No	1. Is the FS information-set isomorphic (in part at least) with the essential information-set from the URS?	See 2
	2. Does the FS information-set contain:	
No	redundancy/irrelevance?	
Yes	omission?	Annex A list
Yes	ambiguity?	Annex B list
Possibly	error?	Annex C list
Yes	3. Does the FS information-set contain solution design unacceptably?	Annex D list
Yes/NA	4. Are user i/f formats detailed; equipment constraints also?	
	5. Are language and format 'reader-friendly' for	
No	users?	Too abstract
Possibly	technicians?	for design
Doubtful	6. Are i/o features clearly described as Agency, Media, Form, Format, Rate, Error?	Error features are lacking
	7. Are the following (if required) detailed	
No	Security/Integrity?	Essential
No	Performance:Degredation?	Essential
N/A	Efficiency?	
N/A	Portability?	
No	8. Should this FS be authorised in its present form?	

noticed that the checklist is entirely application-independent, although the 'specific detail' annexes referred to will of course contain the detail of defects.

Although compliance is a mandatory requirement, its object comprises an entirely application-dependent and optional set of issues, and its determination is less than absolute. These points require further elaboration.

The contents of the FS must include, as well as a sufficient description of inputs, features, functions, and outputs, a definition of any other operating characteristics required. Some examples are:

Performance: specifically, the response time of different parts of the system if these are critical in any way.

Security: specifically, any requirements for privacy (avoidance of unauthorized access) and/or integrity (avoidance of data corruption or loss).

Portability: specifically, the type and configurations detail of any equipment that the software may have to work on, other than that for which it was developed.

The performance requirements are limited to the domain of time (access/response) and not space (object-code size), since the latter is best regarded not as a requirement but as a constraint. In fact, Weinberg and Schulman (1974) pointed out that both time and space optimization requirements may have the most severe effects on quality. Implementing such requirements – even if successful at the compliance level – is often achieved at the expense of 'modifiability'. The reason for this is that either one (or both) may be taken as the dominant objective at the design/coding stages of a software development, to the extreme detriment of 'good design practice' and possibly 'good programming practice' also. The best way to avoid this is to design and code the system for these optimization requirements within a properly considered and balanced design (see Chapter 7). If then the software is not compliant in the performance sense, it should be 'tuned' at the code level (e.g. by speeding up frequently used routines, writing parts in assembler, etc.) or even re-designed. When this is done from the security of a good design in the first place the effect on modifiability can be controlled.

The specific reliability aspects of a software system were defined by Myers (1976) in the following ten points:

1. Mean Time Between Failures (MTBF), defined by type of failure (system, user feature, specific functions) and severity.
2. Mean Time to Restart (MTR) after failure.
3. Goals for the number of software errors, categorized by severity and time of discovery.

4. Consequences of systems failure (or less) on critical functions.

5. Tolerable data loss in the event of failure.

6. Vital information to be protected from failure.

7. Necessary fault-detection functions.

8. Necessary fault-correction functions.

9. Necessary fault-tolerant functions.

10. Detection and recovery from user errors and hardware failures.

The list is extremely useful for several reasons. Firstly, the first three on the list are metrics for compliance of the sort used as acceptance criteria in some contracts for hardware supply. In fact, as discussed below, these are not usually meaningful things to specify for a software system, as there is nothing (other than threat of what may happen) that they add to the scope or detail of requirements.

Others on the list refer to aspects of privacy or integrity and must be specified explicitly and in detail if they are to be implemented (and therefore the subject of compliance). It should be noted that some of these features, for example 10, may be detailed by prototyping (URS and OSD types as described in Chapter 4). Other features may not emerge until the Architectural Design and, when this is so, they cause substantial change-control activity. Users (clients) sometimes take a dim view of this, although they take an even dimmer view of a system that has not been adequately thought out in systems engineering terms and is then fully implemented. The Myers checklist, 4–10, should be used at the specification stage to elicit as much detail as possible, in the full knowledge of all parties that the questions are essentially ones of design and must be asked again at that stage.

As for portability of software, the point has been made in Chapter 7 that this is better regarded as portability of design than of code. It is a fallacy to regard portability as being a matter of harmonizing the choice of equipment architectures and using a popular high-level language. The portability of a software system may be enabled in this way, but will not be ensured. For time-critical systems particularly, there may be a failure in compliance if too simplistic an approach is taken to portability. Our advice is to make the issue specific as to type and configuration of target equipment, and then test the portability as a parallel exercise at the α- and β-test levels (see Section 9.5). Any problems experienced will have to be reviewed at the design and code level for the transported system, and a variant version of the software may exist as a consequence.

As pointed out elsewhere, the FS should not contain undemonstrable requirements, i.e. ones whose effects are not evident, or that lack metrics for their determination; it should therefore be possible to determine the compliance of a software system. However, this raises the question of whether or not software systems can be proved categorically correct. This somewhat contentious issue, already touched on elsewhere, is discussed in Section 9.5. However, a suitable line to take here is that compliance will be demonstrated by testing, and that the result will be a 'degree of confidence' rather than a categorical certainty about the status of the software.

9.4.2 Modifiability

The modifiability of a software system is crucial for two reasons: corrective maintenance and new-version changes. Unlike the issue of compliance, this mandatory criterion may not be precisely specified, nor may it be simply demonstrated by using the system.

Along with some other desiderata (such as 'testability', 'reconfiguration', 'structuredness' – all generally related to each other and to modifiability), there is no suitable metric in this case. In specifications, and in the contracts (or pseudo-contracts) that depend on them, it is unwise to require indefinite properties such as 'the software will be highly reliable, extremely modifiable, easily reconfigurable, well structured, eminently testable' and so forth. To do so is to set up the basis for contention, as the matter will inevitably be one for value judgement outside an established framework of mensuration. In short, the FS must avoid the undemonstrable in stating its mandatory requirements ('hard' as distinct from 'soft' statements). If this is not observed, the problem is essentially this: who is to say (and on what basis) that a software system is modifiable with ease, some difficulty, or extreme difficulty? After all, any software system is modifiable – all one has to do is patch ADD X for SUB Y in the object code and that fixes it, doesn't it? The issue is not whether changes can be made to software, but whether they are likely to degrade the previous status (compliance and modifiability) in the process.

As with a hardware system the matter is one of design and construction (coding in this case) and not entirely analogous to hardware engineering in the general sense; the engineering quality is an issue which can only be decided by a peer-group. This does not mean that only the implementation team can judge the matter (after all, their view would be entirely subjective); nor can the independent QA group for that matter; managers and others, if familiar with good design and coding practice, can add value at the time of structured walkthroughs, and even decide by inspection whether a software system is likely to be of high, medium or low quality with regard to its modifiability.

However, in order to demonstrate the modifiability of a software system, a more intensive method is required than that of inspection. In fact to do QA on this aspect of software, one must put oneself in the position of a software engineer who, although unfamiliar with the system, is asked to modify it, perhaps years after its development and long after its authors have gone. What usually happens (after a period of recrimination, during which the unfortunate software engineer blusters and pleads to get out of the task but accepts some bribe in the end) is depicted in the six basic steps of Figure 9.1.

The judgemental approach usually starts at the bottom level, trying to use the system and looking at the code listing. It may be evident at this stage (step 2 in the schematic), that the system is a dreadful mess, in which case the process may stop with the software engineer saying, in effect, that the software is too badly structured and/or undocumented for any changes to be made with confidence. For that reason the 'good programming practice', mentioned in Chapters 7 and 8 are highly important. The state of the code listing is not just a cosmetic matter; it may be the obstacle at which an adverse judgement on modifiability is made (the argument of the heart of Ledgard's book. Ledgard (1987)).

Beyond this point the process involves orientating with the FS, familiarizing with the design, and then attempting a modification. The first should be no problem if the FS has been properly done; otherwise, the process may abort once more. We have known extreme instances when the FS was written for the first time at this point! There were no modifications made, needless to say, but the 'system' was put into production in a status hardly even justifying the designation 'prototype'! To proceed; orientating with the FS is easier if a subset of this is made defining the software system (see 'Documentation' in Section 10.1). Then the design is inspected, and this is usually the most hazardous step of all in determining software modifiability – so much so that we have taken to

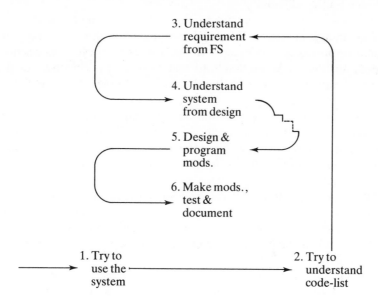

Fig. 9.1 Judgemental method for demonstrating modifiability.

asking for a view of design very early. If it is absent from the available documents, or manifestly inadequate (as a lot of pseudocode-like designs are for this purpose), then the process aborts – the software is not modifiable with confidence. If, on the other hand we can inspect the design and find it informative, then some clearly limited disturbance to the software may be tried.

We have explained the judgemental method of determining software modifiability at some length, because it highlights the need for good software engineering practice and its management throughout the lifecycle. Peer-group judgement of this sort is essential, and is in no way different at the QA level for modifiability, although the QA group should be familiar enough with the system not to have to proceed 'bottom-up'. Quality determination of modifiability (or 'reliability' if the issue is so phrased) by software engineers is reminiscent of the old use of canaries in coalmines to detect toxic gases underground. In effect they are determining whether or not they would dare to modify the software.

The history of software engineering is full of instances of software engineers metaphorically keeling over at the sight of another person's software. Just as often, the questions of modifiability/reliability have not been raised at all, and program patches have been inserted in any case.

9.4.3 Reliability

As already defined, reliability is a concept which involves both compliance and modifiability.

If a software system does not work as its requirements specification prescribes, then it is non-compliant; if it begins to work satisfactorily but then, due to previously undetected categorical errors in its construction, fails to do so, then it is unreliable to that degree; if occurrences of this kind are infrequent, the system may be deemed sufficiently reliable, but otherwise it may not.

If a software system is deemed to be unmodifiable, this is because an expert has judged, perhaps on the basis of practical trials, that to modify the system would result in a degradation of its previously established compliance and modifiability – in short, that its reliability would be adversely affected.

Having said these things, it is surprisingly difficult to say much more about software reliability other than how different the concept is from its apparent analogue in hardware engineering, and how 'good software engineering and management practice' tend to increase the chances of achieving acceptably reliable software.

To many, particularly those who are not specialists in software engineering but have a hardware (electronics) background, this is incomprehensible and sounds like special pleading. In fact it is not, and the reasons for it are not difficult to find. Many hardware products are made up of quite basic, standard components that are mass produced in a manner enabling average failure statistics to be determined. On the basis of these statistics, the failure expectation can be determined – as a compound probability – for modules comprising these components ('assemblies'), and for whole systems of assemblies. These statistics are confidence levels for the reliability of the hardware, and are expressed as Mean Time Between Failures (MTBF). Another average – Mean Time To Repair (MTTR) – is also often possible to determine for such a system.

For software, such standard components are lacking. Even the re-use of a system module is likely to be limited to new versions of the system for which it was written, and even the slightest change renders it, in effect, a different component. The supposed virtue of software that it is 'flexible' leads to many such changes, and the concepts of large-scale re-usability of software modules across different application types, for which they might be thought appropriate, is not well developed. Consequently MTBF and MTTR figures are not appropriate for software systems.

For a hardware system we may say that it has an MTBF of 999.9 years and an MTTR of 3 days, for example. The limitation of these figures is obvious even for hardware; their main use is in marketing ('Our XYZ product has an MTBF of a million years, and an MTTR of one second'), and as definite contract provisions ('Your XYZ product will not fail for a million years and its MTTR will not exceed one second – or else . . .'). Few if any software suppliers would contract product or project software on this basis (nor, for that matter, should makers of customized VLSI circuits, for the same reason). Outside the range of virtual machine facilities, few software systems are extensively used by a large number of users in different types of environment, and large sample-size failure statistics are consequently missing.

Another essential difference between hardware and software is that hardware wears out (physical depreciation, wear and tear, breakage), whilst software 'wears in' (progressive detection and correction of errors, increasing intervals between software failures – at least in high-quality software). This effect is depicted in Figure 9.2.

If MTBF and MTTR are what cannot be used as confidence indicators of the reliability of a software system, what can be used? With acknowledgements to Pressman (1982) we list the following three current areas of research into metrics for software reliability:

1. Analogy with hardware reliability models. A review of several such approaches (in particular those of Shooman *et al.*, and Wolverton *et al.*) are given in Thayer *et al.* (1978). We regard this approach, in general, as unsuitable, for the reasons already given.

2. Error calibration, or 'seeding'. A number of known errors are introduced into the software, and tests are then undertaken on the

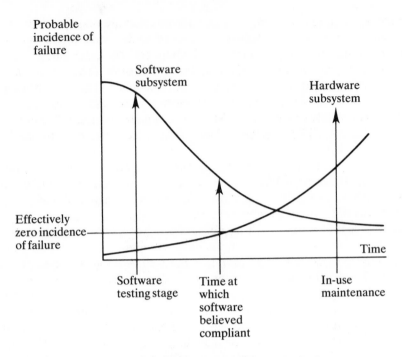

Fig. 9.2 'Ideal' software error incidence behaviour.

basis of which the code is 'calibrated'. Thus if, of 100 introduced errors, 50 are found plus one otherwise unknown error, then we might infer the existence of one other unknown error.

Whereas 'seeding' is a legitimate and useful way of disturbing a software system to investigate its modifiability (e.g. of 100 introduced errors 50 were found, plus 150 otherwise undetected errors = unmodifiable software), the use of it for calibration is highly questionable. There may be extremely complex causal chains involved, and problems in repeating error conditions, particularly for concurrent software systems.

3. Reliability models based on properties of software design or construction at the coding level. These are discussed further.

Of the models attempting to give some measurement of expected reliability – if only through achieving acceptably low levels of complexity – those of Halstead (1977) and McCabe (1976) have already been described, in outline, in Section 5.5.2. Accepting that it is likely that there is a correlation between complexity of construction and reliability in software engineering, it has to be said that neither of these complexity metrics seems to have gained widespread acceptance; in fact the Halstead model has been subject to reappraisal recently.

Another model, specifically for software reliability, is due to Thayer *et al.* (1978). This sets out a relationship for the 'Total Complexity Metric' C(TOT) as:

$$C(TOT) = L(TOT) + 0.1C(INF) + 0.2CC + 0.4C(I/O) + (-0.1)U(READ)$$

where:

L(TOT) is a Logic Complexity Metric;
C(INF) is an Interface Complexity Metric between programs;
CC is the Computational Complexity;
C(I/O) is the input/output complexity;
U(READ) is the readability or uncomplexity metric of code listings.

Each of the sub-metrics is defined in terms of the program-code characteristics. For example:

$$L(TOT) = LS/EX + L(LOOP) + L(IF) = L(BR),$$

where:

LS = number of logic statements;
EX = number of executable values;
L(LOOP) = loop complexity from a table of calibrated values;
L(IF) = a measure of IF statement complexity from a table of calibrated values;
L(BR) = number of branches divided by 1000.

This, and other approaches, are set out in Thayer *et al.* (1978). At the present time models of this sort are still in the research domain, and we are left with the question: how is reliability to be assessed in software engineering? In fact, as with modifiability, we are left with no real metric. Consequently it is ill-advised to guarantee the reliability of software, other than for small S-type systems (see Section 9.5) or other software systems (if of high quality from the start) that, having been in extensive and varied use for a long time, have had most of their defects detected and corrected. In these cases, the record of monotonically increasing intervals between detected errors can play a useful rôle in statements of the software's reliability.

Admittedly, none of this helps much in a composite IT-system development when hardware engineers say 'Our ABC hardware will have an MTBF of a hundred years; what do you mean, your mickey-mouse XYZ software will have to be run for a year before we know whether or not it's likely to fall apart?' That – as they say – is in the nature of software engineering.

9.5   Quality demonstration by testing

Some theoreticians assert that programs can be proved to be categorically correct (or incorrect), and this is true up to a point as we have said elsewhere. The preconditions for this are formidable, however, if one is to avoid the trap that 'logic is nature's way of allowing one to go wrong with confidence.'

These preconditions include a categorically correct FS (otherwise a correct implementation will be incorrect by derivation), in a language suitable for assertions in it to act as operands in a process of logical inference, working towards a coded system that is (*a fortiori*) correct by computation at each step; and finally a method of demonstration (program) that is itself categorically correct.

These limitations tend to make program proving an activity at the small S-system level as defined, after Lehman (1980), in Section 2.3. In fact Lehman asserts the property of S-systems that they are provable through the totality and invariance of their specification. At the present time, this is an area of research (as we have said before) requiring the following to be achieved if it is to have widespread effects in software engineering in general:

1. Suitable 'formal' languages will need to be developed; if these are to extend much above the coding stage of the lifecycle they will have to be suitable for design (likely to enrich steps in that process) and specification (to enable users to authenticate and authorize the FS).

2. A way must be found around the problem of proving the proof program.

Lehman (1980) raises the interesting conjecture of making all non-S-type systems (which he classes as A-type systems, either P- or E- or composites, in other words) into aggregations of S-systems by methods of 'partitioning and structuring'. He goes on to write

> If this is true then no individual programmer should ever be permitted to begin until his task has been defined and delimited by a complete specification against which his completed program can be validated.

This prospect is some way distant yet, if indeed it can ever come about (the questions of 'partitioning' and 'structuring' need particularly careful scrutiny with respect to intuitive, good design practice). As well as Lehman's work (which is rightly a stimulus to research in this area), the interested reader may find an account of formal methods in Alagic and Arbib (1978). In addition there are advanced research systems coming into being – perhaps the best known of which is the 'Gypsy' system due to

Good *et al.* at the University of Texas, Austin. Our own approach finds some support in the papers of Naur (1982), and Perlis *et al.* (1979). Briefly summarized, it is as follows.

In the absence of categorical proof methods on a widely available and practical basis, the alternatives – testing and demonstration – are the required methods for validating software systems. The object of these methods was well summarized (if, perhaps, unintentionally) in an aphorism attributed to Dijkstra (in Buxton *et al.*, 1969):

> *Testing can show the presence, but never the absence of errors in software.*

In fact, given the lack of practical means in most cases to show the absence of errors in software, it is necessary that testing methods should be good enough to show the presence of errors in it.

There are two levels on which software systems should be tested, and these are presaged in the descriptions of VV&C and the quality processes of control, inspection and assurance (Section 9.2). They are:

1. Testing at the subjective level, by the authors of the software.
2. Testing at the objective level, by an independent software quality assurance agency.

The first of these may be described as 'benevolent' testing, and the second as 'adversarial' testing. It is under these designations that we discuss them further.

9.5.1 'Benevolent' testing by authors

The following are prerequisites for author-level testing of software:

1. The purpose of the software should be explicitly clear, for example by means of module specification containing some FS-type material as well as design.
2. The software should be intrinsically testable in other respects than that its purpose is clear; thus it must be well designed and coded (see Chapters 7 and 8), and well documented in all respects (see Section 10.1).
3. There should be an overall strategy for author-level testing. As described below, this may comprise a top-down or a bottom-up method, or a hybrid of the two.
4. There should be a detailed plan for the orderly and rational testing of the software, by its authors, up to and including the final test at this level – the 'α-test'.

   The only way that such a plan can be done is on the basis of the software design, and the only time to do it is when design has progressed to the level at which the modularity of the software is clear, if that is still somewhat short of software module design as described in Chapter 7.

This dependency is made evident on the lifecycle schematic (Figure 3.4).

5. There should, of course, be adequate provision and organization of resources such as software engineers and software development environments as described elsewhere.

As many of these issues are dealt with in other parts of this work, we will not duplicate them here. The strategic issues of top-down and bottom-up testing are discussed further.

Top-down testing involves the creation of a test framework for the software that simulates external stimuli (such as user inputs), and comprises a set of software 'stubs', which represent the main software modules to be made and which merely act and react in a simple manner to the real behaviour of software systems components. Then, as the real programs come into being in some partial state of testedness by their authors, stubs are replaced by real routines which are then progressively tested in combination with each other within the framework.

An example is given in Figure 9.3 depicting a possible top-down testing strategy for the hospital monitoring system (see Figure 5.5).

Conversely to this method, bottom-up testing involves a gradual accretion of programs into a more complex entity to be tested and, thereafter, a further accretion as more programs are produced in partly tested form by their authors, and so on until the whole of the software (and its test environment) is associated and ready for its comprehensive α-tests. Schematically the process can be depicted as shown in Figure 9.4 (again using the hospital example). In practice, there is little to choose between the two strategies.

Most small and medium-sized systems seem to be tested on a bottom-up basis. Many large and very large software systems seem to be tested on a top-down or quasi top-down basis, although there is some natural confusion between this and so-called 'black-box' testing (see Section 9.5.2) in quality assurance.

The relative costs of the two approaches are by no means dissimilar, so a choice cannot normally depend on that factor. By and large, the choice of a testing strategy comes down to a matter of personal (team) style, and we have no further comment to make other than:

1. Make sure there is an explicit strategy of one sort or another and that it is competently reflected in the detailed test plan (see 4 above).

2. Under all circumstances avoid 'big-bang' testing as either an explicit or default practice. Using the previous example, big-bang testing can be depicted as shown in Figure 9.5.

Order of replacement

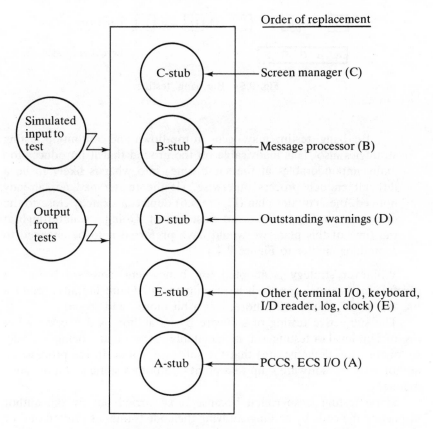

Fig. 9.3 'Top-down' testing.

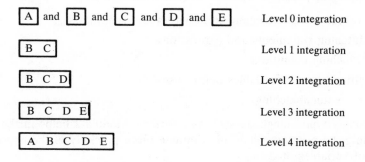

Fig. 9.4 'Bottom-up' testing.

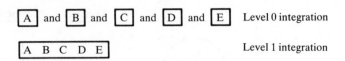

Fig. 9.5   'Big bang' testing.

'Big-bang' testing may occur in top-down and bottom-up testing strategies also. It is inadvisable on the ground that it introduces too many imponderables at the same time, into what is likely to be a difficult enough process otherwise. (If the reader had not already noticed, the activities plan (Figure 5.6) depicts a strategy close to the one shown in Figure 9.4 – too close in fact. Doing a walkthrough at the time of this plan, we would have preferred it to be changed to something similar to Figure 9.4.)

Whatever strategy is adopted for 'benevolent' software testing, a careful, incremental approach is recommended. Quite literally: 'build a bit, test a bit', 'build a bit more, test a bit more', and so on.

The subjective testing of software by its authors is a necessary but insufficient level of testing as it is, inevitably, benevolent – being basically to 'prove' (i.e. demonstrate) that the software works. In the process, an author tests the software – up to a point – in both a static and a dynamic manner.

Static testing is so called because it is carried out by the author inspecting the code by reading/studying the code listings as printed out, or displayed on a screen. The process is materially assisted by the adoption of a good programming language with a well-developed compiler, and 'good programming practices' as described in Section 8.2.

Particular points to look for in static testing are:

- Correct use of statement terminators and separators
- Matching statements and expressions
- Branching conditions
- Initialization of variables before use
- Parameter matching

A strongly typed language such as Pascal or Modula-2 helps further by enabling the programmer to discriminate more precisely in the expected uses of variables or data.

Dynamic tests, such as are carried out top-down or bottom-up, commence with programs that are partly tested statically by their authors. The first levels of dynamic testing usually involve:

- Exercising each branch of all conditionals

- Exercising input and output functions, both inside and outside expected ranges
- Exercising all computation functions and logical manipulations of data

The author usually 'forces' the program to execute in the expectation of an outcome that may or may not occur, and also tries to induce unexpected outcomes anyway, such as may occur with data values out of range. The program is seeded with such 'forcing' instructions and with 'trace' instructions such as output statements. These are designed to demonstrate the parts of a program executed and the value of parameters at that time as diagnostics of its operation. The seeding instructions are removed by the author before submitting the module for further incremental testing of the dynamic type (top-down or bottom-up as the case may be), along with other subjective authors of the software system-to-be.

The static and dynamic testing of software by its authors acting within a definite strategy and to an explicit test plan, and the static testing of designs and code by team colleagues other than the author of a module (design review and code reading) comprises the quality control of the software. This quality control terminates in an α-test.

The α-test generally constitutes as exhaustive a dynamic test of the whole system (both hardware and software involved), as is feasible in the time available and called for by the severity of consequences if the system fails.

As well as this dynamic test, the α-test attempts to show that the system is usable and modifiable. Thus the authors of the system attempt to play the user's rôle by trying the system with both valid and invalid inputs and usages.

A particularly valuable thing for authors to do as a part of α-testing is to seed each others' code with known errors, as part of a planned exercise in evaluating the reliability and modifiability of the system. However well done this is, it is not totally revealing about modifiability, as the authors know the system too well at this stage of the lifecycle.

The whole process of author testing of software is seen as subjective for the obvious reason that the authors of programs, when determining their dynamic tests or performing the static inspection of code, have a tendency to be 'blind' to error. Often an error is incorporated into the test in exactly the same way as it occurs in the code. To some extent this subjectivity is mitigated by 'design review' and 'code reading' within the CPT, but the author-team is still correctly held to be subjective towards the system in its totality.

The general attitude of demonstrating that the creation works is natural and the implementation team is much worse if it is not present. As a result, the α-test is regarded as a thoroughly necessary but essentially benevolent attempt to demonstrate that the system works and is of requisite quality in other respects. Its outcome is therefore not held to be a status of validation for the software nor, *per se*, its verification (see Sections 9.6.1 and 9.6.2).

9.5.2   Adversarial testing by independents

As for author testing of software, there are several prerequisites for independent-level testing:

1. There should be a strategy for the objective testing of the software. In general this concerns the quality assurance of the system and involves the determination and execution of 'black-box' and 'white-box' tests. These are both described further below.

2. The purpose of the system should be fully evident, particularly the user features and their expected responses, so that black-box tests can be fully planned and performed.

3. The design of the system must be fully evident, as must the construction of the code, in order that white-box tests can be fully planned and performed.

4. There should be a detailed plan for the independent tests. This can be done only after the FS for black-box testing, and only after detailed software design down to module level for white-box tests. The final step is a β-test of the software system, which should succeed the α-test. The β-test comprises such black-box and white-box tests as are called for in the strategy.

   The satisfactory outcome of both α- and β-tests may be taken as sufficient for the software system to be classed as 'valid'.

5. The organization and staffing provisions for quality assurance in general, and independent software testing in particular, must be available. These are described further in Section 9.6.

Much of the substance of this has already been described, or will be elsewhere (for instance, the documentation requirements bearing on black-box and white-box testing will be dealt with in Section 10.1). The strategic issues of black-box and white-box testing are discussed further.

In black-box testing, a software system is seen as a closed entity with defined interfaces to the outside (or 'exogenous') world. The system is tested on this basis only, being subjected to as many permutations of correct or incorrect usage, external accident, 'flood testing' (in the sense of saturation loading), and so forth as may reasonably be done.

Very frequently, the 'behaviour space' of possible usage is exceedingly large and, as a result, black-box testing can end up either as an inconclusive set of tests done relatively quickly and inexpensively or, on some relatively rare occasions, a comprehensive generation of possible external stimuli by elaborate and expensive simulators.

Usually, black-box tests are a compromise between the total behaviour space problem and that which is reasonably achievable, and one ends up doing the most likely subset of inputs and observing the system response against the expected behaviour. These tests include all those relating to 'user friendliness' features; if these are not defined properly then the behaviour-space problem will be the worse. Black-box testing requires a high degree of familiarity with the FS, and is a highly useful means of determining the compliance of a software system. It is, however, far from the totality of independent tests for software quality.

In white-box testing, the software is seen as a holistic system, a set of connected or partly connected components – as is the case – rather than as a closed system as in black-box testing. Also, in contrast to the requirements of black-box testing, white-box testing requires a full and detailed knowledge of the software design and code structure (the 'endogenous' world), rather than an appreciation of the FS only.

An independent white-box test of software should constitute the following:

- Independently determined and executed static and dynamic testing of the software. Static testing of this type is incorporated in independent Quality Inspection (already defined in Section 9.2 and to be treated further in Section 9.6). This, and dynamic tests of modules, combinations of modules, and the whole system are analogous to those for author tests but approached from the 'objective' viewpoint of showing that the software does not work.

- Seeding the code with known errors, not so much to calibrate the error expectancy (as described in Section 9.4.3), but to try to induce error and unexpected behaviour in the software as a means to assessing its quality – in the sense of modifiability – at a judgemental level.

- Attempting a change to the software in the form of a removal of part of it (with some compensation if only via 'stubs'), and some addition to it (other than a 'stub'). This will, if done competently, throw light on the quality issue of modifiability of the software system.

- A thorough quality assurance of the deliverable documentation as this is defined in Section 1.1.

The independent, 'objective' testing of software can generally be done only if sufficient subjective testing has preceded it – otherwise it is a waste of time. A competent software engineering organization performs a sufficiency of subjective testing (ending in an α-test), then a sufficiency of objective testing (ending in a β-test). The software is, in the event of sufficient and positive tests of this sort, said to be quality controlled and quality assured (unless 'certification' is required too), and it may be declared to be in the 'valid' state defined in Section 9.2. (This is true, incidentally, whether or not it has been 'verified', although good practice requires that this too should be the case so as to maximize the chance of successful α- and β-tests.)

Independent testing of the kind described is said to be 'objective' because it is devised and done by others than the author-team, and its purposes and methods are 'adversarial'. This does not mean that the attitudes of independent, quality assurance groups need be malignant in any way, but that the whole ethos of this level of testing software is to try to falsify the software. If a successful α-test says, in effect, that the authors think that their system works, a successful β-test says that an independent agency believes this assertion to be justified on the basis of good evidence (and conversely in the case of an unsuccessful β-test).

9.5.3   Confidence in tested software

Most software systems of any reasonable size and complexity probably contain some residual errors, even after exhaustive testing and years of apparently successful usage. These may be at one of two levels:

1. Subtle differences between an implementation and its documentation for whatever reasons. Since a software system includes its deliverable documentation (whether contractually called for or not), a discrepancy between them constitutes an error.

2. Undetected, categorical errors in the software.

In addition to this, the software may be unmodifiable and intrinsically unreliable in the sense that the slightest disturbance of it, such as via categorical error, or modification for maintenance or for a new version, or hardware failure, may cause propagated effects up to the level of a substantial failure.

Rather than speak of 'correct' software in the unqualified sense, one should rather speak of reasonably 'believable' software. Rather than say that software is error free, the most one can usually say is that the conditions under which the next errors will be manifested have not yet arisen.

The whole process of software testing is, or should be, an exercise in confidence accretion. Gradually the bugs in the software should be flushed out of the system by the most exacting tests and, thereafter, real usage at a level that fully exercises the features and functions of the software. In an ideal world – to which one should aspire – a well-made software system would behave as depicted in Figure 9.1, the average time to the next detected error would increase monotonically, and furthermore the obscurity of 'bugs' would increase also.

In practice the picture may be somewhat different. If the software is badly made in the first place, then detection and correction of errors may be a non-convergent process; the modifications effected may fundamentally disturb the behaviour of the system. The notion of a non-convergent process is depicted in Figure 9.6, in which a relatively ideal error-detection histogram is contrasted with a problematical one.

Keeping statistics of error incidence will help to determine if the software is converging to some 'believable' level of error freedom, but only if 'time' is understood to be that duration during which the software is being rigorously tested or exercised in real (or realistic) circumstances. The mere passage of time will say nothing about the convergence or divergence of a software system to (or from) credibility. For that reason the horizontal axis in Figure 9.6 represents time in the qualified sense as described above.

A final cautionary note is in order. A client (or surrogate) will want a categorically correct and unequivocally reliable/modifiable system and may, moreover, say so in the URS/FS and contract. It is in the nature of software engineering that such ideals, whilst aspired to, cannot be reached in most practical cases. Nor, even if they were reached, could the fact be established beyond question. It is not sensible to specify absolutes in the sense of the unquantifiable, untraceable quality criteria. By far the best approach to software quality, for all parties, is to specify and contract for things that are 'traceable' to some extent during the lifecycle (so that QC practice *can* do something about them, and QI procedures can ensure that they actually *do so*) and are demonstrable at the end (so that QA can take place).

A requirement is said to be 'traceable' at a certain lifecycle stage if something can be demonstrated about it. Thus features and functions are 'traceable' at the FS stage and during design, but they may become less clearly traceable at the coding level. At the end of the coding stage, however traceable or otherwise, the features and functions specified in

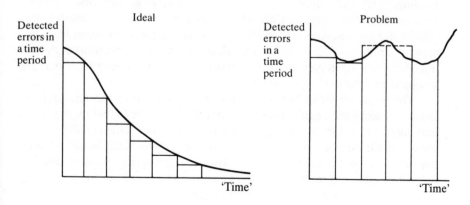

Fig. 9.6 'Ideal' and divergent error incidence behaviour.

the FS must be demonstrated. Other requirements, such as amorphous imperatives that the software must be 'efficient' or 'eminently testable' and so forth, will not be traceable beyond their point of specification. The 'efficiency' issue, or optimality as it sometimes becomes, has been commented on elsewhere. Often, there is little or nothing to indicate, at design level, that this requirement is present, and only a lot of highly compressed and 'clever' assembler-code thereafter.

9.6   Quality Control, Inspection and Assurance practice

Software engineering contains three subprocesses whose purpose is to ensure the quality of the object of that process – the software system. They are, as identified in Section 9.2:

- Quality Control (QC)
- Quality Inspection (QI)
- Quality Assurance (QA)

So fundamentally important are these to software engineering as a whole that, although much of the subject matter has been touched upon in one form or another, we summarize the basic elements of these three in the following sections.

9.6.1   Quality Control (QC)

This is the subjective verification and validation of the software by its authors and, being subjective, does not serve either to verify or to validate the software; nonetheless it is a necessary part of the process.

The methods of QC include peer-group design review and code reading, and the subjective testing of software as described above. Overall, it is the responsibility of the chief programmer to ensure that good software engineering practices – including those of team management – apply, and the deliverable documentation is monitored by the librarian. The strategies and actual testing at the integration level may be assigned to a 'tester' in the CPT.

The problem described in Section 6.4, concerning the comprehensibility of software engineering for general management 'below the line', may become a largely delegated process (but not entirely delegated; management must still manage). Beyond the architectural design stage of the lifecycle, the quality of the software engineering process and its outcome become a matter of explicit method (QC), within the CPT, and this should be independently ensured (QI/QA).

The end point of QC is an α-test, which should be done in a palpably satisfactory way before the quality assurance β-tests proceed. The determination of sufficiency in the α-test is the final act of independent quality assurance (QI), and (all other aspects of QI being satisfactory) signals that the software engineering process undertaken has been verified.

9.6.2   Quality Inspection (QI)

This is the objective verification that the software engineering process has been competent undertaken. The methods of QI include inspection of the CPT plans for design review and code reading, and an appreciation of the strategies and detailed plans for subjective testing; furthermore QI will observe the adequacy of management-level documentation (see Section 6.2) and deliverable documentation (see Section 10.1). As well as inspecting the plans for design reviews and code reading, QI staff should attend some (or, if need be, all) of them, and even schedule tests if they are lacking. The absence of good QC practice, or any major lapses from it, should result in the independent QI/QA agency posting a 'deficiency report'. This should, in the first place, be to the CPT itself but – in the event of continued inaction – the deficiency report should be repeated, with progressive escalation within the management structure.

The combination of QC and QI can be seen as the necessary process of verifying the software engineering process. The end point of QI is the inspection of the α-tests as done by the author team which, if competently done, may result in the system being declared 'verified' in terms of the process involved in its creation, and the independent QA β-tests will commence.

An essential part of determining QA tests – the understanding of design and code structure so as to devise white-box tests – occurs as a result of the QI activities of the independent quality-assurance agency, so long as it is the same people doing both QI and QA.

9.6.3   Quality Assurance (QA)

There are two parts to QA in principle (although in some cases the second of these is absent):

1. The independent β-testing of software, as already described.
2. The end-client acceptance trials, including sometimes an on-site operational period under warranty ('free' maintenance cover by supplier).

The first of these is generally carried out by the supplier's own QI/QA organization, whether for a product or a project as defined in Section 2.3. Its QA methods are those of black-box and white-box β-testing and its end point, following a successful β-test, is the status of 'valid' for the software system and its documentation.

As well as doing the β-tests on the implemented, α-tested and quality-inspected software, the independent QA group must have commenced their involvement early in the lifecycle. The key point concerned is that at which the FS becomes available in its settled form suitable to be signed-off. It should be an act for independent quality assurance to review this document for its general and apparent adequacy. This should provide the insight into requirements to provide the basis for black-box testing activities of QA, whilst the ongoing QI from architectural design to α-test should properly provide the basis for white-box testing. Even after successful verification and β-tests, the software should be declared 'valid' only if its deliverable documentation is approved by the QI/QA team.

In case of some projects the end-client may hold acceptance trials for the system, in addition to any QC, QI/QA undertaken by the supplier. Furthermore, even after successful trials, the system may have a running-in period usually covered by a warranty for free maintenance by the supplier. Client acceptance trials are generally very much more like black-box tests than white-box tests, although a client would be wise to investigate the modifiability of a software system by disturbing it in some controlled fashion. The end point of client acceptance trials is often a certificate of acceptance, and the end point of the warrantied running-in period is the declaration (in one form or another) that the system is 'certified'.

9.6.4 Organizing for QI/QA

Many supplier organizations in the IT field, for products or projects incorporating software, have quality groups for hardware but not software components. We offer the following brief guidelines on some of the main issues of setting up QI/QA groups for software engineering:

1. It is extremely important for management to overcome some suspicion amongst software engineers that an independent QI/QA group is in some way a 'police force' or 'espionage service' about their practices. A feature of good management is to establish and encourage the notion of one common objective towards which all parties contribute. An important enabling factor for this is the careful selection of staff for the QI/QA groups.

2. In staffing a QI/QA group it is inadvisable to recruit new employees (software engineers) into the group. Firstly, QI/QA staff should be conversant with the product (or project) technology to a high degree, as well as being competent software engineers. This is unlikely to be the case in new recruits.

   Secondly, QI/QA staff should be well known, respected and liked in the company if the problems of 1 are to be avoided. If possible,

QI/QA staff should be appointed out of technical implementation groups, where they can be more easily replaced by newly recruited staff. Possibly even better is the notion of 'staff rotation', on a fairly long-term basis, but with the intention to return after a few years to the implementation sector. Staff transfer/rotation should be a part of positive career development; nothing so broadens the technical horizon of software engineers as a spell of QI/QA work.

3. For deficiency reporting to be effective as a part of QI, as well as for the authority of final QA to have real meaning, the independent quality groups should have a separate reporting structure in the organization, to an equivalently high level as that of the implementation team; having both report to the same person relatively low down in the organisation hierarchy tends to nullify the effects of independent QI/OA.

9.6.5   Quality and the single-author team

Unless specifically provided, QC is not possible in the case of software developed by one person working alone. Nonetheless, QA should be provided for – either by an internal but 'independent' agency, or by external contracting. Given the provision of a QA function in this way, what should then happen is that the QA group performs QI as in the normal case, so far as making sure that general matters such as lifecycle ordering of activities, archiving, etc., are performed.

Furthermore, the QI/QA group should act as the adversarial agency for design review and code reading, in the absence of other CPT members to act in this way, and should ensure a proper approach to software testing by the author up to α-test level. In some cases, the rôle of independent QI/QA becomes that of a surrogate CPT member for QC rather than an agency for independent testing.

There is nothing intrinsically wrong with this truncation of QI/QA functions, so long as the QI/QA agency is held clearly accountable for the verification and validation of the system. Thus, for example, β-testing may be foregone entirely in some cases if the QI/QA agency is thoroughly convinced of the value of α-tests. Nonetheless, any subsequent evidence to the contrary is the responsibility of the QI/QA group, and not a matter of blame for the α-testing procedures of the single-author team.

9.6.6   The cost of quality

Quality costs money, but the price for poor quality may be far higher – even (in some cases) unquantifiable.

The two issues of quality cost and potential price for systems malfunction or failure are ineluctably linked as the dyad on which decisions bearing on quality should be made. Early in the lifecycle – at the URS stage say – the consequences of malfunction must be detailed. These will then predicate any special means and methods for quality control, inspection and assurance. For instance, if loss of human life is a possible consequence of failure, then extremely elaborate β-testing may be required before the system goes into usage – such as simulators to generate the possible 'behaviour-space' for black-box testing. In these cases, the cost of quality may be justifiably high, in the range 60–150% of the whole development cost of the system.

In more normal cases, the provisions of 'good software engineering' practice, comprising QC and the intermittent QI/QA activities of a relatively small number of independent 'adversaries', amounts to something in the order of 30–35% of the total development cost. For some rather non-critical jobs such as 'games' software for personal computers, the cost of quality may be in the QC practices of the authors and thus may seem a marginal amount. The results have been known to show it.

Chapter 10   Additional management issues

Synopsis

The basic problems of managing the software engineering process, and suggested approaches for dealing with them, are set out in earlier chapters of this work. The following issues remain outstanding and form the substance of this chapter:

- Deliverable documentation (Section 10.1).
- Software maintenance, new versions, and configuration management (Section 10.2).
- Software personnel issues (Sections 10.3 and 10.4). We incorporate some comments and guidelines on recruiting and retaining software staff, appraisal, and software engineering education.
- Contract issues; these are dealt with in Section 10.5 and incorporate some definitions of contract types, in software engineering, for retailing or retaining supply.

10.1   Deliverable documentation

We distinguish between two types of documentation in software engineering, namely that necessary for the management of the software development, and that describing the software system and necessary for its usage, operation and amendment for maintenance or new versions.

The first of these, the management documentation, is the subject of Section 6.2, where the necessary items are defined and described. The second category, generally referred to as 'deliverable documentation' is that which – as its name implies – is part of a software system delivered as a product or a project. To whom the documentation will be delivered depends on the level of the document and on the nature of the software system, whether product or project. This is described further below.

Deliverable documentation usually comprises three levels of manual:

1. the user's manual;

2. the operator's manual;

3. the maintenance manual.

There is, in general, no difference in the scope of these documents in the case of products or projects; merely that the destination of one of them is different in some cases.

User's and operator's manuals are delivered to clients in the case of both products and projects. On the other hand, the maintenance manual is very rarely delivered to clients for a product, and certainly never if the supplier has a contract covering maintenance and guarantee of the product. In the case of projects, the maintenance and other manuals are often part of the contracted supply in order that the client may maintain and amend the system on his own behalf.

The users of a software system are the people who activate and supervise (and on some but not all occasions provide) the inputs to the system. The operators of a software system are the people who activate and supervise the operation of the equipment on which the software executes. In some cases, the users and operators are the same people.

In other areas such as embedded systems and closed-loop control applications, users and operators as we have defined them may be far removed from the software, or may not be human agencies at all so much as other subsystems and so on.

We describe the user's and operator's manuals as for separate, human agencies.

10.1.1   The user's manual

The user's manual should comprise three parts:

1. A synopsis of the URS describing what the system is supposed to do, and its main features and functions as these may be exploited by the user. This is, in general, a textual description in natural language only and will certainly exclude software engineers' languages and notations, special implementation terminology, pseudocode and so forth.

   On the other hand, if special terminology is incorporated, it is in the applications language rather than that of implementation, and may even contain algorithms insofar as the user is likely to comprehend them and may have reason to do so.

2. Clear formats and instructions for user input to the system. This section must specify the input media precisely, and describe all essential inputs to get the system to work in the first place, and any optional inputs for exploiting the features of the system.

   The contents of this section will be largely textual, in natural language, but some diagrams (such as how input commands appear on the screen), should be included if appropriate – i.e. in the case of a user/operator as one and the same person.

3. Clear formats for output from the system. This section may be very largely or even entirely diagrammatic. Typically, screen formats are described by drawing them.

As well as the expected outputs from legitimate use of the system, screen formats to show diagnostics in the case of incorrect usage such as illegal input may be included if appropriate – i.e. in the case of user/operator as one and the same person. Figure 10.1 shows an example of output screen format, from the user manual of a hospital patient and general alarm-monitoring system; another example (from a different implementation of it) may be found in Section 4.4, and further examples may be found in Chapter 11.

In general, the user's manual is not a large document. Furthermore, its essential information is (or should be) available early in the lifecycle. For instance, the URS synopsis is probably the preface to the FS anyway (see Section 4.4); also, details of the inputs and outputs across the user interface will probably have been settled (perhaps by prototyping in the URS stage), to avoid the frightful expression 'user friendly' in the FS. It is always advisable to have subjective matters, such as concern the users, well defined and 'signed-off' as designs of input and output formats.

Whether the user's manual should be done early in the lifecycle is a matter of style in different organizations. The arguments for doing it as early as possible include:

SECTION CODE	FLOOR	ROOM NO.	PATIENT NAME	DOCTER ASSIGNED	NURSE ASSIGNED	ALARM PULS	ECG	BP	TMP	SMK
D	2	36								*
A	1	21	BROWN	SWIFT	BRONTE		F			
E	6	4	JONES	WOOLF	AMIS	C				
B	2	107	KELLY	WAUGH	AUSTEN	C				
B	3	62	PAUL	GASKELL	DICKENS			S		
A	2	14								*
C	1	3	TWIST	DICKENS	GASKELL	F				

(LIST CONTINUES: TYPE "MORE" FOR OTHER MESSAGES)

ALARMS   S = SERIOUS, C = CRITICAL, F = FAIL; * = SMOKE ALARM

Fig. 10.1   The user interface: screen format.

1. Very little additional effort is required, being only that to compile and make 'cosmetic' what is already available for, and in, the FS.

2. As it can be done early and easily, why not do it to get it out of the way? Leaving it until later may put it in a lifecycle stage already overburdened with other activities. Also, deferred documentation tends to become defaulted-on documentation.

3. It is unlikely to be a volatile document in the sense of being subject to a lot of rapid change unless, that is, the FS is in general volatile. Change control tends to reduce this problem.

4. The users will be gratified by considerations of their interests; ratifying the user's manual does wonders for co-operation between users and software engineers – as does the URS level prototyping on which it is often based.

Our recommendation is clear; do the user's manual at the FS stage. We have seen excellent user's manuals, embodied in the FS with great advantage, 'signed-off' and subject thereafter to change control.

The problems of upgrading a user's manual in the event of substantive change to the system or its user features is minimal in the current epoch, given the availability of word-processing equipment or features within the PSE (see Section 8.3).

10.1.2   The operator's manual

The operator's manual should contain two types of information:

1. Instructions on how to start the system, and how to stop it in the event of human intervention being required. Likewise, how to restart the system after it has been stopped for whatever reason.

2. The output formats of diagnostic messages concerning error and other fault-detection features.

The range of instructions represented in 1 may be relatively simple ones, such as 'bootstrap' instructions for a personal computer, up to the exceedingly complex level of a full Job Control Language (JCL) for a mainframe computer; the one will be a simple screen format of instructions when the machine is turned on, whereas the other may be a large volume of textual descriptions of the JCL for a major computer facility.

As to diagnostic messages, these should incorporate all the items that are designed and implemented into the system for detecting and reporting the violations of 'security', as defined in Chapter 9.

The diagnostic features of a system may vary in complexity from the relatively simple tests for input error up to exceedingly elaborate provisions for protection against hardware failure and the propagation of software errors throughout the system.

Unlike the user's manual, the material for the operator's manual is not necessarily all basically available at the FS stage. User's input errors, their diagnosis and associated error messages can, to a large extent, be specified as a result of URS prototyping. That part is relatively straightforward. Similarly, perhaps, with the privacy aspect of security. However, as said in Chapter 9, the integrity aspect of security is often very far from evident at the FS stage, and becomes an issue of substance only at the architectural design stage.

For some systems not containing (nor likely to contain) elaborate error-detection features, the operator's manual can be written at the FS stage and – in these cases – the arguments applying in the case of the user's manual apply equally here; we recommend that for such systems the operator's manual is written as early as possible, i.e. at the FS stage. It is not normally incorporated in the FS as its material is basically inappropriate to that document.

In other cases, the issue is far less clear. By the time the information for 2 above is fully available, the implementation may be considerably progressed. In these cases our advice is to draft a version of the operator's manual towards the end of the detailed software design phase, and put it under the same form of documentation version control as for the maintenance manual (whose contents are extremely volatile – see Section 10.1.3 below). In these cases, the operator's manual will have to be generally tidied up and made 'cosmetic' towards the end of the subjective testing phase, e.g. during the performance of α-tests.

The operator's manual is generally a mixture of natural language text, and diagrams such as screen formats for error diagnostic messages. The use of technical implementation languages and notations should be avoided, although, as with the user's manual, there is a strong temptation to software engineers to use things like pseudocode, as it is so easy to type in and edit on even a primitive PSE. Nonetheless, given the interests of the people for whom the document is intended, such temptation should be resisted.

10.1.3 The maintenance manual

The maintenance manual is essential if modifications are to be done to a software system – as is normally the case for both corrective maintenance and new versions. So fundamentally important is maintenance document-ation that it is often a specifically contracted item in project-type supply, and default in this aspect of supply can cause cancellation with fault against a supplier.

Whether contracted or not, and whether for a project or product, the maintenance documentation should be a clearly defined technical objective for the CPT as this construction is described in Chapter 6. Not that this has to any great extent been the prevailing practice in software engineering to date, excepting such cases when the force of an external client's contract has clarified the matter conclusively and early in the lifecycle. Basically, software engineers do not like doing documentation; on the other hand they are the first to comment when encountering badly documented software not of their making. We will return to this point later in the current section.

Basically, a maintenance manual should contain four classes of material:

1. A definition of the software should be provided. This commonly takes the form of extracts from the FS corresponding to the features and functions implemented in software. They may be enhanced by a version of the software taxonomy from the OSD, so long as this has not been invalidated by later, real design.

2. The detailed software design must be incorporated. This may include an overall architectural design of the system, hardware and software, in whatever notation (or admixture of them) is appropriate.

   All 'steps' in the software design should be detailed, as well as the notations appropriate at these steps, the design should be annotated in natural language to indicate any particularly hidden features of the design, such as optimality.

3. A reader-friendly and well-commented code listing must be included. This should be directly related by nomenclature to the lowest level of design documentation; in this case nomenclature means more than just notation, so pseudocode designs are not necessarily the answer. Section 7.3.3 and Chapter 8 contain some guidelines in the matter of good self-documenting code practices and the reader is further referred to Ledgard (1987).

4. Test plans; data and results from the authors' subjective testing to α-test level, and from the adversarial (independent) β-tests, should be incorporated.

The maintenance manual is likely to be voluminous. For large and very large systems its hard-copy version may comprise several large books of the different materials. The form of it differs from section to section, as can be expected given their contents. These sections are described further.

The software definition section is basically textual with a few diagrams, such as the OSD software taxonomy and an overall architectural design. As the likely readers of maintenance manuals will be software engineers themselves, there is no strong objection to this part of the maintenance manual being in a specialist language, such as pseudocode, so long as its terminology (i.e. the syntax subset) is generally familiar. In this case, the FS extracts will need converting from their original form of natural language, and considerable care will have to be taken not to commit errors in the process; the better practice is merely to extract a subset from the FS in its original form. Under no circumstances should the matter be made an excuse to do the FS (or high-level design) in pseudocode in the first place.

The design section should contain all software designs, from architectural design down to detailed designs of program modules. In our approach, this will entail the graphical/textual representation form from several 'steps', for medium-sized software systems upwards. For small systems it may be the detail design in something like BS 6224, pseudocode or structured flowcharts, and have utilized its own 'language', which is probably best chosen as one of several diagrammatic notations. The process of design, being a highly intuitive one in most cases and one that involves many levels of simultaneous compromise, may still be difficult to follow even given detailed diagrams. This 'mapping' problem is endemic and leads to design decisions becoming hidden, more by accident than intent. The achievement of efficiency criteria is often a notable case in point. The requirements structure (as evident in the format of the FS) should be preserved through the design stage, if this can be done without distorting the considerations for a good solution. It is helpful when changing software systems to have its design correspond with the form of the requirements so far as possible.

For this reason in general, it is well advised to annotate design steps, to give some idea to a reader at a later time what particular objectives and problems were being dealt with at this stage of design. This annotation may be in natural language or (as is more often the case) pseudocode, so long as this latter is reasonably familiar to all software engineers.

The design section may contain a rich assortment of notations. For example, one may have MASCOT diagrams and Petri nets from the architectural design stage (if it is a process-orientated system with concurrency), MASCOT and CCITT-SDL as one proceeds down the detailed software design, BS 6224 at the module design level, and pseudocode specification of programs.

When this occurs, a clear indication of the type of notation and its symbols and rules as used is a valuable appendix to the design section of the maintenance manual.

The code-listing section must be directly mappable with the lowest level of the design section. In general, it is impossible to map a code listing to the FS and highest levels of design because of the process of transformation undergone in the design process itself; furthermore, in the absence of an explicit design, it is generally impossible (other than for small and simple systems) to derive a rational design for a program by working upwards out of the code listing. In this respect, software engineering and hardware engineering are substantially different. The necessity to make the code-listing level of the maintenance manual a clear and readable document has been established elsewhere; the schematic diagram of Table 9.2 demonstrated why. The first impression gained of the modifiability of a software system will include a value judgement by a software engineer, probably not its author, of the code listing.

Ledgard (1986) has stressed the 'human factors' aspect of programming, and in Chapter 8 we have offered some brief guidelines on good programming practice. Figures 10.2 and 10.3 represent examples of fairly bad and somewhat better code listings respectively. Source: S. Selwood.

Neither of these examples is 'self-documenting code' as described in Section 7.3.3. The tendency of code listings to explain the code (often unnecessarily) is clear from both examples, and points up the need for higher-level design documents. The fact that one example is in a high-level language and the other in assembler code is not entirely without significance. Many IT applications on self-hosted micros provide little opportunity for readable, cosmetic code listings.

In general, though, the greater problem is the attitude of software engineers who tend to denigrate 'cosmetics', and resist and resent any attempt to influence them in this aspect of good software engineering practice. One mark of the amateur programmer is that he or she thinks code is self-documenting when it is in the state of Figure 10.2.

The test-history section of the maintenance manual is to enable original tests to be repeated during software maintenance, or whilst modifying code for a new version. The contents of a test history are described further:

1. A description of the subjective test strategy undertaken by original

```
*
ACNSEC  RSECT   ROM
*
ACNBL1  MOV     A,£H'FO'        Mask for MS nibble
        ANL     A,@RO           Get MS nibble
        SWAP    A               Swap left/right nibble
        ADD     A,R7            Add R7 and MS nibble
ACNBL2  MOV     @R1,A           To IIC buffer
        DEC     R1
        MOV     A,£H'OF'        Mask for LS nibble
        ANL     A,@RO           Get LS nibble
        ADD     A,R7            Add R7 and LS nibble
        MOV     @R1,A           To IIC buff
        DEC     R1
        DEC     R0
        RET
```

Fig. 10.2   Code listings: example of bad practice.

Routine description:
> *Read status {S1}*
> **if** *(BB=0) {self-generated interrupt}* **then**
> **Do** *nothing*
> **else begin**
>> **if** *(AAS=0) {arbitration lost only}* **then**
>> *Read byte to release SCL {S0}*
>> **else begin** *{addressed as slave}*
>> **repeat**
>>> *Read status {S1}*
>>> **if** *(TRX=0) {receiver}* **then**
>>> **begin**
>>>> **if** *(AAS=0) {data byte received}* **then**
>>>> **begin**
>>>>> **if** *(No. wanted > 0)* **and** *(AD0=0)* **then**
>>>>> **begin**
>>>>>> *Read byte {SO}*
>>>>>> *Store byte*
>>>>>> *Decrement no. wanted*
>>>>>> **if** *(No. wanted = 0)* **then**
>>>>>>> *Store received packet*
>>>>> **end**
>>>>> **else**
>>>>>> *Read byte to release SCL {S0}*
>>>> **end**
>>>> **else begin** *{addressed as slave}*
>>>>> *Read data to start reception {S0}*
>>>>> *Initialise no. wanted*
>>>> **end**
>>> **end**
>>> **else begin** *{transmitter}*
>>>> **if** *(AAS=1) {addressed as slave}* **then**
>>>>> *Initialise read pointer*
>>>> **if** *(LRB=0) {ack}* **then**
>>>>> *Send data {S0}*
>>>> **else** *{no ack}*
>>>>> *Quit using bus*
>>> **end**
>>> **repeat**
>>>> **Read** *status {S1}*
>>>> **until** *(BB=0 or PIN=0)*
>> **until** *(BB=0) {stop condition}*
> **end**
> **end**

Note: The read pointer is not initialised in this routine because there is only one byte to send.

Fig. 10.3   Code listing: example of better practice.

authors (i.e. top-down or bottom-up) should be included, along with the detailed test plan as enacted by the authors, from simple dynamic tests, through the steps of integration, to α-test.

The input data, expected results, and output from dynamic tests (where these can be detailed) should be given; otherwise, for less deterministic tests, a description of the test and the behaviour of the system should be provided.

2. A description of the objective test strategy undertaken by an independent QI/QA agency (i.e. black-box and white-box components of β-tests) should be shown, along with the details of black-box and white-box tests specifying input data, expected result, and output from the tests where these can be detailed; otherwise, for less deterministic tests, a description of the test and the behaviour of the system should be provided.

3. Client acceptance trials, and operating history, should be detailed, including the details of acceptance trials specifying input data, expected results, and output from the tests where these can be detailed; otherwise, for less deterministic tests, a description of the test and the behaviour of the system should be provided. Customer (or general 'field') reports of faults and corrective measures after installation for a project, or general release for product, should be included.

The form of this section of the maintenance manual will be largely textual (in natural language and, perhaps, pseudocode) for the description of tests, and both textual and numerical for input and output.

It is clear that the different components of a maintenance manual will come into being at different lifecycle stages, in that their basic material will exist in the archive in a more or less volatile form. For instance, the software definition material will be available, and minimally volatile, from architectural design stage onwards. We recommend that this section of the maintenance manual is compiled, and clearly labelled as the top level of the document, at the start of the detailed software design stage.

The main virtue of this is to provide a clear understanding of the scope of software to be made, and also to signify the start of maintenance documentation by getting one of its sections over and done with; in view of the exigencies of compiling other levels of the maintenance manual, and the problem of delayed documentation becoming defaulted-on documentation, doing the software specification section as early as possible is a wise precaution.

Design, code-listing and test-history sections of the maintenance manual are highly volatile materials during the implementation activities of the lifecycle. It makes no sense to try to keep a deliverable (cosmetic) version of much of this material during the creative stages of software engineering, because the normal rate at which code and design are corrected and changed is very high.

On the other hand we do recommend that:

1. The maintenance manual should be planned, within the CPT, from the start of implementation; it should not be left as an 'understood' requirement. Its four basic sections should be foreseen, and the first one (software specification) completed early – see above.

2. The design, code and test sections will, of course, be archived for reasons of general visibility. Archived versions should be updated as a continuing activity, and preserved in this form and in the immediately preceding version (see Section 3.3).

3. Towards the end of the subjective testing phase, the whole set of maintenance documentation should be consolidated and put in its reasonably cosmetic form for delivery. The missing elements of test history should be provided for in the format, to be filled in later.

   Consolidating documentation out of the archive into the maintenance manual should be a serious job, competently undertaken – not just a chore for junior members/trainees in the CPT. Under no circumstances should the consolidation of documentation be taken as an excuse to create the basic material for the first time.

As well as ensuring that the maintenance manual can be compiled in the manner recommended, another strong reason for updating the design, coding and testing material in the archive is to act as an insurance policy against accidents during the implementation. Accidents, in these terms, are generally staffing matters such as CPT members becoming available for one reason or another.

About the worst thing that can happen during a software development is that software engineers fall ill, or leave, during the stage when code is partly written and author-tested. When the designs and code listings are missing or invalid (and even worse if there is no adequate specification), the whole endeavour is endangered. For some software systems, the security and integrity of archive material during the development, and thereafter its deliverable documentation (under configuration management) is so crucial that the choice of PSE/configuration management support systems is largely determined by that consideration.

The problem of updating a highly volatile documentation set during the development of a major software system was, in former epochs, the legitimate excuse of software engineers to leave documentation until the end of the job. All elements of deliverable documentation, other than the code listing, required manual updating, re-typing, etc. The results were endangered developments and largely defective documentation done in haste (if at all) after the job, by people who wanted to get on to their next software engineering task.

Nowadays the facilities of a PSE will provide some electronic means of updating documentation, except in the case of small, relatively primitive, self-hosted micros. The one exception to this electronic facility for software engineers is in the area of design. Few of the diagrammatic notations described in Section 7.3 are as yet fully implemented within PSEs. As no one notation is universally advantageous over lifecycle stages and different applications, this should not be taken as the reason to adopt an implemented version of one or the other to be used as 'standard' practice. Nor, in order to 'solve' the design documentation problem, should pseudocode be adopted, just because the PSE of almost all computers will support it easily.

For the design part of deliverable documentation, the ideal PSE would incorporate several implemented notations, possibly even down to code generation and system reconfiguration level. A subset of the ten notations listed in Section 7.3, depending on the application mixture, would be a good start.

Until then, the updating of the design level of deliverable document-ation may well be a laborious, manual activity. Managers, chief programmers, CPT members and software engineers in general should recognize this, and ensure that – however laborious – the design documentation does get updated and properly incorporated in the maintenance-manual part of deliverable documentation.

10.2   Maintenance, new versions, and configuration management

After a software system has been validated (and certified if this is required), it is regarded as operational. For a project, this may be a contractual milestone such as the beginning of a warranty period, during which any defects in the system are corrected within the originally contracted price; for a product the system will appear as an item in a sales catalogue and, ultimately, will be sold and delivered to clients under some appropriate guarantee terms.

In either case the change of status (in our status matrix terms as previously employed) for validation or certification from 0 to + means that the software should be maintained in a continuing fashion, and that the E- loop property of the system will begin to operate in the sense that the system may begin to be obsolete. In fact it may be somewhat obsolete at the time it is validated, particularly if there is a substantial backlog of unimplemented changes that have been left in order to get the system finished in its present form.

The issues of maintenance to correct detected errors, and new-version policies to deal with requirements evolution, require careful organization and technical provisions. The importance of this is signified by the proportion of cost attributable to software maintenance alone. Such figures as are available (they are, naturally, treated with some sensitivity by companies) indicate that, new versions apart, the ratio of development to maintenance costs for software systems is in the order of 60 : 40 (see Boehm, 1981). Others put this ratio at 50 : 50 or even (Putnam, 1982) at 40 : 60. The figure is, of course, not static; there has been a progressive increase in the fraction due to maintenance as software systems have become more widespread, large and complex (and because many of these have been made by amateur programmers). Boehm's figures indicate that this progression has been continuous since Epoch 1, the comparable ratio for 1955 being in the order of 95 : 5. There will be some value to which the ratio will converge asymptotically. Perhaps SDI ('Starwars') will provide a paradigm of the form $x : 3x$ or some such. Given the scope of SDI (anything between 30 and 100 magastatements is possible), the '$3x$' component should be an interesting affair for the humble maintenance man with his screwdriver and oilcan. Thirty thousand person-years of maintenance effort, perhaps?

For new versions, the picture is less clear, and the problem has come to be seen more as one of how to make software more 'new-versionable', and how to decide that a new development altogether is required, rather than a new version.

10.2.1 Software maintenance and release policy

The maintenance of a project may be undertaken by the user organization, or may be contracted by it to the supplier organization (or even an entirely separate company – although this is rare for obvious reasons). For a product, the maintenance is a matter for the supplier's field-support group. In either case there is likely to be a migration of responsibility for the software, from the people who made it to the people who will maintain it. Even in the case of a supplier contracting to maintain software developed as a project, staff assignments and availability change over a period of time. The migration of responsibility for a software system moving out of the development stage into the maintenance stage places great emphasis on the quality of the deliverable documentation, and this in turn means that the deliverable documentation must be seen as an integral part of the software system. It must, in fact, be fully quality assured, and here it must be said that most software systems we have seen should undoubtedly have failed the software β-test. The software may be + status but its documentation may be very emphatically −!

Not only must the documentation be adequate, but it must also be maintained in this status. The organization provisions to achieve this are self-evident; competent software staff doing the maintenance, and competent managers ensuring that maintenance changes to the software

are properly reflected at all levels of the documentation.

The technical requirements for maintenance are more complex; as well as an adequate PSE, as required for software development in the first place (for maintenance may involve re-development of a part of the system), the facilities must include tools for making documentation updates relatively easy to do. This is discussed further in Section 10.2.3.

For projects, unique systems for single end-client organizations, maintenance changes to software are usually effected for all copies of the software in existence. This is often relatively easy to achieve, as the user environment is restricted to a single organization (or a limited number of related companies), and propagation of even small changes to the software is not difficult to organize.

For products, the situation is somewhat different. There may be numerous copies of a software system (perhaps millions in the case of 'virtual computer' facilities), and their geographical distribution may be from Afghanistan to Zanzibar, so to speak. The sort of question that arises is: 'In the case of that very obscure bug that Fred found last Thursday (well he would wouldn't he?), necessitating a one-instruction change – for ADD X read SUB Y – should it be the cause of a new release of the software and its documentation to all 350 000 clients?'

We have referred earlier to new versions accommodating E-type system changes to requirements, and this is dealt with below. The instance quoted above concerns a form of 'new' release for corrected error – a somewhat different concept. A paper by Lehman (1980) suggests a statistical method for determining the release frequency for new E-type versions, and this is discussed, as appropriate, in the section below. We distinguish these versions from their Maintenance counterparts (M-type versions) in the following.

Determining policy for M-type version releases for software products may be far from straightforward. Factors such as the rarity of occurrence of different types of error, the potential severity of consequences (a minor spelling error in a screen message for instance, right up the scale of effect to system failure), the cost of re-issuing software and its documentation, and the effect on the supplier's reputation, all have to be balanced. Each software system in a product has its own 'equation' in these terms.

10.2.2   New (E-type) versions and release policy

Lehman (1980) has enunciated five 'laws of program evolution'. These are:

I. *The 'Law' of Continuing Change.* A program that is used and that (as an implementation of its specifications) reflects some other reality, undergoes continued change or becomes progressively less useful. The 'change or decay' process continues until it is judged more cost-effective to replace the system with a re-created version.

II. *The 'Law' of Increasing Complexity.* As an evolving program is continually changed its complexity increases as its structure deteriorates, unless work is done to maintain or reduce it.

III. *The 'Law' of Program Evolution.* Program evolution is subject to a dynamics which makes the programming process, and hence measures of global project and systems attributes, self-regulating with statistically determinable trends and invariance.

IV. *The 'Law' of Conservation of Organization Stability (Invariant Work Rate).* During the active life of a program, the global activity rate in the associated programming projects is statistically invariant.

V. *The 'Law' of Conservation of Familiarity (Perceived Complexity).* During the active life of a program, the release content (changes, additions, deletions) of successive releases of the evolving program is statistically invariant.

The author goes on to cite some evidence for Laws III–V from a paradigm – a large, batch program for general-purpose data-processing comprising 1.3 million source-code instructions (assembler) and 4800 program modules. It is beyond our scope here to comment further on the statistical nature of this work, which its author scrupulously identifies in places as excluding some considerations and providing only 'phenomenological' (i.e. not causally established) apparent relationships. For this reason we set aside the 'Fundamental Law III' as awaiting more widespread confirmation.

The main import of the other four is that requirements change over time and, if the software representing them is not also changed it becomes progressively unusable; if it is changed then it either becomes more complex in the process, or changes have to be more extensive in order to maintain (or reduce) the original complexity level. The work rate and amount-of-change rate remain roughly constant over the lifecycle of an evolving system (given that requirements changes do result in software changes).

Lehman calls this the 'meta-system' behaviour of software, implying that it is less a matter for management decision than accommodation. This view is both intuitively plausible and well known amongst developers of medium to large and very large software systems (for small systems as defined in Chapter 2 'Law I' often becomes a simple question of totally re-writing the software).

There is, as already described, a substantial difference between the issues involved for maintenance (M-type) releases and these evolutionary (E-type) releases of software. The imperative for M-type releases is commercial in the tactical sense of contract requirement or possible customer alienation through faulty software; one would hardly re-issue large numbers of a games-playing system (such as in the Chapter 11 'case study') for a minor screen-format error, but one would feel compelled to withdraw and re-issue a software system likely to fail and electrocute several hundred hospital patients.

The imperative for an E-type release is usually commercial in the strategic sense: the enhancement of market position, client relationships (and the consequent deterioration of competitors' standing, it is hoped), by improving a software system in terms of the suitability of its features and functions.

Apart from these differences in purpose, and some inevitable differences in scale as a result, there is no distinction of technical issues between M- and E- releases of a software system.

A central question in software evolution is that of how much change one can safely make to a system before invoking a re-development policy; is it 5% of modules, 25%, 50%, 75%? Of course there is no general-case answer to this, although that does not prevent the question from being asked.

Judgementally, there is no reason why the possible proportional change should not be very high for well-made software. Here the considerations of modifiability as described in Chapter 9 are significant. For systems where competent, objective software engineers deem the software 'modifiable with confidence', changes to substantially above 50% of modules may be effected. It should be noted, though, that the coda to Lehman's 'Law II' will limit the amount of change possible. It will not only be a matter of subtracting X modules and adding Y modules, but also of changing Z modules in order to preserve the good structure of the software (or even improve it). Beyond some point in doing X and Y, the changes required (expressed as a percentage of modules needing change) will approach 100%. It may be that even minor levels of change – removal of a few percent of old modules and addition of a few percent of new modules – causes changes to all, or nearly all, modules. In the example due to Lehman (1980), 'release 19' had involved a fraction of 0.55 of the modules changed in an incremental growth of about 0.1 in the number of modules.

In this case it is a reasonable inference that the software was poorly made in the first place and is of low modifiability. This was very much a condition in Epochs 1–3, but recent years have seen some improvement in some software development companies, although it is only five years since we saw one 'megastatement' system (again in assembler) the first version of which was so badly made that it absorbed a major part of software resources to do E-type releases of even small code-size changes.

In the case of both M-type and E-type releases of software, a vital matter is the administration of documentation sets, their updating, and correlation with product classification and clients where the different product classes are installed. This is known as configuration management for software systems and is described in the following subsection.

10.2.3 Configuration management

When a definitive version of a software system has been made and its validation is complete, a record must be kept of subsequent changes to the software, and a corresponding documentation set made for the changed system. In general, this is known as 'configuration management' of a software system, and may be part of a more general configuration management procedure for hardware and software.

Configuration management for products and projects is basically the same, in that there is no essential difference in objectives and basic means. Where the two may differ is in the following:

1. For projects, there may be a migration of responsibility between supplier and client if the former maintains the system for some time. Potentially at least, this can cause confusion when the supplier sets up and maintains a configuration management system and then, subsequently, maintenance transfers to the client.

2. The problem of migration should not occur for products. Following the validation of a product by the supplier's own product maintenance group (via QA procedures of β-testing), the system and its deliverable documentation should be entirely taken over by the supplier's product maintenance group. The configuration management system should be pre-planned, and then set up and maintained by the product maintenance group from the end of β-testing onwards.

In general, a configuration management system (nowadays either electronic or at least electronically supported) requires the following:

1. A general software product or project name. For instance, in the case of the hospital patient and environment alarm-monitoring system, we may have HPEAM or HOSPALARM or something of the sort.

2. A version numbering system for the E-type release status of the software. Thus HOSPALARM/7 might indicate version 7 of the system. This number will probably grow slowly (in months or years).

3. An M-type release numbering system in cases of software products or projects requiring an overall system-release for sets of corrected errors. Thus HOSPALARM/7.4 might indicate the fourth overall M-type release of version 7 of the software.

4. A set of software modules comprising a version, with their individual version and M-type release statuses. Thus HOSPALARM/7.4 might comprise (using the module designations in the example in Section 5.4):

HOSPALARM/7.4: A/7.1
B/2.10
C/6.3
D/1.19
E/1.27

The module M-type release number may grow quickly (in days or weeks possibly), and may become large although, given the usual size of software modules, beyond a certain point a re-write will be clearly called for. At the general M-type release level, in this case ·4 the number will grow at a rate determined by release policy.

5. 'Deliverable' documentation-sets (as described in Section 10.1) will need to correspond with each E-type version release, each general M-type release if appropriate, and the exact version and M-type release status of the software modules comprising it.

Thus, within the configuration management system under HOSPALARM/7.4 we would either find the exact documentation sets for D/1.19 and A/7.1 (along with the others) or pointers to the documents if they are filed in another fashion; e.g. under 'All HOSPALARM Module D versions and correction releases'.

6. A file of customers, and the products (version and release) they have last had delivered. Thus: VICTORIA HOSP (NY)/HOSPALARM/ 7.4.

7. An infrastructure organization to maintain and operate the configuration management systems.

8. Electronic means to facilitate configuration management.

The example given may make the issue of configuration management seem awfully simple. It is far from simple in practice. Our example concerned a small E-type system of around 2000 source statements of code. It is doubtful whether there would be any new versions of the system, although there may be plenty of M-type releases. The version of modules (e.g. A/7) is entirely fictitious; is it likely that there would be seven evolutions of the sensor software?

In the case of medium, large and very large software systems, the configuration-management requirements may involve many new versions over the lifetime of the software and lots of M-type releases, leading to considerable product complexity for a potentially large number of modules. The computer requirements for electronically supported configuration management systems are fairly simple to enumerate:

1. Good file-handling and general management facilities.

2. Enough archival store for all the expected projects and products, for all of their evolutions over their lifetime.

3. A security arrangement to prevent accidental (or other) access to the

configuration management system (this may be at two levels; general access and product/project specific access).

4. Word-processing, edit, and design notation update facilities for making documentation changes. (*Note*. We reiterate that, of these, the one concerning design is largely lacking.)

5. Possibility for on-line, concurrent access by software engineers and others (e.g. product marketing and support staff).

There can be no prescription for a configuration management system. Suppliers of mainframes and large minicomputers have 'virtual computer' facilities covering most of the items listed, but the issue of equipment procurement is seldom so simply determined. For instance, PSE requirements other than for configuration management play a rôle. Figure 10.4 depicts an Apse (Ada programming support environment) after Reiffer (1982).

Acquiring a PSE/configuration management system to support multi-product/project development of medium-sized to large software systems, is likely to prove expensive. On the other hand, the cost of not providing these facilities adequately could be enormous in terms of the difficulties

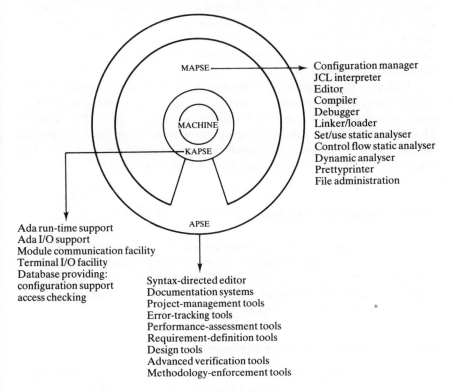

Configuration manager
JCL interpreter
Editor
Compiler
Debugger
Linker/loader
Set/use static analyser
Control flow static analyser
Dynamic analyser
Prettyprinter
File administration

Ada run-time support
Ada I/O support
Module communication facility
Terminal I/O facility
Database providing:
configuration support
access checking

Syntax-directed editor
Documentation systems
Project-management tools
Error-tracking tools
Performance-assessment tools
Requirement-definition tools
Design tools
Advanced verification tools
Methodology-enforcement tools

Fig. 10.4   PSE and configuration management systems.

of doing software development in the first place, and configuration management thereafter. (Incidentally, given the facilities, the archive and deliverable documentation can be kept under the configuration-management systems during development, e.g. HOSPALARM/0.) We make the strongest recommendation that adequate PSE/configuration management systems are procured and provided in all IT development organizations.

Apse, IPSE and other developments are likely to prove useful for large-scale software development and configuration management in the future. The Ada language and its environments (as depicted in Figure 10.4) is one area with adherents, and another one is the Integrated Project Support Environment (IPSE) of the British 'Alvey' initiative.

No less important, and as often under-provided, are the organization and staffing infrastructures for configuration management. Someone has to set the system up; someone (or many) must make sure it is always used and properly used. There is a tendency for good configuration-management practice to lapse. In this respect an electronic-based system has advantages over a manual one, as it can more easily become a part of software engineers' habitual practice to do configuration management as an extension of software development done within the electronic environment. The ISTAR lifecycle-management system, based on a 'contract model', and any others of its type will be particularly important (where used) for inculcating and preserving this and other aspects of good software engineering practice.

However it is supported, configuration management is essential. The dangers are obvious; imagine a service call at three o'clock on a Sunday morning reporting a catastrophic software failure from the Victoria Hospital, New York. And no one knows whether they have the payroll software or the alarm system, nor which version of whatever it is has just gone wrong. 'Where's the documentation? Send for Fred!'

10.3 Personnel issues

In this section we offer some general comments on the issue of recruiting and retaining software engineers. Whilst different companies' practices will vary in the matter of personnel management, some aspects are specific to software engineering and these issues should be appreciated and used to determine individual policies.

10.3.1 Recruiting software engineers

The general observation of skill-shortage in software engineering obscures differences in supply and demand for different levels of staff (in terms of experience and relevant, vocational education), and different application types. Those specific skill shortages should determine policies in recruiting, retention and education at company level, and managers and personnel officers are advised to acquaint themselves with the market conditions for the kind of software engineering staff required.

Indicating surplus of supply over demand by +, balance by = and shortfall by −, a typical (if hypothetical) picture may be represented by the skills matrix shown in Table 10.1.

Although this is a hypothetical example, it embodies a truism at the present time in many countries; the most severe skill shortage is in the chief programmer area for advanced IT applications in embedded, real-time systems. This situation is not likely to be alleviated in the near future in our view. The remedy may, in part, lie in education policy and some comment is offered on the subject in Section 10.4.

In the circumstances, there is much pressure on companies to recruit and retain their software engineers in the best and most competitive fashion possible. Not all companies are used to operating in a 'sellers' market' for technical staff, and the following remarks are offered with that in mind. To stand a chance of recruiting staff of any type one needs:

1. *An adequate advertising campaign*
   Advertising is a specialist business; amateurs often make elementary errors in determining frequency, media, and design of advertisements. As a general principle in the layout of advertisements, they should not be too textually dense, nor should they emphasize company information over matters of immediate interest to the applicant (job type, level, place, money).

2. *A minimal delay before making an offer*
   In a highly competitive market for 'rare resources', the shorter the elapsed time between an applicant's response to an advertisement and receipt of an offer, the higher the probability of positive outcome. Some large companies with multi-level, consensual processes can take weeks (and even months) to complete their bureaucratic moves with an applicant. This is seldom successful as, for the rarest resources (such as chief programmers for real-time systems) a lead time of 4–6 weeks is usually maximal; first-class

Table 10.1   The buyers and sellers market for staff.

Application type	Experience level (yrs)			
	0–3	*4–7*	*8–11*	*11–*
Business data processing	−	=	+	+ +
Scientific computing	−	=	+	+
Embedded, real-time systems	−	− −	− − −	− − −

applicants with a spirit of 'get up and go' will, beyond this point, have got up and gone.

3. *A competent interviewing practice*
An exacting, oral interview at the technical level is more often than not a strong attraction to first-class software engineers. The objective is to get the applicant talking. An interviewer should basically prompt; a bad interview has the interviewer doing most of the talking.

On the other hand, the applicant's claims of technical experience must be thoroughly 'β-tested' in the conversation; a useful device is to have a checklist of technical questions to ask. We have known questions such as 'What does the term "type" mean as applied to a variable or data item?' produce a totally different impression from that of the carefully prepared recital of technical experience. Another good idea is to set applicants a short, written essay in order to establish the applicant's literacy (essential in software engineering).

4. *Competitive employment terms and conditions*
The basic terms and conditions of employment depend on a balance between company practices as established, and the 'market rate' for the resource concerned. In some cases, 'standard' remuneration packages have to be amended by addition of a 'scarce resource' market supplement of some sort, and this can cause much contention in companies employing other types of technician. As well as the remuneration package, potential employees are much concerned to know the possible career development path for software engineers in the company; a notional career development is described in Section 10.3.2.

Above all other considerations, recruiting staff will require that a clear distinction is made in the employer's company between what is really needed, and what may be wanted on the other hand. Many companies make the mistake of advertising for 'need' and interviewing/offering for 'want', particularly if some inconvenient market rate in the remuneration package is required. Before recruiting software engineers (or any other staff) a job description should be written; this should be the real need and not some synthetic 'want'. All else should flow from that understanding.

10.3.2   Retaining software engineers

We wish to make two specific points about retaining software engineers as distinct from the general principles determining the employment volatility of staff, of which the following five are the major ones:

1. job satisfaction;

2. remuneration package;
3. general working conditions;
4. career development opportunity;
5. location, particularly the facilities for the employee and associates/dependants.

For a particular position with a particular company, most of these factors will be 'given' in the sense that the conditions are already determined; the most that can be done will be to improve on some *status quo* – e.g. factors 2 or 3 within limits.

A main, positive factor in employing software engineers – one that most certainly can be determined by management – is that concerning career development. Whilst this will change from place to place, being perhaps linked to other professions such as electronic engineering in some companies, the following points should generally apply:

1. A career-development scheme should exist for software engineers within an employer company. Given the relative youth of the profession, a career-development philosophy is likely to be better if meritocratic for software engineers, rather than heavily structured and bureaucratic. A notional career-development scheme is described in Figure 10.5. Career development should be a topic at the interview in the first place.
2. Staff appraisal should take place on a regular basis, and be related to the theoretical career development opportunity of the person appraised. This is discussed further below.

A notional career trajectory for software engineers, showing some provisions for education and refreshment in the main subject, is given in Figure 10.7 based on the notional career development schematic in Figure 10.5.

Staff appraisal is a crucial and difficult issue, often the subject of considerable misunderstanding. We offer the following notes on the subject without suggesting that it is in any sense a matter of well-established technique. Staff appraisal is too subjective for this to be possible.

There are, basically, two types of appraisal – connected but none the less distinct:

1. *Annual review of remuneration and other benefits*
   This includes any salary increment, bonus, profit-sharing or other matters bearing on remuneration; it may also concern share-option issues and pension rights, holiday entitlements, etc.
2. *Job-performance appraisal*
   This is the joint evaluation of professional (software engineering)

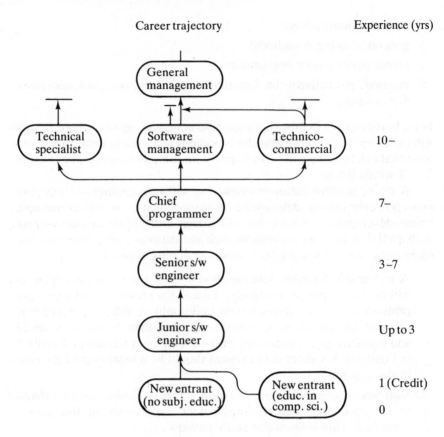

Fig. 10.5 A notional career development scheme.

performance, between an appraisee and technical management staff. The period of review may, or may not, be annual; it may for instance be determined by a task duration.

Although job appraisals and the annual review are obviously connected, it is generally a mistake to allow remuneration discussions into the discussion of performance. Consequently, it is good practice to have the appraisal before the review.

Whereas the annual review may be done by general management, job-performance appraisal is a technical, peer-group matter and must be undertaken by technical management, chief programmers, etc. Even so, appraisals should be formal in the sense that a record is kept of the main points covered. Thus, subsequent appraisals can note any change for the better (or worse) in the performance of the appraisee.

It is generally good practice to appraise software engineers shortly after appointment. About three months after the software engineer joins a company (at whatever career stage as depicted in Table 10.1), a manager – general or technical in this case – should have a relatively informal appraisal to review the settling-in process and initial attitudes as seen from both sides.

Then, at perhaps 6–9 months, a technical appraisal proper should be attempted. On the one hand this will give an appraisee a decent chance to rectify any perceived shortcomings; on the other hand it will enable the employer company to rectify some of its recruiting mistakes early. (How does your company rectify its recruiting mistakes – which everyone makes to some extent? Does it appraise them out or bake them in?)

Appraisal is basically a dialogue between technical peers. That is not to say that the participants are 'equal' technically or hierarchically. The period may be fixed, i.e. annual and preceding the review, or it may be based on epochs in the sense that a suitable task-driven occasion determines the period. In this last case, an 'epoch' should not be too long. People working on, say, a five-year software development should have appraisals with greater frequency than at the five-year period.

Software engineers do not normally resent fair and reasoned comment on their performance, however 'negative' this may be. Most good practitioners tend, without realizing it, to epitomize Pope's lines: 'Know then thyself, presume not God to scan/ The proper study of mankind is Man.' The peer-group software team construction outlined in Chapter 6, and its practices, help materially in this attitude. In fact we have found that the best software engineers become highly demotivated if they are not constructively appraised.

The formality of appraisal, and the technique overall, are greatly assisted by the existence of a checklist of items for the appraisal. An example of such a checklist is shown in Figure 10.6. Appraisals may take one to two hours in the case of junior software engineers, up to three or four hours for more senior people. A most important feature of staff motivation/retention is the clear identification, at appraisals, of the sort of subject education and refreshment that professional software engineers may need (and should have) at different career-development stages.

10.4 Software engineering education

Irwin Edman believed that education is the process of casting false pearls before real swine. Worse, few topics, in the general area of computing, have excited so much comment and dissent amongst practitioners and academics as has software engineering education. The main problem has been to decide two basic questions:

1. What is a suitable curriculum for teaching software engineering? In particular, there has been (and is) a problem to discriminate clearly

Appraisal of: *JOHN SMITH*, by: *MARY JONES*, on: *January 21st, 1986*

	Ex.	*VG*	*G*	*Mod.*	*Unsat.*	*Weak*	*Poor*
Technical factors							
1. Specifications		*					
2. Designs				*			
3. Coding				*			
4. Testing						*	
5. Documentation					*		
6. Modification				*			
7. Design review (as author)	*						
8. Design review (reviewer)							*
9. Code reading (as author)			*				
10. Code reading (as reader)							*
11. Chief programmer	(Not applicable in this case)						
13. Overall co-operation in team					*		
General							
14. Punctuality			*				
15. Dependability					*		
16. Co-operation with management	*						
17. Quality of written reporting	*						
18. Quality of oral reporting				*			
19. Interest in firm/div/dept.	*						
20. Initiative		*					
21. Interest in self-improvement	*						
22. Sense of responsibility				*			
23. Mgt. performance or potential					*		

Fig. 10.6 Staff appraisal example.

between software engineering and computer science as subjects of study, whereas their classifications as fields of endeavour is much more straightforward.

2. What is a suitable source for software engineering education? In particular, can and should the subject – given its adequate definition – be taught in secondary and tertiary education establishments such as schools, polytechnics and universities?

Our views on these matters are set out below. In particular, we offer some remarks on the general problem of software engineering education, the issue of education requirements at different staff levels, curricula for suitable courses, and the problem of adequate sources.

10.4.1   The general problem

At one level it is surprising that a problem of defining distinct curricula exists between software engineering and computer science, as the two are quite easily classifiable as fields of endeavour. The object of software engineering is to make high-quality software for practical applications and under economic constraint, utilizing good (software) engineering and management practices in the process.

The object of computer science includes basic research into theoretical principles of software engineering practice, as well as matters such as computer hardware architecture, and the theoretical bases for information management and numerical computation; in the process a corpus of knowledge is built up in these areas and is underpinned by subject matter from physics and mathematics (and recently – for AI-epistemology and its derivates such as cognitive psychology).

In principle the matter is simple and straightforward, and can be represented in a convenient analogy; the practically useful aspects of computer science research should infuse and inform software engineering practice just as mathematics and physics (mechanics, properties of materials, etc.) sustain engineering in general.

One of the main problems obscuring this understanding is that computer science curricula and courses abound at secondary and tertiary education levels (schools, and polytechnics/universities), whilst software engineering as a subject is virtually non-existent in the education sector in most countries, for reasons elucidated below. One result of this is that the programming part of computer science, as widely taught, is taken by many people (including some computer scientists) as the totality of software engineering. The supposition is established that nothing further is needed for practising as a software engineer than a decent computer science course.

In fact, nothing could be more misleading; whilst a computer science education is a fine basis from which to begin a software engineering apprenticeship, and unimprovable as the basis for a career in computer science, it is not a qualification in software engineering. One would not (or should not) commission a graduate physicist to build a bridge, say, as his or her first job.

Another problem besetting the issue of software engineering education is the basic one of whether there is a real subject of software engineering at all. The matter was summarized a decade ago by Wasserman (1976) as follows:

- Software engineering education must force the student to synthesize computer science principles with available tools and techniques (including management factors).

- Education in software engineering is fundamentally different from education in computer science.

- Although some things in software engineering can be presented through lectures and reading, they are strongly reinforced by having the students 'get their hands dirty'.

In short, software engineering can be 'caught but not taught'. This rather formidable aphorism is almost literally true; software engineering cannot be taught as an *a priori* subject such as, for example, mathematics. In this respect it resembles a craft.

In the weaving industries, before automation of the process took place, a young aspirant weaver was shown how to weave and generally helped to learn the craft by 'sitting next to Nellie', where that worthy was a highly experienced weaver. As Wasserman points out, an explicit part of software engineering education is for practitioners to 'get their hands dirty'. We would add that a strong CPT-like, peer-group structure, operating modern software engineering practices with a good PSE and towards a real (or realistic) software objective, is the best craft environment of all. In this respect, the chief programmer (or master software engineer), and other senior CPT team members act as 'Nellie'.

Software engineering has become a vogue subject for many academic institutions over recent years, where basic computer science courses have been extended and amended, and then designated 'Software Engineering'. With some exceptions this approach has basically fallen short of software education in any meaningful sense.

The urge to do something is, of course, very strong. Education funding is not altogether easy to come by in general; also many central government initiatives in IT stress the importance (correctly) of software engineering. For instance, the first so-called 'Butcher Report' on IT skills shortage in the United Kingdom (already cited in Chapter 1) gives the following 'disaggregated' list for IT subjects at education level:

- Computer science (especially software), electronic engineering, software engineering, mathematics, physics, materials science, systems engineering, other engineering (especially mechanical, design and production), etc.

The challenge is now to get the matter of software engineering properly established, in terms of plausible curricula and methods for software enabling it to be learned. (*Note.* This really means 'learned' as distinct from 'taught'.) As commented by Jensen *et al.* (1979), in the context of a curriculum for software engineering education suggested by the IEEE, the results of amalgamating bits of computer science curricula with parts of engineering courses will most probably produce a better-trained computer scientist, not a software engineer. Just so. We have known of academic departments changing their designation from computer science (with little other noticeable effect) to exploit the fashion in IT.

10.4.2   Staff requirements

In Chapter 1 we identified three populations whose activities might affect the software engineering process. We define these now as follows:

- *Practitioners*. Software engineers or amateur programmers (but not 'hobbyists'), and their technical managers, who have had software engineering education/experience at some stage of their careers.
- *Contiguents*. Other vocational specialists, and their managers, such as electronics hardware engineers who work on contiguous parts of composite systems containing software subsystems; if these staff program at all, they are probably 'amateur programmers' within the previous category.
- *Management* (and others). Any general management including legal, commercial, accounting, production and quality engineering, administrative and other staff, having little or no understanding of software engineering but bearing responsibility for some parts of the process of developing software.

In many organizations, defective software engineering involves all three of these populations; in general it involves the first and third. In these circumstances, to deal with the problem at one level only is not likely to lead to any noticeable improvement in the quality of software engineering as a process, or its products. Where the need exists, education should address:

- the primary-skill education of practitioners,
- a secondary-skill requirement for contiguents,
- a strong level of orientation for management.

As follows from comments in Chapters 1 and 3 of this work, an objective in determining curricula, methods and education programmes should be to provide a common conceptual framework, and basic vocabulary between the populations where the process of software engineering is concerned. For this reason, an education programme should be coherent – however provided – in the matter of basic material and methods.

10.4.3   Suggested guidelines and curricula

Two guiding principles should be held in mind when planning software engineering education curricula and methods.

1. The object of education is a process of bringing out the latent talents

of the student rather than putting in the acquired wisdom of the teacher, although the latter is often a necessary precursor.

2. Software engineering, being essentially a craft having little canonical literature and few 'laws', must be learned as a set of skills rather than taught in a didactic, pedagogical fashion. In Oscar Wilde's dictum: 'Experience is the name we give to our mistakes.' (The authors of this work are, on that scale, extremely experienced; perhaps this book is a further instance)

With that in mind, and recalling also the need for coherent material between several levels of education course, we define a 'core curriculum' as follows:

1. Definitions in software engineering; products, projects and prototypes; S-type, P-type and E-type systems, and a thorough grasp of the lifecycle ordering of events in software engineering. This will be the conceptual framework for the subject and the courses.

2. Specification and outline design. The stages of conceptualization, URS/FS, and OSD/software taxonomies. Prototyping and feasibility.

3. General management control procedures. Archiving, structured walkthrough, change control, CPT organization and methodology, and management control documentation. The problem of comprehensibility of the software engineering process 'below the line'.

4. Principles for good design and programming. Introduction to the principles of good design (after Constantine *et al.*) and structured programming (after Dijkstra, Jackson *et al.*). Introduction to a subset of design notations, such as SADT, MASCOT, SDL, BS 6224, etc.

5. Software effort and timescale estimating. Discussion of estimating practices, with emphasis on parametric models research and the recommended FS/OSD stage method of notional activities planning.

6. Software quality definitions and quality criteria; organization for quality control, inspection and assurance. Software validation and practices in subjective and objective testing.

7. Specific management issues in software engineering. Deliverable documentation; version control and configuration management issues; staff recruiting, retention and education; contracting software services.

It will be immediately obvious that the core curriculum corresponds to the structure and content of this book. Whether this book is adequate for it is another matter.

Further than the core, all courses described below should contain a practical exercise (whatever other practicals they embody), as a vehicle for practising matters such as specification, OSD, archiving, estimating and planning, team organization and CPT type practices. It should also include exercises in design principles and notations. Typically, this practical – known as a 'normative' exercise for its effect within and across courses – comprises a defective URS for some quite complex requirement, such as might be the case for the hospital system already extensively mentioned earlier. Finding (or inventing) normative practicals for the core curriculum is a difficult task; a balance must be found between what can be done in a reasonably short time and what would obviously comprise a non-trivial URS.

The courses described below form a minimal, coherent education programme in software engineering, comprising:

- A primary-skill course in software engineering for practitioners. This is in the form of an exceptionally intensive 'master class' in the subject.

- A refresher course for senior software managers, chief programmers and other senior staff.

- A curriculum for secondary-skill education as required by 'contiguents'.

- An orientation course for managers and others as described above.

In the description of courses given below, the terms 'residential' and 'modular' (or non-modular) are employed. These terms have the following meanings. A 'residential' course is one where the students will be located, together, at a place where they will not be disturbed by day-to-day working or business interruptions. A consequence of this will be that group-based project work can be done at irregular hours if need be. A 'modular' course is one which can be done in parts, with some discontinuity between the parts. Some courses can be scheduled in that way; others requiring the strong and continuous establishment of 'themes' and substantial practical exercises would suffer from discontinuity.

Primary skill and refresher courses should be a part of rational career development for software engineers. This point was made in Section 10.3.2 concerning staff appraisal, where a notional career development schematic was suggested for software engineers.

Figure 10.7 shows that same schematic, with an indication of the points at which the two education courses, and others, may well apply.

A 'basic programming' course is usually a 4–6 week course, full time or part time (but non-modular) and comprising: an introduction to basic computer hardware architecture, binary arithmetic and Boolean algebra, simple PSE facilities such as available on a good microcomputer (or small minicomputer) system; assembler-language programming and a good high-level language introduction (such as Pascal); the principles of good design and structured programming; introduction to good programming practice after Ledgard (1987). Beyond this, aspiring software engineers need to begin their apprenticeship as shown in the schematic.

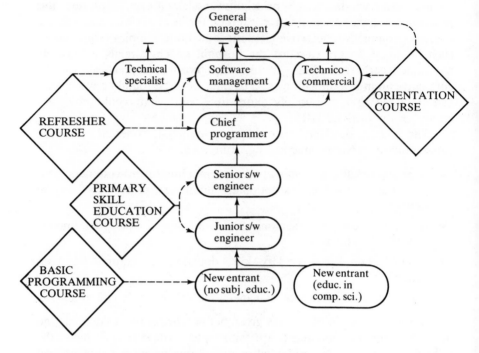

Fig. 10.7 Career development and continued education.
(*Note*: The read pointer is not initialized in this routine because there is only one byte to send.)

Table 10.2 A coherent course programme.

	Duration (days)	Form (Modular, residential)	Facilities for practicals
Orientation	7	Residential, non-modular	Self-hosted micros with UCSD Pascal
Secondary skill	10	Residential, modular	Self-hosted micros with UCSD Pascal
Refresher	10	Non-residential, modular	Access to an advanced PSE
Primary skill	35	Residential, non-modular	Access to a good mini based PSE

The other courses defined should, in our view, have the provisions shown in Table 10.2.

The four courses in Table 10.2 can be described, in summary, as follows:

1. *The primary-skill education course*

    This course is, effectively, a master class in software engineering for practising programmers with usually between 2 and 6 years of experience, even if it is intermittent programming as for some amateur programmers. The course should comprise the core curriculum (with normative practical), plus additional lectures, in considerable depth, in design; practice in programming; modern developments in languages and PSEs, human factors and the user interface; and the behavioural aspects of the CP.

    From the end of the first week to the close of the course, there should be an intensive, team-based practical exercise comprising all lifecycle activities, from specification to α-testing and QA (β-testing). This practical will consume some 60% of total course hours of student time, and a lot of computer time.

    A suggested reading list for this course could comprise: a good, basic book on software engineering; one on the basic principles of programming; an introduction to modern languages (e.g. Pascal, Modula, Ada); and source works or papers on estimating (e.g. Boehm, 1981), design, and quality.

    Evaluation of attendees should be based on a tutor's appraisal of general course participation, an evaluation (by the tutor acting as surrogate client in the main practical), and an examination; our practice has been to set two rather severe three-hour written papers.

2. *The refresher course*

    This may be a 2 × 5-day, modular course for software managers, chief programmers, etc. – particularly if they have never done the primary skill course or equivalent. The first week of the course should comprise the core curriculum (with its normative practical); if necessary some pre-reading (and prior practice) in a modern programming language should be done – for example an introduction to Pascal or Modula and some practice on a microcomputer.

    The second week should comprise a second 'normative' practical at the specification and design level, and lectures on specialist topics of particular interest, such as (if appropriate) database technology, communications technology, design of concurrent systems, future developments in hardware and software (e.g. Ada at the language level), and so forth.

    There should be no in-course reading task but a suitable basic book on software engineering should be used for post-course reading and reference.

The ratio of theory to practical work should be about 65 : 35 in terms of student hours; there should be little computer usage other than for familiarization with language (Pascal) and PSE principles. Individual evaluation may be by written examination and must include both technical and management issues.

3. *A secondary-skill course*
This is a 10 day (2 × 5 days), residential course, which may be modular, for technicians with little experience or knowledge of programming. Pre-reading for the course may include general introductions to the problem of software engineering (as currently found in Brooks (1975) and Weinberg (1971)), and an introduction to modern high-level languages (as found in Smedema *et al.* (1985)).

The first week should comprise a part of the core curriculum (items 1–5 earlier, in fact), including its normative practical, and a substantial introduction to programming with hands-on practice, in a language such as Pascal or Modula, on a good microcomputer. The second module should reprise the core curriculum, with a different normative practical to the same (design) level; furthermore there should be presentations of case histories in software engineering (positive and negative) from the technical application area appropriate to the attendees.

The ratio of theory to practical on this course, including the programming practice and the two 'normative' exercises, is in the order of 50 : 50 in terms of student time. There should be no in-course reading, but a suitable basic book on software engineering should be distributed for post-course reading and reference.

It is not appropriate to evaluate attendees individually on this course.

4. *An orientation course*
This is a 7–10 day, residential and non-modular course for management and other staff who may lack knowledge and experience of software engineering. Pre-reading for the course should be at the general level of introduction to the problems of software engineering, as set out in 3 above.

The course should comprise the 'core curriculum' with its normative practical, plus 2 to 3 days of lectures on and practice in programming, using UCSD Pascal on a good microcomputer. The ratio of lecture to practical work on this course, including both the programming and the normative exercise, should be about 70 : 30. Whilst there will be no in-course reading, a suitable basic book on software engineering should be distributed as post-course reading and reference.

It is not appropriate to evaluate attendees individually on this course.

A question sometimes arises concerning vocational re-orientation of staff in organizations having too much of some type of specialization, and too few software engineers. A surplus of mechanical or electronic engineers, natural scientists and so on, can happen when a fundamental change occurs in the technological basis of a well-established product line.

In general, the matter should be seen in exactly the same way as for a new entrant to the software engineering career structure. There is basically no way of predetermining aptitude, so the best approach is to give the staff concerned a programming course such as that described after Figure 10.6, and then some actual software engineering to do – preferably in a strong environment such as a 'Peer-group CPT'. The 'yield' from this process (percentage of successful converts to software engineering), will be very strongly a function of age and previous vocational education level.

Policies to effect a miracle cure to a staffing problem in this area, by propelling senior and other staff – some perhaps lacking academic education in a technical subject – into programming courses do no favours to either company or people. Furthermore, effectively starting people off again at the bottom of a career-development trajectory may act as a demotivating factor in many cases.

10.4.4 Education sources

It is difficult to envisage software engineering as a full subject to be treated at secondary or tertiary education levels as represented by schools, polytechnics and universities. The reasons have already been indicated in several of the foregoing sections and are summarized as follows:

1. Software engineering is a craft to be learned, rather than a subject to be taught. To some extent (as in the primary-skill master classes), software engineering can be presented as a systematic framework, within which some principles can be explained and much practical experience can be consolidated. The best demonstration of this is that, whilst the principles of programming can be taught to a large extent, software engineering is far more than just programming and cannot be taught in the same sense.

2. Academic staff are often themselves insufficiently experienced in real-life software engineering for realistic simulation of practical exercises, CPT environments, management/user/client rôle playing, contracting and so forth. The theoretical grasp of computer-science principles is no substitute, even though it may play an invaluable part in educating computer scientists and, up to a point, others such as electronic hardware and software engineers. We recognize that this

viewpoint will find disfavour in some quarters, and we stress that the problem is not a universal property of academic level courses but a danger to be avoided.

3. In general it is difficult to see how institutions geared to provide for and measure individuals' cognitive abilities (and their application) can be expected to provide adequately for and test achievement in a subject in which the major criterion for 'success' is the result of a team endeavour.

These difficulties are widely known and have been extensively treated by others such as Jensen and Tonies (1979), Sommerville (1985), and Wasserman (1976). Sommerville's approach, and others like it, notably in the USA, recognize that software engineering is not a full curriculum study in academic institutes, and also that it is not computer science even though cognate with it.

Given that academia in general has not (could not have) provided software engineering education, in the sense of delivering competent software engineers to business and industry, and given the fundamental importance and urgency of the subject for IT in general, there is a very clear need for some alternative approach. In our view, a considerable weight of responsibility in the matter rests with business and industry, who are the employers of software engineers (and other participants) whose education needs are involved.

The difficulty with this thesis is that business and industry are difficult to organize in the matter of consensus about means and methods, and tend to become suspicious about commercial advantage. Other difficulties involve the determination of curricula in a competent fashion (there being some danger of amateur software educators, unsuitable content, unreasonable compression, etc.), and the high cost of releasing staff to attend courses. Overall, though, the fundamental problem is the lack of sources for education programmes of the sort described above.

Not least of the factors within this problem is that there are so very few possible tutors for software engineering courses who are both competent and available. Our hope is that this work will serve some small purpose in clarifying these matters, as well as assisting in the process of software engineering education wherever, however, and by whomsoever this is done.

10.5 Contracting

Many firms making and using software in the IT sector in general either sell their software as products or services, or purchase software as products or services, or do both. In the present section we offer guidelines on the following topics:

- pricing software products and services;
- contract types, their basic form and the management issues from the purchasers side;
- some criteria for selecting a software supplier.

10.5.1 Pricing software products and services

To be able to price a software product, or service, with reasonable hope of a business return on the transaction, one must be able to determine its development cost. There are basically three instances to consider: one concerning software products, and two concerning software projects. However, in all cases (including those of prototypes and research) the basic costing method is the same.

The components of cost in software engineering, as in other engineering, are those of people's time allocated to the development and the materials they use. Normally, the main part of software engineering costs are these people-based costs (computed as the product of person-hours, and a cost factor comprising the hourly salary rate plus an overhead to recover general costs), plus the cost of computer time (which, for a shared PSE over different jobs requires an identification and logging procedure). For a product, the price is then determined by setting a realistic target for sales, and amortizing the whole cost accordingly (including any prototyping, research, pre-marketing activity and an aspired profit level).

For a project one may have a 'fixed-price' contract, in which the price will have been fixed well before the costs are known (at FS stage for instance), or a 'time-and-materials' contract in which case the costs and price are identical and charged in a continuing fashion (such as monthly). The terms 'fixed-price' and 'time-and-materials' are defined further below. The exigencies of setting prices for fixed-price contract supply are set out at length in Chapter 5, along with a recommended method for estimating the cost (effort) with acceptable accuracy.

Costs do not normally exceed price in time-and-material project-type supply, but may well do so for products and fixed-price project-type supply. When this happens for a product, the assumed sales level should be increased if this is reasonable, or the price per unit product should be increased, or a combination of both should be done if feasible. If none of this is reasonable, then the product has been put beyond the level of cost-plus-profit recovery and it may have to be cancelled.

When cost over-run occurs on a fixed-price supply project, the matter may be negotiable with the client (if, for instance, there are reasonable extenuating circumstances – preferably covered in the contract), but if not the job loses money and that is that. A further comment on how to act in these cases is offered below.

10.5.2 Contract types for software services

There are two basic types of contract for software engineering services as distinct from products. These are:

1. Time-and-materials (T&M) supply. In general this is an informal kind of contracting, based more on a definition of resources needed and the duration of that need than for a specific and defined task to be done. The contract form is often a simple letter with little intended legal status between the parties, defining the people to be assigned, the duration and commercial terms as hourly (or daily) charge-out rate, travel and subsistence expenses (if applying), materials, taxes and so forth. Staff-replacement and contract-termination clauses are usually informal, and payment terms are monthly in arrears of person costs and materials accrued. This form of contracting, of superficial attraction in many cases, is sometimes known derogatorily as 'body shopping' and supplier firms do not always enjoy a high reputation in software engineering.

2. Fixed-price-and-timescale supply (FP&TS). In general, this is a very much more stringent kind of contracting based on a definition of the task to be done and the cost/timescale to do it. The contract is generally a formal, legal instrument as distinct from the casual letter of agreement used in T&M assignment.

    A variant of 'fixed-price' is the 'cost-plus-fixed-fee' form of contract, in which the price to be reimbursed is clearly disaggregated into basic costs, overheads, materials, and profit margin, and the first three reimbursed before the last named. Table 10.3 shows the typical clauses of a fixed-price contract and its essential appendices.

    A fixed-price-and-timescale contract almost always has the greatest possible significance as a legal instrument. Thus, it should be properly executed by contract lawyers; as in the other matters, intervention of amateurs can be disastrous. The intention should be an equitable representation of interest preserving the reasonable rights of the parties, and this should be achieved as clearly and unambiguously as possible if a lawyers' field day is to be avoided.

There are four rather severe possibilities for cancelling a fixed-price contract; cancellation by the client, with or without fault of the supplier, and cancellation by the supplier with or without fault of the client. The conditions under which these may be exercised, and their consequences such as liquidated damages, must be defined with great clarity in the contract. The subject of damages, particularly, should be a matter of reason and care when being defined. If the client is contracting services as a part of product development, then it may be impossible to indemnify the company against supplier failure to the totality of possible loss and

Table 10.3 Clauses in a fixed-price contract.

Clause

Preamble

1. Definitions
2. Scope of the agreement
3. Mechanism for variations to scope
4. Delivery period
5. Mechanism for variation to delivery period
6. Contract price
7. Mechanism for variation to price
8. Other costs
9. Terms of payment
10. Obligations to the client
11. Specific obligations of supplier
12. Acceptance trials
13. Liability for damages
14. Damages to the system on the client site
15. Force majeure
16. Warranty and maintenance
17. Property and risk
18. Confidentiality/publicity
19. Cancellation
20. Infringement of third party rights
21. Employment offers to staff
22. Settlement of disputes
23. Applicable law
24. Entire agreement

Appendices

A. Functional Specification
B. Delivery period, contract price and payment terms
C. Project Management procedures including a change-control mechanism
D. Documentation standards
E. Acceptance trial procedures
F. Acceptance certificate (specimen)

---

damage. For instance contracting a $10 million p.a. software house, with a cancellation clause (with fault) specifying $50 million (for lost product sales) is, however justified, meaningless. The object should be to set the supplier vulnerability at a level likely to concern but not threaten.

From the supplier's side, fixed-price contracting is a matter of asserting one's estimating and management competence. In general, software and systems houses that are prepared to bid FP&TS terms (given a competently done FS), enjoy a justifiably higher reputation in software engineering than do 'body shops' (if they survive their own faults of mis-estimating, defective contracting, and project mis-management that is).

Before a supplier offers to carry out T&M work, he must decide whether it is the type of work he can do, and whether he has the resources available to do it.

In the case of FP&TS contracts the matter of whether or not to bid (and if successful to do) a job, depends crucially on the adequacy of specifications available. One of the worst situations to be in is that of being asked to bid prematurely. In this case a supplier can adopt one of the following postures.

1. *No-bid.* This means intimating to the client that one will not offer for the job concerned. Usually a polite letter is better than a blank silence. When done courteously, failing to bid does not generally lose reputation or future bidding prospects. When done in an un-cooperative way (no response at all, or a hostile one), then reputa-tion and future prospects do suffer. This is known as a 'destructive no-bid'.

2. *Bid-and-be-damned.* Effectively this involves, if too early in the lifecycle, 'price-to-win' techniques used as effectively as possible.

    Loss leading, keeping staff occupied if other workload is low, 'getting a foot in the door' of a new market, all are reasons for early bidding. The most prevalent reason though is that marketing/sales staff too have budgets and targets, and these may be so grossly stated as to overlook the quality of a sale in the sense of its viability in logistics, technology and contract.

    Jobs bid too early in the lifecycle (before FS/OSD stage) for fixed-price contract should have their cost to do established as early as possible (to ± 20% at FS/OSD stage; ratified to ± 10% at Software Design stage). Thereafter, one can either take the consequences on the chin and do the best possible irrespective of real cost and its over-run; or one can try to trim costs (and probably degrade the quality of supply and, in the long term, one's reputation); or one can try to manipulate a client into the belief that a second contract (for 'new version' modifications or maintenance say) is needed, and load the losses from the first contract into the second one. Manifestly, the first of these courses of action is the only one which makes real commercial sense, however 'smart' the others may seem to be in the short term.

3. *Constructive no-bid.* This is a most desirable option which involves bidding non-compliantly but for a well-argued reason. Thus if called upon to bid fixed-price at a very early URS stage (often called the 'commercial spec') one may – for example – make a short offer, in

which the FS phase is T&M estimated, and a budgetary estimate is indicated for the subsequent implementation. This should be accompanied by an argument that the likely high variance on estimates is in the interest of neither party, and that a binding FP&TS estimate will be made for a contract on completion of the FS. The arguments to give against underbidding are the two obvious ones on the client's behalf; that it creates pressures on any supplier to 'cut corners', and that no client should be happy at a supplier's losing money as it may, ultimately, affect the stability of supplies from that firm.

Constructive no-bidding loses a lot of jobs, but if done thoroughly and with probity, and if technically well argued, the posture also gains a lot of jobs. In all events, an ethical and technically competent constructive no-bid almost always enhances a company's reputation – far more than some of the meretricious devices listed in (b) above. The method of constructive no-bidding is really an exercise in client (or market) education into the realities of complex systems/software engineering projects. Commercial departments of companies vulnerable to the twin forces of premature underbidding on the one hand, or lost markets on the other should, perhaps, offer their clients courses for orientation and even education in software engineering as a part of marketing.

10.5.3 Selecting software suppliers

A client organization, contemplating contracted supply of software engineering services, may either contract supplier staff in to do work under the management of the client personnel and at the client's site (usually on a T&M contract), or the client may contract a specific job to be done.

In this latter case, the arrangement will – most likely – be a fixed-price supply, not under the client's direct management, and perhaps not even done at the client's site during the implementation.

The attractions of T&M 'contracting in' are deceptive; client managers tend to argue that it provides them with greater control over the supplier staff. On the other hand there is much defective contracting of 'body-shop' services for specious reasons such as apparent cheapness.

On the other hand, fixed-price supply sometimes seems, incorrectly, to be a more problematical relationship for the client for various reasons: the need for adequate FS; the formality of contracting; the seeming loss of direct control in off-site development; supplier's own means and methods, etc. In fact, fixed-price supply done properly is one of the better ways of getting software made given the choice of a competent supplier.

The basic criteria for supplier choice may be summarized as follows (assuming the overall financial stability of the company):

- High technical ability of its staff, with credible actual or latent ability in the technologies required.
- Credible real or latent (learning) ability of its staff in the applications area.
- A systems engineering attitude to the problem, such as evidence of caring what the realities of the system will be, not just how to computerize an intellectual construct of the problem.
- Understanding of the lifecycle ordering of activities, and project/ product distinction, phasing, specification change control, etc.
- Evidence of use of modern software methods and facilities as conducive to software quality.
- Professional, but otherwise highly co-operative relationship (client: supplier) at personnel levels.
- Awareness of the need for (and limitations of) competent contracts.
- Reasonable cost and commercial provisions (not a payment schedule of 90% now and 10% later).
- Possibility to interview the staff put forward to do the job – whether or not it is 'contracting-in' or 'contracting-out'.
- Reference clients nominated by the supplier.

A particular matter for determination on this list is 'reasonable commercial provision' for payments on a fixed-price (or cost-recovery) contract. Basically, the payment schedule should fit the work accretion profile for the job. Otherwise, one of the contract parties is financing the development unreasonably.

Provision must be carefully made for consequential slippage of payment milestones if these are linked to project activities (i.e. supplier's fault = tough luck; client's fault = pay up at the originally scheduled time; if a supplier's slippage causes the client to lose money then penalties may be involved). Of all matters that it is essential to beware, the one of determining the timescale and cost for fixed-price supply is by far the most dangerous. The reader will, by now, be aware that the FS/OSD stage is the earliest time at which this can be done in general. In some cases, e.g. when system-security aspects require architectural design to have proceeded, even the FS/OSD stage may be too early.

10.6 A checklist for good software engineering practice

Management

- Is there an adequate statement of the task, of sufficient status (e.g. contract or pseudocontract), and does it define the type of task (project, product, prototype, research)?

- Are the processes of requirement specification and technical feasibility properly undertaken (including prototyping as necessary)?
- Is there an adequate, formatted and up-to-date archive?
- Are software engineers involved early enough in the lifecycle, i.e. FS/OSD at latest?
- Are there updated activities plans and status matrices?
- Are there accurate estimates of effort and timescale, done at OSD stage and re-done at software design stage?
- Is there an adequate cost-reporting system?
- Is there an adequately orientated general management, confident enough to be 'pro-active' in its management rôle?
- Are management-led, structured walkthroughs being done?
- Is the user/client (or surrogate) relationship in good order?

Implementation

- Is there a signed-off FS and is it quality assured?
- Is there an explicit change control mechanism and does it work?
- Is there an architectural design and a clear definition of the software engineering task within it?
- Is there a clear CPT structure (or other equivalent), with explicit task assignment?
- Is there an explicit design for the software, done 'stepwise with improvement'?
- Are design reviews and code reading planned in detail and being done?
- Is there an explicit philosophy for author testing, and an explicit test plan?
- Is the deliverable documentation defined and coming into being at the right time?

Quality

- Is the QA agency explicitly identified early enough (FS stage)?
- Is QI taking place and being effective?
- Is there an explicit philosophy for β-testing, and an explicit plan for any black-box/white-box testing?
- Are the black-box/white-box tests defined and ready at the right time (before the end of α-testing)?

Resources

- Are the quantitative and qualitative aspects of the software team(s) adequate for the task concerned?
- Are any suppliers properly chosen and contracted?
- Are the software development and support facilities adequate?
- Are staff working conditions and general motivation adequately provided?
- Is post-installation software maintenance planned and provided for adequately?

This checklist can be used throughout the lifecycle, although individual issues can only be expected to be positive at and beyond the appropriate lifecycle stages.

Chapter 11 Case study: extracts from an archive

Synopsis

In this chapter we set out to show some examples of the archived traces of early lifecycle activities such as, *inter alia*:

1. Invitation to tender, URS, client correspondence and contract.
2. CPT formation, meetings and correspondence.
3. The FS and OSD.
4. Estimates and notional plans.
5. Management-control documents; activities plans and status matrices, cost (effort) control.
6. Design.

We do not present the whole content of any archive section, nor the whole set of sections, for the obvious reason of their volume. There follows, therefore, the sort of selection we would make if called in to 'audit' a software engineering task such as the one described.

Explanatory note

This is not an example concocted for this book; in the course of the last several years we have engaged in the sort of 'coherent' education programme described in Section 10.4 above and, in particular for the present purposes, we have devised and given the 'master classes' in software engineering described as primary-skill education for practitioners. As the readers will recall, we recommended a severe practical exercise as the backbone (so to speak) of this level of education – something taxing but achievable, in the timescale available, to all lifecycle levels.

We have found that games, such as chess and some that are playing-card based, are particularly suitable for this purpose (although it must be said that by 'chess' we mean a subset that excludes the P-type system property of 'intelligent' play by the machine).

Rather than choose chess, with its connotations of intellectual difficulty, we have chosen one of the card-game alternatives – Cribbage. It may be argued that too few people have ever heard of this game let alone played it; in a way that is part of our purpose too, as in real life software engineers are constantly confronted with unfamiliar applications.

Cribbage is a game of some antiquity (being attributed to the early seventeenth century poet, Sir John Suckling), and is generally played, as a basis for a mild form of gambling, in British public houses – along with darts, dominoes, skittles and other rituals perhaps not quite so suitable for computerization. It should not be thought that the game is trivial for it most certainly is not (if anything, it is the 'cricket' of card games on account of its arcane rules). Nor should it be thought British; one of the authors has played against Americans, Dutch, and others.

Given all of these things, the great advantage is that the game is fun to learn and play, and as a task for our purpose has the great advantage of being exactly implementable. In this respect it is on the boundary line of small and medium-sized as an S-type system.

The line we have adopted is that of abstracting salient documents from the archive, as though we were 'auditing' a software development as the external QI agency (see Chapter 9). In fact the whole archive (of which we have several real-life examples) amounts to a prohibitively large quantity of material, including code listings for about 3000 source statements of Pascal.

The schematic diagram (Figure 11.1) depicts our process of extraction from archive material filling two large ring-binders. Apart from extracting material and tidying it up somewhat, we have labelled each page (for the reader's convenience), in the upper left-hand corner, with an abbreviated reference to the archive section order we have adopted – e.g. (5.OSD). Normal page numbering is preserved as in other parts of the book. The extracts from the various sections of the archive are presented in the following order:

Section 1   Contents list
Section 2   CPT meetings
Section 3   URS and client correspondence
Section 4   FS(and User manual)
Section 5   OSD(software taxonomy)
Section 6   Management-control information
Section 7   Quality
Sections 8–12 These sections are not presented in full but some important points concerning the specification of a new version are given.

The ordered, QI extracts from the archive begin forthwith; we leave readers (so to speak) in the hope that they will not be deterred from trying to understand the requirement by the singularity of the application –

Extracts presented in our 'ideal' order for a single-level Archive (i.e. not divided between 'Technical' and 'Management' sections, and excluding code listings and testing information)	Order (section) in which the material existed in the actual archive – showing omissions from, and combinations of content
1. Content list	Missing
2. Software team (CPT) meetings	7
3. URS and Client Correspondence	1 and 14 respectively
4. FS (including User Manual); Change Control in chronological order	FS and User Manual in 2; Change control missing 5, 7,
5. OSD (software taxonomy only); estimate based on notional activities planning	3 and 9 respectively
6. Management control information; plans/ status matrices/cost (effort) accretion	Missing plans 10; missing cost information
7. Quality procedures, structures, correspondence	Missing
8. Software Design; top-level (architectural) and detailed	4 and 5 respectively
9. Code listings (omitted for space reasons here)	Separate volume
10. Authors test plans and actual tests (omitted for space reasons here)	13
11. Deliverable documentation (omitted here other than User Manual in 4)	Missing
12. Next version preliminary specification	Missing

Fig. 11.1   Ideal versus real archive.

what example, above a trivial level, would not be alien to some readers? We hope, also, to spread the game of cribbage.

Last, are the designs correct? What might follow is the biggest design review in history. Readers finding lacunae in the design should not rush to inform the publisher – kindly though this might be meant; the implementation did in fact work (including the new versions which are intimated so as to make an S-type example more clearly an E-type one). On the subject of errors, we claim that any that exist are a matter of our deliberate policy, to keep the reader alert; this disreputable device will not be unknown to anyone acquainted with the authors, who have developed its use into a fine, meretricious art . . .

(1. Cont.)

SECTION 1
CONTENTS LIST

(1. Cont.)

The archive content is, and will be preserved, in the following order:

1. Contents list.
2. CPT meetings (chronological).
3. URS and client correspondence (chronological).
4. FS (and User manual); contract; change-control correspondence (chronological).
5. OSD (software taxonomy); estimates and plans.
6. Management-control information; activity plans, status matrices and cost (effort) control graphs.
7. Quality; procedures, structures, correspondence (chronological) for QA (reviews, etc.) and other (QI, etc.).
8. Design; top level, detail.
9. Code listings in two separate volumes: 'current'; 'previous'.
10. Author(CPT)-level testing; plan and actual tests.
11. Deliverable documentation:
    * User's manual (including Operator's manual) as in 4.
    * Maintenance manual as separate, formatted volume for:
          software specifications
          designs
          code listings
          test information
12. New version information.

(2. CPT)

**SECTION 2
CPT MEETINGS**

(2. CPT)

MEMO   From: Jo   **DATE**   W 1

              To: Bill, Sid and Sarah   D 1

              cc: Archive file (Sect. 2
                     provisional)

Inaugural meeting of CPT

As you have heard, we have been assigned to make a card-game system for a client 'MacBuxton'. The CPT will be myself (as chief prog.), Bill, Sid and Sarah. Bill and Sid will join the team in the next couple of weeks when finished on the PV/21-6 job.

I've checked we can all make it, so our first CPT meeting will be at 10.00 hours on Wednesday next in the downstairs conference room (i.e. D3/W1 on our project-dating convention). I don't want to be too formal, but some of us haven't worked together before and we all want to do this next job right (not like PV/21-4, for instance). Suggested agenda:

1. Agree agenda.

2. Archive format (see attached suggestions – this, or its agreed variant, will be archive content 1).

3. Discuss specificaton (see attached invitation to tender – this will go in archive content 3 or variant).

4. Team rôles (if clear). Librarian.

5. Other topics.

If you want to change this, don't write – do it under 1 at the meeting.

CP.

(2. CPT)

MEMO   From: Librarian   **DATE**   W 1

               To: CPT   D 4

               cc: Arch. Sect. 2

Yesterday's meeting – minutes

Main points only:

1. Archive content agreed after modification; archive file set up with agreed contents list at start.

2. Rôles. Librarian job roster. Weekly assignment as follows: me (Sarah), Sid, Bill, repeats. Anyone missing (e.g. ill) then next person on schedule and no compensation arrangements, swopping, etc. Just tough on the next in line. Who does archive 6? (Answer: CP with quick and dirty timesheets from all, before 10.00 on each Monday – sorry, D1!).
   No point in other rôles yet.

3. Discussed URS. What is cribbage?? Bill doesn't like the sound of the 'next version' given the timescale. (*Action:* CP to try to find out more about it.) Tried to play the game. (*Note:* buy cards and a pegging board.) Sid will bring his copy of 'Hoyle'.

4. Next actions. CP + Lib. to start on draft FS (target D1/W2 – i.e. next Mon.) All to meet after work tomorrow to play more cribbage for an hour.

Next CPT meeting D5/W2.

Lib.

(2. CPT)

MEMO   From: Sid   **DATE**   W 2

To: CPT (Crib.)   D 1

cc: Arch. (2) via Lib.

I have some good news and some bad news (assign as appropriate). Is there a bug in the URS Appendix B? Example gives A/3/3/8 with 8 as drawcard scores 12. I make it score 8 (answers on a postcard etc.).

Another thing is the chance of infinite loop if a lunatic player challenges computed score for ever. See attached flowchart (Diagram 2.1) for solution. Unless there is a prompted *decision* to over-ride computed score or accept computed one we could be here all night, as they say. Another question: Will user want changes from autoscore to manual claim during a game?

Now the good news. I can't make the next meeting because of re-scheduled beta-tests on PV/21-6. Pity I'm Librarian next week.

Sid.   (Encl. Flowchart (Diagram 2.1))

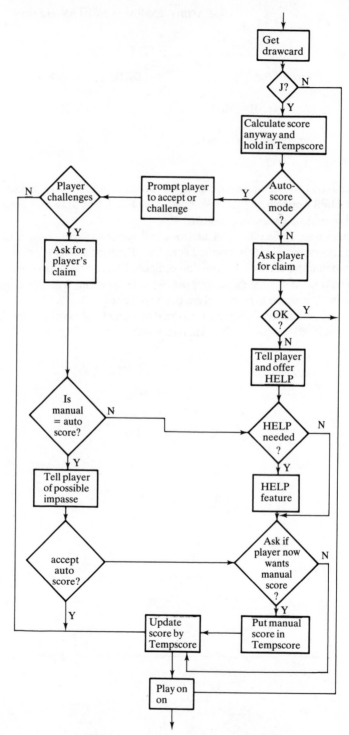

Diagram 2.1 Flowchart of requirements.

(2. CPT)

MEMO   From: CP   **DATE**   W 2

To: Cribteam   D 3

cc: Arch. (2) via Lib.

Several issues on cribbage job:

1. Attached draft FS for comment at Friday's meeting. We must send it for comment a.s.a.p. to the client. Please read, etc.

2. Bill became available today and will do draft OSD to be discussed at Friday's meeting.

3. Had a meeting with client about versions, timescales and screen formats (see Arch. (3) note). As a result Sarah has been doing I/O prototypes on our VAX and meets client tomorrow to demonstrate. Report at Friday's meeting.

4. Sid's bad news has got worse – he's not going to be available at all for us. PV/21-6 has extensions apparently (or over-run more likely). So it's just the three of us.

5. As you can see, I've suggested a PC; if we do it on that I suggest Pascal since we all know it.

CP.

(2. CPT)

MEMO	From:	Bill	**DATE**	W 2
	To:	Cribbage		D 4
	cc:	A (2) via Lib.		
		(Note: A = Archive)		

One or two things bugging me:

1. I'm not happy with the reference to a PC in the FS; it may be OK for Version 1 but what about Version 2? We may find ourselves modelling the universe on a notched stick! My guess is 5K of Pascal source for Version 1, but you'll see I've not done code size yet on the OSD.

2. That timescale looks hairy. I don't see us doing Version 1 in less than 4 months now Sid's gone. Then Version 2 . . . ('and, of course, payroll!') . . . by when? Which Christmas did he have in mind?

3. Now there's no Sid it's just me and Sarah as dogsbody Librarians; how about the CP taking Sid's place?

Bill   (Encl. Draft OSD)

(2. CPT)

MEMO   From: Lib   **DATE**   W 2

        To: Cribteam   D 5

        cc: A (2)

Minutes of last meeting.

1. CP to act for Sid in Librarian roster.
2. Draft FS agreed (and sent to client for comment).
3. Draft OSD discussed, revised and code size done (see A(5) input).
4. Architecture design discussed and drafted (see A(8) input).
5. Screen layout agreed (Sarah and client). S. to draft User's/Operator's manual.

Actions

(a) Self to do activities plan/estimates. Note format for status matrix now in A(6).

(b) Self and Bill to do design; Sarah to join a.s.a.p.

(c) Sarah to get client to sign FS (including User's manual).

No further traffic under this section. All future project team notes under other section concerned.

Jo

(3. URS)

SECTION 3
URS AND CLIENT CORRESPONDENCE

(3. URS)

* AN INVITATION TO TENDER *

Offers are invited for the development and delivery of a computer-based, VDU-operated card game – CRIBBAGE – to be implemented to the enclosed specifications (see (a) below).

Our company is in the business of retailing computer-based games through commercial outlets in various countries. Several of our main distributors have required, and are expecting delivery of our new catalogue of games not later than **three weeks** before the Monday of Christmas week. It follows that the successful bidder will be the one that offers:

1. A convincing system.

2. One that is generally operable on the main PC equipment currently available.

3. An implementation within the timescale indicated.

The general terms and conditions of supply will be the following:

(a) A basic, screen-based cribbage game for two players will be developed first. This is described in the annexed specification (with its two appendices), and the whole of this is known as **Version 1** of implementation.

(b) Version 1 must be fully implemented and demonstrated to us in successful acceptance trials – which we shall determine – in the minimum possible time, since there will be a **Version 2** of requirements to be implemented (and similarly demonstrated to our satisfaction) before the final end date of three weeks prior to Christmas week beginning. Version 2 is, as yet, undefined.

(c) The software must be portable. Suppliers may assume that the target equipment will be standard (MSX) type, 16-bit microcomputer equipment, in 256 Kilobytes of RAM configuration, and having available a set of high-level languages such as BASIC, FORTRAN, PL-M, Pascal and Forth.

(d) Your offers for Version 1, on which we intend to base fixed-price-and-timescale contracts of supply, must be with us on or before April 17th. – in writing, and fully authorized from your side. Your price must be fully detailed. Contracts will be placed by us on or before May 1st.

I need hardly add that successful supply in this case will place your company at great, potential advantage with us in terms of future supplies of this sort. I remain, on behalf of MacBuxton & Associates,

Yours faithfully,

(3. URS)

SPECIFICATION FOR VERSION 1 OF CRIBBAGE GAME

Rules, and an example of play, are set out in Appendices I and II below. Your system must be fully compliant in all respects with these rules for Cribbage. Furthermore, your system must:

1. Enable two-handed cribbage to be played with all hands, boxes, etc. fully displayed on the screen in Version 1. The screen format should be fully 'user friendly', in the sense of being cosmetic (pleasing) and obviously self-explanatory.

2. Your system will be menu driven. In other words, the user(s) will be offered a simple set of clear choices of facilities and clear instructions on how to use them – all done by user-friendly screen messages. Apart from menu options to start and end games, there will be three major facilities required in Version 1, and these are described in 3 below. Another menu driven option is described in 4 below. The menu features will undoubtedly be extended in Version 2.

3. In Version 1, a choice will exist as to how scores are entered (for rules, see Appendix 1). In one option, a score may be claimed by user input. In this case, your system must always show a prominent 'prompt' message calling for claims. In the other option, scores may be computed by the system and entered automatically. In this case your system must always show a prominent 'confirm' message indicating the score, and requiring explicit user confirmation. Apart from these two additional menu options, you must provide a 'Help' feature for analysis of false claims (in the case of manual score input) and justification of computed scores in the case of non-confirmation).

4. There are several points during play at which cards are shuffled, cut, etc. Following all these acts of (effectively) randomizing the deck, users must be able to request the card deck to be displayed on the screen.

5. Use a convention of A,2,3, . . . , J,Q,K to depict cards, and C,H,S,D to depict suits (clubs, hearts, spades, and diamonds, respectively).
   Thus AD = Ace of diamonds, 7H = seven of hearts, etc.

6. During play, the screen should show a cribbage pegging board of the form shown in Diagram 3.1.

Diagram 3.1 Cribbage board (screen depiction).

(3. URS)

Scores must be indicated by means of two 'pegs' (i.e. extra-illuminated points) per player, the front 'peg' indicating the score. All user scores are shown by taking the back 'peg' forwards of the front peg by the amount of the score. Play begins at the left-hand, outer line for each player and scoring goes round the player's set of peg-holes twice until one player has totalled (or exceeded) a score of 221. Also during play, the use of cards must be dynamic in the sense that discards into the 'box' (see rules) must be seen to leave the 'hand' field of the player concerned, and enter the 'box' field. The box field itself must be dynamic, being assigned to each player in turn.

There should be a central 'game field' on the screen where cards played in the 'small games' (see rules) appear. When a small game is over, it should be indicated as 'closed' in some way. When hands are being scored, cards will be replaced from the game field into the players' 'hand' field.

7. As well as showing scores via the peg-board on the screen, they should be shown also numerically for each player. Likewise, the running total of card values in 'small games' should be shown and must revert to zero before every new 'small game' (see rules).

8. The screen must, at all times, have a field designated for diagnostic messages in the case of user input error; these messages must be short, textual and helpful.
The field may or may not be used for your 'Help' feature (see 3 above) at your discretion – so long as our injunction for fully 'user-friendly' output is preserved.

Appendix 1 Rules of Cribbage

1. The game is played between two opponents.

2. The usual card deck is used, i.e. 52 cards, 4 suits, no Jokers or 'wild' cards.

3. Firstly, the deck is 'shuffled' by one of the players (it doesn't matter who) and a draw is made for who has the deal in the first place. A typical 'draw' convention would be:

> 'Ace counts low, high card wins', or
> 'Ace counts low, low card wins', or
> 'Ace counts high, low card wins', or some other agreed convention (it hardly matters).

4. The dealer deals six cards each after the deck has been re-shuffled (by the dealer) and cut (by the non-dealer). The residual deck from the deal is placed back on top of the remainder of the cut deck.

(3. URS)

5. Each player retains four cards (which usually comprise his best, or potentially best, hand), and discards two cards into what is called 'the box'. This will act as an additional hand for the dealer. Neither side knows what the other discards into the box until the dealer scores the contents of the box. Usually, the non-dealer avoids discarding useful cards into his opponent's 'box'.

6. The non-dealer cuts the deck and the dealer turns up the card thus exposed. If it is a Jack (J) the dealer scores two.

7. The two players then play a small game against each other as follows:

   (a) Each card has a value in this play, Ace = 1, 2 = 2, etc., ..., J = Q = K = 10, as well as its type (e.g. Queen, Ace, etc.).

   (b) A score of two points accrues to a player whose last play completes an addition of the value of the cards played equalling 15 exactly. Thus in the following case
   Player 1 / 5H, 5C, KH, KD
   Player 2 / AH, AD, AC, JD
   Player 2 leads JD and Player 1 replies 5H and scores two points accordingly (since J = 10 + 5 = 15).

   (c) Play proceeds until an aggregate value of 31 is reached by summing the values of the cards, or until neither side can proceed without violating 31. The person playing last card scores two points (if 31 exactly is reached) or one point if 31 is not reached.
   Play restarts after reaching 31 (or the nearest number to it without exceeding it).
   Thus in the above hand:

Player 1	Player 2
	JD
5H (= 2 points)	AH
KD	AD
(can't go)	AC
(can't go)	(no more cards)

   In this case Player 2 scores one point for the last card played (he also scores two points for a pair since two sequential cards played are the same type, Aces, and this is explained below). The first player still has two last cards, and now plays (say)

KH	(no more cards)
5C	(no more cards)

   and the player scores one for the last card played + two points for making a total of 15 on this play.

(3. URS)

(d) During the play, other methods of scoring occur. Runs of more than two cards in a sequence count for each card in the run. Runs need not be in perfect sequence, thus 2, A, 3 is a run and would score three points. If a player now adds a 4, then it is a run of four and scores four points. If the player added a 2 at this stage then a run of three would have occurred (2, A, 3, 2 of which the first card is now not relevant). Runs need not be the same suit and if they are, no additional scores apply. Face cards retain their value of 10 for counting the play score (15s, etc., 31 maximum, etc.) but retain their distinct characters for runs. Thus, K, Q, J in that order bring the game total to 30 (10 + 10 + 10) but count three score points for the player of the last card (the J) for the run K, Q, J. Pairs score two points during play, if played in sequence. Three of a kind score six points during play, if played in sequence. Four of a kind twelve points during play, if played in sequence.

8. After the play and its scoring are complete, the players score their hands. Note, the draw card at step 7 does not play a rôle during play, but does play a rôle in scoring the hands.

9. The non-dealer scores his hand first. The rules for 15s (scoring 2 points) and runs, pairs/triples/quadruples are the same as in 7d above.

 Flushes (all cards of the same suit) play no rôle in the 'game' but can play a rôle in hand and box scoring (see below). A flush of all four cards (i.e. being of the same suit) in the hand scores four points; if the draw card is the same suit, the flush scores five points; flushes of less than four of a kind of suit in the hand do not count.

 A jack in the hand, if of the same suit as the draw card, scores one point.

 The draw card is regarded as a fifth card for each player when scoring his hand, and can be added to cards to make 15s, runs, multiples and (as described) flushes.

10. When the non-dealer has scored his hand, the dealer scores his hand (as in 9 and then scores his 'box' (the four discarded cards plus the draw card in exactly the same way as in (9) except that – for boxes – a flush must be all *five* cards of the box + draw card (and it scores, of course, five points).

11. When both dealer and non-dealer have scored their hands and the box, then the dealer (and box) passes to the opponent, and the whole sequence (beginning with a 'shuffle' by the dealer and a 'cut' by the non-dealer) proceeds as described in 4 onwards.

12. The game ends when one player's score of points (accumulated during play and by scoring hands and boxes) reaches or exceeds 121. Thus, the sequence (in the 'Play'), scoring the hands and box and even turning up the draw card can be vital in determining who will win a game if the scoring is very close as both players approach the score of 121.

(3. URS)

Appendix 2 A full example of one hand of cribbage

1. Start. A player shuffles and declares 'Ace high, low card wins'. The other player (let's call him Player 2) cuts a 7, the first player then cuts a 9, and Player 2 has first deal and the box. Player 2 reshuffles the deck and Player 1 cuts it; Player 2 then deals six cards each starting with a card for his opponent and proceeding a card a time in sequence.

2. The resulting hands are (say):

   Player 1: 4H, 4D, 6S, 6D, QC, KD.
   Player 2: AH, 3D, 3C, 8S, JH, QD.

   Now both of these sets of cards are poor hands as they stand, but both have high potential. Player 1 holds four points (2 each for the pairs) and Player 2 also holds four points (2 for the pair and 2 for a '15' made up of the A + 3 + 3 + 8). However, Player 1's hand would be vastly improved if he discarded the two court cards (Q and K) and then a draw card of 5 emerged. In that case he would hold a spectacular twenty-four points made up by four combinations of the run 4,5,6 (= 12 points), two pairs (= 4 points) and four combinations of '15' made up of 4 + 5 + 6 (= 8 points). On the other hand, discarding the two court cards may be a bit dangerous as it is his opponent's 'box' and they may be useful in helping to make runs as they are adjacent cards (. . . ,Q,K).

   Player 2 can also have his hand improved if he discards the court cards (J and Q) and then a draw card of either 3 or 8 emerges. In the case of a 3 as draw card he would hold a score of twelve comprising three combinations of '15' made up of A + 3 + 3 + 8 (= six points) and the triple of three 3s (= 6 points). In the case of an 8 emerging he would score twelve points also but this time four combinations of '15' made up of A + 3 + 3 + 8 (scoring 8 points) and two pairs (scoring 4 points). Furthermore it is his 'box' and a discard of the court cards may be useful to him because they are adjacent (. . . ,J,Q,. . .).

   So Player 1 discards the Q and K and Player discards the J and Q – each hoping for a favourable 'draw card' to emerge. Remember that neither player knows the other's discard until the 'box' is counted.

3. The non-dealer (Player 1) now cuts the deck and the dealer turns over the top card revealed (the 'draw card'). If this is a J then the dealer (Player 2) would score two points.

   However, in this case it is the 9 of hearts and both players-hopes are disappointed (as is often the case in cards). However, it is by no means a useless draw for either side as the scoring will show.

4. The 'play' now commences. The non-dealer must lead. He has to decide which card to lead in total ignorance of his opponent's hand (except that it cannot contain any of the six cards dealt to him, nor the draw card – but this information is seldom of much use).

(3. URS)

In the event, Player 1 leads with a *4*. The game total (note, not the player's score) is now 4. This puts his opponent in some trouble; if he replies with an Ace, then the game score will be 5 and there will be a high probability that his opponent will be able to complete a 15 and therefore score two points; on the other hand if he replies with 3 then he leaves himself open to a run (scoring three for his opponent) if the other holds either a 2 (in which case the run would be 4, 3, 2) or a 5 (in which case the run would be 4, 3, 5). So, the opponent (Player 2) replies with the *8* from his hand. The game total is now 12 $(4 + 8 = 12)$.

Player 1 now sees that a reply of a 6 would leave him vulnerable to a run if his opponent holds a 7 (the run being 8, 6, 7 and scoring three for Player 2, and still being within the limit of the 31 game total, i.e. $4 + 8 + 6 + 7 = 25$).

Player 1 replies with his other 4. The game total is now $4 + 8 + 4 = 16$ and no scores have been made by either side.

Player 2 now faces a problem of using his 3s since Player 1 has just used a 4 and a run may easily occur given a sequence of . . . ,4,3, . . . So, with a light heart he can play one of his sixes (game total now 23). So he plays a *6*.

Player 2 is now in a similar position; no vulnerabilities (to 15 or to runs) and he only has three's anyway. So he plays a *3* (game total = 26). At this point Player 1 cannot play as his last card would take the game total beyond 31. So he has to 'pass' (scoring no points for a last card in this game).

Player 2 can still play and does so with his last card 3. The game total is now 29 and neither side can play further (Player 1 is holding a 6; Player 2 has no more cards left).

So Player 1 scores one point for his last card in this game (note if the game total had been 31 exactly at this stage then the last player would have scored two points, not one). He also scores two points for two of a kind (in this case 3s played in sequence).

Since there are still unplayed cards, another game begins, with the non-player from the last round beginning.

This game is very brief. Player 1 leads his last 6 and scores one point for his last card as Player 2 has no cards left. At this point the game stands at 01:03 points scored during this play.

Note, the draw card has not played a rôle during the 'play'.

5. The scores are now taken for the hands and the box. The non-dealer (Player 1) scores first. He can now take all points from his hands + the draw card. Thus he has at his disposal:

   4, 4, 6, 6

and

   9

Thus he scores eight points, made up of two 15s $(6 + 9 = 15$ for each of the two 6s) which scores four points, and 2 points each for the pairs (4s and 6s).

(3. URS)

Player 1 now has 9 points from this round (1 for the game and 8 for his hand).

Player 2 now takes his hand in which (with the draw card) he has:

A, 3, 3, 8

and

9

Thus he scores six points, made up of two 15s (A + 3 + 3 + 8 and 3 + 3 + 9) scoring four points, plus two points for the pair of 3s. At this stage his score is 9 points from this round (3 from the game and 6 from his hand). However, he can now also score the 'box'. This acts like a present, a bonus. In it (in this case) he finds:

JH, QC, QD, KD

and

9H

(note the suits are important and must not be lost sight of). This 'box' scores nine points for Player 2 as follows: two runs of three (JH, QC, KD and JH, QD, KH) = six points; two points for the pair of Qs; one point because the J is of the same suit as the draw card (see rule 9 in Appendix 1). At this stage Player 2 has a score from this round of 18 (= 3 + 6 + 9) against Player 1's score of 9.

6. Player 1 now shuffles, Player 2 cuts, Player 1 deals and the whole process is repeated.

   Note 1   In the above, neither side has a flush (all cards of one suit) in either hand or box. (Suits are not significant within the 'game play' up to 31).

   Note 2   There are two very exceptional cases in scoring. The maximum score in a hand or box is 29 points comprising

   5, 5, 5, J (of same suit as drawcard)

   and a draw card of

   5

   Furthermore the only score which it is not possible to have in a hand or box (between 0 and 29) is a score of *19 points*. No combination of runs, flushes, 15s or J points can ever amount to this score. For this reason, in real-life play, a player will sometimes declare a score of 19 if he has zero; it is a small joke amongst the grandmasters of cribbage.

(3. URS)

MEMO   From: CP   **DATE**   W 2

To: Client   D 5

cc: CPT members
A (3) via Lib.
Manager.

Summary of main points of today's meeting

1. The URS contains two errors. Firstly – in (6) of the specification – it says scores go to 221 or over: this should be 121 as said in rules. Secondly – in the sample game of Appendix 2 – the cards 1 + 3 + 3 + 8 with drawcard of 8 scores 8 points, not 12 as stated.

2. Client confirmed following timescale:
   * Contract by May 1st.
   * First version beta-test (by client) by June 30th.
   * Definition of Version 2 by August 30th (delay because of holidays).
   * Contract for Version 2 by Sept. 15th.
   * Beta-test (by client) on Version 2 on or before Nov. 15th.
   It was pointed out that the features of Version 2 would have to be limited to those achievable in the timescale.

3. Client indicated the following probable Version 2 features (not limiting):
   * 'Intelligent' play by computer (i.e. to act as a player or players).
   * 3- and 4-handed play as well as 2-handed with the computer being any number of the players (up to all of them) in each case.
   * Save game/retrieve game during play. This will require a game identification input as well as input of players' names (as needed for Version 1 incidentally).

4. On portability, client will think about the problem. It was suggested that beta-tests on both Versions should be on single, nominated equipment and that further Versions (3, 4, etc.) should be done to 'port' to given equipment. CP stated the view that these 'porting' versions would not take more than one person month/two elapsed weeks in each case so long as (c) under 'An invitation to tender' of URS applies in full.

5. *Actions*
   Draft FS to client by Friday this week (done).
   Mock-up screen layouts to be displayed on our VAX on Tuesday of next week, and draft user's manual to client before Wednesday next.
   Commercial offer to client before Wednesday next.
   Meeting at client premises, 10.00 on Thursday next.

(4. FS)

SECTION 4
FS (AND USER MANUAL)

(4.FS)

FUNCTIONAL SPECIFICATION

Introduction

The system required is to allow users of a VDU-based computer system of some sort (as yet unspecified, but see Annex (i) below) to play games of two-handed cribbage. The rules of cribbage are set out in a *Modern Encyclopedia of Card Games* (pp. 95–100 inclusive) and these rules for two-handed play will be taken as definitive.

In the first instance, as we understand it from the client MacBuxton & Associates, the requirement is for a tutorial system for beginners in the game. This specification is for that purpose entirely and for no other unless subsequently changed by a mutually acceptable, authorized process.

Features

The main features and functions required are summarized as follows and detailed to greater level, where appropriate, in subsequent sections of this document:

1. The users (players) will have the set of features and facilities available as a (screen) menu from which selection will be possible by simple and clear (keyboard) input. Formats for the screen display of this menu, and for the keyboard input, are set out in the User's manual attached as Annex (ii) below. Erroneous input for menu selection will be clearly diagnosed by a screen message.

2. In normal ('Play') mode, users (players) will be able to enact all the parts of a normal game of cribbage in the sequence in which they should occur. Each stage will be prompted by a screen message (see Annex B – User's manual). Erroneous play will be diagnosed by a simple screen message.

3. The mode of play may be determined at the start of a game to be either automatic (computer-based computation) of scores requiring ratification by user input before being aggregated, or manual score claims. In the event these latter are wrong, a diagnostic message will be shown on the screen, and this will offer to show the correct claim and how it is made up. In the event of the user not ratifying an automatically computed score, the same diagnostic message will be shown, with the addition that the user will be asked to enter a 'claim'.

   In the event that the user continues to enter a 'claim' wrongly or not ratify a computed score, a message will be displayed requiring a decision to enter the computed score or to override it via the claim.

(4.FS)

4. A HELP facility will be provided to compute a correct score and display it, on menu request of the user, along with an analysis of the way it is comprised.

5. As an extension of the HELP feature, and one separately accessed from the menu, the user will be able to ask for an example game to be played. This facility (EXAMPLE) will have all the features of a game of two-handed cribbage and will merely require players to make a simple keyboard input to activate each stage. If required, a recorded score from EXAMPLE may be challenged, and the usual HELP feature (4) invoked.

6. After the steps in a game requiring shuffling or cutting the cards (randomization), the user will be asked by a screen message if the deck is to be displayed. If not, the game will proceed. If so, the deck will be shown and the game (or other menu option) will proceed by user input. The formats for these messages and displays are set out in Annex B – User's manual. This feature (DECK) will be generally available as a menu item also (see below).

7. Games may be terminated during play (or any menu item) by the invocation of a menu item (QUIT). This will re-offer the menu as at the start.

8. If a game is not terminated by QUIT it will, whether a user (player) game or an EXAMPLE, proceed until one side scores 121 (or more) points before the other side in terms of the order of scoring as set out in the rules.

9. An exit from the cribbage system altogether will be possible by invoking the EXIT option at any stage of PLAY, EXAMPLE or HELP.

The way in which the foregoing features will work is represented in the schematic below. It must be stressed that this is not a design of the system-to-be necessarily, so much as an explanation of the features 1–9 above. The following diagram is known as a 'state transition' sketch and merely depicts the main states of usage of the features and how they are related in logic.

STATE 0: Machine turned on; call up CRIBBAGE system. Menu shows three choices only: PLAY (1), EXAMPLE (1) and EXIT (5).

STATE 1: PLAY (or EXAMPLE) is invoked.
The user features for this are generally described in (A) below. At each step including when a winner is known, the menu offers choices for DECK, HELP, QUIT and EXIT.

STATE 2: DECK is invoked.
This displays the randomized card deck on the screen. The menu then offers RETURN (which resumes PLAY or EXAMPLE as appropriate), QUIT or EXIT.

STATE 3: HELP is invoked.
The user features for this are generally described in (B) below. The

(4.FS)

menu offers RETURN (which resumes PLAY or EXAMPLE as
appropriate), QUIT or EXIT.

STATE 4: QUIT is invoked.
This automatically resumes STATE 0.

STATE 5: EXIT is invoked.
This automatically exits from the CRIBBAGE system altogether.

A schematic description of these features and their relationship is shown in
Diagram 4.1.

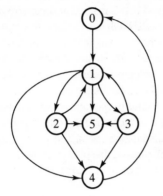

Diagram 4.1   State transition of requirement.

Notwithstanding that cribbage is officially defined and described, and
furthermore has been described in the client's own way in the URS, we offer the
following amplification of requirement for the PLAY (and EXAMPLE) features.
(*Note.* The HELP facility is described under 'STATE 3' above.)

(A)   PLAY and EXAMPLE

At the start, the user must turn the computer on, at which point the STATE 0 menu is
shown, along with a message advising the user how to proceed.

Assuming that EXIT is not chosen, and that either PLAY or EXAMPLE are
chosen, the sequence occurring is as described in the following. (*Note.* We give
this sequence as for PLAY but it is in no way different than for EXAMPLE other than
that a complete, pre-saved game is replayed, step by step, omitting user-play and
merely requiring a simple input to cause the next step to occur. This feature does
not involve the computer in playing cribbage in the 'intelligent' sense.)

When PLAY starts, a simulated card deck is randomized and users are
required to input two players' identifications within a fixed format, in which any
keyboard characters are allowed in any order or amount, so long as the total for one
player does not exceed ten characters. Furthermore, the players are required to

(4.FS)

decide whether scoring shall be automatic (computed) or by manual claim for the whole game.

The users are asked to decide on a convention (Ace high/low and high/low draw wins) to determine first deal/box. The result is signified by the enhancement of that player's name on the screen and the placing of the box field under that player's name on the screen.

The cards are then randomized again and the users are asked by a screen message if they are to be displayed (DECK).

On resumption of play, each side is dealt 6 cards which are fully visible in a hand field on the screen (see User's manual in Annex (ii) below). Users are then prompted to discard two cards each into the box, the convention in this case being (since play is fully visible) that the box-holder discards a card, then the other player a card, then the box holder, etc. When this is done – each step being prompted on the screen – a drawcard is selected at random and displayed in a special field on the screen. If this is a Jack then 2 points are claimable for the dealer.

The process of small games now commences as in the rules. Each time a score is appropriate, a message is displayed to this effect. In manual scoring this requires a numerical claim and in automatic scoring it requires a confirmation of the computed amount. In small games false play (such as offering cards not in the hand, refusing to play when it is possible to do so) or violating a small-game total of 31, will be diagnosed and refused.

The scoring of points won by drawing the drawcard, during small games, and by scoring hands and boxes is entirely as prescribed in the rules.

All invalid input (violation of keyboard formats) and false play will be diagnosed and messages displayed to that effect in a field for that purpose on the screen. When one side, playing in its correct turn, has scored over 120 points, the game stops and a message WINNER is displayed. Further play in this game is prevented from that point onwards.

(B)   The HELP feature

This feature displays on the screen a computed score for the last step taken (*note*: it may be a step in the play with no legitimate score occurring) and shows its composition if indeed a score is appropriate. In the case of user claims (manual score input as distinct from computed scores), the feature will ask for the composition of claim to be input and will then indicate the errors as well as the correct score and its composition. In the case of the user contesting a computed score in the automatic scoring mode for a game, then the feature will require the user to enter a claim and its composition (justification), and will then treat the matter as one of false claim. The user will then be required to decide which of the scores (the computed one or the claim) is to be allowed. In the case of the latter, that player's score will be qualified (by an * against it) for the duration of the game, as being questionable. Only one qualification (*) will be shown against a score, however many false claims are entered in it during a game.

(4.FS)

ANNEX (i) to the Functional Specification

Computer equipment

There is a general requirement for the system, comprising the above features and functions, to be operable on any 16-bit microcomputer in the normal category of personal computer or home computer such as those from IBM, Atari, Sinclair, Apple, Commodore, Acorn, Philips, etc. Without prejudice, we indicate that the version indicated above, plus its foreseen extensions in Version 2 as indicated to date, could be developed for a 256 kbyte RAM computer of this sort with Pascal.

However, we deem it best to assume the development of Version 1 as described above, and Version 2 when fully defined, in UCSD Pascal on a multi-user VAX host computer operating VMS and having 3 × VT 100 screens. It is with that working assumption that this FS is made and any bids, contracts, etc. to which it is part are submitted.

ANNEX (ii) to the Functional Specification: The User's/Operator's manual

1. The game of cribbage

The CRIBBAGE system is one of a set of computer-based games in the MacBuxton Catalogue under the heading PUB, available on a wide variety of personal computers and systems of larger scope such as those indicated in our literature.

The game of cribbage is of great antiquity, being attributed to the poet Sir John Suckling. It is generally played amongst friends in British public houses as a basis for small-stake gambling. In many places there are teams of players who compete against other teams in a local league structure.

It is our most sincere hope that the users of this little game will get hours of enjoyment from the art and sport of this ancient pastime – not least of which hours will be spent in working out the rules of play.

For this reason we have attached, as Part 3 of this manual of usage, a complete extract from the *Modern Encyclopedia of Card Games*, which describes Sir John's creation with great lucidity.

2. How to use the computer CRIBBAGE

In this section we set out how the system may be used in outline (2.1), the special forms of screen format you will see according to which feature you are trying to use (2.2), and the messages you will see on the screen and the format of your input required at these times (2.3).

(4.FS)

2.1   Features of the CRIBBAGE system

The system is initiated by starting up the computer with the CRIBBAGE disk installed as described in the manufacturer's manual for your machine. The first thing you will notice is a 'welcome' message (see 2.2 and 2.3 below).

If you now press the RETURN key on your keyboard you will be presented with the menu of choices for beginning. This screen format is shown in 2.2 below and requires you to choose between PLAY, EXAMPLE and EXIT. How to choose these by keyboard input is described in 2.3 below. If you make an error in working the keyboard by inputting a wrong character, hitting the wrong key(s), etc., a diagnostic message will tell you and advise the correct action. In some cases, of course, you may enter a wrong choice on your part quite permissibly; the system cannot detect and diagnose this for you. If, at the start, your choice is for the EXIT option, then the computer will leave the CRIBBAGE system altogether and revert to its operating system, whose messages will then be displayed as per the manufacturer's manual for your equipment. To re-start CRIBBAGE, re-load the disk and follow the manufacturer's instructions for calling up the system.

The choice of PLAY will begin a sequence of prompted steps towards and within a game of cribbage between two players. The reader is cordially invited at this point to become familiar to some extent with the rules of the game as set out in Section 3 below. From this point onwards it is understood that the object, terms, rules of play, and complex scoring conventions are understood, if not fully familiar to the user.

At the outset of PLAY, a prompt message on the screen asks for players' identifications (see 2.3 below). Determination of dealer (first box holder) is done by prompting messages on the screen followed by user inputs – all described below. Cards are dealt, discarding to the box done, a drawcard selected, small games played, and hands and boxes are scored – all involving messages on the screen at each step prompting the next move. All opportunity to score is indicated by a screen message and must be responded to. All the screen message formats and input (keyboard) response formats are set out in 2.2/2.3 below.

The methods of scoring during an entire game will be a matter of user choice at the start, the options being either user input of claims or the computer's computation of scores. If the first is the case, and a wrong claim is made, then that fact will be indicated by a message. The user can either then accept the computed score or ask for HELP. The HELP feature will show the correct score and how it is determined. In this case of a user challenging the computed score when that feature is operating, the user will be required to claim and indicate the composition of the claim.

The system will then indicate the correct score and its composition, and will require a decision as to which score is to be used. If the user over-rides the computed score with a wrong claim, the score of that player will be qualified by means of an asterisk for the rest of the game, indicating false play (i.e. cheating).

(4.FS)

When one side, playing in correct sequence, exceeds a total score of 120 that side wins, a special message is displayed, and that game stops. At any step in a game, the HELP feature may be invoked and, when completed, will offer RETURN, QUIT or EXIT (i.e. exit from the CRIBBAGE system altogether, as already described).

As well as HELP, the user may select a menu entry to display all the cards in their order (DECK). This feature is to check the randomization of cards. DECK will offer – when used – either RETURN, QUIT or EXIT. One cannot go from DECK to HELP or elsewhere in the system (nor can one go from HELP to DECK for that matter).

The other option (EXAMPLE), available at the start, is a tutorial feature in which a full game is replayed step by step with the computer doing all the scoring, etc. The user need only press the RETURN key on the keyboard to invoke the next step. Play is otherwise identical to that in the PLAY feature, and the user can choose the same menu options as for that mode.

2.2   Screen formats for the basic features of 'CRIBBAGE'

There are two basic screen formats:

1. The screen layout during PLAY or EXAMPLE.
2. The screen layout for displaying the randomized cards (DECK).

These are incorporated in one screen format defining fields and their usage for different purposes in the two modes (1) and (2). This basic screen layout is shown in Diagram 4.2, and Diagram 4.3 shows an example.

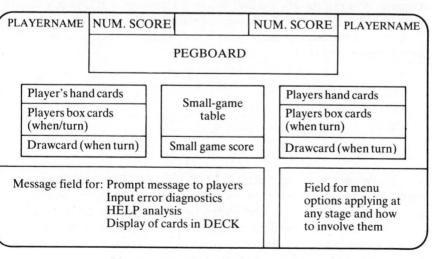

Diagram 4.2   Screen format: general.

(4. FS)

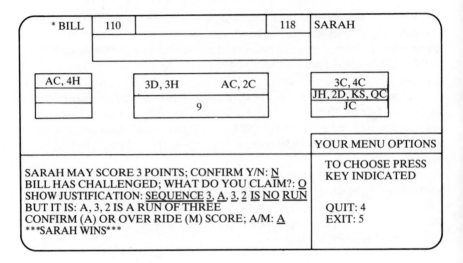

Diagram 4.3   Screen format: actual.

2.3   Commands and other Keyboard input formats

At the outset, having loaded the CRIBBAGE disk, the message:

    * WELCOME TO THE MACBUXTON CRIBBAGE SYSTEM *

is displayed on the screen in the field for messages, etc. (see 2.2 above), and menu options are offered in the adjacent field. To select a menu option at any stage, you must type MENU followed by the appropriate numerical code.

In general, the menu options have the following form and are chosen by pressing the key indicated:

PLAY	0
EXAMPLE	1
HELP	2
DECK	3
QUIT	4
EXIT	5

In the first instance, the options will be PLAY (0), EXAMPLE (1) or EXIT (5) and a simple key will take you to one of them. During the usage of the system these options will change depending on which feature you are using, but the keyboard convention remains the same. If you make an error in menu selection, such as pressing a letter or a special character or an out-of-range number, then a diagnostic message will appear in the message field saying:

(4. FS)

* INPUT ERROR ON MENU SELECTION, CHARACTER . . .NOT
ALLOWED, MAKE PROPER CHOICE PLEASE *

If you make an error in typing MENU itself there will be a general diagnostic
message shown (used in other cases too) saying:

* UNKNOWN INPUT, PLEASE CHECK YOUR FORMAT AND RE-TRY *

This is known as the general input-error diagnostic.

Further keyboard inputs from the user will be required during play in order to
indicate, as response to prompts, cards played in small games, discards to the box,
claimed scores, etc.

The convention for cards is to indicate the value first and suit second, i.e. 2C for
the two of clubs. Spaces between the characters (e.g. 2 C) will not cause an input
error. Suits may be indicated in upper- or lower-case text (2c or 2C). As the system
is arranged there will never be an occasion in PLAY (but there may during HELP)
for a player to input more than one card at a time without an intervening prompt.
When, in HELP, this might be the case, cards are separated by a comma – thus
2C, AH, etc.

If an error is made in either character of a card input, a message will be
displayed to that effect:

* INPUT ERROR ON CARD, CHARACTER . . . IS WRONG, PLEASE
CHECK AND RE-TRY *

If a card is indicated illegally (i.e. the player doesn't have it) then a message will be
shown:

* YOU ARE USING A CARD NOT IN YOUR HAND, PLEASE
CHECK AND RE-TRY *

Analogously, messages will be shown for illegal input of scores; thus a claim of (say)
a7 as a score will lead to an error message

* INPUT ERROR ON SCORE, CHARACTER . . . IS WRONG,
PLEASE CHECK AND RE-TRY *

A wrong claim will be signified by a message calling for a decision on how the user
wishes to proceed.

* YOUR INPUT CLAIM OF 9 FOR BOX-SCORE IS WRONG, DO YOU
WISH FOR HELP FEATURE: Y/N? *

and if so:

* THE CORRECT CLAIM IS 8 (2 × RUNS OF 3 + 1 PAIR) DO YOU
WISH THIS (A) OR YOUR CLAIM (M) TO BE USED?: A/M? *

In some instances, the user will be asked to justify a claim (i.e. when challenging a

(4.FS)

computed score). Here the convention is to indicate the number of occurrences of a scoring event (e.g. 2 × RUNS as above) and link all such by a plus. The user need not type the event identifier in full but may use the following code:

Pairs (two of a kind)	P
Trebles (three of a kind)	T
Quadruples (four of a kind)	Q
Run of 3	R3
Run of 4	R4
Run of 5	R5
15	15
Flush	F
Jack (hand or box: 'hat')	J1
Jack (drawcard: 'heels')	J2

In HELP (or the scores challenge part of it) the following message type may appear:

> * YOU CLAIM 3 × RUNS OF 3, INDICATE THE CARD TYPES INVOLVED PLEASE *

The input will then be as already described for PLAY, i.e.

> AC, 2D, 3H + AC, 2D, 3S + AC, 2D, 3C

Note the use of + between different parts of this format.

Other examples of user input include responses to message queries such as Y/N (yes or no) and A/M (automatic or manual scoring). For an example of this latter during PLAY, and at the beginning of this feature, the user will receive a screen message saying

> * YOU MAY CHOOSE AUTOMATIC SCORING (WITH USER CONFIRMATION FEATURES) – WHICH IS CALLED 'A' – OR MANUAL ('M') SCORING BY CLAIMS WHICH THE COMPUTER WILL CHECK. THIS CHOICE ONCE MADE CANNOT BE CHANGED FOR THIS GAME. WHICH IS IT TO BE? A/M? *

3. The rules of Cribbage

(Here follows an extract from *Modern Encyclopedia of Card Games*.)

4. Authorisation

This Functional Specification is authorized in its entirety by:

THE CLIENT (for MacBuxton & Associates)	....
THE SUPPLIER (for Lead Balloons Inc.)	....
DATE	....

(4.FS)

Contract   between, on the one hand MacBuxton & Associates (The Client), and Lead Balloons Inc. (The Supplier), being hereinafter referred to as The Parties: Who, by execution of this document on the date set out hereunder have agreed that:

1. Said Supplier shall provide to said Client software and its documentation for a computer-based system, for playing the game of Cribbage at a visual display unit (VDU) as part of a computer system and, furthermore:

2. The supplier shall provide the Cribbage software as defined in Annex (i) hereto (The Functional Specification) only, and shall not provide computer equipment nor its essential operating software, languages and so forth. The Cribbage software shall be supplied in a fully tested fashion with its documentation (User manual/Operator manual and a Maintenance manual), and the software so defined and the documentation so defined shall constitute The Supply, and furthermore:

3. The Supply shall be deemed to be delivered when satisfactorily tested by The Client, such a test being deemed the Beta-test and Acceptance Trial. Said Client shall only test the features specified in Annex (i) hereto and, in the event of compliant behaviour of the system, shall complete said tests in one day and shall not unreasonably delay, defer or refuse acceptance.

   In the event that the Supplier offers the System for the Test and Trial, and the Client is unable or refuses to beta-test the system, then Arbitration as set out below will ensue.

4. The Supply as defined will be done for a Fixed Price of $40 000 (forty thousand) to be paid as $10 000 on contract signature, $20 000 on successful Test and Trials, and the residue one month after that date. The Price so quoted is inclusive of all taxes, fees and charges, and no other amounts shall accrue to the liability of The Client without explicit consent of both Parties.

5. The Supply will be offered for Test and Trial on or before June 30th of the current year.

6. Variances to the Supply, The Price, The Timescale or The Test and Trial procedure must be arranged in writing, and approved by both Parties, having approved officers of their companies execute the variations.

7. Cancellation. Neither Party can cancel against the other without fault on that other party's side being alleged. To attempt to cancel without fault is to incur fault. If The Client cancels this contract for reasons of established fault by The Supplier, said Supplier shall reimburse all moneys paid at that time plus a damage of $20 000 (twenty thousand).

   If The Supplier cancels this contract for reasons for established fault by The Client, said Client shall reimburse all moneys outstanding on the Contract, to its

(4. FS)

total amount (whether these have been incurred as costs by The Supplier or not at that time) plus a damage of $20 000.

8. Force Majeure. Either Party may discontinue the Contract without cancellation in case of established factors, acting as 'force majeure', that prevent the Contract or the Supply or both.

9. Arbitration. In the case of dispute, Parties will submit the issue or issues to arbitration of the Chamber of Commerce of Ruritania, and shall accept the ruling of that body.

10. The whole of this Contract is arranged, executed and shall be fully determined for all purposes within the Republic of Ruritania.

Signed on behalf of: The Client   ....
                       The Supplier ....
                       Date   ....

Attachments: Annex (i) The Functional Specification (incorporating User Manual). This document is initialled on every page by the signatories hereto.

(5. OSD)

SECTION 5
OSD (SOFTWARE TAXONOMY)

(5. OSD)

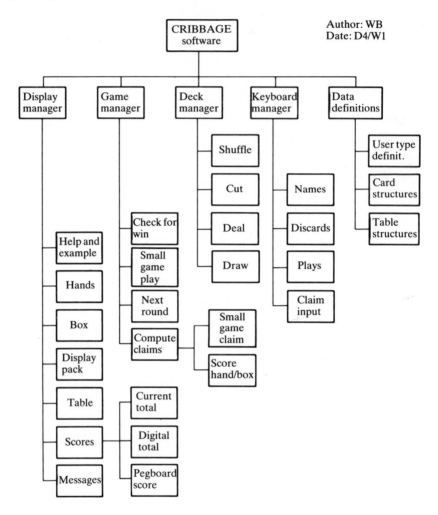

Diagram 5.1 A draft OSD software taxonomy.

(5. OSD)

		EST. PASCAL STATEMENTS	
DATA DEFINITIONS:	(TO BE DONE BY JO)		
	USER TYPE	100	
	CARD STRUCTURES	50	
	TABLE STRUCTURES	100	
			250
DISPLAY MANAGER:	(TO BE DONE BY SARAH)		
	HANDS	50	
	BOX	50	
	SCORES : CURRENT TOTAL	25	
	: DIGITAL	25	
	: PEGBOARD	200	
	DISPLAY PACK	150	
	TABLE	100	
	MESSAGES	100	
	HELP AND EXAMPLE	150	
			850
KEYBOARD MANAGER:	(TO BE DONE BY JO)		
	NAMES	50	
	DISCARDS	50	
	PLAYS	100	
	CLAIMS INPUT	50	
			250
GAME MANAGER:	(TO BE DONE BY BILL)		
	SMALL GAME	150	
	COMPUTE CLAIMS : SMALL GAME/DRAWCARD	200	
	: HANDS BOX	200	
	CHECK FOR WIN	50	
	NEXT ROUND	100	
			700
DECK MANAGER:	(TO BE DONE BY BILL)		
	SHUFFLE	100	
	CUT	50	
	DEAL	50	
	DRAW	50	
			250

ESTIMATED CODE SIZE: 2300
CONTINGENCY (10%)   + 230
                       2530   SOURCE STATEMENTS OF PASCAL

Diagram 5.2   Software codesize estimates based on OSD.

(5. OSD)

MEMO	From:	CP		**DATE**	W 3
	To:	Manager			D 1
	cc:	CPT			
		A (5) via Lib.			

Commercial estimates for Cribbage – Version 1

On the basis of the enclosed activities plan I estimate an effort of 43 × 3 = 129 person days to do the task from FS to beta-test, excluding QA. This is subject to:

(a) No substantial changes to the FS.

(b) Staff continuity.

(c) Computer access.

To increase the estimate for prior work (URS/prototypes; FS) and QI/QA, I suggest an addition of 40 person days for the first, and 20 person days for the second (see quality plan). A total effort bid of 129 + 40 + 20 = 189 person days would be appropriate. The total timescale for this is 60 days, 43 being for the implementation phase from FS onwards. Assuming we get the go-ahead for this at our meeting with the client next week, and assuming that we get the contract by May 1st, the acceptance should be scheduled for day 43 after that.

(Encl. Netplans)

Module (see URS)	Key	Activity Type	Key
Display Manager Module	A	Summarize URS (do prototypes)	1
Keyboard Manager Module	B	FS	2
Data Definitions	C	Software design (overall)	3
Games Manager Module	D	Software module design	4
Desk Manager Module	E	Design review	5
		Code module	6
		Read code	7
		Test plan	8
		Test code	9
		Integrate and test code	10
		Documentation (general)	11
		Documentation module	12
		α-test	13
		β-test	14

continued

(5. OSD)

Part	1	2	3	4	5	6	7	8	9	10	11	12	13	14
System	10	5	2					3			2		1	2
A				5	2	15	2		5			1		
B				3	1	5	2		2	2		1		
C				2	1	3	0		0			1		
D				2	1	10	2		3	3		1		
E				3	1	5	2		2			1		

Resource	Activities assigned (ordered but not completely synchronised)
Team	3
Sarah	1 A4 A6 A9 A/B/C/D/E/ 10 12
Sarah and Jo	A5 A7 A/B/C/10 11
Jo	2 B/C4 8 B6 B9
J0 and Bill	B/C5;D/E5 B/E7 D7
Bill	2 D/E4 E6 E9 D6 D9
QA	A/B/C/D/E5 A/B/E 7 D7 13

Diagram 5.3 Activities key and assignment to team members.

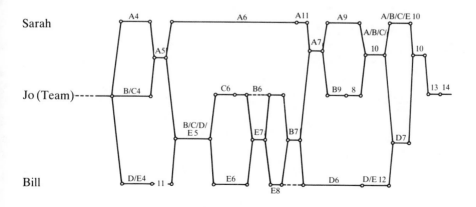

Diagram 5.4 Activities plan.

(6. MAN)

SECTION 6
MANAGEMENT – CONTROL INFORMATION

(6. MAN)

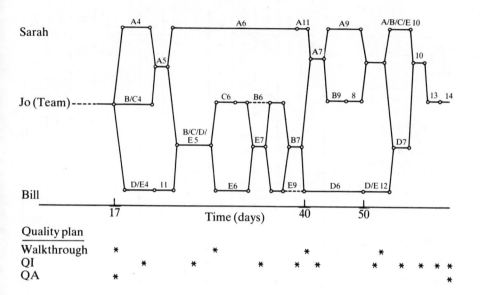

Diagram 6.1   Derived quality plan.

(6. MAN)

STATUS

DATE D5/W4

MODULE/PROG	Ideas & gen	Arch. des.	Mod. des.	Prog. des.	Review	Code	Read	Prog. test	Int. test	Int. test	Int. test	Doc.	Alpha-test
A	+	+	+	o	–	–	–	–	–	–	–	–	–
Hands				o	–								
Box				o	–								
Scores: (current)				o	–								
(digital)				o	–								
(pegboard)				o	–								
Display pack				o	–								
Table				o	–								
messages				o	–								
Help & examples				o	–								
B	+	+	+	o	–	–	–	–	–	–	–	–	–
Names				o	–								
Discards				o	–								
Plays				o	–								
Claims				o	–								
C	+	+	+	+	–	–	–	–	–	–	–	–	–
User type				+	–								
Card struc.				+	–								
Table struc.				+	–								
D	+	+	o	–	–	–	–	–	–	–	–	–	–
Small game				–	–								
Claim: (small-game)				–	–								
(Hand/Box)				–	–								
Check win				–	–								
Next round				–	–								
E	+	+	+	o	–	–	–	–	–	–	–	–	–
Shuffle				o	–								
Cut				o	–								
Deal				o	–								
Draw				o	–								

Diagram 6.2 Status matrix (a).

(6. MAN)

STATUS
DATE D5/W5

MODULE/PROG	Ideas & gen	Arch. des.	Mod. des.	Prog. des.	Review	Code	Read	Prog. test	Int. test	Int. test	Int. test	Doc.	Alpha-test
A	+	+	+	+	+	o	-						
Hands				+	+	o	-						
Box				+	+	o	-						
Scores: (curr)				+	+	o	-						
(dig)				+	+	o	-						
(pag)				+	+	o	-						
Display pack				+	+	o	-						
Table				+	+	o	-						
Messages				+	+	o	-						
Help & examples				+	+	o	-						
B	+	+	+	+	+	-							
Names				+	+	-							
Discards				+	+	-							
Plays				+	+	-							
Claims				+	+	-							
C	+	+	+	+	+	o	-						
User type				+	+	o	-						
Card struc.				+	+	+	-						
Table struc.				+	+	+	-						
D	+	+	+	o	-								
Small game				+	-								
Claim: (small)				+	-								
(Hand/B)				+	-								
Check win				o	-								
Next round				o	-								
E	+	+	+	+	+	-							
Shuffle				+	+	-							
Cut				+	+	-							
Deal				+	+	-							
Draw				+	+	-							

Diagram 6.3 Status matrix (b).

(6. MAN)

STATUS
DATE D5/W6

MODULE/PROG	Ideas & gen	Arch. des.	Mod. des.	Prog. des.	Review	Code	Read	Prog. test	Int. test	Int. test	Int. test	Doc.	Alpha-test
A	+	+	+	+	+	o	−						
Hands				+	+	+	−						
Box				+	+	+	−						
Scores: (curr)				+	+	+	−						
(dig)				+	+	+	−						
(pag)				+	+	+	−						
Display pack				+	+	o	−						
Table				+	+	+	−						
Messages				+	+	−	−						
Help & examples				+	+	−	−						
B	+	+	+	+	+	o	−						
Names				+	+	+	−						
Discards				+	+	+	−						
Plays				+	+	+	−						
Claims				+	+	o	−						
C	+	+	+	+	+	+	−						
User type				+	+	+	−						
Card struc.				+	+	+	−						
Table struc.				+	+	+	−						
D	+	+	+	+	+	o	−						
Small game				+	+	o	−						
Claim: (small)				+	+	+	−						
(Hand/B)				+	+	+	−						
Check win				+	+	−	−						
Next round				+	+	−	−						
E	+	+	+	+	+	−							
Shuffle				+	+	−							
Cut				+	+	−							
Deal				+	+	−							
Draw				+	+	−							

Diagram 6.4 Status matrix (c).

(6. MAN)

STATUS
DATE D5/W7

MODULE/PROG	Ideas & gen	Arch. des.	Mod. des.	Prog. des.	Review	Code	Read	Prog. test	Int. test	Int. test	Int. test	Doc.	Alpha-test
A	+	+	+	+	+	o	−						
Hands				+	+	+	−						
Box				+	+	+	−						
Scores: (curr)				+	+	+	−						
(dig)				+	+	+	−						
(pag)				+	+	+	−						
Display pack				+	+	+	−						
Table				+	+	+	−						
Messages				+	+	+	−						
Help & examples				+	+	o	−						
B	+	+	+	+	+	+	−						
Names				+	+	+	−						
Discards				+	+	+	−						
Plays				+	+	+	−						
Claims				+	+	+	−						
C	+	+	+	+	+	+	−						
User type				+	+	+	−						
Card struc.				+	+	+	−						
Table struc.				+	+	+	−						
D	+	+	+	+	+	o	−						
Small game				+	+	+	−						
Claim: (small)				+	+	+	−						
(Hand/B)				+	+	+	−						
Check win				+	+	+	−						
Next round				+	+	o	−						
E	+	+	+	+	+	+	−						
Shuffle				+	+	+	−						
Cut				+	+	+	−						
Deal				+	+	+	−						
Draw				+	+	+	−						

Diagram 6.5 Status matrix (d).

(6. MAN)

STATUS
DATE D5/W8

MODULE/PROG	Ideas & gen	Arch. des.	Mod. des.	Prog. des.	Review	Code	Read	Prog. test	Int. test	Int. test	Int. test	Doc.	Alpha-test	
A	+	+	+	+	+	o	−							*
Hands				+	+	+	−							
Box				+	+	+	−							
Scores: (curr)				+	+	+	−							
(dig)				+	+	+	−							
(pag)				+	+	+	−							
Display pack				+	+	+	−							
Table				+	+	+	−							
Messages				+	+	+	−							
Help & examples				+	+	o	−							
B	+	+	+	+	+	+	+	o	−					
Names				+	+	+	+	+	−					
Discards				+	+	+	+	o	−					
Plays				+	+	+	+	−	−					
Claims				+	+	+	+	−	−					
C	+	+	o	−	−	−	−	−	−					**
User type				−	−	−	−	−	−					
Card struc.				−	−	−	−	−	−					
Table struc.				−	−	−	−	−	−					
D	+	+	+	+	+	+	o	o	−					
Small game				+	+	+	o	o	−					
Claim: (small)				+	+	+	o	o	−					
(Hand/B)				+	+	+	o	o	−					
Check win				+	+	+	o	o	−					
Next round				+	+	+	o	o	−					
E	+	+	+	+	+	+	+	+	−					
Shuffle				+	+	+	+	+	−					
Cut				+	+	+	+	+	−					
Deal				+	+	+	+	+	−					
Draw				+	+	+	+	+	−					

Diagram 6.6   Status matrix (e).

(6. MAN)

STATUS
DATE D5/W9

MODULE/PROG	Ideas & gen	Arch. des.	Mod. des.	Prog. des.	Review	Code	Read	Prog. test	Int. test	Int. test	Int. test	Doc.	Alpha-test
A	+	+	+	+	+	+	+	o	–				
Hands				+	+	+	+	o	–				
Box				+	+	+	+	+	–				
Scores: (curr)				+	+	+	+	+	–				
(dig)				+	+	+	+	+	–				
(pag)				+	+	+	+	+	–				
Display pack				+	+	+	+	o	–				
Table				+	+	+	+	+	–				
Messages				+	+	+	+	+	–				
Help & examples				+	+	+	+	+	–				
B	+	+	+	+	+	+	+	+	+	–			
Names				+	+	+	+	+	+	–			
Discards				+	+	+	+	+	+	–			
Plays				+	+	+	+	+	+	–			
Claims				+	+	+	+	+	+	–			
C	+	+	+	+	+	+	+	o	–				
User type				+	+	+	+	o	–				
Card struc.				+	+	+	+	o	–				
Table struc.				+	+	+	+	o	–				
D	+	+	+	o	–	–	–	–					***
Small game				o	–	–	–	–					
Claim: (small)				+	+	+	+	–					
(Hand/B)				o	–	–	–	–					
Check win				+	+	+	+	–					
Next round				+	+	+	+	–					
E	+	+	+	+	+	+	+	+	+	–			
Shuffle				+	+	+	+	+	+	–			
Cut				+	+	+	+	+	+	–			
Deal				+	+	+	+	+	+	–			
Draw				+	+	+	+	+	+	–			

Diagram 6.7   Status matrix (f).

(6. MAN)

STATUS
DATE D5/W10

MODULE/PROG	Ideas & gen	Arch. des.	Mod. des.	Prog. des.	Review	Code	Read	Prog. test	Int. test	Int. test	Int. test	Doc.	Alpha-test
A	+	+	+	+	+	+	+	+	+	−	−	+	
Hands				+	+	+	+	+	+	−	−	+	
Box				+	+	+	+	+	+	−	−	+	
Scores: (curr)				+	+	+	+	+	+	−	−	+	
(dig)				+	+	+	+	+	+	−	−	+	
(pag)				+	+	+	+	+	+	−	−	+	
Display pack				+	+	+	+	+	+	−	−	+	
Table				+	+	+	+	+	+	−	−	+	
Messages				+	+	+	+	+	+	−	−	+	
Help & examples				+	+	+	+	+	+	−	−	+	
B	+	+	+	+	+	+	+	+	+	o	−	o	
Names				+	+	+	+	+	+	o	−	o	
Discards				+	+	+	+	+	+	o	−	o	
Plays				+	+	+	+	+	+	o	−	o	
Claims				+	+	+	+	+	+	o	−	o	
C	+	+	+	+	+	+	+	+	+	o	−	o	
User type				+	+	+	+	+	+	o	−	o	
Card struc.				+	+	+	+	+	+	o	−	o	
Table struc.				+	+	+	+	+	+	o	−	o	
D	+	+	+	+	+	+	+	+	o	−			
Small game				+	+	+	+	+	o	−			
Claim: (small)				+	+	+	+	+	o	−			
(Hand/B)				+	+	+	+	+	o	−			
Check win				+	+	+	+	+	o	−			
Next round				+	+	+	+	+	o	−			
E	+	+	+	+	+	+	+	+	+	o	−	o	
Shuffle				+	+	+	+	+	+	o	−	o	
Cut				+	+	+	+	+	+	o	−	o	
Deal				+	+	+	+	+	+	o	−	o	
Draw				+	+	+	+	+	+	o	−	o	

Diagram 6.8 Status matrix (g).

(6. MAN)

STATUS
DATE D5/W11

MODULE/PROG

	Ideas & gen	Arch. des.	Mod. des.	Prog. des.	Review	Code	Read	Prog. test	Int. test	Int. test	Int. test	Doc.	Alpha-test	
A	+	+	+	+	+	+	+	+	+	+	+	+	+	
Hands				+	+	+	+	+	+	+	+	+	+	
Box				+	+	+	+	+	+	+	+	+	+	
Scores: (curr)				+	+	+	+	+	+	+	+	+	+	
(dig)				+	+	+	+	+	+	+	+	+	+	
(pag)				+	+	+	+	+	+	+	+	+	+	
Display pack				+	+	+	+	+	+	+	+	+	+	
Table				+	+	+	+	+	+	+	+	+	+	
Messages				+	+	+	+	+	+	+	+	+	+	
Help & examples				+	+	+	+	+	+	+	+	+	+	
B	+	+	+	+	+	+	+	+	+	+	+	+	+	
Names				+	+	+	+	+	+	+	+	+	+	
Discards				+	+	+	+	+	+	+	+	+	+	
Plays				+	+	+	+	+	+	+	+	+	+	
Claims				+	+	+	+	+	+	+	+	+	+	
C	+	+	+	+	+	+	+	+	+	+	+	+	+	
User type				+	+	+	+	+	+	+	+	+	+	
Card struc.				+	+	+	+	+	+	+	+	+	+	
Table struc.				+	+	+·	+	+	+	+	+	+	+	
D	+	+	+	+	+	+	+	+	+	+	+	o	(+)	*
Small game				+	+	+	+	+	+	+	+	o	(+)	
Claim: (small)				+	+	+	+	+	+	+	+	o	(+)	
(Hand/B)				+	+	+	+	+	+	+	+	o	(+)	
Check win				+	+	+	+	+	+	+	+	o	(+)	
Next round				+	+	+	+	+	+	+	+	o	(+)	
E	+	+	+	+	+	+	+	+	+	+	+	+	+	
Shuffle				+	+	+	+	+	+	+	+	+	+	
Cut				+	+	+	+	+	+	+	+	+	+	
Deal				+	+	+	+	+	+	+	+	+	+	
Draw				+	+	+	+	+	+	+	+	+	+	

Diagram 6.9 Status matrix (h).

(6. MAN)

MEMO	From:	CP	**DATE**	W 4
	To:	Manager		D 1
	cc:	A (6) via Lib.		

Cost reporting on CRIBBAGE project

I propose to supply you with an effort rather than cost report on a fortnightly basis.
You will, therefore, have the first on D1/W6 and then others on D1/W8 and D1/W10.
The report will be simple, graphical depictions of actual effort against estimate, and
a 'weighted actual' histogram to show the value of the effort at that time. Please note
that overtime is not impossible if we are to meet this tight schedule. I shall
aggregate overtime hours (on the curve and the histogram) at 150% of time booked,
to give an idea of cost overspend by remunerating staff at time-and-a-half for excess
hours.

CP.

(6. MAN)

Author: CP
Date   : D5/W5

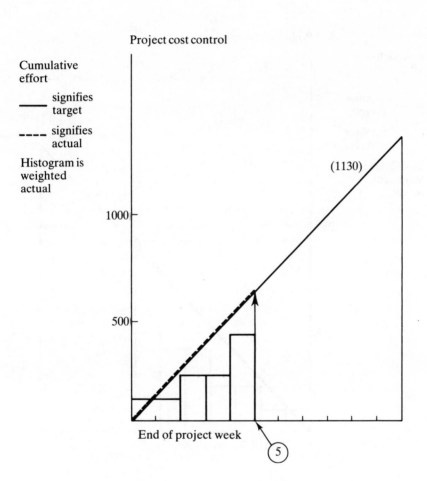

Diagram 6.10   Cost control (1).

(6. MAN)

Author: CP
Date   : D5/W7

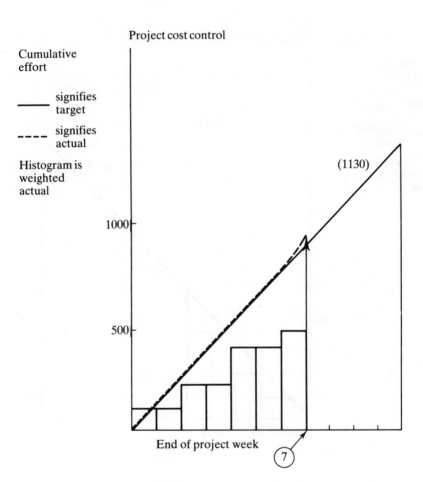

Project cost control

Cumulative
effort

_____   signifies
target

- - - -   signifies
actual

Histogram is
weighted
actual

(1130)

1000

500

End of project week

⑦

Diagram 6.11   Cost control (2).

(6. MAN)

Author: CP
Date   : D5/W9

Project cost control

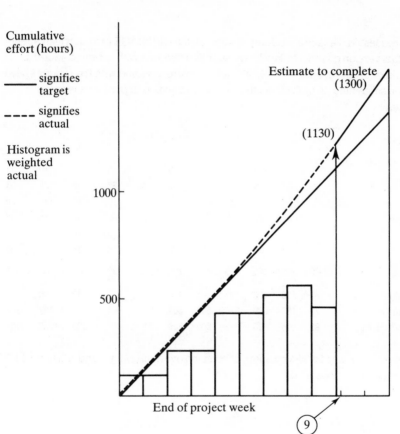

Diagram 6.12   Cost control (3).

(6. MAN)

MEMO	From:	CP	**DATE**	W 11
	To:	Manager		D 5
	cc:	A (6) via Lib.		

As requested, I attach a summary of effort on the CRIBBAGE project which ended its first version contract today. I have supplied two, one with overtime added as booked (i.e. not at time-and-a-half), and one corresponding with the reports I have been submitting. In both cases, the excess is indicated in parenthesis and is in hours.

Person					Project week						
	1	2	3	4	5	6	7	8	9	10	11
CP	35	35	35	35	35	35	35	35	35	35	35
								(10)	(15)	(35)	(20)
Sarah	35	35	35	35	35	35	35	35	35	35	35
							(10)	(20)	(10)		
Bill	10	35	35	35	35	35	35	35	35	35	35
Total	80	105	105	105	105	105	105	125	130	135	145
Weight.( )Tot.	80	105	105	105	105	105	135	165	142	150	165
Cum.Tot.	80	185	290	395	500	605	740	905	1047	1197	1362
Est.Cum.Tot.	80	185	290	395	500	605	710	815	920	1025	1130

The over-run was 20.55% on effort, accounting overtime at time-and-a-half (or 13.7% on straight hours booked).

(7. QUAL)

SECTION 7
QUALITY

(7. QUAL)

MEMO   From: Manager   **DATE**   W 4

           To: CP   D 1

           cc: Client
                 A (7) via Lib.

Quality functions for the CRIBBAGE project

Our client, MacBuxton & Ass., have enquired for details of our quality practices.
    This note stands as a definition for the CPT and an indication to the client.
    You will undertake

1. design reviews

2. code reading

at suitable stages, and this – in both cases – will be by explicit assignment. I note the
activities plan coincides with this. Further, you will thoroughly test the software to
an explicit schedule; again I note that the plan shows such a schedule.
Reviews/readings, plus the testing up to and including alpha-tests, comprises your
own Quality Control (QC).
    Our quality department will inspect this process (QI) and will report at the time
of alphatests (if otherwise all right in the meantime) and at any time before that if a
defect in your procedures or their quality is detected.
    When the process by which your software has been verified (up to and
including the alpha-test) has been completed, it will be subject to a client beta-test.

Manager

(7. QUAL)

MEMO   From: Sid (Quality dept.)   **DATE**   D4   W 11

To: Manager
cc: CP
A (7) via Lib.

Final QI report validating CRIBBAGE software

There having been no earlier occasion to communicate, herewith is my final system verification report.

1. Being assigned as intermittent, independent quality inspector for the CRIBBAGE software I had various contacts with the CP and CPT in general from D1/W4 onwards.

2. I attended all design reviews and code readings (including repeats on modules C and D) and can declare them satisfactorily carried out in all cases.
   Errors were found at both designs and code reviews (readings) there being one of very great severity in module D. Module C was found to have been implemented in a slightly different manner to that specified and a re-do was necessary. Both these faults have been cleared up, but the one for D continues to concern me due to the haste of reimplementation.

3. Author, integration and alpha-testing have been adequate. I attended all integration and alpha-tests and confirm their adequacy to demonstrate compliance. I note that no 'disturbance' tests were planned or done to test modifiability. The deliverable documentation is done, I have inspected it, and it is good (except D).

4. I note that all Lifecycle stages were properly done, in the proper sequence, and well archived. The code size estimates at OSD stage were optimistic. The actual was 3274 source statements (excluding data, etc.) against 2530 as estimated (+13%).

Sid

(8. DES)

SECTION 8
SOFTWARE DESIGN

(*Note*. This section contains the high-level architectural ideas and a state-transition representation of the whole system, then BS 6224 representations of two programs in particular, and a pseudocode description – to just above code level – for one of them. Obviously, there is a whole set of BS 6244 diagrams and pseudocode specifications for all programs of the complete system. We have chosen just the one 'track' in the whole design.

  This section is, therefore, about one-tenth of the total Section 8 content and is to illustrate the design process rather than provide the whole corpus of design material.)

(8. DES)

AUTHOR: CP
DATE   : W2/D4

Very (!) top-level architectural design: first ideas

Main sequencer
Administrates
game phases.
Handles command
START

| Log-on player names | Main game Cut for deal Deal hands Draw card | Small game Play in turn Check legal play Request score and claim Repeat if cards left | Compute Score hands Score box | Commands HELP DECK RESUME EXAMPLE CLAIMS |

Deck manager
Data: 52 card
    deck
Functions: Cut,
    Shuffle,
    Deal
    6 cards

Table manager
Data: Players hands,
    box,
    cards on table
Function: Play one card
    Reassemble
    one hand

Scorer
Function: Score
    sequence,
    Score one
    hand / box,
    Signal
    winner

Input handler
Receive keyboard chars.
Validate format as card,
position, claim or
command name

Display manager
Maintain visual version
of hands, table, scores,
pegboard, messages

Machine: IBM-PC (hardware & software)

Diagram 8.1   Architectural design (A).

(8. DES)

AUTHOR: CPT (all)
DATE   : W3/D5

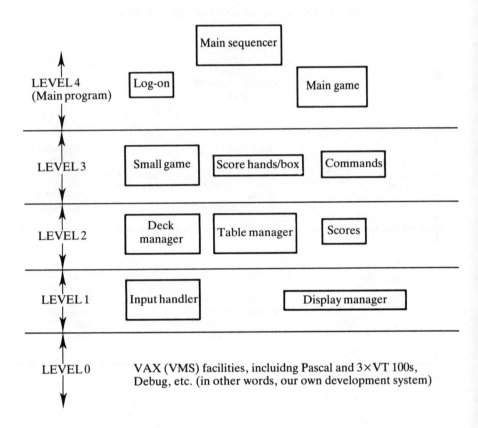

Diagram 8.2   Architectural design (B).

(8. DES)

AUTHOR: Bill
DATE   : W35/D4

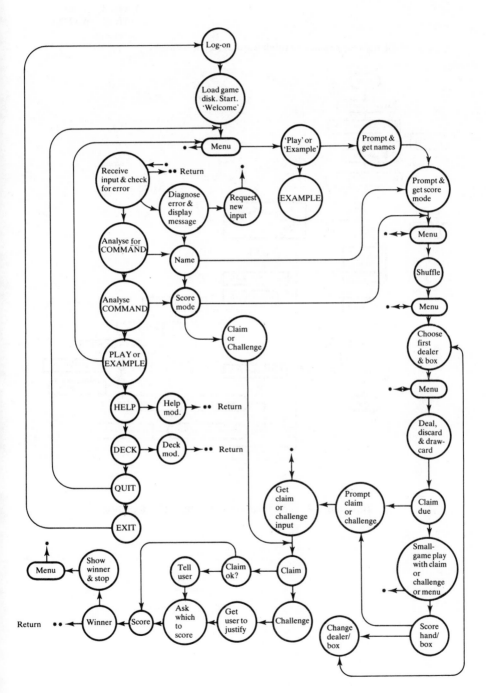

Diagram 8.3 Architectural design (C) – state transition.

(8. DES)

AUTHOR: Sarah
DATE   : W3/D5

BS 6224 Schematic of overall features (top level logic)

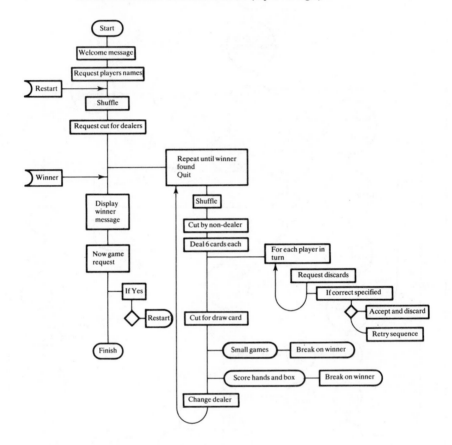

Diagram 8.4 Top-level design – BS 6224 depiction.

(8. DES)

AUTHOR: Bill
DATE   : W5/D3
Review by   on

Design of small games sequencer

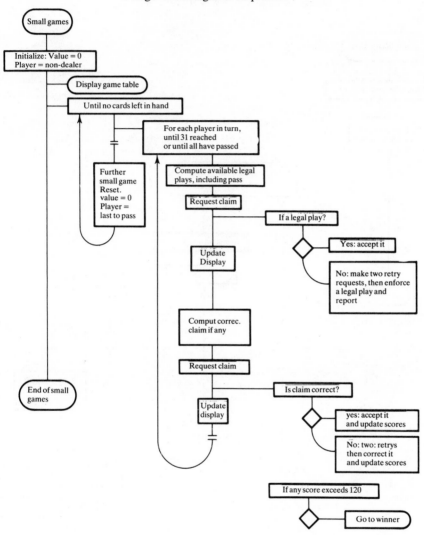

Diagram 8.5 Subsystem design (A) – BS 6224 depiction.

(8. DES)

AUTHOR: Bill
DATE   : W5/D4
Review by

Design of hand and box score program

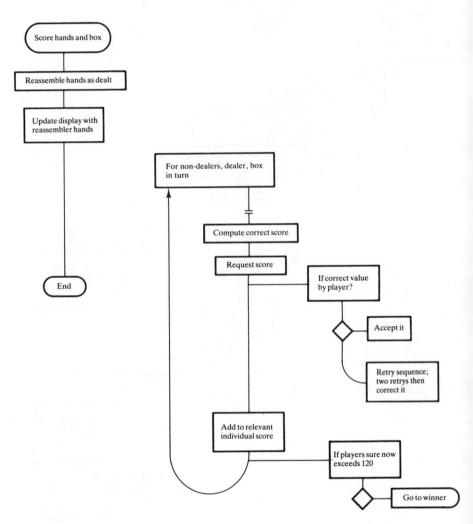

Diagram 8.6 Subsystem design (B) – BS 6224 depiction.

(8. DES)

Author: Bill

Date: W5/D5

Review by on

'Scorer' Module Spec. and Design

Users: small games and 'score hands and Box' modules

External Procedures: Compute claim (called after each play)
Compute hand
Compute box
Display claims (called by the DISPLAY command to show detailed scoring)

Design notes:

The data structures used but not changed by this module are those representing the hands as dealt after discards, the box and draw card, and the cards (copies of those in the hands) in order as played on the table.

The module owns an internal data structure: a table showing on each line a score contribution, and the identifiers of the cards producing that contribution. The Display claims procedure displays this table.

An internal procedure Evaluate takes as parameters a group of cards and scores pairs, triples, fours and runs depending on the value of n.

Pseudo code

procedure Evaluator (takes a group of n cards as played)
        if all n cards of same rank **then**
        if n = 4 **then** score 12
      else if n = 3 **then** score 6
      else if n = 2 **then** score 2
      else sort cards into order
      if all n cards as sorted are in successive rank then score n
    end Evaluator

procedure Compute claim
        Compute current total value of cards played so far;
        if current value = 15 **then** score 2
        if current value = 31 **then** score 2
        call Evaluator (last two cards played)
        call Evaluator (last three cards played)

(8. DES)

>   **call** Evaluator (last four cards played)
>   **end** Compute claim

procedure Compute hand (takes a group of five cards as parameters)
>   **For all**combinations of two, three or four cards from the group
>   **call**   Evaluator (on each combination)
>   **For all**combinations of four cards
>   **if**   all four of same suit **then** score 4
>   **For**   each card in the group
>   **if**   it is a Jack of the same suit as the drawcard **then** score 1
>   **end** Computehand

procedure Compute box
>   **call**   Computehand (group of four discards and the draw card)
>   **if**   (group of four discards and the drawcard) all of same suit **then**
>   score 5
>   **end** compute box
>   **end** Score Module

This concludes the extracts from an archive as performed by an independent QI agency on the CRIBBAGE project.

As said at the start, the extracts do not comprise the whole of any one section, nor the whole set of sections. Particularly depleted in this respect is Section 8, at which point the volume of material (design followed by code) begins to increase rapidly. We hope, however, to have shown enough of the design process.

Sections 9–11 of the archive from which we have selected are far too voluminous for either reasonable extraction or incorporation. What is of interest, however, is the issue of a 'next version'.

In the case we have considered, Version 1 (as defined in Section 4) was to be followed by Version 2 to be done under stringent timescale conditions. This requirement is summarized below and constitutes a major set of additions, some of which place great stress on the basic architecture of Version 1.

In the event, it was found that, although Version 1 had been compliant and reliable, it was not so easily modifiable, and major rewrites of Version 1 software took place. As compared with an effort over-run of 20% on Version 1 (or 13% depending on how overtime was accounted), Version 2 had an effort over-run of 68% (43%), and moreover violated timescale by a small amount (15% or so).

Not least, the impact on staff was very severe.

(9–12)

VERSION 2 – SPECIFICATION   DATE: Sept. 16th

1. The system will allow three- and four-handed play. This will require changes to the screen format and these must be agreed with the client before being implemented. Choice of the mode (2-, 3- or 4-handed) will be, like that for auto or manual scoring, a prompted user input after choice of PLAY – not a menu item.

2. HELP, EXAMPLE and DECK will remain as menu options, along with PLAY, QUIT and EXIT, and the menu will be extended for the features described below.

3. Games may be saved at any stage of PLAY; this requires user input of a game identification at the same time as players' names are input. This feature (SAVE) will be available as a menu option from PLAY (but not EXAMPLE), HELP, and DECK. It will terminate by RETURN (to where it came from), QUIT or EXIT.

4. Saved games may be retrieved at any stage of PLAY, by means of a menu option RECALL. This feature can be invoked from PLAY, EXAMPLE, HELP and DECK; it will prompt the user to decide what is to be done (except in the case of EXAMPLE) with the current position – i.e. SAVE it, or lose it. A recalled game will set up the position at the time it was saved and one may then access PLAY (to play on), QUIT or EXIT. Accessing DECK, HELP or SAVE (again) must be done through PLAY. If manual PLAY is accessed it will require another identification input in case the resumed game is going to be saved again.

References

Alagic, S. and M.A. Arbib, 1978. *The Design of Well Structured and Correct Programs*. New York: Springer Verlag.

Allworth, S.T., 1981. *Introduction to Real-time Software Design*. London & Basingstoke: Macmillan.

Baber, R.L., 1982. *Software Reflected*. Amsterdam: North-Holland.

Bauer, F.L., 1972. *Software Engineering*. Amsterdam: North-Holland.

Ben Ari, M. 1982. *Principles of Concurrent Programming*. Englewood Cliffs, NJ: Prentice-Hall.

Benington, H.D., 1956. 'Production of large computer programmes', Proc. ONR Symposium on Advanced Programming Methods for Digital Computers, pp. 15–27.

Bergland, G.D., 1981. 'A guided tour of program design methodologies', *IEEE Comp. J.*, **14**, pp. 13–37.

Birrell, N.D. and M.A. Ould, 1985. *A Practical Handbook for Software Development*. Cambridge: Cambridge University Press.

Boehm, B.W., 1981. *Software Engineering Economics*. Englewood Cliffs, NJ: Prentice-Hall.

Boehm, B.W., 1984. 'Software engineering economics', *IEEE Trans. on Software Engineering*, January, **SE-10(1)**, pp. 4–21.

British Standards Institution, 1982. Guide to Structure Diagrams for Use in Program Design and Other Logic Applications, BS 6224.

Brooks, F.P., 1975. *The Mythical Man-Month*. Reading, MA: Addison-Wesley.

Butcher, J. (MP), 1984. *Information Technology Skills Shortages*. First report of the committee proceedings.

Buxton, J.N., 1980. *Requirements of Ada PSE (Stoneman)*. US Department of Defense, OSD/R & E, Washington.

Buxton, J.N., P. Naur and B. Randall, 1969. *Software Engineering Techniques*, Proc. NATO conference, Rome. Published by the Scientific Affairs Division, NATO, Brussels.

Cho Chin-Kui, 1980. *An Introduction to Software Quality Control*. New York: John Wiley.

Constantine, L.L. and E. Yourdon, 1979. *Structured Design*. Englewood Cliffs, NJ: Prentice-Hall.

DeMarco, T., 1982. *Controlling Software Projects*. New York: Yourdon Press.

Deutsch, M.S., 1982. *Software Verification and Validation*. Englewood Cliffs, NJ: Prentice-Hall.

375

Dijkstra, E.W., 1977. 'The Impact of Microprocessors', IFIP Congress, published in *Gesellschaft für Mathematik und Datenverarbeitung Spiegel*, **7(4)**, pp. 8–11.

Dolotta, T.A., 1976. *Data Processing in 1980–85*. Chichester: John Wiley.

Glaser, E.L., V. Illingworth and I.C. Pyle (eds), 1983. *Dictionary of Computer Science*. Oxford: Oxford Science Publications.

Glass, R.L., 1979. *Software Reliability Guidebook*. Englewood Cliffs, NJ: Prentice-Hall.

Halstead, H.M., 1977. *Elements of Software Science*. New York: Elsevier.

Healey, M., 1976. *Minicomputers and Microprocessors*. Sevenoaks, Kent: Hodder & Stoughton.

Herd, J.R., J.N. Posla, W.E. Russell and K.R. Steward, 1977. 'Software cost estimation: study results'. Final Technical Report RADC-TR-77-220, Vol. 1. Rockville, MD: Doty Associates Inc., June 1977.

Hoare, C.A.R., 1984. 'Programming – sorcery or science?'. *IEEE Software*, pp. 6–16.

Jackson, M.A., 1983. *System Development*. London: Prentice-Hall.

Jensen, R.W., 1984. 'Estimating software costs'. Inst. of Dataprocessing Management, lectures, Rome 1984.

Jensen, R.W. and C.C. Tonies, 1979. *Software Engineering*. Englewood Cliffs, NJ: Prentice-Hall.

Jonkers, H.C.M., 1982. *Abstraction, Specification and Implementation Techniques*. Mathematisch Centrum Amsterdam.

Ledgard, H.F., 1987. *Contemporary Software – Thieves and Thickets*. Addison-Wesley (in preparation).

Lehman, M.M., 1980. *Programs, Programming and the Software Lifecycle*. Dept. of Computing and Control, Imperial College, London.

Lehman, M.M., V. Stenning and W.M. Turski, 1984. 'Another look at software design methodology'. *ACM Software Engineering Notes*, **9(2)**, pp. 38–53.

McCabe, T., 1976. 'A software complexity measure', *IEEE (Software) Trans.*, **2**, pp. 308–320, December.

McDermid, J. (ed.), 1985. *Integrated Project Support Environments*. Peter Peregrinus Ltd, London, on behalf of IEEE Software Engineering Series 1.

Mayo, J.S., 1983. *IC Design Automation: Key to Future Technology*. High Technology Publications, pp. 17–21.

Metzger, P.W., 1981. *Managing a Programming Project*. Englewood Cliffs, NJ: Prentice-Hall.

Miller, E.F., 1972. *A Survey of Major Techniques of Program Validation*. General Research Report RM-1731, p. 4. Santa Barbara, CA: GRC.

Mills, H.D. and F.T. Baker, 1973. 'Chief programmer teams', *Datamation*, **19(12)**, December, pp. 58–61.

Myers, G.J., 1975. *Reliable Software through Composite Design*. New York: Van Nostrand Reinhold.

Myers, G.J., 1976. *Software Reliability*. New York: John Wiley.

Naur, P., 1982. 'Formulation in program development'. *BIT*, **22**, pp. 437–453.

Naur, P. and B. Randell, 1968. 'Software engineering', Proc. NATO conf. Scientific Affairs Division, NATO, Brussels.

Nelson, R.A., L.M. Haibt and P.B. Sheridon, 1983. 'Casting Petri-nets into programs', *IEEE (Software Engineering)*, **SE-9(5)**, pp. 590–602.

Norden, P.V., 1963. 'Useful tools for project management', in *Operations Research in Research and Development* (B.V. Dean, ed.). New York: John Wiley.

Parnas, D.L., 1972. 'On the criteria to be used in decomposing systems into modules', *Comm. ACM*, **15(2)**, pp. 1053–1058.

Perlis, A.J., R.A. De Millo and R.J. Lipton, 1979. 'Social process and proofs of theorems and programs'. *Comm. ACM*, **23(5)**, pp. 271–280.

Pressman, R.S., 1982. *Software Engineering – A Practitioner's Approach*. New York: McGraw-Hill.

Putnam, L.H., 1982. 'Software cost estimating, and lifecycle control'. *IEEE Catalog*, Los Alamitos, CA.

Reiffer, D.J., 1974. 'Computer Program Verification/Validation/Certification'. The Aerospace Corp. Report (TOR 0074(4112)5), pp. 18–23, Los Angeles, CA.

Reiffer, D.J., 1982. 'Increasing Software Productivity'. Conference London April 22–23, 1982. Institute of Data Processing Management.

Smedema, C.H., P. Medama and M. Boasson, 1985. *The Programming Language Pascal, Modula, Chill, Ada*. London: Prentice-Hall.

Sommerville, I., 1985. *Software Engineering* (2nd edn). Wokingham: Addison-Wesley.

Staffurth, C. (ed.), 1969. *Project Cost Control using Networks*. The Operational Research Society/The Institute of Cost and Works Accountants.

Thayer, T.A., M. Lipon and E.C. Nelson, 1978. *Software Reliability*. Amsterdam: North-Holland.

Ullman, J.D., 1982. *Principles of Database Systems* (2nd edn). Computer Science Press.

Veryard, R., 1984. *Pragmatic Data Analysis*. Oxford: Blackwell Scientific Publications.

Walston, C.E. and C.P. Felix, 1977. 'A method of program measurements and estimation', *IBM Systems J.*, **16(1)**, pp. 54–73.

Wasserman, A.I. and P. Freeman (eds), 1976. *Towards Improving Software Engineering Education*. New York: Springer Verlag.

Weinberg, G.M., 1971. *The Psychology of Computer Programming*. New York: Van Nostrand Reinhold.

Weinberg, G.M. and E.L. Schulman, 1974. 'Goals and performance in computer programming', *Human Factor*, **16**, pp. 70–77.

Weiner-Erlich, W.K., J.R. Hamrick and V.F. Rudolfo. 'Modeling software behaviour in terms of a lifecycle curve: implications for software maintenance. *IEEE (Software Engineering)*, **SE-10(4)**, pp. 376–383.

Weitzman, C. 1980. *Distributed Micro-minicomputer Systems*. Englewood Cliffs, NJ: Prentice-Hall.

Wexelblat, R.L. (ed.), 1981. *History of Programming Languages*, ACM Sigplan Conference 1978. New York: Academic Press.

Wolverton, R., 1974. 'Cost of developing large-scale software', *IEEE Trans. on Computers*. Reprinted in Putnam (1982), pp. 282–303.

Yourdon, E., 1979. *Managing the Structured Techniques*. Englewood Cliffs, NJ: Prentice-Hall.

Index

Activities planning 108 seq.
alpha test 251
Alvey Directorate 224
amateur programming 4
appraisal, staff 283 seq.
APSE 224
archive, the project 33 seq.
ASPECT 224

beta test 252
big bang testing 248
black box tests 252
bottom up estimating 105
bottom up testing 248
budgetary estimates 130

calling structure diagrams 192
career development 283
CCITT-SDL 196
change control 41 seq.
code reading 152
complexity models 116
compliance as quality criterion 236
configuration management 277
concurrent systems 175
CPM 108

data dictionary 200
dataflow diagrams 184
Delphi estimating method 130
design reviews 152
design structure diagrams 203

ECLIPSE 224
EEC 225
employment terms and conditions 282
entity relationship analysis 54 seq.
E-type systems 22
executable specifications 74

fixed price contracts 298
formal methods 178
formal specifications, languages for 72
functional decomposition 171
functional specification, example 75 seq.

guidelines (vs. standards) 11

HIPO method 54
hobbyists 4

information hiding 165
Information Technology, definition 2
interviewing practice 282
ISTAR 225

JSD method 54, 174
JSP 174

librarian 150

maintenance 272 seq.
maintenance manual 265
MASCOT 189
mean time between failures 238
mean time to repair 238
meta system behaviour 275
metrics for reliability 238
micro development systems 221
modifiability as quality criterion 236

Nassi Schneiderman diagrams 204
notation, definition 168

object oriented design 172
operator's manual 264
orientation courses 294

P-type systems 22
parametric cost models 113 seq.

"Parkinsonian" estimates 102
PERT 108 seq., 140
Petri nets 176, 194
primary skill courses 293
process oriented design 174
productivity factors 106
PSEs 85, 219 seq.
pseudo code 201

quality assurance 231, 257
quality control 231, 256
quality inspection 231, 257
quality criteria 236 seq.

refresher courses 293
representational notations 49
resources bar chart 132

S-type systems 22
SADT 54, 187
SDL 196
secondary skill courses 294
self documenting code 202
self hosted systems 221
single author systems 43
SMALLTALK 223

software complexity models 116
software crisis 5, 9
software engineering, definition 14
software lifecycle 28 seq.
state transition diagrams 196
status matrix 143
structure driven design 174
structured programming 212
structured walkthrough 36 seq.
supplier selection 301
system sizes 23

taxonomies 84 seq.
taxonomy for software sizing 87, 94
tester 151
time and materials contracts 298
toolsmith 150
top down estimating 105
top down testing 248
transform driven design 173

user manual 262

visibility of software process 17

white box tests 252

3167